Hy Resnick, PhD
Phoebe Sade Anderson, MSW
Editors

Human Services Technology: Innovations in Practice and Education

Human Services Technology: Innovations in Practice and Education has been co-published simultaneously as *Journal of Technology in Human Services,* Volume 20, Numbers 1/2 and 3/4 2002.

Pre-publication REVIEWS, COMMENTARIES, EVALUATIONS . . .

"SKILLFULLY EXPLORES THE GROWTH AND EVOLUTION OF COMPUTERS IN THE HELPING PROFESSIONS. . . . Remarkable in its scope, touching on areas previously untouched by technology such as therapy, conflict resolution, and drug addiction, as well as training and administration. AN EYE OPENER."

Harold Weitz, MS,
Senior Consultant,
INDP Consulting Company
(formerly with IBM, the NYC Housing Authority, and the Urban Research Center at Hunter College)

More pre-publication
REVIEWS, COMMENTARIES, EVALUATIONS . . .

"RICH AND ORIGINAL. . . . A timely and pioneering contribution to the emerging field of technology for the helping professions. . . . INTRODUCES A HOST OF INNOVATIVE SOFTWARE APPLICATIONS that will be valued by human service practitioners and educators, by the computer shy and the technophile alike. Highly stimulating, readable, and thought-provoking. . . . I RECOMMEND IT HIGHLY."

Pauline I. Erera, PhD,
Associate Professor,
School of Social Work,
University of Washington

"HIGHLY RECOMMENDED to human service professionals, teachers of at-risk youth, and anyone interested in developing software for social service purposes. . . Demonstrates ways in which access to services can be greatly increased . . . describes development processes for determining effectiveness. If traditional classroom training was to undergo the participatory development and testing that was done for many of these projects, I believe student outcomes would be greatly improved."

Bonnie Hovel, MSW, ACSW,
Owner, GroupWyse Organizational Development Consulting Firm,
Bellevue, Washington

"This book provides you with a full manual in each of the specific spheres of the various human relation professions, as well as the technical specificity required within each sphere of practice. In reality, this book is an updated manual of contemporary practice with a full and clear review of competence requirements and the empirical research evaluation of each practice endeavor."

Henry W. Maier, PhD, DShc,
Professor Emeritus,
University of Washington

"AS AN EDUCATOR, I WAS STIMULATED. As a psychologist, my 'sacred cows' were seriously challenged. As a businessman, I was inspired to create a new product. As a practical doer, I will keep this book as a reference. As a professional, I was proud of the number of human service colleagues who are not satisfied to teach as they were taught, who challenge us to go beyond the known and familiar."

Ron R. Short, PhD,
Author,
Learning in Relationship: Foundation of Personal and Professional Success

Human Services Technology: Innovations in Practice and Education

Human Services Technology: Innovations in Practice and Education has been co-published simultaneously as *Journal of Technology in Human Services*, Volume 20, Numbers 1/2 and 3/4 2002.

The *Journal of Technology in Human Services* Monographic "Separates"

(formerly the *Computers in Human Services* series)*

Below is a list of " separates," which in serials librarianship means a special issue simultaneously published as a special journal issue or double-issue *and* as a "separate" hardbound monograph. (This is a format which we also call a "DocuSerial.")

"Separates" are published because specialized libraries or professionals may wish to purchase a specific thematic issue by itself in a format which can be separately cataloged and shelved, as opposed to purchasing the journal on an on-going basis. Faculty members may also more easily consider a "separate" for classroom adoption.

"Separates" are carefully classified separately with the major book jobbers so that the journal tie-in can be noted on new book order slips to avoid duplicate purchasing.

You may wish to visit Haworth's Website at . . .

http://www.HaworthPress.com

. . . to search our online catalog for complete tables of contents of these separates and related publications.

You may also call 1-800-HAWORTH (outside US/Canada: 607-722-5857), or Fax 1-800-895-0582 (outside US/Canada: 607-771-0012), or e-mail at:

getinfo@haworthpressinc.com

Human Services Technology: Innovations in Practice and Education, edited by Hy Resnick, PhD, and Phoebe Sade Anderson, MSW (Vol. 20, No. (1/2)(3/4, 2002). *"This book provides you with a full manual in each of the specific spheres of the various human relation professions, as well as the technical specificity required within each sphere of practice. In reality, this book is an updated manual of contemporary practice with a full and clear review of competence requirements and the empirical research evaluation of each practice endeavor." (Henry W. Maier, PhD, DShc, Professor Emeritus, University of Washington)*

Using the Internet as a Research Tool for Social Work and Human Services, edited by Goutham M. Menon, PhD (Vol. 19, No. 2/3, 2002). *Explores ways to use the Internet in many aspects of social work research, including the development of online studies and psychological testing.*

New Advances in Technology for Social Work Education and Practice, edited by Julie Miller-Cribbs, PhD, (Vol. 18, No. 3/4, 2001). *"A valuable tool for educators who want to introduce students of social work to the numerous applications of technology within the field. . . . Goes a long way toward helping social work become proactive in its approach to technology integration within the field." (Sharon D. Johnson, PhD, Assistant Professor, Department of Social Work, University of Missouri, St. Louis)*

Using Technology in Human Services Education: Going the Distance, edited by Goutham M. Menon, PhD, and Nancy K. Brown, PhD (Vol. 18, No. 1/2, 2001). *"A refreshingly realistic and balanced collection. . . . Highlights many innovative efforts in both education and practice. Will be extremely valuable in courses on technology in social work, or for courses examining emerging trends in social work practice." (Paul P. Freddolino, PhD, Professor and Coordinator of Distance Education, School of Social Work, Michigan State University, East Lansing)*

Human Services Online: A New Arena for Service Delivery, edited by Jerry Finn, PhD, and Gary Holden, DSW (Vol. 17, No. 1/2/3, 2000). *Focuses on the ways that human services are using the Internet for service delivery, social change, and resource development as more and more agencies can be found on the Internet.*

Computers and Information Technology in Social Work: Education, Training, and Practice, edited by Jo Ann R. Coe, PhD, and Goutham M. Menon, PhD (Vol. 16, No. 2/3, 1999). *Discusses the impact that recent technological advances have had on social work practice and education. Social workers and educators will discover ideas and projects that were presented at a week long conference presented at the University of South Carolina College of Social Work. This unique book covers a wide range of topics, such as different aspects of technology applied to assist those in helping professions, how computers can be used in child protective cases in order to practice more effectively, social services via videoconferencing, and much more.*

Information Technologies: Teaching to Use–Using to Teach, edited by Frank B. Raymond III, DSW, Leon Ginsberg, PhD, and Debra Gohagan, MSW, ACSW, LISW* (Vol. 15, No. 2/3, 1998). *Explores examples of the use of technology to teach social work knowledge, values, and skills across the curriculum.*

The History and Function of the Target Cities Management Information Systems, edited by Matthew G. Hile, PhD* (Vol. 14, No. 3/4, 1998). *"Essential reading for anyone invested in improving the coordination and delivery of substance abuse services in large metropolitan areas." (Albert D. Farrell, PhD, Professor of Psychology, Virginia Commonwealth University, Richmond)*

Human Services in the Information Age, edited by Jackie Rafferty, MS, Jan Steyaert, and David Colombi* (Vol. 12, No. 1/2/3/4, 1996). *"Anyone interested in the current state of the development of human service information systems of all types needs to read this book." (Walter F. LaMendola, PhD, Consultant, Wheat Ridge, CO)*

Electronic Tools for Social Work Practice and Education, edited by Hy Resnick, PhD* (Vol. 11, No. 1/2/3/4, 1994). *"Opens a new world of opportunities for readers by introducing a variety of electronic tools available when working with various clients." (Ram A. Cnaan, PhD, Associate Professor, School of Social Work, University of Pennsylvania)*

Technology in People Services: Research, Theory, and Applications, edited by Marcos Leiderman, MSW, Charles Guzzetta, EdD, Leny Struminger, PhD, and Menachem Monnickendam, PhD, MSW* (Vol. 9, No. 1/2/3/4, 1993). *"Honest reporting and inquiry into the opportunities and limitations for administrators, managers, supervisors, clinicians, service providers, consumers, and clients . . . A well-integrated and in-depth examination." (John P. Flynn, PhD, Associate Director for Instructional Computing, University Computing Services and Professor of Social Work, Western Michigan University)*

Computer Applications in Mental Health: Education and Evaluation, edited by Marvin J. Miller, MD* (Vol. 8, No. 3/4, 1992). *"Describes computer programs designed specifically for mental health clinicians and their work in both private practice and institutional treatment settings." (SciTech Book News)*

Computers for Social Change and Community Organizing, edited by John Downing, PhD, Robert Fasano, MSW, Patricia Friedland, MLS, Michael McCullough, AM, Terry Mizrahi, PhD, and Jeremy Shapiro, PhD* (Vol. 8, No. 1, 1991). *This landmark volume presents an original and until-now-unavailable perspective on the uses of computers for community- and social-change-based organizations.*

Computer Literacy in Human Services Education, edited by Richard L. Reinoehl and B. Jeanne Mueller* (Vol. 7, No. 1/2/3/4, 1990). *This volume provides a unique and notable contribution to the investigation and exemplification of computer literacy in human services education.*

Computer Literacy in Human Services, edited by Richard L. Reinoehl and Thomas Hanna* (Vol. 6, No. 1/2/3/4, 1990). *"Includes a diversity of articles on many of the most important practical and conceptual issues associated with the use of computer technology in the human services." (Adult Residential Care)*

The Impact of Information Technology on Social Work Practice, edited by Ram A. Cnaan, PhD, and Phyllida Parsloe, PhD* (Vol. 5, No. 1/2, 1989). *International experts confront the urgent need for social work practice to move into the computer age.*

A Casebook of Computer Applications in the Social and Human Services, edited by Walter LaMendola, PhD, Bryan Glastonbury, and Stuart Toole* (Vol. 4, No. 1/2/3/4, 1989). *"Makes for engaging and enlightening reading in the rapidly expanding field of information technology in the human services." (Wallace Gingerich, PhD, Associate Professor, School of Social Welfare, University of Wisconsin-Milwaukee)*

Technology and Human Service Delivery: Challenges and a Critical Perspective, edited by John W. Murphy, PhD, and John T. Pardeck, PhD, MSW* (Vol. 3, No. 1/2, 1988). *"A much-needed, critical examination of whether and how computers can improve social services . . . Essential reading for social workers in the field and for scholars interested in how computers alter social systems." (Charles Ess, PhD, Assistant Professor of Philosophy, Morningside College)*

Research in Mental Health Computing: The Next Five Years, edited by John H. Greist, MD, Judith A. Carroll, PhD, Harold P. Erdman, PhD, Marjorie H. Klein, PhD, and Cecil R. Wurster, MA* (Vol. 2, No. 3/4, 1988). *"Provides a clear and lucid perspective on the state of research in mental health computing." (David Servan-Schreiber, MD, Western Psychiatric Institute & Clinic and Department of Computer Science, Carnegie Mellon University)*

∞ ALL HAWORTH BOOKS AND JOURNALS
ARE PRINTED ON CERTIFIED
ACID-FREE PAPER

Human Services Technology: Innovations in Practice and Education

Hy Resnick, PhD
Phoebe Sade Anderson, MSW
Editors

Human Services Technology: Innovations in Practice and Education has been co-published simultaneously as *Journal of Technology in Human Services*, Volume 20, Numbers 1/2 and 3/4 2002.

The Haworth Press, Inc.
New York • London • Oxford

Human Services Technology: Innovations in Practice and Education has been co-published simultaneously as *Journal of Technology in Human Services*™, Volume 20, Numbers 1/2 and 3/4 2002.

Cover design by Thomas J. Mayshock Jr.

Library of Congress Cataloging-in-Publication Data

Human Services Technology: Innovations in Practice and Education / Hy Resnick and Phoebe Sade Anderson, editors.

p. cm.

"Co-published simultaneously as Journal of Technology in Human Services, volume 20, numbers 1/2/3/4 2002."

Includes bibliographical references and index.

ISBN 0-7890-1700-8 (hard : alk. paper) – ISBN 0-7890-1701-6 (pbk: alk. paper)

1. Social work education–Technological innovations–United States. 2. Social service–Technological innovations–United States. I. Resnick, Herman, 1930- II. Anderson, Phoebe Sade. III. Journal of technology in human services.

HV11.7 .H86 2002

361.3'071--dc21 2002001519

Indexing, Abstracting & Website/Internet Coverage

This section provides you with a list of major indexing & abstracting services. That is to say, each service began covering this periodical during the year noted in the right column. Most Websites which are listed below have indicated that they will either post, disseminate, compile, archive, cite or alert their own Website users with research-based content from this work. (This list is as current as the copyright date of this publication.)

Abstracting, Website/Indexing Coverage . . . . Year When Coverage Began

- ***ACM Guide to Computer Literature*** **1992**
- ***Applied Social Sciences Index & Abstracts (ASSIA) (Online: ASSI via Data-Star) (CDRom: ASSIA Plus) <www.csa.com>*** **1993**
- ***Behavioral Medicine Abstracts*** **1996**
- ***BUBL Information Service, an Internet-based Information Service for the UK higher education community <http://bubl.ac.uk/>*** **1995**
- ***caredata CD: the social and community care database <www.scie.org.uk>*** **1994**
- ***CINAHL (Cumulative Index to Nursing & Allied Health Literature), in print, EBSCO, and Silver Platter, Data-Star, and PaperChase. (Support materials include Subject Heading List, Database Search Guide, and Instructional video) <www.cinahl.com>*** **1995**
- ***CNPIEC Reference Guide: Chinese National Directory of Foreign Periodicals*** **1995**

(continued)

- *Computer Abstracts* **1995**
- *Computer Literature Index* **1994**
- *Computing Reviews* **1993**
- *Education Process Improvement Ctr, Inc (EPICENTER) <http://www.epicent.com>* **1995**
- *Educational Administration Abstracts (EAA)* **2002**
- *Engineering Information (PAGE ONE)* **1995**
- *FINDEX <www.publist.com>* **2000**
- *IBZ International Bibliography of Periodical Literature <www.saur.de>* **1996**
- *Index Guide to College Journals (core list compiled by integrating 48 indexes frequently used to support undergraduate programs in small to medium sized libraries)* **1999**
- *Information Science Abstracts* **1992**
- *INSPEC <www.iee.org.uk/publish/>* **1992**
- *Internet & Personal Computing Abstracts <www.infotoday.com /mca/default.htm>* **2000**
- *Library & Information Science Abstracts (LISA) <www.csa.com>* **1994**
- *Periodica Islamica* **1994**
- *Psychological Abstracts (PsycINFO) <www.apa.org>* **1992**
- *Referativnyi Zhurnal (Abstracts Journal of the All-Russian Institute of Scientific and Technical Information–in Russian)* **1992**
- *Sage Public Administration Abstracts (SPAA)* **1992**
- *Social Services Abstracts <www.csa.com>* **1992**
- *Social Work Abstracts <www.silverplatter.com/catalog/swab.htm>* **1992**
- *Sociological Abstracts (SA) <www.csa.com>* **1992**
- *SwetsNet <www.swetsnet.com>* **1999**
- *Violence and Abuse Abstracts: A Review of Current Literature on Interpersonal Violence (VAA)* **2002**

(continued)

Special Bibliographic Notes related to special journal issues (separates) and indexing/abstracting:

- indexing/abstracting services in this list will also cover material in any "separate" that is co-published simultaneously with Haworth's special thematic journal issue or DocuSerial. Indexing/abstracting usually covers material at the article/chapter level.
- monographic co-editions are intended for either non-subscribers or libraries which intend to purchase a second copy for their circulating collections.
- monographic co-editions are reported to all jobbers/wholesalers/approval plans. The source journal is listed as the "series" to assist the prevention of duplicate purchasing in the same manner utilized for books-in-series.
- to facilitate user/access services all indexing/abstracting services are encouraged to utilize the co-indexing entry note indicated at the bottom of the first page of each article/chapter/contribution.
- this is intended to assist a library user of any reference tool (whether print, electronic, online, or CD-ROM) to locate the monographic version if the library has purchased this version but not a subscription to the source journal.
- individual articles/chapters in any Haworth publication are also available through the Haworth Document Delivery Service (HDDS).

Human Services Technology: Innovations in Practice and Education

CONTENTS

ABOUT THE EDITORS

Hy Resnick, PhD, is Professor Emeritus at the University of Washington School of Social Work. His major areas of expertise are electronic technology in human service practice and education, organization development, group work, group processes, and international social work. Dr. Resnick has organized and coordinated numerous Planned Change conferences with Russian, Asian, and Eastern European colleagues and is currently working with COLSA (College of Labor and Social Affairs), a Vietnamese governmental teaching institution that trains social workers in rehabilitation settings.

Dr. Resnick's book (co-authored with Rino Patti), *Change from Within: Humanizing Social Welfare Organizations*, is used in universities, community colleges, and training institutions in the United States and overseas. A second book, entitled *Electronic Tools for Social Work Practice and Education*, was published by The Haworth Press, Inc. in 1994. He has designed and produced two software multimedia programs with his company SWATT (Social Work and Technology/Training–Website www.swatt.org)–one for use in social work practice with at-risk youth called "BUSTED" and the other called "BETTER LISTENING" for use in social work education.

Dr. Resnick has conducted seminars and workshops for non-profit and profit-making organizations in countries around the world including Australia, Israel, Greece, New Zealand, Russia, Scotland, Uzbekistan, and Vietnam. He lives with his wife and family in Woodinville, Washington.

Phoebe Sade Anderson, MSW, completed her master's degree in social work at the University of Washington in 2000. In addition to her interest in the technological advances within the field, she has spent much of her time working on the social policies and systems in Washington State. Professionally, Ms. Anderson has been involved in organizing, advocating and lobbying for welfare reform and the rights of low-income people; she is presently the Chairperson of the Board of Directors of Fair Budget, a statewide not-for-profit organization that addresses these needs. Most recently, she has been working to improve the child welfare arena, particularly the experiences of children in out-of-home care. Initially, she worked as a policy analyst for an agency working to reform the child welfare system in Washington. Presently, Ms. Anderson is the Educational Advocacy Coordinator for a non-profit agency in the Seattle area; she is developing and running a pilot program focused on increasing the educational outcomes of adolescent foster youth.

Ms. Anderson would like to thank her family for all of their continuous love and support.

Preface

The software presented in the first section, focusing on practice, can be said to have its roots in efforts which took place almost a half century ago when a small group of innovative scientists interested in computers and helping people began to think of ways to merge the two fields.

Joseph Weizenbaum, one of the scientists and a MIT professor of computer science, introduced the first breakthrough computer program as an experiment which attempted to imitate a Rogerian approach to counseling, using a natural language processing system. Although critics have emphasized ELIZA's inability to truly replicate the tonal quality of voices and its insensitivity to vocal nuances, Weizenbaum never meant for ELIZA to be a substitute for the personal element in counseling. His interest was solely in scientifically exploring computer-human interface. In fact, when psychiatrists suggested that ELIZA might be an acceptable substitute for human therapy, he was so appalled that he shifted his research to focus on the problems created by the mechanization of human characteristics and talents.

Some computer driven programs developed in the 60s and 70s were intentionally designed to be used in the helping professions. These programs varied in the theoretical underpinnings employed in their design, which were based on the therapeutic orientations of their developers. Colby, Watt and Gilbert (1960) and Taylor (1970), for example, designed their computer assisted programs employing a psychoanalytic approach. They all had in common the motivation to experiment with computers as a potential aid to therapy. Their programs were also meant mainly for demonstration purposes rather than for providing a finished computer assisted counseling application. The creators of these programs believed their advantages lay in the consistency of the computer

[Haworth co-indexing entry note]: "Preface." Resnick, Hy, and Phoebe Sade Anderson. Co-published simultaneously in *Journal of Technology in Human Services* (The Haworth Press, Inc.) Vol. 20, No. 1/2, 2002, pp. xvii-xxi; and: *Human Services Technology: Innovations in Practice and Education* (ed: Hy Resnick, and Phoebe Sade Anderson) The Haworth Press, Inc., 2002, pp. xvii-xxi. Single or multiple copies of this article are available for a fee from The Haworth Document Delivery Service [1-800-HAWORTH, 9:00 a.m. - 5:00 p.m. (EST). E-mail address: getinfo@haworthpressinc.com].

"therapist" who never became tired, angry or bored, was available at all times of the day, AND had no existing personal problems.

The next wave of computer driven programs designed for clinical use focused on assessment of general and specific problem areas. For example, programs were introduced which assessed alcohol and drug abuse, sexual dysfunction, and a client's risk level for committing suicide (Greist 1973). In 1978, Wagman and Kerber introduced PLATO DCS. Thought to be the most comprehensive system to date, it was based on cognitive theory and modeled on the logic pattern of computers. The advantages for such assessment systems were in the standardization of the presentation of questions and in the fact that clients were thought to be more likely to divulge sensitive information to a computer than to a human.

Some of the most widespread computer applications in the helping professions during the 1970s and the 1980s were attempts to deal with career counseling and career guidance topics. As of 1980, there were at least twenty-five computer assisted guidance systems available. These systems focused on providing career information and guidance functions, namely in the forms of assessments of values, skills and interests and decision making instructions. Other related programs were designed to increase academic motivation, improve study skills and assist individuals in eliminating behaviors that limit academic performance, such as test anxiety and procrastination. Specifically, CASSI (Computer Assisted Study Skills Instruction System) was one of the major programs in the 1980s for these problem areas.

In the mid to late 1980s, a shift occurred when software began to be utilized in training professionals in the counseling field. These programs were able to monitor the user's understanding of the material, provide users with feedback, and allow for users' determined pace and direction of learning. Quite quickly, this use of the computer and this training approach progressed into a model of direct training for the clients who were then able to deal with their problems working alone. An example of this type of application was described in 1988 by Denton who produced a program of computer aided video instruction to help psychiatric in-patients adapt to the post-discharge experience using a problem solving approach.

Between the early 1980s and the present day the use of computers as an adjunct to the therapist in Cognitive Behavioral Therapy (CBT) has rapidly grown, specifically for such diagnosed disorders as depression, anxiety, obsessive-compulsive disorder and stress. Because CBT is based on the assessment of symptoms and the offering of exercises and homework tasks, the use of desktop, laptop, and hand held palm computers has lent itself well to this form of therapy. For example, a client is able to assess his own symptoms and carry out the prescribed and monitored exercises through the computer program. The procedures are well defined and target specific behaviors in a systematic way. This usage is most effective for a client away from the therapist and/or used to support or supplement the work of a human therapist.

A significant advantage of technology for clinical purposes is in its solution to the problem of distance. The telephone, the computer, and the Internet have minimized the challenges faced by inaccessibility and reluctance to participate in face-to-face therapy. Telephone therapy for groups and for individuals has long been a useful tool. Most recently the use of online support groups has grown dramatically. Some people seem to be more comfortable seeking help from their computers at home and some are just unable to access any help locally. The ease of electronic communication regionally, nationally and internationally has greatly increased non-face to face clinical work (while also raising ethical questions about the use of technology in the social work field).

Most recently, computer games and simulations have progressed onto the technological platform of social work. For work with children, computer games have proven especially helpful because they allow the children to express themselves in an environment of fantasy where they are more comfortable. Many computer games use extraordinary elements such as vibrant graphics which connect with a child's own recreational use of popular computer games. But in addition to fantasy-like games, programs meant to help youth in problem solving and decision making are becoming popular. From drug education to AIDS/HIV prevention, schools, organizations and agencies are beginning to use such software.

Some of the most innovative work has been in virtual reality, although this type of computer intervention is still highly costly and not readily feasible for many. Practitioners have focused on resolving issues of fear and anxiety through the use of a virtual environment and realistic stimuli. The visual graphics are stunningly real and offer a level of interactivity not often possible in the real world for many clients.

Electronic technology also has a history in public and higher education which can be summarized as consisting of three phases. Phase I dates back to the 20s and 30s when educators began introducing sound and still images into the classroom employing wire recorders and slide projectors. The purpose of introducing these technologies was–as is true today–to make the classroom experience more interesting and dramatic, thereby enhancing learning by highlighting a point, clarifying a complex issue, or making an historical event more real.

Phase II can be said to occur in the 40s, 50s and 60s, when moving images were brought into the classroom utilizing initially 8 mm cameras and later the much more powerful and sophisticated 16 mm camera (later video camera or camcorder) to capture real life as it moved and interacted. Because of the latter technology's increased sophistication, scenes were displayed onto screens with dramatic impact for the learner. Although both Phase I and Phase II technologies did indeed bring change to the students' experiences, these technologies still kept students in the role of passive learner–but still listening to instructors while sitting. It was only when interactivity came to be seen by educators and computer specialists as central to "true" learning (not only for passing tests) that Phase III really began.

Phase III had many false starts in the 70s and 80s but finally took off in the current decade with the advent, acceptance, and high utilization of an array of electronic technological tools that could effectively facilitate not only interactivity but also make available the entire world of information via the Internet. An additional payoff is the ending of dependence of an agreed upon central site for learning. Learning, via the Internet, can now take place from home, a car, a boat, a plane, or even near a swimming pool. All the advantages of this phase made possible a profound change in the classroom experience of the student–from a role of passive consumer of information to a role of active, if not proactive, seeker of information. Students, in this new role, move toward being independent learners, relying less on the instructor to acquire information and more on themselves to achieve that goal. Instructors consequently shift from their primary role of information giver and resource provider to the less dramatic but still useful role of information processor and facilitator/navigator (instructor as "guide on the side" rather than the "sage on the stage").

The first order consequences of these shifts for both the student as learner and instructor as professor are predictable and may be profound–students will learn better, and be more prepared to use information that technology has provided for them in life. Some (or many) instructors will struggle with a changed role and reduced status in society. Modern societies will benefit but higher education (read social work education) will be transformed in ways still difficult to predict.

As technology is more and more accepted, the potential for its use within human services is endless. What has been especially interesting to watch is the reaction of the field to the integration of computer-driven models of treatment, education and administration. In a profession based on human interaction, the usage of computers and technology over the past four decades has been a slow process. We are, however, at this point, undoubtedly in the middle of a transformation in the way social work practitioners and educators employ technology in their daily work.

Hy Resnick
Phoebe Sade Anderson

Introduction

This is the second edition of a volume dedicated to the belief–a belief once novel now increasingly accepted–that social work will be changed, perhaps dramatically, by the introduction of electronic technology into its practice and education.

The first edition (*Electronic Technology in Social Work Practice and Education*, published in 1994) presented articles describing software recently developed–some still in the prototype stage–which were designed for human service purposes. One of its aims was to introduce readers to an array of software programs–however primitive in design and technology–that provided a view of the first wave of computer driven programs that were designed to support and enhance social work practice and instruction.

At the same time it provided the reader with a vision of what the future might hold with respect to the use of electronic technology and social work in practice and education. By doing so it was hoped that the field would become more receptive to the idea of using electronic technology in its work. If social work is to be significantly modified by electronic technology in the near and foreseeable future,[1] then these electronic "inventions" need to be brought to the attention of the profession to help them get ready to use this technology to best advantage–sooner than later!

Another aim of the first edition was to encourage social workers and educators (and non-social workers interested in technology for human service purposes) to begin using, and perhaps for some, designing and producing computer driven interventions in their work with clients and students. Finally, the first edition was published in order to encourage deans and department heads of social work agencies and educational institutions to begin modifying their budgets–if not their thinking–to include funds for the support that is needed if technology is to be utilized in their organizations.

[Haworth co-indexing entry note]: "Introduction." Resnick, Hy, and Phoebe Sade Anderson. Co-published simultaneously in *Journal of Technology in Human Services* (The Haworth Press, Inc.) Vol. 20, No. 1/2, 2002, pp. 1-3; and: *Human Services Technology: Innovations in Practice and Education* (ed: Hy Resnick, and Phoebe Sade Anderson) The Haworth Press, Inc., 2002, pp. 1-3. Single or multiple copies of this article are available for a fee from The Haworth Document Delivery Service [1-800-HAWORTH, 9:00 a.m. - 5:00 p.m. (EST). E-mail address: getinfo@haworthpressinc.com].

There were those of us who predicted–yearly, regularly and probably overoptimistically–that electronic technology would infiltrate itself into the mainstream of social work and lead to great changes in how we did our work.[2] We were often disappointed when so little seemed to be happening in the profession. For example, there were few publications on the subject of electronic technology and social work, little attention was paid to technology at local and national conferences, and most telling of all, few rebudgeting negotiations were taking place in decision makers' meetings.

Actually, a great deal was happening in the underculture of our profession–individual instructors, practitioners and social work "techies" were working on their own projects with little institutional support–a la Edison, the Wright brothers, Dr. Ehrlich, and others too numerous to mention. We were, in these informal venues, developing software; publishing thin journals; participating in poorly publicized, funded and attended side-conferences; dreaming up ways to use the Internet in classes; writing articles and books on the parameters and issues of the future of technology in social work.

These small–but beautiful–activities are typical of the way innovations are initiated and accepted by individuals in different parts of a country, usually unconnected and uncoordinated, until one day they become the basis of a new paradigm of a profession or a science. Indeed that is what has happened in the last five or six years. These "inventions" have led to changes in our work with clients and students and are the basis for this collection (and others recently published).

This second edition will have the same major foci as the first. Specifically, to present social work (and other human service professions) with a range of articles which describe software programs, telephone, video and Internet innovations but now with more sophisticated technology, smaller size, easier applicability, reduced prices, and with the capacity to utilize more advanced multimedia platforms/environments which support and, arguably enhance, social work practice and instruction.

It is also assumed in this edition that social work readers will be stimulated to use computer driven programs to enhance their practice and education, and hopefully, readers of the second edition will soon be designing their own online courses and/or developing multimedia programs that will better fit their clients' needs than traditional methods of practicing and instructing.

Social work education, institution, and agency administrators too will find in these multimedia and online programs evidence that indeed computer driven interventions and online programs are out there, are usable and are enhancing social work practice and education. There is also every reason to believe they may also be cost effective.

In this edition, as was true in the first, the volume is divided into two main sections–technology and social work practice, and technology and social work education. The practice section deals with the clinical work (including administration) of our profession–the education section includes articles describing technological innovations in social work education.

NOTES

1. Butterfield,W.H. (1998) Human Services and the Information Economy in Raymond, F., Ginsberg, L. and Cohagen, D. eds. Teaching to Use and Using to Teach. NY: The Haworth Press, Inc.

2. See following article for an extreme perspective on the impact of technology on the social work profession: Kreuger, Larry & Stretch, John. Commentary. *Social Work*, October 2000, pp. 457-461.

Introduction to Technology for Social Work Practice

Hy Resnick
Phoebe Sade Anderson

The contributors to the first half of this collection are human service educators and practitioners whose articles focus on software they have developed for work with youth and adults. These articles were selected for inclusion in this edition for the following reasons:

- The designers/authors had produced software (text based mostly) for human services purposes in the past and so their current work represents the progress that technology has made in our field. These designers/authors are the second stage innovators whose work needs to be recorded.
- These programs are being used by professional helpers and are actually employed in various human service programs to support practice (software programs described in the first edition were mostly demonstration models).
- Some of the software programs included had been subjected to increasingly rigorous and formal evaluations, the outcomes of

[Haworth co-indexing entry note]: "Introduction to Technology for Social Work Practice." Resnick, Hy, and Phoebe Sade Anderson. Co-published simultaneously in *Journal of Technology in Human Services* (The Haworth Press, Inc.) Vol. 20, No. 1/2, 2002, pp. 5-10; and: *Human Services Technology: Innovations in Practice and Education* (ed: Hy Resnick, and Phoebe Sade Anderson) The Haworth Press, Inc., 2002, pp. 5-10. Single or multiple copies of this article are available for a fee from The Haworth Document Delivery Service [1-800-HAWORTH, 9:00 a.m. - 5:00 p.m. (EST). E-mail address: getinfo@haworthpressinc.com].

which indicate the utility of properly designed software in our profession.

- They represent the internationalization of technology in the human services as well as the interconnectedness of our field. The software described in these articles were developed, tested and utilized in Australia, Canada, Israel, Finland, the United Kingdom and the United States.
- These programs are now more user friendly, employing more sophisticated technology to create well-designed software for a variety of uses: a play-therapy tool, a child welfare aid, an educative/preventative intervention for a variety of issues and as a problem-solving program in a school setting.

ELECTRONIC TECHNOLOGY USED IN WORKING WITH YOUTH

The opening article by Louis L. Aymard, a clinical psychologist in the United States, describes a software program called "Funny Face" obtained through the shareware process and originally designed for entertainment/commercial purposes. In this article, Aymard describes how he makes use of this software program with pre- and latency-aged children. Working in a private clinic as a play therapist, he uses the computer and the "Funny Face" program to attract and introduce his pre- and latency-age children. Aymard uses the computer and "Funny Face" to attract and introduce his patients to his version of play therapy using the computer as a toy, not a machine (he places the computer with an attractive screen in the toy table). He also uses "Funny Face" as a projective technique, to make masks and to engage in socio-dramatic play. His goal in his use of the program is to teach children about identifying and expressing feelings in a constructive way.

Les Cowan, a Scottish social worker and computer program developer, takes a story well known in the UK and turns it into an engaging multimedia program for 6th graders dealing with the trauma of being placed in foster homes or with adoptive parents. The program, called "Bruce's Multimedia Story," focuses on a puppy with whom the children can identify who is leaving his mother to enter the unknown world. "Bruce's Multimedia Story" (and a second software program called "Billy Breaks the Rules" which he designed for older youth) uses many cartoons, delightful music as background, and voice-over to help the child talk to his social worker about feelings which the cartoons about the puppy elicit. These two programs represent the continuation of Cowan's work in the UK to introduce electronic technology to British social work with children.

Michael Gropper, a social work administrator in Israel, describes "Say No with Donny," a software program he has developed, produced, tested, and disseminated in Israel for at-risk Jewish youth (and a slightly revised version for Arab youth). Gropper developed the software program from the ground up for sixth graders as an alcohol and drug preventative. Using a variety of personal change theories to underpin his design, Gropper presents a central character, Donny (or Samir in the Arab version), as a big brother role model for the 6th grade user with which to identify. Donny is programmed to tell them about the people, events and issues that can influence the way young people think about alcohol and drug use. A guided group process, integral to the use of the program, is designed to facilitate the conducting of the software in an agency or a school setting.

"Talking It Out: A Computer-Based Mediation Process for Adolescents" is a software program developed by Kris Bosworth, an educational psychologist who has produced and tested a number of software programs to be used therapeutically with youth. In "Talking It Out," she uses concepts from the mediation literature to create a youth-managed software driven mediation process to be used in a school or agency setting. "Talking It Out" is her creative effort to help teens in schools use computer technology to settle disputes peacefully. A distinctive feature of this software is the use of an animated panel of teens who advise the participants in their choices and decision-making.

Ann Wilder and Dick Schoech's article describes a software program designed to educate youth about HIV and AIDS, especially youth with parents who have HIV or the AIDS virus. Their article also emphasizes their creative use of a youth group as a member of their design and production team to test the belief that young people listen or learn best from their peers.

These five articles commonly describe how electronic technology is used in work with youth of all ages. But they differ in a number of ways, including:

- practice sites where these programs are utilized (private clinic in the US, public child welfare in Scotland, and school and agency setting in both Israel and the United States).

- how they are developed–some adapt popular stories or commercial software for children to therapeutic goals, others create new software with therapeutic purposes in mind.
- how they are to be facilitated–using guides to facilitate a group, to be used independently, and to be used interactively by client and practitioner.
- their goals–some have treatment objectives, others are prevention focused, and some have educational objectives.

These differences are indicative of the wide range of ways in which electronic technology can be used in work with youth.

The next part of this section shows how electronic technology can also be used with adults.

ELECTRONIC TECHNOLOGY USED IN WORKING WITH ADULTS

The next six articles in this section describe software programs designed for use in working with adults.

In the first article, Andrea Meier, Clinical Assistant Professor at a School of Social Work in the United States, discusses her use of the Internet to answer two questions: (1) can the Internet deliver social support, and (2) can online support groups help social workers manage job stress? Beginning with a pilot of MSW students and growing into a larger study of practicing, master's level social workers, described in this article, Meier utilized her extensive research on organizational behavior, occupational stress, coping theory, social support, and the use of online groups. This article offers useful insight into a model of working with adults, but also addresses the key issues of integrating technology into all levels of social work, specifically peer support.

Jerry Finn, an American social work educator who has been a pioneer in conducting research in the use of electronic communication for therapeutic purposes, and Mary Banach, a social work educator and practitioner, developed this article as a response to the lack of research and clarity of the legal implications of therapeutic online services in the United States. In this important work they identify legal and ethical issues with which human service professionals will have to contend in the near future as online services continue to be offered by social agencies and private professionals. They offer a range of professionally sound and practical ideas to deal with these issues.

Kate Collie and Davor Čubranić, an art therapist and a computer scientist from Canada, introduce a novel use of electronic technology and art therapy in working with patients suffering from traumatic illness. They describe a computer-aided distance art therapy program which they, working with a cross discipline team of ten others, designed and produced. They conceive of this effort as a form of telehealth, an electronic activity that is increasingly being used in the health fields with certain populations including homebound, rural inhabitants, and those that value privacy.

Telephone counseling, a low tech program described by Maxine Rosenfield, a counselor working in the UK and currently in Australia, is designed to help shut ins or similarly homebound clients. She contrasts telephone counseling with both telephone hotline and face to face traditional counseling to highlight the distinctive elements of this new but increasingly used mode of electronic helping.

Marja-Leena Mielonen, a Finnish psychiatrist, and her colleagues describe and illustrate another use of electronic technology in professional helping commonly called telepsychiatry, or more descriptively, interactive video conferencing. This type of technology involves a psychiatrist at one end in an urban hospital or facility and patients and/or their families at the other who are seen for assessment, planning or treatment purposes. Especially interesting is the description of Mielonen et al.'s use of an interactive video conferencing session focused on patient care planning between psychiatric staff and family members of a patient.

A final article written by Joseph E. Garcia and L. Floyd Lewis, who are members of the management faculty at a major university school of business in the United States, and Ann L. Hallock, a social worker, is included in this practice section because of the importance of staff meetings to human service practitioners and supervisors. They describe an electronically supported approach to conducting staff meetings. Lewis et al. developed an electronically-supported program called *Meeting Works*™ which helps improve the efficiency and effectiveness of staff meetings. Lewis and Garcia developed *Meeting Works*™ over twenty years ago and have been engaged in testing and revising it ever since. *Meeting Works*™ has been utilized by social service agencies (Casey Family Programs), profit-making organizations (Boeing, IBM, Weyerhaeuser) and public agencies (National Park Service).

Computer programs for the human services have typically been designed for work with children, and certainly the entertainment computer industry has devoted much of its interest and resources to developing programs for youth–with great success. This section focusing on electronic technology and work with adults contains a surprising number of articles which describe software programs intended for use with adults–a population whose needs may also be served by human service oriented software programs.

"Funny Face": Shareware for Child Counseling and Play Therapy

Louis L. Aymard

SUMMARY. "Funny Face," an off-the-shelf children's computer game, is used in play therapy and counseling with preschool and latency age children by the author/designer, who also serves as the therapist. *[Article copies available for a fee from The Haworth Document Delivery Service: 1-800-HAWORTH. E-mail address: <getinfo@haworthpressinc.com> Website: <http://www.HaworthPress.com> © 2002 by The Haworth Press, Inc. All rights reserved.]*

KEYWORDS. Play therapy, child counseling, computers, technology, youth

INTRODUCTION

The hardware and software spawned out of Silicon Valley in the late 1970s has had a profound impact upon almost every facet of American

Louis L. Aymard, PhD, is affiliated with the Arnold-Severn Center, 528 College Parkway, Suite G, Annapolis, MD 21401 (E-mail: laymard@friend.ly.net).

[Haworth co-indexing entry note]: "'Funny Face': Shareware for Child Counseling and Play Therapy." Aymard, Louis L. Co-published simultaneously in *Journal of Technology in Human Services* (The Haworth Press, Inc.) Vol. 20, No. 1/2, 2002, pp. 11-29; and: *Human Services Technology: Innovations in Practice and Education* (ed: Hy Resnick, and Phoebe Sade Anderson) The Haworth Press, Inc., 2002, pp. 11-29. Single or multiple copies of this article are available for a fee from The Haworth Document Delivery Service [1-800-HAWORTH, 9:00 a.m. - 5:00 p.m. (EST). E-mail address: getinfo@haworthpressinc.com].

life. The personal computer has become indispensable in government, industry, education, and homes. One of the largest consumers of digital technology is the academic community. Creative teachers at all levels of education incorporate the computer into the classroom because they realize its value in communicating with children of the Digital Age. This boon in computer utilization in many segments of our society stands in stark contrast to computer use by counselors and child psychotherapists.

The impetus for using computers in psychotherapy with children appeared almost 15 years ago. In a classic article about computers and child therapy, David Allen (1984) described how "Ultima," an adventure-fantasy game for the Apple II computer, aptly engaged latency-age children in counseling and produced psychosocial gains such as enhanced self-concept and a sense of mastery. In the ensuing years, other pioneers (Canter, 1987; Casey & Ramsammy, 1992; Clark & Schoech, 1984; Favelle, 1994; Gardner, 1991; Johnson, 1984, 1987; Kokish, 1994; Margolies, 1991; Oakley, 1994; Resnick, 1994; Sherer, 1994; Sisson, Mayfield & Entz, 1985) reported very positive psychotherapeutic outcomes when using computers with children. Several themes pervade this burgeoning group of seminal studies. First, the computer was not a "turn-off" for children but rather a "hook" to involve them in counseling or play therapy. Second, the computer was not deleterious to the children's therapy because the presenting problems remitted. Finally, none of the researchers found compelling evidence that the computer is therapeutically contraindicated for children or adolescents.

Given the documented support for computer use in child psychotherapy, one might wonder why few mental health professionals incorporate this technology into their work with children. Survey research (Kepner & Thompson, 1995) conducted in Maryland provides a preliminary answer to that question. Play therapists who practice in schools, health departments, public agencies and university settings were queried about the use of computers with children. Only twelve percent of the therapists who responded (N = 51) reported that they regularly use the computer in counseling sessions with children. However, 68 percent of the respondents indicated that they *would* use the computer, but felt inhibited by the lack of time for adequate training (34%) or the expense of the equipment (21%). A correlative hypothesis, advanced by the author, is that mental health professionals conceive of computers as electronic workstations while their child clients believe the computer is a toy.

This chapter will chronicle how the author used a cartooning computer game in play therapy sessions with preschool and latency-age children. The children were clients in a child psychology practice at a private mental health setting in the Baltimore-Washington metropolitan area. The children's presenting problems included anxiety disorders, learning disabilities, attention deficit disorder, oppositional defiant disorder, sexual abuse and adjustment disorders to parental separation and divorce. It is important to emphasize that the computer was never the singular intervention used in the course of the children's therapy.

The hardware was a Dell Latitude laptop computer with an active-matrix color display. It was placed on one of six colorful plastic crates securely fastened to each other and the wall to form a console in a play therapy room. An Epson Stylus Color 600 printer was adjacent to the computer. The COM port at the rear of the laptop computer was input for a mouse-pen that allowed children to manipulate the cursor by dragging its small track-ball across a mouse pad. An important factor in the successful utilization of this technology was that the computer was nestled among the toys in the play therapy room so that it resembled an electronic arcade. It was *not* placed on the clinician's desk, giving it the appearance of an office machine.

USING SHAREWARE FOR CHILD THERAPY

Children's software is plentiful in computer outlets, toy stores, and discount houses. It comes in scintillating packaging, with colorful artwork, and supporting documentation at a price between $30.00 and $60.00 per title. A review of children's software, produced commercially in the United States, yielded an impressive list of 2,961 titles (Wolock et al., 1998). It is conceivable that child counselors and play therapists could spend hundreds of dollars building a software library.

An economical alternative to investing lots of money in children's computer programs is shareware. Shareware is actually a marketing technique based on the consumer concept "try before you buy." It is a boon for child therapists who wish to purchase software at bargain prices. Computer neophytes may be curious about where to find shareware. Some vendors advertise online. Exploring the Web with any of the major search engines will harvest myriad sites that feature shareware. Other firms market shareware titles in computer periodicals.

Although there are no published criteria to guide counselors and play therapists in selecting shareware, answering the following questions may provide some structure to the process.

1. Is the shareware compatible with the computer's operating system and peripherals? A wonderful craft-making program will be useless if it can't be configured to print on the office printer.
2. Does the shareware have bugs or glitches that cause a system crash at certain points when it is in use? Two safeguards against this are using shareware that is recommended by a colleague or selecting a title that one may try for several weeks before paying the vendor.
3. Can the shareware be adapted for a variety of psychotherapeutic purposes? The "Funny Face" program, described in this article, may be used as a game, to introduce children to play therapy, to make masks, or to help children ventilate repressed feelings.
4. Is the shareware easy to install? Some programs require a large investment of time to get them working properly. That is a luxury few professionals can afford.
5. Is the shareware easy to use? If a program is too complicated to master, most likely it will frustrate both the child and the therapist.
6. Does the shareware have visual appeal and/or multimedia features? Children are accustomed to playing fast-paced video games with excellent graphics and sound. A shareware program with older bitmap graphics will be a turn-off for them.
7. Is the shareware really a bargain, i.e., well-priced? A $15 shareware game is not a good deal if one can purchase an older commercial version of the program, with lots of features, for $20.00.
8. Is the shareware compatible with one's treatment philosophy? Counselors and play therapists should explore all aspects of a program before using it with children. The shareware may contain language, graphics or other material that is incompatible with one's treatment philosophy.
9. Does the shareware vendor offer technical support? This is very important if problems arise in the installation process.

"FUNNY FACE"

"Funny Face" is cartooning shareware described by its creator as "software that stimulates creativity!" (Zamora, 1992). It is ideally suited for younger children (3 to 9 years of age) who have trouble separating from their parents and feeling comfortable during the early stage of play therapy. When the program loads, it plays a catchy tune and the screen flashes with a kaleidoscopic display of odd-looking faces, each of which appear sequentially for a few seconds. Clicking the left mouse button clears display and takes the user to the screen in Figure 1. [Note: "Funny Face" operates on the Windows 95 and 98 platforms. As of this writing there is not an Apple Macintosh edition of the shareware; however, the newer Macs run some Windows programs.]

Four icons appear on the right- and left-hand sides of the screen. Clicking on each produces a pop-up menu with a variety of pre-drawn features in image libraries that can be combined to produce literally millions of different faces. The paint icon at the lower right-hand corner provides a palette of hues to color the faces. An interesting feature of the software is that the pictures can be stored in two different file formats. The default option produces a "Funny Face" proprietary file (.ffp) that is designed to occupy very little disk space (approximately 100 bytes). The program also saves pictures in a bitmap file format (.bmp) for exporting to word processors, desktop publishers or creativity software.

CLINICAL APPLICATIONS OF "FUNNY FACE"

Introducing Children to Counseling or Play Therapy

The first play therapy session brings children into an unfamiliar setting, with a stranger, under ambiguous circumstances. Under those conditions, who wouldn't be anxious, reticent, passive aggressive, or any of the descriptors found in the clinical literature that characterize children's initial resistance to play therapy? A computer loaded with games, a paint program, and creativity software is an effective way of introducing children to play therapy. "Funny Face" is an excellent program to use if a counselor or therapist is seeing a young child for the first time. Its opening screen is captivating. Children are often more attracted to it than they are to other toys in the play therapy room. They are curious about the faces flashing on the screen. When they realize they are looking at a computer game, a click of the mouse transforms an uncomfortable experience with a stranger into playtime in an electronic arcade.

FIGURE 1. The Opening Screen of "Funny Face."

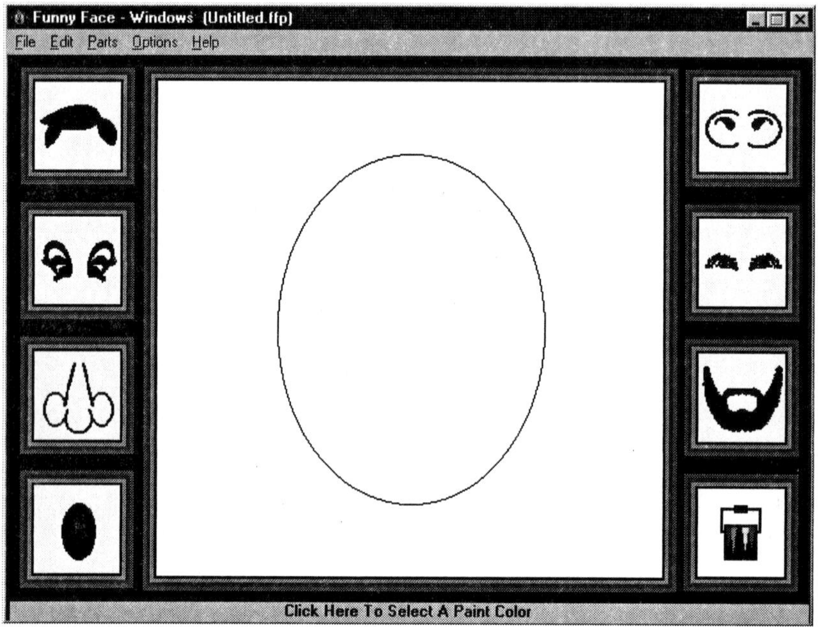

"Funny Face" as a Projective Technique

Projection is defined in psychology and psychiatry as an intrapsychic mechanism in which an individual rejects consciously accessing aversive thoughts, affects or memories and instead transmits them outside of the self onto others or external stimuli. Drawings, storytelling, responses to thematic apperception cards and inkblots have been commonly used as projective techniques. The validity of projective techniques with children is a subject of some controversy in the play therapy literature. Barnes (1996) articulately exposes the rationale behind the opposition to projective tests in *The healing path with children: An exploration for parents and professionals.*

> Despite the lack of empirical evidence for the use of projective techniques, they are used pervasively in the field of play therapy. Play therapy training programs and texts are full of such projective and interpretive methods. There are even those who foolishly be-

> lieve that projective techniques actually enable an outsider to determine the state of children's psychological functioning, right down to past trauma and conflicts. (Barnes, 1996, p. 176)

Barnes' analysis of projective techniques is a cogent admonition that child therapists should not rely upon personal intuition about what is happening at any point in time within a child's inner world. Nevertheless, experienced therapists often derive valuable diagnostic clues from the content and process of children's behaviors during an assessment or psychotherapy session. A little girl who sits at the computer and says, "I'm not sure if I can play this game," may be telling the therapist about her diffidence in new situations or projecting her cognitive perspective about life.

It is not the author's contention that "Funny Face" is a psychometric tool. The faces children create with the software should never be used for diagnostic purposes. That would constitute the same level of psychotherapeutic malpractice as diagnosing a personality disorder from a drawing or a sculptured clay artifact. Notwithstanding, the affect, cognition and behaviors that children express when playing "Funny Face" will be important clues about how they approach learning, challenges, problem solving, competition, frustration, or any of the vicissitudes of life.

Catharsis and Affective Expression

Two important goals of child counseling are to teach youngsters how to identify and understand feelings and to facilitate their expression of powerfully-charged affects that emanate from conflict, trauma, domestic discord or any significant psychosocial stressors they have encountered during the developmental process. The Make-A-Feelings-Face is a creative way of using "Funny Face" to achieve those psychotherapeutic objectives, particularly for children who are unable or unwilling to articulate their feelings about life experiences, interpersonal conflicts or traumas. Children must first be introduced to the game by the therapist and then allowed to experiment with making faces and printing them. When the child is familiar with the program's features and comfortable playing "Funny Face," the therapist can invite them to "make a feeling face." Depending upon the child's age, ego strength, defensiveness and history, the therapist must decide whether to suggest that the face will represent how the child feels or whether it will be an alter ego. In the former case, if Peter got into a fight at school and comes to the session angry, the therapist might say, "Peter, make a face that shows how you were feeling during your fight with Tommy today." In the latter case, a six-year-old girl who is confused, overwhelmed and unwilling to say anything about her parents' divorce could be encouraged to draw a face that shows how someone feels when they hear that a mommy and a daddy are getting a divorce. After seeing the face they created, children are often expansive in their discussions about the feeling related to it. For purposes of continuity with the course of treatment, some therapists may ask the child to begin each session by making a face that shows how he or she is feeling on that particular day.

Mask-Making and Sociodramatic Play

The print feature of "Funny Face" produces a bitmap image that is not of superior quality, but the picture is quite adequate for working with children in counseling sessions. The printed image is about 39 square inches (256 square centimeters), an area that corresponds roughly to the size of a young child's face. When the "Funny Face" image is cut into an oval, it covers a child's face like a mask. Holes can be cut around the eyes with scissors. Gluing the mask to a small wooden stick allows a child to use different faces during a play episode. Also, holes can be punched near the sides of the mask to attach it to the child's head with an elastic band. If a child wants to use a mask in several sessions, covering it with laminate sheets or clear contact paper makes it durable. The therapist or counselor can also use "Funny Face" to create different masks for sociodramatic play or to teach children about identifying certain feelings.

Saving "Funny Face" Files

The Funny Faces created by children can be saved on the computer's hard drive or stored on floppy diskettes. The author uses colored floppy diskettes with decorative labels for two reasons. First, it gives children a sense of belonging because the therapist is saving their art on a special diskette. Second, it obviates the concern that a child might inadvertently retrieve another child's files in a directory on the computer's hard drive.

The issue of confidentiality is very critical when storing electronic data created by children in therapy sessions. Naming a "Funny Face" file with a child's surname is inadvisable. That compromises the confidentiality of the therapeutic process if the file is accessed by anyone other than the therapist or the child. Like any clinical material, the diskettes should be stored in a locked cabinet.

CASE EXAMPLES

The clinical utility of "Funny Face" is not inherent in the software. It is derived from the creativity of the therapist as well as the child's unique psychodynamic process that is operative at the time he or she plays the game. Pseudonyms are used in the following cases. Information about the children has been edited cautiously to ensure the privacy and confidentiality of the families involved.

Managing Children's Resistance to Therapy with "Funny Face"

Brett was more resistant than most seven-year-old boys about coming to counseling. Anticipating he would cause big trouble, both parents accompanied him to the appointment. As the therapist greeted them, Brett was crouched under the table in the waiting room. His father carried him, kicking and screaming, into the office. Brett crossed his eyes, stuck out his tongue, and made grotesque faces. He was unimpressed when the therapist told him there was a room full of toys next door in which they could play. The initial session with Brett and his family was useful to observe the parent-child dynamics. The second appointment with Brett and his parents occurred on a frigid, wintry night. Brett came in without a fuss but refused to remove his jacket. He sat with it zipped up over his head, like a turtle hiding in its shell. This time Brett heard the therapist say that there was a computer in the playroom. A head with disheveled hair popped out from the jacket. He bolted into the playroom and chuckled when he noticed "Funny Face" on the computer screen. The therapist told Brett that he could try any of the toys or games. "You'll let me play with your computer?" he asked. "That's what it's there for," replied the therapist. Brett drew the face in Figure 2.

Brett's Funny Face bears a remarkable resemblance to the grimaces he made in the first session. His behavior was outrageous when things didn't go his way. Gradually family, friends, and teachers began distancing from him. In the sessions that followed, Brett's attention shifted away from the computer to therapeutic board games. He communicated openly and directly with his therapist about his insecurities. Brett thought he was weird, but over time the pictures he made with "Funny

FIGURE 2. A Face Created by a 7-Year-Old Oppositional Boy.

Face" assumed a kinder, gentler countenance. It was "the hook" that engaged Brett in the initial play therapy sessions.

Using "Funny Face" in an Assessment

Paul was eight years old when his parents brought him for a psychological evaluation. They observed radical changes in his behavior after he returned from a visit with his maternal grandmother during summer vacation. Paul's naturally gregarious manner gave way to reclusive behaviors. Instead of playing kickball with the neighborhood children, he spent hours alone in his room. He began making suggestive comments to his younger sister and to other girls in the neighborhood.

Paul was oppositional at the intake session. He mocked the toys in the playroom. Fortuitously, "Funny Face" was displayed on the computer screen. Paul became curious and asked what it was. The therapist explained that it was a computer game for making faces and asked if he wanted to play with it. After spending some time experimenting with the program, he created the haunting face in Figure 3. He colored the whites of the eyes red as though they were bloodshot and chose a zipper for the mouth. As rapport built between Paul and the psychologist, later he disclosed that his maternal grandmother insisted upon bathing him and fondling his genitals during the visit with her. As is often the case with incestuous abuse, Paul was sworn to secrecy by the grandmother who told him that she would be put in prison if he told anyone about their bathtub play.

Computer games are digital media for children to act out the dynamics of intrapsychic life, as are crayons, clay, sand, toys and other play materials. In that context, "Funny Face" has value as a projective technique. When guided by the child's psychodynamic processes, the game has the potential to offer a clinician invaluable clues about unique interpersonal and intrapersonal life issues.

Discussing Family Business

Each session, when the therapist greeted six-year-old Will, he leapt from his seat in the waiting room and ran down the corridor to the playroom. He and his younger sister lived in an affluent community. His mother was a corporate vice-president. At home she was passive and uninvolved in Will's life. She deferred to her husband's judgement about child rearing. His parenting philosophy was that children are like horses: Break their spirit and everything else will fall into place. Will's parents were concerned that he had a learning disability. Teachers couldn't keep him focused during class periods. He was failing all of his subjects in school. Extensive psychoeducational testing revealed that Will had no serious learning problems. In the early phase of the counseling, the therapist taught Will's parents positive behavior management techniques. Concurrently, he came for play therapy to resolve the issue of his plummeting self-esteem due to school failure. Will knew his parents were coming for some kind of coaching sessions about how to take care of children. Will was a garrulous boy who always had stories to tell, but he rarely talked about his family. As life at home and in school improved, Will used the "Funny Face" program to "talk" about family business. A lengthy silence followed after he drew the face in Figure 4. Will looked at the therapist and said, "He's a scared guy." "He looks scared," the therapist replied. Will continued, "He's scared because he gets his butt beat and I used to get my butt beat before my parents came to you for those lessons." "Funny Face" was the medium Will

FIGURE 3. A Face Created by a Sexually Abused Boy at an Intake Session.

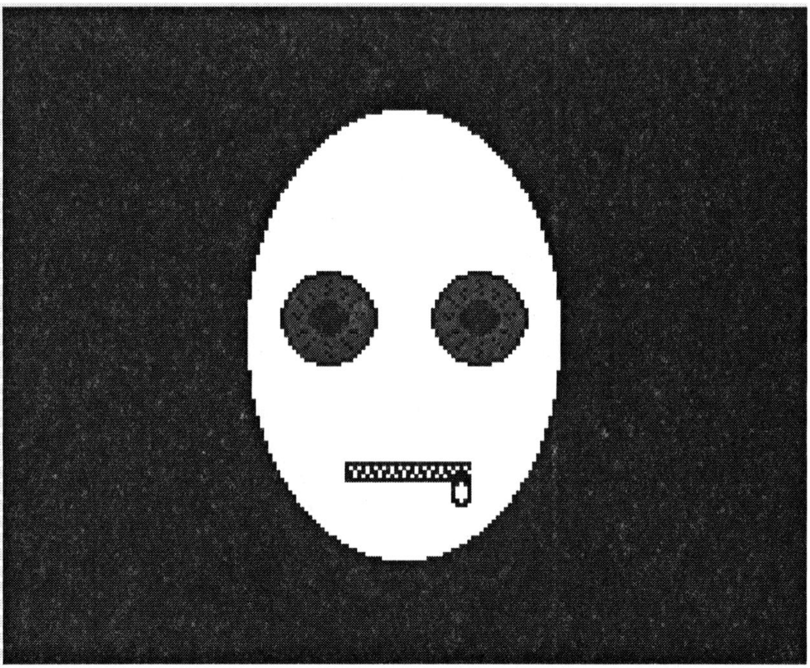

needed to publish his family story. Subsequently, the therapist assured him that his parents were learning how to nurture children and manage his behavior positively.

Kara's Chaotic Family Life

Life in Kara's family was terrifying and chaotic for a five-year-old girl. Her mother was diagnosed with paranoid schizophrenia, but refused to enter treatment. As the intensity of the mother's psychotic episodes escalated, Kara's father obtained custody of the children and was successful in obtaining a court injunction to keep the mother away from the house. Kara witnessed several of her mother's frightening psychotic episodes such as violent fights with her father, dressing in odd clothes, and screaming profanities at neighbors. Once the police were called because the mother had abducted Kara and her brother for two days, driv-

FIGURE 4. A Physically Abused Child's Self Portrait Made with "Funny Face."

ing them aimlessly around a large metropolitan area. Kara was quite taciturn in the initial stages of play therapy. When any reference to the family or her mother came up, she refused to talk.

Kara became obsessed with the "Funny Face" program. At the beginning of a play session, she sat at the computer and said, "Watch me! I'm going to make a picture of a funny man." Although Kara insisted that she was drawing men, often the face on the computer screen was a harrowing picture of a scornful, angry woman. This continued for several months, during which time the therapist witnessed the preponderant place that the vengeful maternal archetype occupied in her psyche. Over time, the female faces Kara made with "Funny Face" were more benign looking. About that time she became less conflicted and played out her frightened and aggressive impulses in sessions. Before termination, Kara talked directly with her therapist about her mother. She took solace in learning that her father had arranged it so that she and her brother would not have to be alone with her mother. "Funny Face" was the toy that enabled Kara to access and express in play therapy the powerfully-charged affects she harbored about her mother.

Erin Makes a Mask

Erin was an internalized, perfectionistic seven-year-old girl whose parents were divorced. She lived with her paternal grandparents and her father, a domineering man who knew little about loving or nurturing his daughter. His bellicose voice and authoritarian style controlled his daughter's behavior, but she paid an enormous emotional price. She was regressed and lacking in confidence. The school counselor reported that Erin didn't want to talk or play when they were together. One day, the counselor invited Erin to play the "Make-A-Feelings Face" on the computer. Although Erin didn't resist, she clearly had other plans for the session. Erin took great pains to produce the man's face in Figure 5. She wanted to print her handiwork. The counselor helped her do that. Erin took scissors and punched holes in the eyes of the face. "It's a mask," she exclaimed. "That's Daddy's angry face." Erin placed the mask over her face. She growled at the counselor, pretending she was a big bad man who could beat him up.

Justin's Termination in Play Therapy

The principal of a private elementary school suggested that Justin's parents take him to see a child psychologist for his school phobia. Almost every session began with Justin playing "Funny Face." It was no surprise that he asked to play the game when he came for his termination session. While the program was loading on the computer, Justin turned to the therapist and said, "I want to take home a picture of you." He glanced at the therapist and smiled when the faces appeared on the monitor. Justin looked back and forth from the therapist's face to the screen. He aptly explained each facial feature he selected with a comment such as, "that looks like your eyes." Several minutes later, Justin had produced the face in Figure 6. He printed two copies of his therapist's portrait. He gave one to the therapist and put the other in his pocket. He said, "I'm taking this picture home to put on the wall in my bedroom." Justin's use of "Funny Face" demonstrates how children use computer software to portray the profiles of significant adults with whom they have strong emotional ties.

FIGURE 5. Erin's Picture of Her Father's Angry Face.

CONCLUSIONS

Principal Points in Review

Adults who have not grown up in the Digital Age use the personal computer as a business tool for word processing, e-mailing, data analysis, or desktop publishing. Reframing the computer as a psychotherapeutic toy for them requires ingenuity, imagination and creativity. Furthermore, the process extends far beyond simply selecting and installing children's software on the office PC. The psychotherapeutic value of the computer for children is patently evident if one reflects upon the goals of child therapy. Admittedly clinicians of different theoretical persuasions disagree about the goals of child counseling or psychotherapy; nevertheless, most would concur that behavior change, personal insight, catharsis, or enhanced prosocial functioning are welcomed outcomes of the work. If one assents to those as legitimate treatment goals for children, then crayons, paper, dolls, sand, games, books or almost anything that is not intrinsically harmful to the child has the potential to facilitate one or more of those goals. The psychotherapeutic value of any toy lies in the

FIGURE 6. Picture of the Author Drawn by a Child During a Termination Session.

creative adaptation of the toy by the therapist, as well as the child's affinity to the toy as integral to his or her journey of self-discovery. When it comes to adapting "traditional toys" for play therapy, mental health professionals have no trouble improvising. The play therapy literature is replete with excellent examples of how artistic materials, books, toys and games have been transformed into therapeutic artifacts (Landreth, Homeyer, Bratton, & Kale, 1995; Schaefer & Reid, 1986).

This chapter is further testimony to what has been documented previously in the child clinical literature. Computer games, skillfully used by creative clinicians, have tremendous psychotherapeutic value for children and adolescents (Allen, 1984; Aymard, 1999; Bosworth, 1994; Canter, 1987; Casey & Ramsammy, 1992; Clarke & Schoech, 1984; Favelle, 1994; Gardner, 1991; Johnson, 1984, 1987; Kokish, 1994; Margolies, 1991; Oakley, 1994; Resnick, 1994; Sherer, 1994; Sisson et al., 1985). Of course all child therapists who use the computer in their work should meticulously monitor *the process* to ensure that there is attainment of treatment goals and resolution of the presenting problem(s) for which the child was referred.

Hopefully, the growing literature that documents the value of digital technology in clinical practice will encourage mental health professionals to summon their creative energies and explore ways of adapting computer programs for psychotherapeutic use. The author has successfully used the computer for drawing, storytelling, craft-making, puppetry, creating animated therapeutic metaphors and game playing with children and adolescents. Further discussion of these topics is available in the online book *From cyberspace to inner space: Counseling children with computers* (Aymard & Kepner, 1998). If there is a caveat about computers and child counseling, it is aptly embodied in the following formula:

1 Computer + 1 Child + 1 Therapist = Effective Play Therapy

Before using computers with children, a therapist should be comfortable using the technology. If he or she is a technophobe, the anxious feelings will be projected onto the child and the outcome will be counter-therapeutic. Almost everyone should be able to identify with the experience of riding in an automobile with a novice driver who anxiously approaches every busy intersection. Furthermore, it is an ethical imperative that anyone engaged in the practice of counseling or play therapy should have extensive training in theories of development, child psychopathology, techniques of child psychotherapy, ethical professional standards and the historical foundations of the field.

Children of all cultures communicate in a universal language called play. All play is a form of storytelling. Whether children are playing a competitive game or romping about freely in the playroom, they are telling us stories about themselves. Those who value the role of technology in counseling children are a new breed of therapists. They courageously join children of the Digital Age on the playground of cyberspace. Children play with reckless abandon both in physical space and in cyberspace. Contemporary child therapists must strive to become acquainted with new dialects in the language of play. Only then will they be able to accompany children on the path of healing towards a better tomorrow.

REFERENCES

Allen, D. H. (1984). The use of computer fantasy games in child therapy. In M. D. Schwartz (Ed.), *Using computers in clinical practice: Psychotherapy and mental health applications* (pp. 329-334). New York: The Haworth Press, Inc.

Aymard, L., & Kepner, T. (1998). *From cyberspace to inner space: Counseling children with computers.* [Online book]. Available: http://www.connectedcounseling.com.

Aymard, L. (1999). Therapeutic applications of computers with children. In C. E. Schaefer (Ed.), *Innovative psychotherapy techniques in child and adolescent therapy* (2nd ed., pp. 271-314). New York: John Wiley & Sons, Inc.

Barnes, M. A. (1996). *The healing path with children: An exploration for parents and professionals.* Kingston, Ontario, Canada: Viktoria, Fermoyle & Berrigan Publishing House.

Bosworth, K. (1994). Computer games and simulations as tools to reach and engage adolescents in health promotion activities. *Computers in Human Services, 11*(1/2), 109-119.

Canter, D. S. (1987, March). The therapeutic effects of combining Apple Macintosh computers and creativity software in art therapy sessions. *Art Therapy,* 17-26.

Casey, J. A., & Ramsammy, R. (1992). *MacMentoring: Using technology and counseling with at-risk youth.* Ann Arbor, MI: ERIC Clearinghouse on Counseling and Personnel Services. (ERIC Document Reproduction Service No. ED 344 179).

Clarke, B., & Schoech, D. (1984). A computer-assisted therapeutic game for adolescents: Initial development and comments. In M. D. Schwartz (Ed.), *Using computers in clinical practice: Psychotherapy and mental health applications* (pp. 335-353). New York: The Haworth Press, Inc.

Favelle, G. K. (1994). Therapeutic applications of commercially available computer software. *Computers in Human Services, 11*(1), 151-158.

Gardner, J. E. (1991). Can the Mario Brothers help? Nintendo games as an adjunct in psychotherapy with children. *Psychotherapy, 28*(4), 667-670.

Johnson, R. G. (1984). High tech play therapy. *A Journal for Remedial Education and Counseling, 1*, 128-133.

Johnson, R. G. (1987). Using computer art in counseling children. *Elementary School Guidance & Counseling, 21*(4), 262-265.

Kepner, T. & Thompson, D. (1995). Use of the computer as a psychotherapeutic toy: A survey of play therapists in Maryland. Unpublished raw data.

Kokish, R. (1994). Experiences using a PC in play therapy with children. In H. Resnick (Ed.), *Electronic tools for social work practice and education* (pp. 141-150). New York: The Haworth Press, Inc.

Landreth, G., Homeyer, L., Bratton, S. & Kale, A. (1995). *The world of play therapy literature: A definitive guide to authors and subjects in the field* (2nd ed.). Denton, TX: The Center for Play Therapy.

Margolies, R. (1991). The computer as social skills agent. *T.H.E. Journal, 18*(6), 70-71.

Oakley, C. (1994). SMACK: A computer driven game for at-risk teens. *Computers in Human Services, 11*(1), 97-99.

Resnick, H. (Ed.). (1994). *Electronic tools for social work practice and education.* New York: The Haworth Press, Inc.

Schaefer, C. E., & Reid, S. E. (Eds.). (1986). *Game play: Therapeutic use of childhood games.* New York: John Wiley & Sons.

Sherer, M. (1994). The effect of computerized simulation games on the moral development of youth in distress. *Computers in Human Services, 11*(1/2), 81-95.

Sisson, L. H., Mayfield, S. A., & Entz, S. (1985). Reaching students through computers: A new therapy for learning and playing. *Journals of Reading, Writing and Learning Disabilities International*, *1*(3), 61-83.

Wolock, E., Orr, A., & Buckleitner, W. (Eds.). (1998). *The elementary teacher's sourcebook on children's software*. Flemington, NJ: Active Learning Associates, Inc.

Zamora, B. (1992). *Funny Face user manual: Installation and operations*. Antioch, CA: Z-WARE.

Interactive Media for Child Care and Counselling: New Resources, New Opportunities

Les Cowan

SUMMARY. A familiar children's story in the UK–*Bruce's Story*, about the adventures of a puppy moving into the unknown world as he grows up–is converted into a multimedia program designed to help children in out of home care talk (or write) about their own experiences coming into the child welfare system and into foster and adoptive families. *[Article copies available for a fee from The Haworth Document Delivery Service: 1-800-HAWORTH. E-mail address: <getinfo@haworthpressinc.com> Website: <http://www.HaworthPress.com> © 2002 by The Haworth Press, Inc. All rights reserved.]*

KEYWORDS. Child welfare, technology, children's stories, foster parents, adoptions, youth

EFFECTIVE COMMUNICATION

Trying to communicate effectively with children and young people can often be a frustrating experience, and child care professionals know very well how complex and traumatic many of the problems young people present can be. A young person under supervision for offending be-

Les Cowan is affiliated with Information PLUS.

[Haworth co-indexing entry note]: "Interactive Media for Child Care and Counselling: New Resources, New Opportunities." Cowan, Les. Co-published simultaneously in *Journal of Technology in Human Services* (The Haworth Press, Inc.) Vol. 20, No. 1/2, 2002, pp. 31-48; and: *Human Services Technology: Innovations in Practice and Education* (ed: Hy Resnick, and Phoebe Sade Anderson) The Haworth Press, Inc., 2002, pp. 31-48. Single or multiple copies of this article are available for a fee from The Haworth Document Delivery Service [1-800-HAWORTH, 9:00 a.m. - 5:00 p.m. (EST). E-mail address: getinfo@haworthpressinc.com].

haviour probably no more wants to be in the interview room than the worker wants to have them there. Such a lack of interest and motivation may render any constructive discussion about the impact and consequences of anti-social behaviour virtually impossible. Alternatively, a child may be in need of therapeutic help in relation to loss of birth family, attachment to new carers and a confusing and traumatic series of life events. The task then is to help a child make sense of confusing, unfair, unmerited and damaging events–hard enough for many adults, never mind a child with less experience and understanding of the world. In either of these cases or in many others, working with children and young people involves serious hurdles to effective communication. That, however, remains the objective, and one of our tasks as social work professionals and researchers is to find a better way of achieving it.

CHILD FRIENDLY TECHNIQUES

As well as the difficulty of the subject matter, the techniques we are familiar with as adults and in adult counselling settings are often quite foreign to younger clients. Face to face cognitive dialogue is key to all sorts of adult interactions but can be an entirely unknown language for children and young people. Many adults will remember from personal experience the lack of impact an adult lecture on improving behaviour can have! In contrast, the natural language of children is essentially experiential, not discursive. Children learn not by talking but by doing. They often express their feelings not verbally but by acting out a range of inner tensions, conflicts and anxieties. They learn about the world not by logically predicting the outcome of a series of actions, but by doing "what comes naturally" and then seeing what happens. Hence children learn by playing and experimenting–whether that means objects, actions or attitudes, acting out various roles and observing the consequences or by trying out a range of behaviours and seeing which works best.

Children's emotional and behavioural issues should not, therefore, be met with a solely cognitive, logical, discursive response and ideally should receive the resources of the most well trained, skilled and experienced counsellors. Even then, however (and allowing that the resource is available), we are still faced with the concept of an adult authority figure talking to the child or young person whose behaviour is perceived as "the problem" with the object of moderating both the behaviour itself and the inner feelings that give rise to it.

Given this disjunction in communication, it may be worthwhile to turn the problem around and ask what is the natural world of the child and how can that environment be used to deal with these sorts of issues. In examining this we have to acknowledge that the world of the child is not static but changes from one generation to the next. Certainly children's lives still involve imagination, music, role play, dolls, toys and many other media, but anyone in contact with children over the last ten years will also appreciate that computer based activities now attract a lot of attention and are highly valued in youth culture. This may mean using computers in education and for school projects, playing games, browsing the web or e-mailing friends. While adults may bemoan the perceived loss of more traditional play activities, children are still experimenting, exploring and expressing inner feelings. It is just that in the later part of the 20th and into the 21st centuries, the environment in which this happens now includes the computer desktop as well as the physical world.

So what is the relevance of this for child care and counselling? The fact that children express themselves through play has not been lost on the helping professions. The concept of play therapy is well established, well used and helpful to many children. However, if we are to reflect the changing media in which children act out their play lives, then the computer environment must also be included, explored and pressed into service. Although traditionally orientated child care workers have often not been immediately receptive to computer based activities for a variety of reasons, it is clear that children are. Therefore, to communicate with them on their own terms, computer based activities must be considered.

In summary,

- communicating effectively with children is not easy and any help available should be considered;
- traditional techniques based on cognitive dialogue are not a natural means of communication for children who tend to learn more experientially and express themselves by actions more than words;
- children's play and learning environment has expanded over the past 20 years to include computer based activities which are valued highly in our culture and towards which many children are positively disposed.

On the basis of this it would seem both natural and worthwhile to consider whether computer applications could be used to assist in care and counselling tasks.

FIRST STEPS

With this in mind, and from the background of generic field social work in late 1980s in the UK, a first experiment in developing child care software was the development of "Optext Adventure System," an authoring environment designed to enable non-programmers to develop computer based material for use with children. Optext produced multiple choice text adventures which could then be used to explore real life issues of action, consequence and outcome.[1]

While meeting with some early success and favourable responses, Optext was still unfortunately a prisoner of computing facilities available at the time. Windows had yet to hit and multimedia was still mainly to do with tape slide sequences and an accompanying soundtrack. Text only, multiple choice adventures, however well conceived in theory, just do not grab the attention sufficiently and hence tend to fail at the first hurdle of play activities–it's got to be fun!

Nevertheless, some worthwhile use was derived, a principle was established and in the meantime, facilities available to software developers were constantly improving. Unfortunately, this improvement still did not seem to be giving rise to a body of published software for use in child care, equivalent to what was becoming available in education. While the reasons for this are many and varied, ultimately it depends on a developer or company taking a risk and investing resources in producing software in the hope that a market will emerge. Finally, in frustration at seeing no sign of products which would meet children's social care needs emerging, Information PLUS was born in 1994 with a specific intention of developing software and creating a market for specialist products aimed at child care and counselling.

The remainder of this paper will focus on our first two attempts at interactive child care resources: *Bruce's Multimedia Story* launched in February 1998 and *Billy Breaks the Rules* launched in March 1999.

BRUCE'S MULTIMEDIA STORY

In order to start both with a manageable project and a resource with some familiarity for current practitioners, it was decided to begin by converting an existing and well-accepted child counselling book into multimedia. *Bruce's Story*[2] has been known in the UK for about 15 years and has sold around 20,000 copies, making it something of a best seller among child counselling resources. The story is primarily aimed at under 10s and follows the adventures of Bruce, "a spaniel sort of dog," as he has to leave his home and family and travel into the unknown in search of new carers and friends. In many ways Bruce's journey mirrors the experience of children coming into the child welfare system and into foster or adoptive families. In using the book, practitioners encourage children to talk about what happens to Bruce, particularly in relation to their own life experience. Worksheets, associated with particular pages in the story, invite children to write down what they would like to say back to Bruce about their own lives.

The aim for multimedia development was therefore to produce an animated children's storybook from *Bruce's Story* where text could be clicked on to be read, pictures would have a range of interesting and engaging animations, and where children would have an interactive opportunity to respond to what has been happening in the story. Goals for the software were twofold–first, for the story to be fun to read and play with and second, for children to gain a therapeutic benefit from what they are reading by means of an adult helper or counsellor encouraging communication based on the story and how it relates to the child's own life. *Bruce's Multimedia Story* is intended for one to one use with a child and adult counsellor or therapist, since children who have experienced this degree of loss and emotional trauma will certainly need adult support in expressing their thoughts and feelings.

INTERFACE AND USABILITY

On starting up *Bruce's Multimedia Story*, the user is first presented with a brief title sequence with original music, animation and a welcome message spoken in an age appropriate voice followed by a simple 4 option menu:

- Start *Bruce's Story*
- Contents
- Instructions
- Information PLUS

Instructions and *Information PLUS* present basic information for the user while the *Contents* option presents a thumbnail of every page and a chance to go directly to a chosen page. *Start Bruce's Story* takes the user directly into page 1.

Given the need to preserve a natural bridge for child care workers familiar with *Bruce's Story* but not with computer software, the decision was taken to keep the final appearance of the software as close to the book as possible. For that reason the screen display preserves the original layout with printed text on the left and the accompanying illustration on the right. Clicking on text has it read in the same age appropriate voice as used for the welcome message and clicking on hot spots in the pictures will run one of about 75 simple animations scattered throughout the story. At the foot of each screen are page numbers which take the user back to the contents screen, and mini "Bruce" icons which control navigation between pages through a further simple animation.

The one area where the software is significantly different in basic format from the book relates to the use of the worksheets. Rather than simply reproducing printed material for use with the software, it was decided to make access to worksheets an interactive part of the programme. Users are therefore able to click on "Bruce's Bones" scattered throughout the story to pop up a "secret message from Bruce." This takes the form of a spoken invitation to reflect on Bruce's adventures in relation to the life experience of the child user. For example, Bruce might say, "I was very sad and scared when I had to leave home. Tell me, have you ever felt like that?" Children can then either simply talk about memories and feelings the question raises with the adult carer working with them or click on another button to launch a simple word processor to type (or have the adult type for them) whatever they want to say. Clicking on the bone again folds down the pop up message and allows the user to resume the story.

While deliberately kept as unobtrusive as possible within the software design, this feature is at the heart of how the software is intended to work. By engaging a child from the point of view of Bruce the dog, the software is intended to open up constructive communication about painful and traumatic life events which a child may find great difficulty in discussing otherwise. Ideally children using *Bruce's Multimedia Story* will feel drawn in to the story and be able to make natural connections between what happens to Bruce and their own experiences. When a child is ready to talk about what may be very painful and personal events, the adult counsellor then has an opportunity to help the child come to terms with these memories and feelings.

PRE-RELEASE TESTING

Following development but prior to release, *Bruce's Multimedia Story* was extensively tested in practice with a number of children and in a number of agencies. This test phase gave rise to a number of conclusions about the benefits of a computer-based resource, as opposed to the same material in conventional book form.

First, an expectation that the use of a computer based interaction would of itself be attractive and compelling was certainly fulfilled. One care worker reported that the child she was working with, David (name changed), obviously enjoyed the play element of the programme and was

> *. . . so eager to get going every time. He was more interested because it was a computer game . . .*

Use of an interactive computer programme with a strong play element was found to be helpful in relation to the child's overall attitude to the work, appearing to facilitate a sense of enjoyment and an ability to relax and participate. Prior to using the programme in an explicitly therapeutic way, the care worker had begun with a number of sessions simply devoted to reading the story and playing with the animations and sound effects. This then led naturally to more therapeutic use:

> *. . . it gave him time to gain confidence enough to ask. When he was playing he was sufficiently relaxed to ask questions–they just came out in the game . . .*

Not surprisingly, this was also a help to the care worker who reported that previously she had found it difficult to find different things to hold David's attention. The play element even gave David sufficient confidence to allow the sessions to broaden to include his foster parent and foster parent's older son. The care worker reported this to have changed the nature of sessions, making them more relaxed and less threatening so that "everybody could join in."

Interestingly, use of a computer programme also subtly changed the power relationship in the interaction. However much a counsellor aims to work "at the child's pace," there is no getting away from the fact that the counselling intervention is essentially the therapist's home territory, not the child's. Using a computer may quite reverse this situation as so many children are more used to computers than many adults, particularly (perhaps) those in the care professions. In turn, this leads to a positive shift in the extent to which the child is in control, a very significant issue in relation to many children's experiences of care. In relation to this, the care worker comments:

> *David kept me right. He used to laugh if I got anything wrong . . . He was helping me.*

Clearly David was enjoying the confidence that came from control, which in turn seems to have been helpful in the overall therapeutic experience. The ability many children have with computers and the fact that only one person can use the mouse at a time changes the balance of control as compared to conventional therapeutic work. For children who have experienced so little control over their lives and circumstances, this may be an extremely important issue.

So playing *Bruce's Multimedia Story* was indeed fun and certainly made for a more productive therapeutic atmosphere. In respect to actual therapeutic value, however, the programme was also found to be beneficial. The care worker reported that David was able to relate well to Bruce, helped by the use of speech in recorded sound clips and animation, all of which helped to bring Bruce to life:

> *He was able to relate to being very like Bruce. He naturally made the connection–that was like me, that happened to me . . . there was so much he could relate to.*

The way in which David was able to relate to Bruce seems to have naturally brought out his feelings and questions and helped the care worker to be open and to give him important information in return. Identification with Bruce also had the unexpected effect of jogging David's memory and bringing back smells, sounds and feelings relating to experiences paralleling those in the story. One point in Bruce's narrative about feeling afraid brought a particularly clear response from David and led to discussion of a range of incidents which had left him feeling afraid. This in turn gave the care worker a valuable insight into how David saw these events and what sense he had been able to make of them:

> *Memories flooded back–you could see that it hurt but he had the confidence to talk about it.*

The care worker was able to use David's opening up to challenge some of his fantasies about the past, for example, that it was his fault that his Mum and her boyfriend argued so much.

> *It has changed his attitude to himself. He no longer looks on himself as bad.*

David's openness and questioning about his past also had the effect of prompting the care worker to do further research and search back in records to answer the many questions David was now posing.

The value of an interesting resource David looked forward to using has already been referred to. The fact that it presented a structured format also seems to have been useful.

> *The programme made it clear where he had gone up to. It was enough to do one page in a session if it was explored properly. Oodles of information came out.*

Overall, it appeared than *Bruce's Multimedia Story* offers a number of specific benefits over conventional use of printed material. Using the computer is attractive and enjoyable, making for a more positive attitude to the therapeutic interaction. Use of the computer may change the counselling power balance, further helping and encouraging the child in terms of confidence, self image and willingness to take risks. An entertaining multimedia environment also makes for a play foundation to the interaction, which is in fact a much more natural learning environment for children than traditional cognitive dialogue. Use of multimedia elements can also go a long way to engaging attention and immersion in the subject matter, further helping children to open up about difficult personal issues and events.

PROFESSIONAL RESPONSE

Since launching in February 1998, *Bruce's Multimedia Story* has been used in a wide variety of settings, including field social work, residential and day care settings, family centres, educational psychology, pre-school care, social work training, fostering and adoption, independent counselling, by parents with their own birth children in cases of divorce and separation (and even moving house) and in family mediation work. Response has been highly positive to date. In terms of general software quality, the package was awarded a Special Mention of Merit in Europrix98, an EU multimedia software competition, and was a regional finalist in the John Logie Baird Awards for Innovation.

In relation to therapeutic benefit, the following review quotations are representative:[3]

> *I have to say that this is probably the most useful bit of material I have ever come across in helping children to come to terms with the moves entailed within the care system and particularly with adoption. I wish it had been around when our first two children were younger.* (Adoption UK Nov 98)

> *Bruce's Story on computer can be particularly helpful with children who find written material difficult and is sensitive to the needs of children and workers alike . . . Especially designed for working with children who are having difficulty understanding changes in their lives, it is an imaginative way of helping open up communication and shared feelings about a child's history and identity . . . Simply put, it capitalizes on children's natural interest in computer-based activities and alleys the fears of the most technophobic social worker.* (Community Care Jan 99)

ACTION AND CONSEQUENCE

Bruce's Multimedia Story deals primarily with events in the past and the resulting thoughts and feelings. While commenting favourably on the potential benefits of using Bruce, many users and commentators also remarked on the need for something dealing with behavioural issues of older children with a view to helping users consider likely future consequences of their present actions. In fact, issues of behavioural choices and the likely outcome of certain courses of action already feature highly in a great deal of work with young people.[4] Unfortunately we know that young people (and indeed many adults) are not likely to be dissuaded from a course of action simply by being told by an authority figure how thing may turn out. Overwhelmingly we learn about the world by doing, not by being told. Many courses of action lead so directly to unhelpful consequences, however, that in the process of learning the lesson, a great deal of damage may be done to relationships, living situations and sometimes even health. Ideally, we would like young people to be able to learn about actions, consequences and outcomes not by going through negative sequences in the real world but in some safer, more protected environment.

Interestingly, the whole concept of the virtual world is one of the things computer technology does best. In computer games and training applications, we can readily find virtual worlds in which users learn about their environment and apply information gained to progress and earn rewards. Learning from mistakes and adopting appropriate strategies to win in a virtual world actually forms the basis of a very popular and common genre of adventure games software. So computer applications can bc good at providing environments in which information can be gained and tactics refined. What the current crop of computer games is not good at, however, is applying this sort of model to real world learning. The world of the computer game is typically fantastic, grotesque, aggressive and competitive–in some ways the very opposite of how we would like to see young people's behaviour developing. For social services this raises the idea of taking the appropriate and relevant techniques and benefits of the virtual world computer game and applying these to real world issues set in real out-of-home settings promoting positive social values.

BILLY BREAKS THE RULES

Following a positive response to *Bruce's Multimedia Story*, the next objective became a software package geared to the social learning needs of older children in the 8-14 age group, focusing on known living situations and known behavioural issues. In due course this became *Billy Breaks the Rules*. In designing an options/choices/consequences resource, the key issues were storyline and user interface. Of these, storyline, although fundamental, was probably less of a problem, since a number of action frameworks had been worked up some years previously as part of OPTEXT Adventure System (see "First Steps" above). *Billy Breaks the Rules* was therefore based to some extent on pre-existing material which itself arose out of direct field social work experience. In order to broaden perspectives and further improve the core storyline, a senior staff development co-worker with a great deal of child care expertise was also invited to join the project.

Because the issues in *Billy* were intended to be relevant to a wide range of children and young people, in care and at home, involved in serious and not so serious behavioural problems, and across a range of ages, it was decided to make the story as widely applicable as possible.

Events are therefore set in a family rather than an institutional care setting (familiar to both groups), begin with a low level issue from which problems can either escalate or improve, and involve a character with no particular specified age. Within the storyline, Billy's actions and their consequences were largely based on the authors' own child care practice experience of where problem flash points arise, the sorts of behaviour they can give rise to, and the sorts of ways in which they can work towards resolution.

In terms of user interface, an important issue was the usability of the software for staff who may never have used a computer before. It was important, therefore, that all control should be mouse based and that the CD should autorun on loading. It was also decided to provide as "clean" a screen as possible without obtrusive navigation buttons. All controls are therefore accessed either by clicking or double clicking pop up thought bubbles containing Billy's choices or any of the four page corners to access Forward, Back, Help and Exit.

The action of the story spans 15 scenes connected by (usually) three choices in each. From these there are 10 possible outcomes, each with 3 "talkabout topics." This scale of action was determined by the need for players to be able to hold in their minds what had gone on up to any current point in the action (ruling out a storyline with hundreds of different scenes) but also without being able to get to a conclusion without having to make a number of significant choices along the way (ruling out a smaller number of scenes). Bearing in mind over 40 different choices across 15 scenes, this makes for dozens of different ways through the storyline.

In scene 1, therefore, Billy is confronted with having stolen money from his foster parents, Tony and Pat and, as a result, has his pocket money (allowance) cut. Billy now has three options expressed in pop up thought bubbles as follows:

- *It's not fair. They should give me enough so I don't have to steal.*
- *It's been ok here. Now I've ruined everything. I'll get sent away.*
- *It's my own fault. I shouldn't have taken it. They might let me have my money if I'm good all week.*

By moving the mouse cursor over a thought bubble option, the user can highlight that choice; by single clicking, the text of the option is spoken in an age appropriate voice, and by double clicking, the user can select that choice and move the action to the consequence of Billy thinking or feeling that way. This in turn gives rise to new choices.

Possible turns within the storyline include Billy withdrawing to his room and not talking to anyone, sitting outside the back door planning to run away, wrecking his room and barricading the door, or deciding to tell someone how he feels. This framework is designed as a social learning environment in which behaviours can be tried out and their likely consequences explored. Unlike in real life, however, choices made in *Billy Breaks the Rules* can be reflected on and talked about, taken back and changed to something else or simply explored for fun without any danger of real and unpleasant consequences.

ROLE OF THE THERAPIST

While the action and options in *Billy Breaks the Rules* are designed for personal learning about life and the likely outcome of certain types of behaviour, the overall concept of the software still vitally depends on therapeutic interactions between the child or young person and a skilled adult counsellor. In fact the user guide spells this out very directly:

> *Billy Breaks the Rules is not intended to be played unsupported and young people playing the game without supportive adult involvement applying the issues are unlikely to get much real benefit. Helper interventions might be along the lines of:*
>
> - *what do you think might happen if Billy does that? Will it help?*
> - *what do you think Billy might be feeling now?*
> - *has anything like this ever happened to you–what did you do?*
>
> *In fact, the gameplay of Billy Breaks the Rules exists only to help young people and helpers think together about relationships, feelings, choices, motivation, and what can be done to improve life situations and choices. Without application, Billy Breaks the Rules may be fun to play (we hope so) but will not impact on the issues.*

The software is therefore not in any way aimed to deliver the intended benefit by itself. This remains a result of skilled human intervention and support.

Billy Breaks the Rules is also of course intended to be fun to play–without which little of the deeper meaning is likely to have any impact. Hence the programme makes extensive use of multimedia elements including over 120 colourful cartoon style animations with plenty of humour, voice clips for Billy, Tony, Pat and others and a high degree of interactivity.

REACTION AND EVALUATION

Within both professional practice and public policy in the UK there is currently an increasing emphasis on "what works"–more formally known as "effective intervention" or "best practices." Clearly that is important for overall strategic directions but also for individual resources. So how do we know that Billy works? First, as a small development company we have to be realistic about how much time and effort can be put into formal evaluation without the resources of an academic research environment. Put simply, with very limited resources, time and money spent on extensive evaluation programmes has to be taken from the development task itself, i.e., we may know that certain sections of the programme work very well, but in finding that out sacrifice the necessary resources to develop the remainder. It is likely that this would be a dilemma for any small developer working in such a new software genre.

Second, the authors came to the task with over thirty years practitioner, trainer and consultant experience, and this found its way directly into the story line, the choice of outcomes for a particular option, and the discussion points included in the programme. In addition to this, early versions were previewed and opened to independent evaluation by other child care professionals and agencies for a completely unbiased view.

Finally, after more than ten years of involvement in the concept and a previous software experiment using some of the same techniques, there is a case for simply pressing ahead with "best endeavours" and ultimately letting the market decide–as it will however much evaluation and analysis precedes a final release. Woody Allen has remarked that "Eighty percent of success is showing up," while *In Search of Excellence* quotes a Cadbury executive slogan: "Ready, Fire, Aim."[5]

As regards post release evaluation, that has principally come from published reviews, and customer reaction. While only on general release for just under 12 months at the time of writing, *Billy Breaks the Rules* has been well received so far. For many child care workers, using Billy Breaks the Rules has been a first experience of computers in child care, and the general response has been one of strong support for the concept. Tangibly, this has so far resulted in *Billy Breaks the Rules* sell-ing to over 100 educational and child care agencies and being selected for inclusion on product catalogues produced by the Scottish Council for Educational Technology and the National Foster Care Association. A number of positive reviews and comments have also been received of which the following is representative:

> *Billy Breaks the Rules I liked even more (than Bruce's Multimedia Story) particularly as the technology is significantly better and more interactive with the child having multiple choices to make with resulting consequences. Again the emphasis is on learning and exploring through fun; which I think is a great combination. It encourages children to make choices and understand the consequences of their actions. I would think it would be very helpful alongside family based work; and communication and problem solving skills.* (Practical Parenting Newsletter: Issue No. 13)

Information PLUS software has also recently been the subject of a feature article in Counselling Today[6] involving wholly independent research of the experience of early customers and their clients:

> *The Coneygree Family Centre works mainly with youngsters who have been abused and are currently living in alternative family situations, according to Clynch. "We try to help them come to terms with their past and adjust to their current situations. We use the games in individual work with the children, depending on their needs. Many are dealing with separation and loss and can identify with the characters on the computer."*
>
> *"These kids are sometimes difficult to engage in conversation," she continued. "But the games get them talking. They really seem to love them."* (Maggie Clynch, Manager of the Coneygree Family Centre in the U.K.)

MARKETING STRATEGIES

In order for computer applications to truly succeed in child care and counselling, it is self evident that resources have to be both developed *and* bought. Software producers must have some confidence that there will be a demand for such a product before resources will be invested in development, and at the other end, someone has to hear about the resource, make a decision, part with their money and use it in practice before users get any benefit. From both points of view, therefore, effective marketing is critical. Since we believe these to be the among the first software products of their kind, this has been especially so without any established distribution mechanism or existing community of buyers.

In marketing terms, therefore, the aim of *Bruce's Multimedia Story* and *Billy Breaks the Rules* has been to create a new category of child care resource and a new demand for this type of resource. Since between both programmes, over 100 UK child care agencies are now using Information PLUS software, this has clearly been achieved at least to some extent, and therefore it may be worth describing the approach taken.

Briefly, the marketing strategy has involved 2 stages; first, a concentration on informing potential buyers, then, second, an attempt to capitalise on this with a more targeted approach. Because of the innovative nature of the products, it was felt that conventional advertising would not be particularly effective and could prove very expensive for little real benefit. Instead Information PLUS has taken the route of demonstrating at as many social work and child care conference events as possible (including HUSITA5 in Budapest) in order to gauge user reaction face to face and begin a process of informing the profession. Allied to this has been submission for professional reviews in the relevant journals and publications.

Once professional comments and evaluation had appeared, it was then possible to look for distribution through the relevant resources catalogues. Although not originally intended for use in educational settings, both products are also now being distributed by the major Scottish educational software catalogue produced by the Scottish Council for Educational Technology (SCET).

Although we continue to believe that new users will be best able to understand and see the application of this sort of software by direct demonstration, it is clearly impractical for this to be the major marketing strategy. Stage 2 of the process is therefore now to distribute a demo CD with samples of both programmes within the UK and internationally to capitalise on conference exposure, published reviews and word of mouth from existing buyers. Our initial experience is that there is a substantial potential market which will be very receptive to high quality new computer based resources, and Information PLUS is therefore currently looking for distribution into non-UK markets subject to such localization as may be necessary.

FUTURE PLANS

Given this market potential, Information PLUS is currently involved in a number of projects which may result in future products within the same general concept framework. In collaboration with our local Health Board, Information PLUS is involved in a bid for funding from Scotland Against Drugs for an interactive behaviour based drugs product. This will not only involve an actions/choices/consequences story line but also background information resources to which users can refer for information to help inform decisions. We have also recently completed a commissioned short demo again using the same format but geared to more explicit offending behaviour. This was planned for demonstration at a major international Criminal Justice conference in the summer of 2000, following which (and depending on delegate reaction) a full scale resource might be developed. Finally we are currently awaiting evaluation feedback on another preliminary demo, this time set out more like an interactive workbook, geared at helping young people about to leave state care gain the skills, motivation and knowledge needed to live independently.

CONCLUSION

The question of use of computer technology in social work has been well theorised upon over the past fifteen years but through most of that time has remained a largely theoretical matter–well established in terms of what should be happening but still with limited implementation in practice. We are now seeing the first signs of computer use in practice becoming a routine reality. It is established that children and young people are often very ready to interact with computer programmes and use these as a way of communicating about personal issues and problems. A computer game or story can provide a productive environment for social learning and the expression of thoughts and feelings. Practitioners and service managers are now seeing the benefits and are ready for more new products and wider application of what is currently available. Barriers of hardware availability and professional competence in using a computer are falling fast and early take up of *Bruce's Multimedia Story* and *Billy Breaks the Rules* suggests that the right products meeting identified needs will be used. It only remains now for developers to produce more and better products and human service professionals to continue responding and adopting new techniques for the benefit of those young people in need of their services and support. As a recent review of *Bruce's Multimedia Story* concluded:

> *Social workers have yet to wake up to the potential from the therapeutic use of computers with children and young people. In computer use in social work, we may be standing on the edge of a new way of working. If Bruce's Multimedia Story is anything to go by, children are more than ready for it.* (Community Care Jan 99)

CONTACT INFORMATION

Bruce's Multimedia Story and *Billy Breaks the Rules* are produced on CD for Mac and PC platforms by Information PLUS, 3, Hill of Heddle, Finstown, Orkney KW17 2LH and cost £34.00 + VAT = £39.95 each. UK postage is £1.50 per order (£2.50 for international orders). Further information and interactive demos of both packages are available at <www.orknet.co.uk/iplus> where the software can also be purchased on-line.

NOTES

1. Optext Adventure System–Software Development in Practice–A Case History: Les Cowan in *Electronic Tools for Social Work Practice and Education,* Resnick (Ed.), The Haworth Press, Inc. New York, 1994.
2. *Bruce's Story:* Maureen Thom and Celia Macliver, Children's Society 1986.
3. The full text of reviews is available at www.orknet.co.uk/iplus
4. Examples include behavioural change programmes for young offenders developed by the Cognitive Centre Foundation (based in Wales). These programmes include decision making in moral dilemma situations aimed at building higher reasoning, challenging the value base and developing the connection between present choices and future outcomes.
5. *In Search of Excellence,* T. Peters and R. Waterman, 1982, Chapter 5, A Bias to Action.
6. New Computer Games Help Aid Adolescents, Counsellors; Counselling Today; The American Counselling Association: Dec 1999, p 20.

Computer Integrated Drug Prevention–Combining Multi-Media and Social Group Work Practice to Teach Inner City Israeli 6th Graders How to Say No to Drugs

Michael Gropper

SUMMARY. The author describes an educational multi-media program to teach Israeli youth to avoid drugs using an older brother model who provides information and advice to youthful Israeli players regarding the adverse consequences of using drugs. *[Article copies available for a fee from The Haworth Document Delivery Service: 1-800-HAWORTH. E-mail address: <getinfo@haworthpressinc.com> Website: <http://www.HaworthPress.com> © 2002 by The Haworth Press, Inc. All rights reserved.]*

KEYWORDS. Drugs, technology, youth, Israel, international social work

INTRODUCTION/BACKGROUND

In 1991, the Institute for the Advancement of Education in Jaffa, Israel initiated a unique and innovative drug prevention initiative in the

Michael Gropper, DSW, is affiliated with the Bar Ilan University School of Social Work, Ramat Gan, Israel.

[Haworth co-indexing entry note]: "Computer Integrated Drug Prevention–Combining Multi-Media and Social Group Work Practice to Teach Inner City Israeli 6th Graders How to Say No to Drugs." Gropper, Michael. Co-published simultaneously in *Journal of Technology in Human Services* (The Haworth Press, Inc.) Vol. 20, No. 1/2, 2002, pp. 49-65; and: *Human Services Technology: Innovations in Practice and Education* (ed: Hy Resnick, and Phoebe Sade Anderson) The Haworth Press, Inc., 2002, pp. 49-65. Single or multiple copies of this article are available for a fee from The Haworth Document Delivery Service [1-800-HAWORTH, 9:00 a.m. - 5:00 p.m. (EST). E-mail address: getinfo@haworthpressinc.com].

heart of one of Israel's poorest and largest inner city communities. The Institute, a community based, non-profit, social service agency, was established in 1982 to help neighborhood Jewish and Arab youngsters from being drawn into a life of crime, delinquency, and prostitution by offering these high risk children therapeutic, social, education, and recreational enrichment programs. The target area is called Jaffa, located at the southern end of Tel Aviv. Jaffa hosts 70,000 residents (60,000 Jewish Israelis and 10,000 Arab Israeli citizens). It also is known for its high poverty and endemic levels of crime and drug addiction amongst many of its population.

At the Jaffa Institute, the author, in his capacity as the assistant director, was responsible for assisting the executive director in writing grant proposals for many of the 20 or so programs that were offered to children who attended the Institute. The author also aided the executive director in thinking about new ideas and development of new programs. Having an extensive and rich background in treating substance abusing clients in the United States, the author began to think of how he could use this specialized knowledge to help the youngsters from Jaffa to deal with the surrounding community pressures to use and abuse drugs.

While drug prevention efforts were beginning to develop in Israel, drug prevention in the schools and community did not exist at the time in the poorest communities like Jaffa. In response, the author began to explore the field of drug prevention and found two program models that were popular in the United States and seemed to be compatible to the Israeli community scene: the DARE program in Los Angeles, which used police officers to teach 5th and 6th grade children drug prevention skills, and the Rand Corporation's Project Alert, which taught 7th and 8th graders to identify and cope with different types of personal and social influences that tempt youngsters to use drugs (Ellickson & Bell, 1990; Pellow & Jengelski, 1991). Both of these models stressed the importance of incorporating social learning theory and cognitive-behavioral principles as central components in teaching children drug resistance skills. Some of these principles include teaching youngsters problem solving and decision making skills, helping them to examine their views and attitudes about drugs and alcohol, learning resistance and coping skills, and strengthening self-efficacy (Bandura, 1977). These same principles were compatible with the model of treating substance abusers that the author personally favored. This model highlights the importance of teaching children self-management skills in dealing with temptations to use drugs which are prevalent in the lives of the children in the Jaffa community (Marlett & Gordon, 1985).

At first, the author thought of bringing Project DARE to Israel. The Israeli police, in fact, were open to the idea, but a lot of bureaucracy in different government ministries prevented this effort from succeeding. Frustrated by his experience with the competing bureaucracy of government ministries, the author came up with an alternate plan to create a viable drug prevention program for the Jaffa community. The agency, located in an old building near the border of Jewish and Arab neighborhoods, had a very attractive computer laboratory facility which provided both educational enrichment to neighborhood youth as well as hours of time spent playing computer games. The year was 1991, and Israeli children were probably ahead of their American counterparts in their interest in computer games because of the tremendous value placed on computer knowledge and mastery found in Israel's different sectors including the educational, military, and business communities. Observing the children in the computer lab over a period of months led the author to believe that the computer could be an even more exciting and engaging teaching agent than police officers if an attractive and fun software program could be created. The author began to believe that the underlying principles of Project DARE could be brought to the agency through the use of some type of an attractive computer software program instead of the traditional use of police officers.

It is important to note that the author's personal background with computers was limited to using word processing programs to write papers. At the time, this author had no awareness of how in tune he actually was to the growing explosion of knowledge and development in the CD-ROM/multi-media world. An emerging multi-media and computer culture was occurring at an unstoppable speed in many parts of the world, including Israel. Health and human social service workers, at first slower than the business community to incorporate high-tech into its operations, began to infuse computer knowledge and applications into their daily operations (Schoech, 1982). This author, utilizing his clinical and administrative background in social work practice, saw the opportunity and the creative potential to create a viable multi-media computer program to teach high risk children the coping skills that are needed to say "no" to drugs (Gropper et al., 1995).

Having the support of the executive director, a proposal was prepared by the author to create a creative computer-interactive drug prevention program for the children of Jaffa, and it was sent to the Jewish Agency of Israel, which funds special innovative projects which contribute to Israeli society. The Institute was awarded a grant of $50,000 to develop and operate the project for one year. A local multi-media company was hired to assist in the development of the software program, which was called "Say No with Donny" (see Gropper et al., 1995). The program took 8 months to develop, and the content and software were developed by the author and the multi-media specialist as well as a small team of agency staff. The uniqueness of the "Say No with Donny" program is that it targets primary drug prevention efforts on a high-risk preadolescence population of 6th graders in a poor community. In addition, it integrates a computer software program into a structured group work intervention format to develop resiliency skills in children. The program, the first of its kind in the world, utilizes both the computer and creative and stimulating group work techniques to teach drug prevention.

The major goals of the "Say No with Donny" drug prevention program are: (1) to teach the child participant knowledge about alcohol and other drugs, (2) address risks and consequences associated with drug taking behavior, (3) discuss attitudes, both participants' own and those of society and how these influence drug taking behavior, and (4) to teach the necessary coping skills, including decision making, problem solving, and resistance skills that help the child say no to drugs.

In 1991, the program was pilot tested on approximately 100 children after the Institute trained its first program facilitators, a small group of counselors and social work students. Since 1991, more than 4000 youngsters, both Jewish and Arab, have passed through the 10-session program. The Arab version of the program, "Say No with Samir," has been given to hundreds of children.

THE ART OF DISSEMINATING EDUCATIONAL INFORMATION

In their book on health promotion, Downie, Fyfe, and Tannahill underscore the need to present health education material in an exciting format and to accentuate the importance of choosing the correct medium to help people remember things.

> People are bombarded daily with a mass of information and only a small proportion of it ever sticks. The information may be ignored; it may be acknowledged, but may not stick; it may stick for a short time and then be forgotten; or indeed, it may stick and remain but be disbelieved or redefined. The aim, then, is to present informa-

tion in a way that will be attractive and have immediate appeal to people, and cause it to be accepted and retained. (p. 111)

Because today's children love to interact with computers, "a primary consideration in developing the "Say No with Donny" program with computer graphic and text program components was to engage and motivate children in a medium of communication that youngsters would understand and relate to in their own contemporary language" (Gropper et al., 1995). The introduction of an attractive and highly stimulating computer software program to teach this material to children is both novel and very exciting for both the children participants as well as the staff that works with the youngsters.

DESCRIPTION OF SOFTWARE AND GROUP WORK SESSIONS

The "Say No with Donny" program combines specialized individual computer instruction with structured small group participation workshops in ten consecutive, 90-minute sessions led by trained counselors and social workers, some of who are doing their field placement at the agency. A user-friendly program created in Windows enables the group leaders and students to work easily and productively through various exercises. The combination of a specialized computer software program and active group participation shows how social group work practice can be combined with an electronic software program in a creative way.

In the "Say No with Donny" program, Donny is the central character, illustrated and presented by attractive and colorful graphic artwork. "Donny was created to represent the central voice and drug free big brother positive, role-model for the participants . . . (he) is presented as a resident from the child's community who represents the desired image, particularly regarding the issue of drug use, that we want the child to have of him/herself when he or she enters the 7th and 8th grade and begins adolescence" (Gropper et al., 1995, p. 97). In each segment, Donny introduces the people, places and issues that can influence the way a child will think about alcohol and drug use, whether it is safe, cool, ok to try, etc. Donny and the group process combine forces to help children learn about internal (psychological, emotional, attitudinal) and external (peer, family, media, and community view of drug use) pressures that often lead vulnerable youngsters to experiment with drugs. Donny is a kid from the neighborhood, and he is presented in the program as an attractive positive role model.

THE ARTWORK AND THE CORRECT IMAGE

In order to create Donny's image, the author and multi-media specialist worked along side a talented graphic artist who was hired to create the artwork for the project. The artist initially provided the project team with different drawings of Donny as she conceived of how his character should look. These initial drawings were shown to several staff and children at the agency Institute, thereby creating a focus group to determine which image would have the most positive and appealing impact. This selection process proved to be successful by the positive feedback that has consistently been given by the children participants concerning Donny's positive appeal. Numerous other visitors from around the world who have seen the program, as well as officials from the Israel Anti-Drug Authority and the Ministry of Education, have found the Donny character to be extremely friendly and inviting to the pre-adolescent age group that the program targeted.

In the "Say No with Donny" program, attractive, drug-free computer characters are contrasted with other computer characters whose use of drugs has made their lives very unattractive. In fact, the literature underscores the educational value of effective drug prevention efforts in contrasting attractive role models who personify non-drug behavior with drug models who are portrayed as unattractive and unappealing (Oei & Baldwin, 1992). All of the characters that were selected for use in the software program were carefully examined and chosen by our focus group team for their capacity to elicit the desired emotional reactions that support the program's goal of contrasting positive and negative role models.

INSTRUCTION BOOKLET FOR GROUP FACILITATORS

The program is highly structured and sequential. An instructional-technical manual was written to give the leaders a clear, step-by-step guide. The manual identifies the session, its objectives, explains exactly what the leader and the children need to do in the 90-minute session, and delineates clear instructions to the leader on how to operate the computer software part of the program. Most sessions follow a similar sequence. Initially, the manual clarifies the session goals for the leader, the children briefly review what they learned in previous meetings, and then the current topic is introduced by either a brief discussion or a game. Next the participant works on a computer activity for 30-40 minutes followed by a role-play or game led by the group leader which helps the child integrate the material learned from the computer. Finally, the children are briefly prepared for the next lesson (Gropper et al., 1995, p. 96).

Each classroom of children that participate in the program is separated into two groups of 15, and to maintain this manageable group number the agency developed a second computer lab. Even at only 15, most of the children worked together in pairs because there were not enough computers for each child. This did not seem to bother the children, and they adjusted very comfortably to this arrangement of working interactively on the computer with a partner.

Originally, the program was designed for use in the agency's two computer labs, but today the program is being given at schools in their own computer classrooms. It is not significant whether the program is used either in the clinical agency or in the school. What is important, however, is that the group leaders are trained in operating and conducting the session, which includes specific knowledge on how to use the software part of the program as well as on how to conduct the post-computer group activity. In order to achieve this goal, the leaders are given several hours of training and are equipped with the program manual which describes how to use the software program and depicts each group activity for the specific session.

PROGRAM CONTENT

The following topics are given to the participants in 10 consecutive sessions. At the start of each session, Donny introduces the topic and tells the children that they are going to meet some interesting people in today's session. Donny's picture appears next to the text that describes the subject of the session. The child participant can interact with either Donny or other characters by placing the cursor on a character portrait, clicking the mouse, thereby enlarging the picture, and interacting directly with the character by asking a question from a menu of questions. The following are brief descriptions of the program content and the computer software presentation that accompanies the topic theme.

1. *Introduction Lesson–Let's Meet Donny*. The children briefly discuss their connotation of the word "drugs" and meet Donny, an older Jaffa teenager. By asking Donny personal questions about himself, the participants establish a rapport with him, a connection that is maintained throughout the program, and is intended to contribute to Donny's positive influence on the participants. The introduction is followed up by a group discussion about drugs where the group leaders try to elicit from the group members their personal and social views about using alcohol, smoking cigarettes, and taking drugs.

2. *What Are Drugs?* Donny and the group leader work together to teach students specific information about drugs. Donny introduces them to people from their neighborhood: a pharmacist, a school principal, an artist, a wine seller, a drug user, and a policeman. These figures each tell the child something about themselves and about drugs. They convey information that challenges the child's preconceptions about what drugs and alcohol do when taken. The characters also try to provide some awareness about the attitude of society concerning using alcohol and other drugs. The children are then asked in the group follow-up what they thought of each character.

3. *Why Do People Use and Abuse Drugs?* Donny discusses both the beneficial and detrimental effects of drugs. Six reasons people use and/or abuse drugs are presented, and students must determine whether the use is warranted or not, therefore heightening his/her awareness about the risks involved in using drugs.

4. *Consequences–Stop and Think!* Too often children are influenced to try drugs because they believe that it is safe, or that it is cool, or in fact that society and most people view the activity as normal. Movies and media often present the "cool" image of drug use. Other times, personal problems in school or with friends and family make drug experimentation very tempting. Using attractive graphic images that follow a story from beginning to end, Donny takes the student through three situations to learn first hand how choices that the student makes can lead to different consequence in his/her life. For example, in one story there is a girl who is sitting at her desk in her home studying for a test when her friends come near her window and ask her to come out and play. If she says yes and leaves her studying, the software takes the child through a visual series of pictures showing the girl having fun with her friends, but then the next day, taking her exam unprepared and worried. The next picture shows the girl getting a failing grade. The other choice of "no" depicts the girl staying in her room, studying, and then receiving an "A" on her exam. Another situation shows a boy riding a bicycle, of-

fered some beer to drink and then having an accident while riding his bike. A second choice shows the boy turning down the offer to drink beer and having a nice time riding his bike. The visual display effectively conveys that actions we choose in life have very real consequences, which is an important concept to learn.

5. *Identifying Pro-Drug Use Pressures.* Donny and the group leader help students to identify drug use pressures (personal, peer, family, media, and community) as the first step in learning the coping skills they will need to say "no."

6. *Media and Community Influences on Drug Use.* Donny helps students identify hidden messages in media advertisements which often influence people to use their products. The media messages are presented on the computer for the child to examine and judge as to what the hidden message is and how this influences the viewers' beliefs, feelings, and behavior. The group activity afterwards asks the children to create their own media presentation to see if they have learned the impact that media has on shaping behaviors. The discussion helps the child make the connection between media influences and alcohol and drug use, including cigarettes.

7. *Peer Pressure–Say "No with Donny."* Students reexamine peer pressure, a major factor that influences them to experiment with drugs and alcohol, and they learn specific drug resistant skills which are graphically portrayed on the computer.

8. *Problem Solving–An Important Skill to Know.* Donny teaches the students a five-step problem solving strategy to deal with problems they face in their lives. Once again, the visual presentation of this important coping skill holds the child's attention.

9. *Solving Personal and Family Problems.* Donny and the students examine common preteen problems (loneliness, boredom, family, and school problems) and Donny helps the children viewers choose and rate four alternative ways to solve such issues. In this exercise, decision making is taught and applied on the computer screen.

10. *Meeting Donny Two Years Later–Using What We Learned!* In the last session, Donny meets the students two years later and tests out what they remember from the program and asks if the program was helpful. Once more, the group activity following the computer interaction involves the children in a discussion of what they thought they learned from the 10 session programs. Each child is then given a Say No with Donny tee-shirt and certificate for their participation.

THE ROLE OF THE FACILITATOR/GROUP LEADER

The response of the children to the program has been extremely positive. Many of the children thank the agency facilitators for having given them the program and acknowledge that these drug resistance skills are badly needed in the neighborhoods where they reside. The group facilitators are equally enthusiastic. Most of them are young, socially idealistic, and in their 20s, post-army, some working as counselors and others doing their field placement in social work at the agency. Their role is extremely important because it is their personal warmth and excitement about teaching younger children drug resistance skills that I believe makes the Donny program work as well as it does. Not only is Donny presented as a big brother hero in the software part of the program, but of equal importance, the leaders' personality and warmth and caring for the children in the group brings the electronic software drug prevention program alive.

> The leader must be warm and friendly as well as active and directive. The group leader should be someone who can represent the values and goals of the program and convey a real concern to the participants about their not smoking cigarettes and experimenting with drugs and alcohol. The group leader should not smoke cigarettes, or else risk the possibility of giving the students a double message about the goals of the program. (Gropper et al., 1995, p. 98)

THE INTERACTION OF THE SOFTWARE AND GROUP WORK PROCESS

While the colorful software program engages and holds the child's attention, it must be stressed that the design team wanted to make the program much more than just a computer software procedure to teach drug prevention. As a social work practitioner with a strong background in group work practice with youth, the author saw the value of reinforcing the computer learning part of the program with group work integration. The goal was to take advantage of the emerging and growing group peer culture found in this pre-adolescent age group and use the intervention process of computer interaction and group work to reinforce a common bond in values against experimenting and using drugs. The leadership training preceding the group intervention with the children also stressed the importance of the leaders' role in taking advantage of the powerful social learning force of pre-teens learning and sharing together a common experience of building some negative values and beliefs against drug taking behavior (Bandura, 1977; Thombs, 1994).

GROUP WORK ACTIVITIES USED IN THE "DONNY" PROGRAM

In the program, two specific group work activities are utilized frequently: "games" and "role-playing." Garvin (1987), writing about the use of games in group work, notes that games tell the leader a lot about how people will react to situations. Games "create situations in which members explore new ways to handle tensions" (Garvin, 1987, p. 127). In the "Say No with Donny" program, games are used continuously throughout the 10 session program "to maintain the interest of the children, to counteract member's anxiety in dealing with the difficult issue of drugs, to reinforce the learning process, and in general, to keep the learning process fun and stimulating" (Gropper et al., 1995, p. 99). Role-playing, the second group work activity used continuously in the program, also has many useful purposes. Garvin (1987) notes that role playing "may help prepare a member for utilization of a behavior outside of the group (behavioral rehearsal)" (p. 127). This transfer of knowledge through role-playing is possible because role-playing a situation helps the child to develop "a perception of judgment of one's capacity to execute a particular course of action required to deal effectively with an impending situation" (Abrams & Niaura, 1987, p. 134). The resulting confidence that comes from role-playing in a group is described by social learning theorists as "self-efficacy" (Bandura, 1977). Self-efficacy is the belief in one's ability to execute the necessary response to a challenge and demand. In the drug prevention field, this would translate, for example, into the belief that one has that if asked to take drugs, the individual would know what to say and/or what to do to not give in to the temptation or pressure to use the drugs. Role-playing is therefore a very important part of the group work of the Say No with Donny program because through role-playing, the children participants can strengthen their self-efficacy beliefs to deal with drug use pressures. In fact, the literature shows that self-efficacy beliefs are proposed to be better predictors of behavior than previous behaviors alone (Bandura, 1977), and therefore help the child to believe in him/herself and know how to handle pressures to use alcohol and other drugs.

PREDICTED RESISTANCE AND COMMUNITY SUPPORT FOR THE PROGRAM

While the program was in the development phase, the author, together with the community social work staff, began to reach out to and meet with the school principals that comprised the 10 elementary schools in the Jaffa community. Since the agency already had an excellent reputation with these schools in providing many morning and afternoon enrichment programs which were held at the agency's community center, it was believed that the principals would be highly receptive to their students' participation in the Donny program. However, the issue of giving drug prevention education to young students, especially with Israel's use of a short teaching day (the average school day was about 8 a.m. to 12:30 p.m.) presented a dilemma for the principals who had to decide how to utilize the short day for their students. Furthermore, meetings with the principals revealed that many of them were in fact reluctant to acknowledge how serious the drug problem really was in Jaffa and openly questioned the necessity of giving this program to their students. These initial meetings with the school officials revealed first hand how much denial there was about drugs in the educational system in the community. Nevertheless, principals from three Jewish elementary schools did agree to have their 6th grade students be amongst the first to take the program at the agency's community center.

The initial reaction by Arab school principals was less successful. In part, this may have reflected a bit of mistrust that had existed between the Arab community and the Institute. In response, agency social workers took a more active approach in reaching out to the Arab community and began to offer many more enrichment services to Arab children. The payoff for the agency's efforts was the agreement of one of the Arab elementary school principals to run an Arabic translated version of the program in an Arab school. The program was called "Say No with Samir." Today in Jaffa, seven of the 10 elementary schools (6 Jewish and 1 Arab) give the program to their 6th grade students at the agency premises.

THE THEORETICAL UNDERPINNINGS OF THE DONNY PROGRAM

As noted previously, the design of the "Say No with Donny" program incorporates many principles from social learning theory (Bandura, 1977) and utilizes many cognitive-behavioral principles to teach children drug prevention skills, i.e., coping skills such as decision-making, problem solving, and resistance skills when tempted to use alcohol and other drugs. "Through a variety of learning techniques including behavioral rehearsal and role-playing, modeling, cognitive restructuring, problem-solving games and exercises, didactic instruction, and coaching, the children are taught how to cope with the pressure to use drugs" (Gropper et al., 1995, p. 93). A central tenet of cognitive-behavioral intervention is the recognition of how the impact of the social learning process that the individual undergoes can influence the way this person perceives and deals with the world (Bandura, 1977). Social learning theory presupposes that cognitive process mediate between behavior and environmental influences. Bandura (1977) calls this mediating process reciprocal determination. In human behavior there exists " . . . a continuous reciprocal interaction between cognitive, behavioral, and environmental determinants. Within the process of reciprocal determination lies the opportunity for people to influence their destiny as well as the limits of self-direction" (Bandura, 1977, p. 7). Accordingly, the concepts of cognitive mediation and self-direction suggest that children, even those exposed to many negative influences to use drugs, can be taught personal responsibility and control over their lives concerning these influences.

Using cognitive psychology principles, Kendall and Braswell (1993) further explicate how the cognitive mediating process in drug prevention education actually works.

> Individuals perceive and make sense of the world and their experiences in it through their cognitive structures. These structures are also referred to as schema or templates. Such a template has an influence on what is perceived, how perceptions are processed, and what information will be remembered in the future. (Kendall & Braswell, 1993, p. 152)

One of the primary theoretical underpinnings of the "Say No with Donny" program is the potential for the computer software program when combined with active group work interventions to provide the internal opportunity for the child's cognitive structures to change in the direction of building structures that could elicit drug resiliency behavior (Gropper et al., 1995). The goal of the "Say No with Donny" program is to take a high risk child and to shape and enrich the "drug prevention cognitive template," that is, the cognitive mediating process, that will give this child the best chance to cope with personal and environmental influences to use alcohol and drugs. Therefore, in order to cope effectively with pressures to use drugs, youngsters need to have an internal cognitive-perceptual structure which correctly activates their ability to see the potential dangers and consequences of using drugs before it is to late, and to implement effective coping skills and resistance skills to deal with the situation. Through active computer simulated learning via the software program, and practice opportunities with the group facilitators, the child can gradually develop his/her confidence to deal with the real future situations when they arise.

PROGRAM EFFECTIVENESS

After its initial inception, the program received many positive reviews by almost every major Israeli newspaper and television stories as well as through content and process evaluations by representatives of the Ministry of Education and the Israel National Anti-Drug Authority. The Israel National Anti-Drug Authority concluded that the "Say No with Donny" program met the highest standards in drug education and recommends the program's implementation in communities throughout Israel. An evaluation study was conducted by Gropper and Harel (1999). A simple multiple time series, quasi-experimental design was used in which 120 children exposed to the pilot program were compared at four different measurement points: baseline, post-intervention, 3 months following intervention, and one year after intervention during the beginning of their 7th grade. Results indicated that the program had a significant positive impact on increasing the recipient's ability to accurately identify substances as drugs, especially concerning cigarettes and heroin in which the effect lasted into the following year. The study also found significant improvements by the subjects in their knowledge about the risks and consequences of drug and alcohol use, an important finding because knowledge about risks and consequences has been shown to be important in mediating future drug use among children (Bachman, Johnston, & O'Malley, 1988; Johnston, 1982, 1985; Johnston, O'Malley, & Bachman, 1987, 1989).

UPDATED VERSION OF THE PROGRAM

In 1998, the agency completed and implemented an updated version of the "Say No with Donny, Computer Integrated Drug Prevention" program. The new program, "About Drugs, No to Drugs," was developed by the Institute for the Advancement of Education in Jaffa with assistance from the Israel National Anti-Drug Authority and the Ministry of Education. During the 1998-99 school year, the new program was given to more than several hundred children from Jaffa and three other Israeli communities. The updated program, while drawing on the same theory and covering almost identical topics as its predecessor, has many new changes. The Donny character has been replaced by an animated, talking computer that appears on the screen and speaks to the child throughout the 10-session program. The program has voice activation, excellent music, and continuous animated interactive graphic sequences that deliver the content and hold the child's attention. The new program structure works very much like the earlier version with 90-minute sessions, about 30 minutes of computer time followed by facilitator led group exercises. Once more, the facilitators are either counselors or social work students. An Arabic and an English version are being developed and are almost completed.

OBTAINING THE PROGRAM

The new version of the program, "About Drugs, No to Drugs," will soon be ready for distribution and sale in the United States, Canada, England and many other countries. The Institute for the Advancement of Education marketing director states that the agency has plans to sell the program around the world and is currently developing its marketing and distribution plan. Anyone interested in learning how to purchase the new program should send inquires to: Dr. Michael Gropper, Golan Center, 198 Achuza Street, Raanana 43560 Israel.

CONCLUSION

The "Say No with Donny" program and the updated version, "About Drugs, No to Drugs" represent a new development in social work practice in the area of health promotion and prevention with youth. Utilizing the electronic computer media to teach prevention to children at a social work community agency program in a poor community is both novel and creative. The integration of group work methods together with a computer program is truly an exciting development for social group work practitioners. There is no question that now as we begin the new millennium, more and more social work practitioners, many of whom are part of the new-age technology generation, will think of creative ways to integrate computer programs into practice with their clients. This new development is both exciting and challenging for the social work profession.

REFERENCES

Abrams, D.B. & Niaura, R.S. (1987). Social Learning Theory. In H.T. Blane & K.E. Leonard (Eds). *Psychological Theories of Drinking and Alcoholism.* New York, Guilford Press.

Bachman, J.G., Johnston, L.D., & O'Malley, P.M. (1988). Explaining the recent decline in marijuana use: Differentiating the effects of perceived risks, disapproval, and general lifestyle factors. *J Health Soc Behav*, *29*, 92-112.

Bandura, A. (1977). *Social Learning Theory.* Englewood Cliffs, New Jersey: Prentice-Hall.

Downie, R.S., Fyfe, C., & Tannahill, A. (1990). *Health Promotion: Models and Values.* Oxford: Oxford University Press.

Ellickson, P.L. & Bell, R.M. (March 16, 1990). Drug prevention in junior high: A multi-site Longitudinal Test. *Science*, 247, 1299-1305.

Garvin, C.D. (1987). *Contemporary Group Work.* Englewood Cliffs, New Jersey: Prentice Hall.

Gerstner, L. (Nov. 15, 1993). The future of technology in education. *Business Week.*

Gropper, M., & Harel, T. (1999). Unpublished manuscript.

Gropper, M., Liraz, Z., Portowicz, D., & Schindler, M. (1995). Computer integrated drug prevention: A new approach to teach lower socioeconomic 5th and 6th grade Israeli children to say no to drugs. *Social Work in Health Care*, *22*(2), 87-103.

Johnston, L.D. (1982). A review and analysis of recent changes in marijuana use by American young people. In *Marijuana: The National Impact on Education.* New York: American Council on Marijuana, 8-13.

Johnston, L.D., O'Malley, P.M., & Bachman, J.G. (1987). *Lifestyle Orientations in Late Adolescence and Patterns of Substance Abuse.* Monitoring the Future Occasional Paper No. 27. Ann Arbor, MI: Institute for Social Research.

Johnston, L.D., O'Malley, P.M., & Bachman, J.G. (1989). *Drug Use, Drinking, and Smoking: National Survey Results from High School, College, and Young Adult Populations, 1975-1988.* DHHS Pub. No. (ADM)89-1638. Washington, DC: Supt. of Docs., U.S. Govt. Print. Off.

Kendall, P.C. & Braswell, L. (1993). *Cognitive-Behavioral Therapy for Impulsive Children.* New York: The Guilford Press.

Oei, T.P.S., & Baldwin, A.R. (1992). Smoking education and prevention: A developmental model. *Journal of Drug Education*, 22(2), 155-181.

Orlandi, M.A., Dozier, C., & Marta, M.A. (1990). Computer assisted strategies for substance abuse prevention: Opportunities and barriers. *Journal of Consulting and Clinical Psychology*, *58*(4), 425-431.

Pellow, R.A. & Jengelski, J.L. (1991). A survey of current research studies on drug education programs in America. *Journal of Drug Education*, *21*(3), 203-210.

Schoech, D. (1982). *Computer Use in Human Services: A Guide to Information Management*. New York: Human Sciences Press.

Thombs, D.L. (1994). *Introduction to Addictive Disorders*. New York: Guilford Press.

"Talking It Out": A Computer-Based Mediation Process for Adolescents

Kris Bosworth

SUMMARY. This article describes the development of a multimedia mediation program ("Talking It Out") that helps young adolescents resolve conflict peacefully. The development and content are described, together with pilot test data from 16 pairs of disputing students. These case studies provide evidence of the popularity and effectiveness of computer-based mediation. *[Article copies available for a fee from The Haworth Document Delivery Service: 1-800-HAWORTH. E-mail address: <getinfo@haworthpressinc.com> Website: <http://www.HaworthPress.com> © 2002 by The Haworth Press, Inc. All rights reserved.]*

KEYWORDS. Adolescents, youth, schools, technology, mediation

Early adolescence is a particularly vulnerable time in development. Young people are experiencing major, rapid developmental changes at a time when society sends them mixed messages about how they should behave. It is essential to provide young adolescents with the information and social skills they need to be successful in their journey toward adulthood. The meteoric rise in youth homicides in the early 1990s and

---

Kris Bosworth, PhD, holds the Smith Endowed Chair in Substance Abuse Prevention in the College of Education at the University of Arizona.

[Haworth co-indexing entry note]: "'Talking It Out': A Computer-Based Mediation Process for Adolescents." Bosworth, Kris. Co-published simultaneously in *Journal of Technology in Human Services* (The Haworth Press, Inc.) Vol. 20, No. 1/2, 2002, pp. 67-81; and: *Human Services Technology: Innovations in Practice and Education* (ed: Hy Resnick, and Phoebe Sade Anderson) The Haworth Press, Inc., 2002, pp. 67-81. Single or multiple copies of this article are available for a fee from The Haworth Document Delivery Service [1-800-HAWORTH, 9:00 a.m. - 5:00 p.m. (EST). E-mail address: getinfo@haworthpressinc.com].

the tragic cases of multiple homicides in schools in the late 1990s have highlighted the need to teach adolescents how to resolve conflicts nonviolently.

A popular approach to teaching conflict resolution skills is mediation (Lupton-Smith et al., 1996; Schrumpf, Crawford, & Bodine, 1997). In mediation, the disputing parties meet with trained mediators, who often are their peers, to proceed through a scripted problem-solving process. Various forms of mediation are currently in use in schools, community organizations, and the juvenile justice system. Strong anecdotal evidence from social workers, educators, and others supports the effectiveness of mediation, although few rigorous evaluations of mediation with adolescents exist (Johnson & Johnson, 1998).

Since the late 1970s the author has been involved with colleagues at the University of Wisconsin-Madison and Indiana University in several projects using technology to teach young people the social skills they need to choose and maintain a healthy lifestyle (Bosworth et al., 1983; Gustafson et al., 1987; Bosworth & Yoast, 1991; BARN Research Group, 1994; Bosworth et al., 1997; Bosworth et al., 1998). Because adolescents are drawn to fast-paced, colorful, energetic media and are the major consumer group targeted for video games and the popular music industry (Funk & Buchman, 1996; Hepburn, 1995), she has focused her research on the appropriate application of the technology in prevention interventions for adolescents. These interests have led her to develop and evaluate several software programs addressing drug abuse prevention, AIDS education, stress management, and related topics.

Unfortunately, much of the software, video games, and even music available to adolescents have violent themes and lyrics. The messages in many of these media are that (1) violence is the way to solve problems, and (2) the key to success is to be more violent than your opponent. These are not life skills that will help young people achieve long-term success in life through cooperation, negotiation, active problem solving, and nonviolent conflict resolution. Because electronic media are so attractive to this age group, however, the author became interested in the potential to harness these formats for teaching students prosocial skills for peaceful conflict resolution, instead of antisocial and counterproductive skills.

With a multiyear development grant from the Centers for Disease Control and Prevention, the author and colleagues developed a software package called *SMART Talk* (marketed as *SMART Team*) to teach adolescents skills for resolving conflict (Bosworth et al., 1996). Designed for distribution through a commercial publishing house (Learning

Multi-Systems), this was a major undertaking that involved a team of researchers, artists, graphic designers, and programmers proficient in C++ programming language. Modules within *SMART Talk* address anger management, perspective taking, and mediation, all important components of conflict resolution. This chapter will describe the content, development, and evaluation of the mediation module named "Talking It Out."

"Talking It Out" is designed for use in a school or agency setting. It can be used independently by adolescents (alone or in pairs), in a group setting, or as a counseling intervention, with pairs of young people in the midst of a dispute being assigned to use the software as an alternative to mediation facilitated by a peer. Thus, "Talking It Out" is a flexible and adaptable tool that can be implemented in many different settings. The professionals in those settings–social worker, counselor, principal, teacher, etc.–play a key role in determining how best to utilize the software in that organizational context.

DESCRIPTION OF THE SOFTWARE

The content of "Talking It Out" is geared for adolescents in grades 5 to 9 (roughly ages 11 to 15), and is intended to achieve the following objectives:

- To provide a process for negotiating conflict between two adolescents
- To increase adolescents' confidence in their ability to find a nonviolent solution to a dispute
- To allow both parties to understand their own and the other person's positions
- To enable the users to identify the barriers to resolution of the conflict
- To assist them in identifying possible solutions
- To facilitate a win-win situation, where both parties feel satisfied with the process and outcome.

The software content was determined by reviewing 11 conflict resolution and mediation protocols. Because no other conflict resolution materials are available in software format, print materials were reviewed to identify the aspects most appropriate for use in a computer format, and the processes described in the books were modified to operate as an interactive interview on the computer. Among the printed materials consulted were *Mediation for Kids* (Peace Education Foundation, 1990), *Mediation: Getting to Win Win!* (Peace Education Foundation, 1994), *Peace Patrol* (*Peace Patrol*, 1994), *Peer Mediation: Conflict Resolution in Schools* (*Peer Mediation*, 1991), *Students Resolving Conflict: Peer Mediation in Schools* (School Mediation Associates, 1984), and *Conflict Resolution: An Elementary School Curriculum* (Community Board Program, 1990). (None of these materials were credited to named authors.) From this review, a mediation model was formulated that embodied the processes most commonly used in existing programs. This draft model was reviewed by two experts in mediation and a focus group of teen mediators who had several years of mediation experience. The final model for "Talking It Out" contained the following steps:

1. Introduction and Ground Rules
2. Telling Each Story
3. Story Verification
4. Generation of Solutions
5. Creation of a Contract.

As in live mediation, the "Talking It Out" model assumes that two disputants will be present at the computer. When two partners access the program together, they are guided through the mediation process as follows:

Introduction and Ground Rules: A graphic character introduces the program, explaining that its purpose is to help "you and your friends learn ways to solve problems and avoid fighting or getting in trouble." The features of a successful solution are laid out:

- nonviolent
- balanced
- possible to do
- easy to see results

At this point, a "Teen Panel" (represented in the software as four graphic characters and based on ten actual peer mediators who consulted in the software development) appear on the screen to give the students suggestions for how to approach the mediation process. Each makes a suggestion, such as "Keep a cool head," or "Go in with a positive attitude." The option to get advice from the Teen Panel appears at several points in the module.

Next, each user has to click "yes" to agree to each of the ground rules listed below. The subsequent screen cannot be accessed until both parties respond "yes" to each of the following statements:

1. "I want to solve the conflict."
2. "I will be respectful."
3. "I will be truthful."
4. "I will keep things confidential."

Telling Each Story: Users decide who goes first. The first person types in his or her side of the conflict, and is able to add or revise the text until the "continue" button is clicked. Then the other user has the opportunity to do the same. Instructions on the screen remind the waiting disputant not to interrupt while the first person types in his or her story.

Story Verification: Each user in turn is presented with the other party's written statement and asked to type in what he or she thinks the other person is saying. Users are encouraged to ask questions for clarification as necessary throughout this process.

Then the person who wrote the statement is asked whether the other party understands it correctly. If not, the person is asked to retell the story in different words. This cycle can be repeated as many times as necessary until both parties agree that they understand each other's positions. This step is important because research shows violent youth tend to have difficulty empathizing with others and making accurate attributions about the motives for others' behavior (Miller & Eisenberg, 1988).

Discussion: Users are invited to identify three issues they need to discuss and enter them in the computer. The Teen Panel again appears to give users advice such as, "Put yourself in each other's shoes," and "What did you learn that was new?" At this point, users engage in face-to-face interaction without accessing the computer to discuss the issues, their feelings, and the conflict. When they are ready to proceed, they click "continue" to access the "solutions" screen.

Generation of Solutions: Each person is asked to enter three things he or she could do to solve the problem. Advice from the Teen Panel is available, if desired. Then the parties are asked to evaluate (1) whether their solutions meet the four criteria of a good solution (described previously), and (2) whether they are willing to do these three things. Anyone who answers "no" to either of these questions is given an opportunity to enter new solutions and evaluate those. Thus, users can cycle through this component of the program several times if necessary until both are satisfied with the solutions.

Creation of a Contract: When both parties agree to their three solutions, these items are embedded in a contract form that lists each person's name and the three items he or she has agreed to do, with lines for signatures and dates. Users have the option to print copies of this contract, so they can actually sign and keep a physical document if they so wish. In situations where students are assigned to complete "Talking It Out," the contract could serve as a record of resolution of the conflict. This is a means of allowing the disputants to complete the mediation process independently and reach their own solutions while maintaining accountability.

REFERRAL PROCESS

"Talking It Out" was initially conceived as part of a universal violence prevention program (*SMART Talk*), applicable and available to all students. During the field implementation in an urban middle school for the outcome evaluation, however, a school social worker and teachers asked whether this module might be an appropriate tool for two students who were in a bitter, ongoing dispute. With this impetus, the evaluation team created a protocol and standardized process that school personnel could use to refer students for computer-based mediation, so that the effects could be assessed:

1. *Initiation of referral:* The person making the referral familiarized the research liaison with the conflict. When referring students with relatively serious disputes that had also triggered formal administrative action (e.g., in-school suspension), the person completed a written referral form. This form documented the nature of the conflict and what administrative action occurred as a result of it.

2. *Screening:* The research liaison reviewed the referral form to determine if computer-based mediation was appropriate. If so, the disputants were scheduled to complete "Talking It Out" within a few days, typically during a regular class period.

3. *Module completion:* Disputants completed the module together. The research liaison determined whether the students were already

familiar with the program, and if they were not, provided a brief overview of the content and purpose. The research liaison remained in the room at a distance, usually doing other work. She did not observe what they were typing, and interacted with the students only when they had questions about how to operate the computer.

4. *Post-mediation interview:* Disputants were interviewed immediately after they printed out their contracts, to elicit their reactions and feelings as to whether the conflict had been resolved. The primary purpose of this interview was to verify that students had in fact completed the process and made progress in resolving their dispute.

5. *Follow-up interview:* The disputants were interviewed individually about a week after using "Talking It Out," to determine the status of their relationship and whether they had implemented the solutions in their contracts.

6. *Report:* The research liaison informed the referring party of the status of the conflict without revealing any confidential information about the process or the resolution.

CASE STUDY OF USE

One of the more serious conflicts involved two white, sixth-grade females. Prior to this altercation, the two generally had been considered best friends; their teacher reported that they spent most of their time in class together, working very well together in groups and one-on-one. The conflict erupted during the transition after fourth-period study hall. The two girls were heard calling each other names and repeating gossip apparently passed on by others ("she said you called me . . . "; "he said you think you can beat me up . . . "; and similar accusations). When the two entered the hallway, the name calling quickly escalated into shouting, then a shoving match. One young woman turned around and punched the other, breaking her nose. They were quickly separated by a nearby teacher and taken to the sixth-grade principal's office.

Each student met individually with the principal to explain what had occurred, and both were punished for their participation in the conflict. The first received a three-day in-school suspension while the second (the puncher) received out-of-school suspension for the same period. After reviewing "Talking It Out," the principal referred the pair for computer-based mediation. Subsequently, a second referral was initiated by a teacher after the two students returned to class.

Computer time could not be scheduled immediately because the girl with the broken nose was frequently absent due to doctor's appointments and recurrent migraine headaches (a result of the injury). The two were scheduled to use "Talking It Out" in a private room 18 days after the conflict. When they entered the room, they still were not speaking to each other, and the teacher who initiated the second referral reported that the atmosphere in the classroom still was very tense "like walking on eggshells."

Both students agreed they were willing to try the program, and when they sat down at the computer together, they quickly began cooperating. One volunteered to read the screen while the other offered to operate the mouse. They continued cooperating for more than half an hour, each even offering the other a chance to tell her story first. On finishing, they printed out their contracts and appeared quite pleased with them.

During the post-use interview, one girl reported that " 'Talking It Out' helped us solve some of our problems. If it weren't for using it, [the fight] probably wouldn't be resolved yet." The other indicated, " 'Talking It Out' really helped us. I misunderstood her and stuff, and now everything is OK." They found the process more helpful than being interviewed by the principal. One commented, "When we talked to the principal, all sides of our problem didn't come out. . . . He just kept asking who started it, and it all happened so fast, I don't think we even knew." The other added, "It is good to be able to write and read our own stories without talking and without an adult getting involved."

The following day the teacher reported in amazement that the tense atmosphere in the classroom had completely evaporated. Both girls were willing to work together in groups and even one-on-one. She said, "I just can't believe that working through 'Talking It Out' has resolved everything for these girls; they are even recommending it to other students in the class to solve their conflicts." For the two months remaining in the school year, this pair again became good friends, with no further conflict occurring between them.

EVALUATION OF SOFTWARE EFFECTIVENESS

The two evaluation studies completed to date have involved the complete *SMART Talk* software, including the "Talking It Out" module. Results of these two studies indicate that the overall *SMART Talk* package is an effective and motivating format for both information delivery and skills building to middle-school students. No differences in use rates could be attributed to gender, ethnic membership, or socioeconomic status. The medium of computer software has potential to engage a population at risk for violence that may not be engaged by traditional prevention approaches. "Talking It Out" was one of the more popular components of the *SMART Talk* package among all the students in the intervention group (n = 195). Those students reported using this component an average of 8.4 times, but whether they were actually using it to resolve a dispute or simply exploring cannot be determined, because these students were not monitored during their use of the computer. The evaluation studies are reported in detail elsewhere (Bosworth, Espelage, & DuBay, 1998; Bosworth et al., 1999), so the following focuses on evaluation data collected from interviews with students who used "Talking It Out."

During the semester that *SMART Talk* was implemented in the urban middle school, sixteen pairs of disputants, 31 students in all (one student was involved in two separate conflicts), were referred. Nine of the 16 pairs monitored were female, five were male, and two comprised one male and one female. Fourteen of the 16 disputes occurred on school property. There were also 14 conflicts that involved some degree of physical contact, ranging from a broken nose and a broken arm, to pushing and shoving, to grabbing money from someone's hand (see Table 1). For purposes of data collection for the pilot study, all but one of the disputants were interviewed again at the end of the semester (in most cases two or three months after use of "Talking It Out").

Among the 16 pairs who were observed using "Talking It Out," none committed repeat offenses or was referred for any disciplinary action (including repeat of "Talking It Out"). One student, however, was referred again with a different person to resolve an unrelated, nonviolent altercation. Of the 15 pairs who participated in the final interview, six said their friendships had improved since the "Talking It Out" experience. Five pairs reported that their relationship had returned to its pre-mediation status, and one pair disagreed, with one party reporting

TABLE 1. Characteristics of Pairs Referred to "Talking It Out"

Pair	Gender of Disputants	Nature of Dispute	Injury	Outcome
1	female/female	escalating name calling	broken nose	resolved
2	female/female	rumor	torn blouse	resolved
3	female/female	rumor	--	resolved
4	female/female	name calling	scratch	resolved
5	female/female	bus conflict	throwing books, etc.	1 party felt resolved/1 felt not resolved
6	female/female	hallway	pushing	resolved
7	female/female	name calling	hair pulled	resolved
8	female/female	hurt feelings	hair pulled	resolved
9	female/female	rumor	pushing	not interviewed
10	male/male	challenge fight	broken arm	resolved
11	male/male	grabbed money	bruise	resolved
12	male/male	pushing in hallway	torn clothing	resolved
13	male/male	challenge fight	grabbing	resolved
14	male/male	rumor	punching	resolved
15	female/male	classroom fight	scratches	resolved
16	female/male	name calling	--	resolved

being friends and the other saying the pair was not friendly. Three pairs reported being distantly civil but not friendly; in these instances it seems that people who disliked each other before the altercation essentially learned to tolerate each other. Most students agreed that their relationships were no worse than prior to the "Talking It Out" experience. In the most positive case, two girls who had not previously been friendly reported becoming "best friends."

When asked whether they had applied the "Talking It Out" principles in other conflicts, 12 students reported having had no opportunity to do so. Seven individuals offered various anecdotal examples of things they had done. Several described ways they had avoided conflicts by thinking about the situation before starting an argument, trying to talk things out instead of getting into fights, and showing more respect for other people. Four students reported using resolution principles during an actual argument, including one who drew up a contract with her sister and another who confronted a friend about a rumor (and discovered it to be untrue). One student reported thinking about "Talking It Out" after a fight and going to the other party the next day to talk things out.

A compelling finding from the interviews was that the students who had experience with live mediation facilitated by a peer *universally preferred* the computer-based experience. They appreciated being empowered to resolve their dispute independently, without having to explain their situation to a third party. Other students perceived that the human mediators had been overly directive, or had taken sides, or had pressured them to apologize before the disputants felt the situation had been resolved. None of the students reported that the presence of the research liaison had interfered with the process in any way.

LESSONS LEARNED

Although the use of "Talking It Out" as an unique intervention within this study was unplanned, project staff quickly developed a protocol that included close observation of the students' work with the software and follow-up with disputing students and their teachers. Several lessons can be shared from this small pilot that may be useful for those interested in developing or using computer-mediated mediation.

1. Privacy and confidentiality were important to the students. Students preferred using "Talking It Out" to traditional peer mediation because of concern for personal privacy. Some were worried that the mediators will share personal information learned in mediation, but for some the concern was more subtle. One student said, "They (mediators) may never tell anyone, but they still know something about you that I'm not so proud of."
2. Initially, the amount of space students had to write their stories was limited. Most students were frustrated by this limitation and wanted unlimited space to tell their story. Not having enough screen space to write was a barrier to problem solving.
3. The use of a printed contract was critical in helping students take the process seriously and to make a commitment to the solution they generated. When interviewed several months after completing "Talking It Out," over 80% of students knew where their contract was. Several carried it with them and others reported having looked at their contract at some time after completing the program.

DISCUSSION

This pilot evaluation indicates that "Talking It Out" can be a powerful intervention in settings where teens might experience conflict. In this study, "Talking It Out" has been used primarily in the school setting, both in counselors' offices and computer labs. Other settings, such as juvenile facilities and community agencies, are also appropriate. The sole constraint on setting of use is presence of the necessary computer hardware (Macintosh with CD-ROM drive).

All instructions for using "Talking It Out" are embedded in the software, allowing adolescents to use the module independently. Field-testing proves that middle-school students had no difficulty using the program without special training or close supervision (Bosworth, Espelage, & DuBay, 1998). Thus, if the software is available on a computer to which young people have free access, they could potentially use the program without adult knowledge or intervention. When conflicts come to adult attention, the adult may wish to have an initial conversation with the disputants to ensure that computer-based mediation is an appropriate avenue for resolution. If the conflict involves a serious infraction, such as theft or physical injury, it may be appropriate to impose additional consequences such as disciplinary action or restitution, in accordance with the policies of that institution.

If two disputants are assigned to use the program (for example, as an alternative to traditional disciplinary procedures), unobtrusive monitoring is appropriate to ensure that they actually complete the process in good faith and reach some resolution. However, among the features that most appealed to young adolescents using the program were privacy and independence in resolving their own dispute.

Reports of student users have been overwhelmingly positive, and some recommended that their friends try it. Initial resistance is possible, especially from adolescents who are required to use the program as part of disciplinary action. Indications are, however, once young people understand the program and its purpose, most will use it willingly, and some will even initiate use.

Why was the computer so popular? Based on students' reports, several reasons can be posited.

Privacy and independence are powerful motivators for adolescents, who often struggle against adult authority and gossip generated by peers. "Talking It Out" offers confidentiality, yet the printed contract can be used for record keeping purposes.

Time constraints are essentially removed with the computer. Disputants can take however much time they wish to write and rewrite, read and reread, process and reprocess their own and the other party's positions before moving to solution seeking.

The computer is a completely neutral piece of machinery that cannot interrupt or comment on what a user types in. Possibly for this reason, several students commented that it was easier to input what they really thought and felt into the computer than to tell their side to an administrator or mediator. As one young woman commented, "We were able to communicate by reading instead of just talking. You know that they will at least read it. I had time to let off steam. It was easier because we were in a quiet place where no one was."

The fact that only one user at a time can use the keyboard gives the other person a "cooling off" period, while minimizing interruptions and arguments in each person's retelling of what occurred. As one student explained, "you have to learn to respect the other person because you can't exactly push their hands aside and start typing."

Written composition may facilitate objectivity: Self-monitoring may be enhanced when adolescents see their words in print–and they have the option to backspace and "unsay" something that did not come out the way they had intended. Spoken language is interpreted on two levels: the words that are spoken and the unspoken messages in body language, inflection, etc. Printed text is devoid of these emotional cues, making it easier for young people to state their feelings without appearing accusatory and to read and respond to the other person's side without becoming defensive. One student commented, "It was like having an argument without talking."

In summary, these case reports suggest that "Talking It Out" is not only an effective tool in assisting adolescents to resolve interpersonal conflicts, but also teaches skills that they are readily able to identify and apply in other situations. Although the program requires at least 45 minutes of concentrated work to complete, students did not complain, and many described it as "fun" and "easy to use." For some, simply writing and reading each other's stories led to resolution. One young man remarked that he was "understood for the first time" by the other party. Classroom teachers corroborated that there had been no disputes among the referred pairs and generally reported a more positive classroom atmosphere.

AVAILABILITY

The *SMART Talk* software package has been published on CD-ROM by Learning Multi-Systems (LMS) in two versions. The standard *SMART Talk* disk contains eight modules that address knowledge, anger management, perspective taking, and dispute resolution. The special-edition *SMART/Cool* CD incorporates three short videos produced by different authors with American Guidance Service.

REFERENCES

BARN Research Group (1994). The BARN system: Use and impact of adolescent health promotion via computer. *Computers in Human Behavior*, 10(4), 467-482.

Bosworth, K., Gustafson, D.H., Hawkins, R.P., Chewning, B., & Day, T. (1983). Adolescents, health education, and computers: The body awareness resource network (BARN), *Health Education*, 14(6), 117-119.

Bosworth, K. & Yoast, R. (1991). DIADS: Computer-based system for development of school drug prevention programs. *Journal of Drug Education*, 21(3), 231-245.

Bosworth, K., Haakenson, P., & McCracken, K. (1997). *Teacher talk:* Capturing innovative teacher voices on the world wide web. *Journal of Technology and Teacher Education* 5 (4)(December), 319-331.

Bosworth, K., Espelage, D., & DuBay, T. (1998). A computer-based violence prevention intervention for young adolescents: Pilot study. *Adolescence, 33* (132), 785-795.

Bosworth, K., Espelage, D., Daytner, G., DuBay, T., Dahlberg, L.L., & Daytner, G. (1996). Using multimedia to teach conflict-resolution skills to young adolescents. *American Journal of Preventive Medicine, 12*(5), 65-74.

Bosworth, K., Espelage, D., Daytner, G., DuBay, T., & Karageorge, K. (In press). The efficacy of a multimedia violence prevention program for early adolescence. *American Journal of Health Behavior.*

Community Board Program. *Conflict resolution: An elementary school curriculum.* (1990). San Francisco: The Community Board Program.

Funk, J.B. & Buchman, D.D. (1996). Playing violent video and computer games and adolescent self-concept. *Journal of Communication, 46*(2), 19-32.

Gustafson, D.H., Bosworth, K., Chewning, B., & Hawkins, R.P. (1987). Computer-based health promotion: Combining technological advances with problem-solving techniques to effect successful health behavior changes. *The Annual Review of Public Health, 8*, 387-415.

Hepburn, M. (1995). TV violence: Myth and reality. *Social Education, 59*(5), 309-311.

Johnson, D.W., & Johnson, R.T. (1998). Conflict resolution and peer mediation programs in elementary and secondary schools–A review of the research. *Review of Educational Research, 66*(4), 459-506.

Lupton-Smith, H.S., Carruthers, W.L., Flythe, R., Goehee, E., & Modest, K.H. (1996). Conflict resolution as peer mediation: Programs for elementary, middle, and high school students. *The School Counselor, 43*(May), 374-391.

Miller, P., & Eisenberg, N. (1988). The relation of empathy to aggressive and externalizing/antisocial behavior. *Psychological Bulletin, 103*, 324-344.

Peace Education Foundation. *Mediation for kids.* (1990). Miami: Peace Education Foundation.

Peace Education Foundation. *Mediation: Getting to win win!* (1994). Miami: Peace Education Foundation.

Peace patrol. (1994). Carson, CA: Jalmar Press.

Peer mediation: Conflict resolution in schools. (1991). Champaign, IL: Research Press.

School Mediation Associates. (1984). *Students resolving conflict: Peer mediation in schools.* Watertown, MA: School Mediation Associates.

Schrumpf, F., Crawford, D.K., & Bodine, R.J. (1997). Peer mediation: Conflict resolution in schools. *Adolescence, 32*(125), 248-51.

Clients as Co-Developers of Multimedia Software: Two HIV/AIDS Training Programs for Kids

Ann Wilder
Dick Schoech

SUMMARY. Most educators using multimedia have difficulty determining how best to structure and present curriculum material to difficult audiences, such as at-risk youth. This article describes a process whereby kids played significant roles as co-developers and subject matter experts in the development of two multimedia training modules on HIV/AIDS for kids ages 6-9 and 9-12. It presents the development process, the resulting software, the results of the formal evaluation, issues,

Ann Wilder, MSSW, CISW, is a Child and Family Therapist in private practice in Tucson, Arizona. She teaches Psychology of Creativity at Pima Community College and is President of the Southern Arizona Association for Play Therapy.

Dick Schoech, PhD, is Professor at the University of Texas at Arlington School of Social Work. He teaches administration, community practice, and computer applications.

Address correspondence to: Dr. Dick Schoech, UTA SSW, Box 19129, Arlington, TX 76019-0129 (Internet: http://www.uta.edu/cussn/ or E-mail: schoech@uta.edu).

The authors wish to acknowledge the AT&T Texas Student Scholars Grant Program and the Levi Strauss Foundation for providing initial funds and the Complementary Medicine Association and the Community Foundation of Southern Arizona for financial support for current marketing and distribution. They would also like to acknowledge all those who have worked on the project, including Pediatric and Family HIV/AIDS staff, Kids Club members, and Research Assistant Eric Hendricks who made significant development contributions through his work as co-developer and member of the development team.

[Haworth co-indexing entry note]: "Clients as Co-Developers of Multimedia Software: Two HIV/AIDS Training Programs for Kids." Wilder, Ann, and Dick Schoech. Co-published simultaneously in *Journal of Technology in Human Services* (The Haworth Press, Inc.) Vol. 20, No. 1/2, 2002, pp. 83-105; and: *Human Services Technology: Innovations in Practice and Education* (ed: Hy Resnick, and Phoebe Sade Anderson) The Haworth Press, Inc., 2002, pp. 83-105. Single or multiple copies of this article are available for a fee from The Haworth Document Delivery Service [1-800-HAWORTH, 9:00 a.m. - 5:00 p.m. (EST). E-mail address: getinfo@haworthpressinc.com].

problems, and lessons learned. It concludes that client involvement in software is effective as well as therapeutic and empowering. However, developing software in controversial areas, such as HIV and AIDS, results in problematic distribution and continued enhancement.

KEYWORDS. Multimedia, kids, children, HIV, AIDS, software

Most educators using multimedia know what they want to communicate and to whom. However, they have difficulty determining how best to structure and present the material, especially to difficult audiences such as kids. This article presents one solution to this problem. It describes a process used to develop two multimedia software HIV/AIDS training modules for kids ages 6-9 and 9-12. In these modules, the kids played significant roles as co-developers and subject matter experts in the software development process.

In the traditional software development process, a core development team outlines the training goals and objectives and then uses a technique such as storyboarding to design all the modules. Text is then written, media secured, and the content is programmed into software. Different technical experts are sometimes added to the core development team during each step in the development process. The product is then tested to determine whether it works as intended. Finally, it is evaluated with users to determine whether the initial learning objectives are being met.

This project used a prototyping development approach. In prototyping, the application is developed through repeated cycles of quick analysis, development, use, feedback, and refinement (Schoech, 1999). The emphasis during prototyping is on quickly developing a trial application. Conventional wisdom and standard practices are ignored for "what works." An initial "quick and dirty" application is developed and presented to key groups for feedback. Prototyping allows users to agree on the look and feel of the application before developers formalize the overall design. In fact, the final application may not resemble the initial design. Prototyping allows users and developers to educate each other about their respective needs and capabilities. The unique development aspect of this project was that the intended user, kids affected by HIV/AIDS, became co-developers in the prototyping process.

THE SITUATION

The Pediatric and Family HIV/AIDS Project (hereafter known as The Project) is a program funded by the Maternal and Child Health Bureau and operated by Catholic Charities of Fort Worth, Texas. The Project provided family centered care for women and children living with HIV and AIDS. As a program evaluation consultant to the Project, one of the tasks assigned to the senior author was to work with Project staff in the formation of an HIV/AIDS resource library for the Project's Kids Club. Kids Club was a psycho-educational support group for children living in families where one or more parents had been diagnosed with HIV or AIDS. Kids Club provided the opportunity for children in similar situations to befriend one another and develop additional support systems by focusing on HIV and AIDS education, preventive health practices, crisis management skills, and recreational activities. Weekly contact with counselors, volunteers, and other kids allowed for open discussion of sensitive topics related to HIV and AIDS. The kids were school age and at varying levels of understanding in the process of accepting the disease as part of their daily lives. Kids Club members were a culturally diverse group. Approximately 50% of Project families were African American, 30% Hispanic and 20% Anglo. Injection drug use was the primary mode of transmission reported by the women who sought services. Over 70% of the families were classified as low income.

Kids living in families where one or more members are HIV positive are often ashamed and confused by the nature of this disease. Attempts to explain the disease or illness of their parent or extended family member can be awkward. Parents are often unable to provide the emotional support that kids need in comprehending the nature of a life threatening illness and potential death of a family member.

When looking for resources for the Project library, the senior author found that most curriculum material for elementary grades focused primarily on teaching preventive health practices (e.g., universal precautions, hand washing, and not touching blood). However, kids were asking more questions about HIV and AIDS because of the recent increase in media attention toward this subject matter. Accurate and concise age appropriate information is crucial if kids are to make healthy decisions that will prevent the spread of HIV and AIDS. Often times people cringe or feel uneasy at the notion of educating kids about HIV/AIDS. Some parents and teachers are uncertain on how to respond to the questions that kids ask. This seems to be related to public misconceptions about the disease and how it is contracted. Even today, after HIV/AIDS has been a part of the language and awareness of the public, people continue to associate this disease primarily with sexual transmission. For kids ages 9-12, much of the literature emphasized explaining disease concepts, how the virus can and cannot be transmitted, and ways to protect the body from exposure to the virus.

Surprised to find only a few text-based books available to educate kids about HIV/AIDS, the senior author saw this area in need of more diverse educational materials. The developer was a graduate research assistant on several software projects and decided to combine her software expertise and graduate course work into developing training materials for kids. She was particularly interested in using computer-based multimedia, because kids have a fascination and ease with technology and love to play computer games.

A literature search revealed that innovators in the field of education have always acknowledged the need for students to interact as much as possible with the subject matter that is being presented. Proponents of active learning often refer to the educational philosophy of John Dewey by asserting that children learn well when they are truly a part of living the experience (Schank, 1993). Piaget presented the idea that learning involves an evolutionary process that incorporates many sensory components reaching equilibrium (Papert, 1993). Quackenbush and Villareal (1988) support creating an open atmosphere for discussion in the classroom where children are allowed to freely ask questions so as not to overwhelm them with information. Thus, educational theory supported the ability of multimedia to impact behavioral change through the interactive study of HIV and AIDS. Additional studies that have addressed theories related to behavior and cognition as concerns in software development include Atkins (1992), Bates (1981), Brown, Collins and Duguid (1989), Dudley-Marling, Owston and Searle (1988), McKenzie (1990), Ransdell (1993), Reiser and Kegelmann (1994), Sewell and Rotheray (1987), and Sponder and Hilgenfeld (1994).

Most of the existing research on human-computer interaction and playfulness has been conducted on children. Webster, Trevino and Ryan (1993) identify a concept known as flow and clarify its relationship to behavioral change with learning. According to this research, the user must have control, attention focus, curiosity, and intrinsic interest for a positive outcome to occur. Such positive outcomes can not only impact learning but also carry over to changes in behavior. This notion is also closely aligned with the progressive educational theories of Schank (1993) who is a strong advocate for a "learn by doing" educational style. He asserts that children and adults are more likely to translate learning into decision making when the learner is able to equate the material to real world experiences and interact at the highest possible level for the task at hand. Multimedia technology provides opportunities for students to interact more than any other technological learning tool. Multimedia applications allow the student to be immersed in hands on, real world situations that require decision making and solution responses (Stansberry, 1993).

THE DEVELOPMENT PROCESS

This section describes the development effort using the typical phases of software development found in the literature.

Phase 1: Locating Political and Financial Sponsors

The first step in the development process was to identify people in key positions who could support and help with the software development. First, the senior author found a supporter in the director of The Project who agreed to allow her to work with children in the Kids Club. Her professor was supportive and accepted the development, documentation, and presentation of an educational software package as a course project. In preparation for his course on *Computer Use in Human Services,* she submitted a student scholars grant request for $1000 to AT&T under the Professor's sponsorship. The grant, which was funded, was to develop and test software that educated kids 9-12 about HIV and AIDS. The software was targeted toward the local public school system. Phase 1 ended when financial, content area, technical, and administrative support were obtained.

Phase 2: Creating the Development Team

Educational software is typically developed by a diverse team playing specific roles. This section describes the team members, their roles, and tasks.

Project management. Project management was carried out by the authors. The senior author primarily coordinated the work and developed the prototype. Her professor structured the project, provided guidance and creative input, and accessed university resources such as hardware, multimedia software, video cameras, video editing software, office space, and supplies. He also provided expertise on intellectual property and copyright issues. The university played a critical management role by providing legitimacy, continuity, sanction, human subjects review, and bookkeeping. A weekly time log was kept documenting time spent in the areas of research, planning and organizing, programming, testing, and travel. Weekly meetings served as a forum for brainstorming, resource acquisition, and prioritization of tasks necessary to reach the goals of the project.

Subject matter experts. Subject matter experts are of two types. One type concerns what to communicate. The other concerns how best to communicate. Both types of expertise can be available in one team or in two separate teams. The unique aspect of this project is that Kids Club members served as communication experts.

The developer, Project staff, and volunteers researched the basic content that kids needed to know about HIV and AIDS. They narrowed the subject matter to specific points and developed learning objectives around these points (see Appendix A for an example). They then developed an initial screen for each learning objective.

Expertise on how to communicate the content was provided by nine Kids Club members between the ages of 9-12. This group consisted of four Latina girls, two African American girls, two African American boys, and one Anglo girl. They performed tasks such as:

- Evaluating the capacities of the software, e.g., viewing commercial games such as "Myst"
- Helping determine the best presentation format
- Helping identify the microworld used to communicate the content
- Identifying age appropriate language
- Helping design the user interface
- Playing with colors
- Giving feedback on multimedia screens
- Finding age appropriate wording for comprehension
- Narrating the text
- Acting in the videos
- Making the software fun

Technical experts. Multimedia projects involve a variety of technical experts, such as computer programmers, scriptwriters, graphic designers, video production specialists, and actors. Since this project had a limited budget, technical expertise had to be provided by the authors. Having limited computer programming expertise required finding user-friendly tools that required minimal coding. "ToolBook," a graphical multimedia development software product, was selected as the development tool and "Arts and Letters" was used for graphic images. With "ToolBook," putting together a multimedia program was similar to assembling a children's book of linked pages constructed with multiple overlays. "ToolBook" also allowed video and sound to be added to any picture, icon, or spot on a page. Other technical tasks were gathering materials, designing graphics, recording kids' voices, and shooting, capturing, and editing video.

Phase 3: Developing the Prototype

Developers presented the theme and basic outline of content for 1.5 hours each week for six weeks to the seven Kids Club members. Between each session, the developers revised the material and incorporated suggestions made by kids the previous week. During the development, the management team met weekly to review progress and to process ideas and changes.

Discussing HIV and AIDS can often result in emotional displays and denial. The developers intentionally encouraged these emotions by listening to and incorporating kids' suggestions, even if they strayed from the initial draft of the storyboard. A creative discovery approach, which was based on consensus, was used each week to elicit opinion from the kids and provide an emotionally safe environment for them to share feelings about the subject of HIV and AIDS. A master's level therapist, working with the Kids Club, was present at each focus group meeting and provided emotional support when needed.

The first two weeks were met with limited enthusiasm by the kids. However, each week thereafter, the kids became more invested in the project as their ideas were brought to life on the screen and their voices were played back for them to hear. This process has a positive effect, because the kids' input was respected and included in the software. During the third week of development, the kids were given the opportunity to record a personal story or testimony related to HIV and AIDS. One child agreed to complete this therapeutic exercise with her counselor. The one recorded voice was played the following week for the kids to hear. Other kids wanted to have their voices recorded, but were not emotionally able to share a personal testimony. Following group discussion with the kids, a consensus was reached to record their voices anonymously narrating the storyboard content in Appendix A. The candid narration of the voices, complete with ethnic accentuation, personalizes the software and honors the bravery of the kids in speaking about a subject that painfully touches their lives.

As the kids saw their ideas being incorporated and listened to their own voices on the computer, they became increasingly invested in the module. This was perhaps the most concentrated and rich segment of the development process. The kids supplied creativity and spontaneity in areas where the developer was "bogged down" or limited in ideas. The kids served as consultants from week to week expanding the scope of the material, providing candor and real life expression to the module's content. Often times the kids encouraged the developer to be more open and direct with the content in areas that were initially approached with caution. Although scholarly resources were consulted on cognition, developmental psychology, and language theory, the kids themselves became the best consultation for age appropriateness of the subject matter and verbal constructs.

Thus, the development process was a concentrated activity that generated creative energy from the kids and the developers. The kids' role became that of muse to the developer who refined and organized their expressive responses to the content of the module. Scripts were written for the kids to read while their voices were recorded into audio files that were used to narrate the module. Other techniques involved offering printed software screens as coloring books for kids to write and sketch their ideas. Playing experiential games was also a useful way to tease out content in the group sessions with the kids. Discussions about using the completed software in public schools resulted in strong reactions from the kids. They wanted to share their experiences so that other children might understand more about HIV and AIDS.

Management met weekly during the development process. Following scheduled timelines was always a challenge for the developers. The creativity and ideas generated by the kids became a rich resource, and the process of incorporating their ideas became more important than adhering to the proposed timelines of the project. Sometimes the level of crisis and chaos happening in the kids' lives impacted the development process. At one point a child's mother died and this participant missed a session. This resulted in the other kids needing time to process their worries about their moms and concerns about their peer. It was clear that their lives were not on hold while the software was being developed. In these situations, the psychosocial needs of the kids took precedent over the timeline for the software development, although the development process became an integral part of their emotional and cognitive processing as well.

The issue of death and dying triggered emotional response in the kids when addressed in the software. For the kids, this was clearly emotionally charged content that presented itself throughout the development process. Group meetings with the kids became a time to air feelings and concerns about their own parents and families that at times generated discussions on sensitive family topics. Reviewing the educational content of the module (e.g., how to get and not get HIV) often triggered disclosure from kids about their own family members and opened the group for questions that might not have arisen from a different subject matter.

Maintaining top-level interest in the development of the module was not a major issue. At one point, the Project staff invited the developer to speak with the local newspaper that ran an article about the development of the software with the kids at the Project. The article brought notoriety to the Project in the community and excited the kids.

Phase 4: Testing of the Prototype

The beta version was presented to the graduate class, at a regional conference for statewide educators, and at a statewide conference related to technology and social work. Initial feedback from the consulting professor and the class was important in identifying issues related to the content and presentation. The class concluded that the kids had helped prepare an overall positive piece of work that needed further development.

Five Kids Club members helped present the module at a region conference to over 300 educators. For many of the kids, this served as a debut for sharing their personal struggle in being affected by HIV. The kids noted that the use of the computer helped them hear themselves providing information about the disease and thus making it "less scary." The module was well received by the audience and many teachers acknowledged that this would be useful in their classrooms. Teachers also acknowledged the political issues related to HIV/AIDS curriculum and the difficulty many school districts were facing at the time in acquiring curriculum that school boards were willing to approve.

The audience at the statewide technology conference was made up primarily of social workers and students. This audience also gave positive feedback on the presentation and supported the use of the module. Members of the audience were taken by the use of the kids in the development process and noted the power of the kids' voices in the presentation of the material. Comments were made regarding the positive aspect of having kids talk to other children about this subject matter.

Since the prototype was well received, the authors decided to seek funding for a formal evaluation of the module, development of a second module for kids ages 6-9, and dissemination of both modules. The Levi Strauss Foundation funded the proposal with a grant of $20,000. This funding supported the hiring of an additional research assistant (see acknowledgements) to help in the evaluation and development. The development of the second module followed the same process described above.

Phase 5: Distribution and Use

Both modules and a teacher's guide were pressed on CD ROM for distribution. Distribution proved to be a time consuming and long-term process. Initial presentations to teachers, principles, parents, and school boards demonstrated that they did not always agree about the subject matter. Rather than work to educate the potential audience or sway their political position regarding HIV/AIDS education, distribution was redirected to human service agencies, counselors, doctors and community HIV workers who had access to children in other settings. However, parental consent for using the module was still requested. Obtaining permission directly from parents was easier than swaying school boards and conservative educators who were often uncomfortable with the content. Although promotion and dissemination activities were refocused, use of the module was sporadic.

After the funding ended, a Web site promoting the software was developed. The Web site generated only a few inquiries. One developer of similar HIV/AIDS educational software expressed similar distribution problems. One Web request from Africa was for the module to be translated into French.

Distribution support was obtained from the Community Foundation of Southern Arizona, a grass roots non-profit organization whose mission is to promote wholistic community health education. With Foundation funds, twenty-five human service providers and community HIV/AIDS educators were identified and asked to preview the software in exchange for a free copy. Preliminary feedback results indicate an overall positive response with regard to the subject matter; however, unlike parents and teachers in Texas, this group of professionals indicated a need for more direct and explicit information about HIV/AIDS and human sexuality. It seems that regional and cultural differences in attitudes about HIV/AIDS is an important factor in distribution of the software. Distribution continues to be one of the most problematic aspects of the software.

DESCRIPTION OF THE SOFTWARE DEVELOPED

The development process resulted in two educational modules, one for 6-9 year olds and one for 9-12 year olds. The 9-12 year old module used a nautical theme to illustrate the concept of HIV as a "pirate" in a microworld format (see Figure 1). Microworld graphics include a lighthouse with a child playing on a coastal beach, tattered paper similar to a treasure map, a pirate, boats sailing on the ocean, seagulls soaring in the sky, and an animated shark attack warning against the dangers of HIV and AIDS. The module contains color graphics, sounds, kids' voices, limited animation, and video. It consists of 24 screens that are clustered into segments as follows.

1. The first segment is composed of five components including an introduction to the module, a statement of learning objectives, the definition of HIV and AIDS, an introduction to the immune system concept, and clarification of how HIV is related to AIDS.
2. The second segment illustrates the pirate, boat and guard metaphors. It also explains the unique nature of the HIV and AIDS disease concept.
3. The third segment states how you can and cannot get HIV and what you can do to keep yourself safe from HIV and AIDS.
4. The fourth segment stresses the importance of personal decision making and the impact of HIV and AIDS on families and communities.
5. The module closes with a personal testimony by a member of Kids Club.

Based on suggestions by the kids, the 6-9 year old module used a jungle theme (see Figure 2 for a typical screen). The final module contained 16 screens. Appendix A presents the goals, objectives, and storyboard of the 6-9 year old module.

FIGURE 1.

EVALUATION AND EVALUATION RESULTS

One part of the evaluation was designed to address some of the issues facing parents and teachers in examining and selecting HIV/AIDS curriculum. The 9-12 year old module was formally evaluated while the 6-9 year old module was being produced. The module and post test were completed by ten parents, eight teachers, two school nurses, a child protective services staff/parents group, and ten 9-12 year old female participants in a summer education program for girls (see Wilder, 1995 for the complete evaluation).

The reactions of parents and teachers to the software are summarized in Tables 1 and 2. Both parents and teachers were very positive about the module and its use. However, all suggested that a parent or knowledgeable adult should be present during use of the software.

A second part of the evaluation focused on kids learning and behavioral change as a result of using the software. This evaluation found that kids learned almost all the expected concepts and their behavior was likely to change in many of the desired ways. Pre- and post-mean scores were compared for the eleven concepts designed to measure kids' learn-

FIGURE 2

ing retention. A difference in pre-post scores at the $p < .05$ significance level or better was noted on two of the eleven concepts. These concepts were *definition of HIV* and *causal relationship of HIV to AIDS*. An increase in post-test scores without significance occurred for five of the eleven concepts. These concepts were *viral, invades the body, communicable germ, immunodeficiency,* and *definition of AIDS*. No change in pre and post-test scores was observed on two out of the eleven concepts, *difficulty of infection by HIV* and *fatality of AIDS*. A non significant decrease in post-test means was observed on two of the most complex of the eleven concepts, *syndrome* and *immunodeficiency*.

Pre and post mean scores were compared for the eleven concepts designed to measure behavioral change. A difference in pre-post scores at the $p < .05$ significance level or less was noted on four of the eleven concepts. These concepts were *unsafe sexual contact with body fluids, casual contact, hygiene* and *emotional concern*. An increase in post-test scores without significance occurred for five of the eleven concepts. These concepts were *prevention, wellness, importance of self, uniqueness of self,* and *wellness*. No change in pre- and post-test scores was ob-

TABLE 1. Reaction of Parents to the Module

1. Parents strongly agreed that:
   a) A multimedia program is a good tool for educating children on HIV and AIDS,
   b) They would allow their child or a child of similar age to view the program,
   c) They preferred their child to view the program with an instructor available to answer questions,
   d) They would give their child permission to use this program at school,
   e) They would support the use of this program in their local public school health or sexual education curriculum,
   f) The subject matter was presented in a non-sexist and non-racist manner,
   g) The subject matter is concrete and presented in a clear and logical format,
   h) The subject matter and its presentation is appropriate for children ages 9-12,
   i) The accents of the recorded voices and the vocabulary helps the program relate to different ethnic populations,
   j) The program is technically simple enough for children ages 9-12,
   k) The pirate, boat and guards metaphor was helpful in presenting the subject matter to children ages 9-12,
   l) Using children to talk to children is helpful in presenting the subject matter to children ages 9-12,
   m) Children ages 9-12 would enjoy using the program, and
   n) Children would perceive the presentation of the subject matter as non-judgmental.

2. Parents agreed that:
   a) Cultural sensitivity is a critical issue in the selection of HIV and AIDS educational software,
   b) The graphics help the program relate to different ethnic populations,
   c) The recorded voices were clear and easy to understand,
   d) The sound, graphics and animation were sequenced in a non-distracting manner,
   e) The instructions for using the program were clear and easy to follow,
   f) The viewing time was appropriate for children ages 9-12, and
   g) Children would perceive the tone of the voices in the program as caring.

3. Parents preferred that their child view this program with children his/her own age. They also preferred a child view the program with a parent or guardian available to answer questions. The parents were indifferent to their child viewing the program with children of the same gender.

served on one of the eleven concepts, *decisions that you make affect other people*. A non significant decrease in post-test means was observed on one of the eleven concepts, *being responsible for your body*. Given the small sample size, the significance levels were better than was expected. In addition, during the evaluation, kids viewed the software in the presence of the senior author or research assistant. An even stronger learning and behavioral change would be expected by kids who use the software as part of a group under the guidance of a trained teacher.

TABLE 2. Reaction of Teachers to the Program

1. Teachers strongly agreed that:
   a) A multimedia program is a good tool for educating children on HIV and AIDS,
   b) They would allow their child or a child of similar age to view the program,
   c) They would give their students permission to use this program at school,
   d) They would support the use of this program in their local public school health or sexual education curriculum,
   e) The program was visually appealing,
   f) The sound, graphics and animation were sequenced in a non-distracting manner,
   g) Cultural sensitivity is a critical issue in the selection of HIV and AIDS educational software,
   h) The subject matter was presented in a non-sexist and non-racist manner,
   i) The subject matter is concrete and presented in a clear and logical format,
   j) The subject matter and its presentation is appropriate for children ages 9-12,
   k) The program is technically simple enough for children ages 9-12,
   l) Using children to talk to children is helpful in presenting the subject matter to children ages 9-12,
   m) Children ages 9-12 would enjoy using the program, and
   n) Children would perceive the presentation of the subject matter as non-judgmental.

2. Teachers agreed that:
   a) The recorded voices were clear and easy to understand,
   b) The instructions for using the program were clear and easy to follow,
   c) More sound, graphics, animation, photographs and video clips would help the program,
   d) The accents of the recorded voices, the vocabulary and the graphics help the program relate to different ethnic populations,
   e) The pirate, boat, and guards metaphor is helpful in presenting the subject matter to children ages 9-12, and
   f) Children ages 9-12 would perceive the tone of the voices in the program as caring.

3. Teachers preferred that their students view this program with children their own age. They also preferred the student view the program with a parent or guardian or an instructor available to answer questions. All of teachers were indifferent to their students viewing the program with children of the same gender.

Results of the current evaluation in Arizona are presented in Table 3. Scores reflect a positive response to the use of the modules and that most tended to agree that the modules were age appropriate and culturally sensitive. Written response from the reviewers indicated a need for more direct and open information about HIV/AIDS and sexuality. The software purposely did not address these issues more directly in order to allow the material to be tailored to the needs of the viewing audience and for the presentation to be enhanced with information from a teacher or community educator who would be present when the software was used. Although opinions of parents, teachers, and professionals would be expected to vary based on geographical location, tailoring materials to meet the needs of every community is not realistic.

TABLE 3. Perception of Ten Community Educators on Cultural Sensitivity, Age Appropriateness, and Use of HIV/AIDS Educational Software in Public Schools.

M	SD	Question (where 1 = strongly agree and 5 = strongly disagree)
1.5	.50	The subject matter is presented in a non-sexist manner
1.6	.49	I would allow my own child or a child I know of the same age to view this program for ages 6-9
1.7	.78	The subject matter is presented in a non-racist manner
1.7	.64	I would allow my own child or a child I know of the same age to view this program for ages 9-12
1.9	.94	I prefer that my child/students view this program with an instructor available to answer questions
2.0	.77	The subject matter is appropriate for children aged 6-9
2.0	.45	I prefer that my child/students view this program by themselves with a parent or guardian available to answer questions
2.0	.77	I would give my child/students permission to receive HIV and AIDS information using this computer program
2.1	.94	A multimedia computer program is a good tool for educating children about HIV and AIDS
2.2	.98	The subject matter is appropriate for children aged 9-12
2.4	1.11	I would support the use of this computer program in my local public school health or sexual education curriculum
4.2	.60	I prefer that my child/students view this program by themselves without an adult present to answer questions

ISSUES, PROBLEMS, AND LESSONS LEARNED

Issues

The content of the software was specifically designed to be used as part of a health based curriculum. However, educating children on HIV and AIDS is a sensitive matter. Given the volatility of HIV/AIDS curriculum, it was difficult to obtain consensus on topics such as personal choice and decision making. For example, one emphasis of the 6-9 year old module was that "you are responsible for your body." However, Child Protective Service professionals and parents had problems with this concept as they taught abused children that they were not responsible for what happened to their bodies. A compromise in terminology was difficult to find.

Another issue concerned the volatility of HIV/AIDS information. For example, one reoccurring theme during the development was the question regarding HIV transmission through the act of kissing. Very little research existed at the time on transmission through kissing. Children wearing braces and having small cuts in their mouths that may bleed became a point of consideration, especially for the 9-12 year old module. The issue of death was a problematic theme with regards to the 6-9 year old module. Some educational and psychological consultants felt that the discussion of death and dying was too mature for a 6-9 year old audience. Research in this area revealed that presenting death indirectly in a metaphor or story was more age appropriate. Differing opinions arose among the developers as to what would be considered "too scary" for a child. The kids, who were most aware of a lifestyle involving daily risk and exposure to HIV, had a higher tolerance for direct information about death, substance use, and sexually transmitted diseases than had children and parents not exposed to HIV/AIDS.

According to a 1987 study by the National Broadcast Association, 91% of the American public support both school and community based HIV and AIDS education (Quackenbush, Nelson & Clark, 1988). However, parents and educators are often at odds on the usefulness of discussing this topic with children prior to adolescence. Often HIV/AIDS is perceived as a subject that is not related to latency age children. Recent state education mandates have been issued to public schools nationwide to provide HIV and AIDS education at every grade level. However, school boards and communities have different opinions about HIV/AIDS education. When the senior author talks about the software, audiences often present themselves as having a certain level of uncomfortability around the subject matter. People often ask questions that seem judgmental such as, "What would you tell a child about HIV/AIDS?" or "How old are you talking about?" or "You don't teach kids how to use condoms, do you?" This has been such an issue that whenever the senior author is in a situation to talk about the software, she starts out with a disclaimer by clearly stating that "this is a health based curriculum that talks to kids about not touching someone else's blood or picking needles up off the ground."

Another issue involved technological expectations. The kids who helped develop the software wanted more bells, whistles, and flash than the developers or the Project could provide. Some kids also had personal behavior problems that impacted technical considerations and the kids' ability to focus and pay attention. Kids wanted to have many things happening on the screen at once that would entertain and excite them. Because of this, it was difficult at times to engage the kids in development process. The more kids were directly a part of the process (e.g., recording their own voices into audio files onto the computer), the more successful the sessions were. Having two facilitators is strongly recommended in order to maintain the engagement with the kids, not only because of attentional deficits but also because of the content directly related to emotionally sensitive areas in their everyday lives.

Technological expectations of parents were also different. Suburban parents tended to think that the software was technically weak and content strong. Inner city parents considered the software content weak and technically acceptable. One guideline consistently found in the literature on this issue is that technology must follow content rather than content begin driven by technology. However, often developers become excited with the multimedia capabilities. This can result in using media for the sake of impression or effect without attention to purpose. The kids often became excited and wanted content to follow technology.

Problem

Staff changes at the Project created communication difficulties for the developers at times. Break down in communication with the Project staff was common during the charged six-week development phase with the kids. The development of the software was viewed as an auxiliary function for Kids Club, where the primary focus was to address HIV/AIDS education and provide peer support. Although the development of the software fit into the goals of the Kids Club, when other issues arose of more importance, the kids focus shifted to accommodate the needs of the group. This became a challenge for the developers, because the agenda of the multimedia project did not always fit the evolving agenda of the kids living daily with the stress of a chronically ill family member.

Another task that proved problematic concerned copyright. Kids and their parents were asked to review and sign a release form allowing use of the kids' names, voices, photographs, and video footage. Using a variety of media was important as some parents were willing to allow their kids' voices to be recorded but not their photographs or videos. Without the parents' consent, the kids were not allowed to participate even though in some cases the kids were eager to disclose personal material. Copyright and intellectual property issues are critical to address up-front as obtaining copyright permission after the fact could be time consuming and difficult.

Another problem involves obtaining enough resources, as educational software projects rarely seem to be completed. One difficult decision problem involves how much of total resources to allocate to development and how much to allocate for distribution and enhancements. An agreement had been made with the Project and Levi Strauss Foundation to not use the software to generate profit. In a sense, this agreement restricted the further enhancements, modification, and distribution of the software. Current technological advances suggest reprogramming and revisions that were expensive. The closer one comes to using cutting edge technology, the more complex the development and the more need for extensive technical support, especially if non-programmers are the developers. One solution to the distribution problem is to redesign the software to run over the Web. However, in this case, use would need to be restricted because the evaluation demonstrated that teachers and parents consistently preferred that a knowledgeable adult be present with kids who were using the software.

Lessons Learned

Clients know best how to communicate with their peers. The idea of using the creative potential of kids in software development was based on the assumption that the kids would have something important to offer. This project found that kids have much to offer. The kids' use of language was the biggest help for the developer. Many times the developer's words used were "too big" for the kids and they helped to revise the vocabulary with terms that made more sense for their age group. This was also helpful in further clarification of the abstract concepts that were presented in the software. The kids made many suggestions for colors and graphics that helped provide more of the excitement and entertainment they were looking for.

Graphics, sound, and video proved to be effective multimedia features. The recorded voices of the kids narrating the software results in a powerful presentation. However, a non-sound option is available for viewers who are unable to hear or prefer to only read the content.

Software development can be empowering and therapeutic for those involved. The development did not take place through a didactic psycho-educational process but rather through an experiential process in which the kids became involved. This was empowering and therapeutic because kids were able to exercise a certain amount of control over the content of the software when they were often powerless over the disease in their everyday lives. The opportunity to co-create, co-develop, and present the software helped them to work with the narrative constructs in their own lives. The staff therapist would report how the kids seemed to be opening up and dealing with their worries after development sessions. Kids seemed to enjoy and feel grounded more than in a standard support group process. This gave the kids something to do and experience that was helpful in working through the issues in their own lives. It was also a way to develop information about themselves and the disease that would be shared with other children. This sharing could be a shaming and embarrassing experience when done in person. The software allowed them to express themselves and deal with the disease in a way that maintained as much anonymity as they desired for themselves.

Enhancements and distribution of human service training software can be problematic. Distribution of software on controversial subjects is problematic. Not only are teachers often too busy to search out and review software, but also adoption involves taking the time to develop new teaching patterns. Another problem is that multimedia contains clearly spelled out curriculum that is open to scrutiny and criticism. The ability to keep curriculum vague may be beneficial to teachers when the subject is controversial.

If designing today, we would make the software run over the Internet, e.g., using streaming audio and video. Thus, the software would be readily available for teachers to examine and use. In addition, enhancements would be easier to make. The software is currently being distributed using multiple financial resources. An extended marketing plan was developed; however, it was not possible to obtain full funding for this distribution. Being able to break the project down into incremental parts that could generate multiple small funding resources was advantageous, because finding small amounts of money for dissemination to targeted audiences is easier than finding larger amounts for general distribution.

CONCLUSION

Computers, learning, and kids go hand in hand. Advances in multimedia have enhanced the ability of software developers and educators to challenge traditional approaches. Papert (1993) notes, "The most powerful use made of computers in changing the epistemological structure of children's learning to date has been the construction of microworlds." A multimedia microworld encourages learning and behavioral change because the world that users are drawn into requires that they develop particular skills. This project demonstrated that multimedia microworlds are effective tools for education about HIV and AIDS, especially if their prospective users are involved in their design.

The Kids HIV/AIDS Training software was co-developed by kids living in families affected by the virus. Disseminating the microworlds designed by the kids is similar to opening their community to others who might become affected or infected with HIV/AIDS. User designed microworlds promote a sense of trust that the developers are sincere and concerned about the users' needs. However, while effective software packages for kids can be developed in controversial areas, dissemination is a long-term process because it involves changing the work patterns, attitudes, and values of adults who control access to the software.

REFERENCES

Atkins, M.J. (1992). Theories of learning and multimedia applications: An overview. *Research Papers in Education*, *8* (2), 251-271.

Bates, T. (1981). Towards a better research framework for evaluating the effectiveness of educational media. *British Journal of Educational Technology*, *12* (3), 214-233.

Brown, J.S., Collins, A. & Duguid, P. (January-February, 1989). Situated cognition and the culture of learning. *Educational Researcher*, 111.

Dudley-Marling, C., Owston, R.G. & Searle, D. (1988). A field-testing approach to software evaluation. *Computers in the Schools*, *5* (1/2), 241-249.

MacKenzie, S. I. (1990). Courseware evaluation: Where's the intelligence? *Journal of Computer Assisted Learning*, *6*, 273-285.

Papert, S. (1993). The children's machine: Rethinking school in the age of the computer. New York: Basic Books.

Quackenbush, M. & Villarreal, S. (1988). *Does AIDS hurt? Educating young children about AIDS*. Santa Cruz, CA: Network Publications.

Quackenbush, M., Nelson, M. & Clark, K. (Eds.). (1988). *The AIDS Challenge: Prevention education for young people*. Santa Cruz, CA: Network.

Ransdell, S. (1993). Educational software evaluation research: Balancing internal, external, and ecological validity. *Behavior Research Methods, Instruments & Computers*, *25* (2), 228-232.

Reiser, R.A. & Kegelmann, H.W. (1994). Evaluating instructional software: A review and critique of current methods. *ETR&D*, *42* (3), 63-69.

Schank, R. (1993). Learning via multimedia computers. *Communications of the ACM*, *36* (5), 54-56.

Schoech, D. (1999). *Human services technology: Understanding, designing, and implementing computer and internet applications in the social services*. New York: The Haworth Press, Inc.

Sewell, D.F. & Rotheray, D.R. (1987). Our children can't do that!: The under-estimation of ability: Implications for software design. *European Journal of Special Needs Education*, *2* (2), 103-110.

Sponder, B. & Hilgenfeld, R. (November, 1994). Cognitive guidelines for teachers developing computer-assisted instruction. *The Computing Teacher*.

Stansberry, D. (1993). Taking the plunge: Is digital media the answer for our failing schools? *New Media, 3* (2), 30-36.

Webster, J., Trevino, L.K., & Ryan, L. (1993). The dimensionality and correlates of flow in human-computer interactions. *Computers in Human Behavior, 9*, 411-426.

Wilder, A. (1995). The use of technology in the education of children on HIV and AIDS: Evaluation of "Let's Talk About HIV and AIDS" Computer Program. Masters thesis, University of Texas at Arlington, Arlington, Texas.

APPENDIX A. Purpose, goals, objectives and storyboard for the 6-9 year old module

Purpose of the module

To use interactive multimedia technology to prevent HIV/AIDS in youth ages 6-9

Goals and objectives of the module

Goal 1: To increase children's (ages 6-9) awareness of health through instruction of wellness concepts

Learning objective #1: After experiencing the module, children will be aware that each person's body is special.

Learning objective #2: After experiencing the module, children will be aware of the need to show more compassion for those affected by HIV/AIDS.

Goal 2: To increase children's (ages 6-9) awareness and understanding of HIV/AIDS through instruction of disease concepts.

Learning objective #1: After experiencing the module, children will be aware of what a virus is.

Learning objective #2: After experiencing the module, children will be aware that HIV/AIDS is caused by a virus.

Learning objective #3: After experiencing the module, children will be aware that HIV/AIDS is a communicable disease.

Learning objective #4: After experiencing the module, children will be aware of how HIV/AIDS is different from other viruses (e.g., lives in blood and how transmitted).

Learning objective #5: After experiencing the module, children will be aware that HIV/AIDS is transmitted through blood.

Learning objective #6: After experiencing the module, children will be aware that HIV/AIDS is a life threatening illness.

Learning objective #7: After experiencing the module, children will be aware that HIV/AIDS can be prevented in children like other diseases.

Goal 3: To increase children's (ages 6-9) awareness and understanding of HIV/AIDS prevention through personal decision making.

Learning objective #1: After experiencing the module, children will be aware that each person is responsible for the decisions they make about their body.

Learning objective #2: After experiencing the module, children will be aware that decisions that they make about their body can affect other people.

Storyboard content outline

1. Opening page–HIV and AIDS-what kids want to know.
2. You are special!
3. What does it mean to be special? (1) You are unique (2) There is no one else like you in the world, and (3) You have your own appearance, abilities, and talents.
4. Part of being special means learning to be responsible and being responsible is hard work. Being responsible mean making good choices and doing what you say you can do.
5. You can make good choices to keep your body healthy: (1) You can eat good foods, (2) You can keep yourself clean, and (3) You can exercise, run, and play.
6. What is a virus? A virus is a germ that you get from someone else. It gets in your body and it makes you sick.
7. What is HIV? (1) A different kind of virus, (2) It's not like measles, chickenpox, cold or the flu, (3) HIV doesn't go away like other viruses, and (4) HIV is harder to get.
8. Right now, there is no cure for HIV, but doctors are working hard to find one.
9. HIV causes the deadly disease AIDS. If a person gets HIV, they can get very sick and die.
10. How can I keep from getting HIV? (1) Needles are not for touching–if you find a needle on the playground go tell an adult instead, (2) Using drugs is not good for your body, and (3) Playing with needles is dangerous.
11. What can I do if I find a needle on the ground? (1) If you find a needle on the ground, go tell a teacher or an adult, (2) Needles are not for touching.
12. What can I do if I'm with someone who gets hurt and starts to bleed? (1) It's okay to help someone, but don't touch his or her blood.
13. What can I do every day to stay healthy? (1) Cover your mouth when you cough or sneeze, (2) Wash your hands.

    Can I be a friend with someone who has HIV? A person who has HIV needs friends just like you. You can be nice and care about them even if they do have HIV.

An Online Stress Management Support Group for Social Workers

Andrea Meier

SUMMARY. This article describes the use of a listserv to make a contribution to that sector of the human service profession which struggles with burnout. The author develops, conducts and evaluates an online support group for social workers. *[Article copies available for a fee from The Haworth Document Delivery Service: 1-800-HAWORTH. E-mail address: <getinfo@haworthpressinc.com> Website: <http://www.HaworthPress.com> © 2002 by The Haworth Press, Inc. All rights reserved.]*

KEYWORDS. Support groups, online training, burnout, stress management

Andrea Meier, PhD, is Visiting Clinical Assistant Professor at the School of Social Work, University of North Carolina at Chapel Hill.

Address correspondence to: Dr. Andrea Meier, University of North Carolina at Chapel Hill, CB#3550, Chapel Hill, NC 27599-3550.

The author extends her thanks to all the social workers who were willing to risk participating in an untested intervention, and especially to the 19 people who completed the study.

[Haworth co-indexing entry note]: "An Online Stress Management Support Group for Social Workers." Meier, Andrea. Co-published simultaneously in *Journal of Technology in Human Services* (The Haworth Press, Inc.) Vol. 20, No. 1/2, 2002, pp. 107-132; and: *Human Services Technology: Innovations in Practice and Education* (ed: Hy Resnick, and Phoebe Sade Anderson) The Haworth Press, Inc., 2002, pp. 107-132. Single or multiple copies of this article are available for a fee from The Haworth Document Delivery Service [1-800-HAWORTH, 9:00 a.m. - 5:00 p.m. (EST). E-mail address: getinfo@haworthpressinc.com].

Technology is the practical application of knowledge (Miriam-Webster, 1984). We often think of technology as the application of scientific knowledge as in computers and the Internet. However, practitioners and researchers apply social science knowledge when they develop intervention technologies, such as support groups. For online support groups, scientific and social intervention technologies are merged. Whether social or scientific, all technologies must undergo many stages of systematic development and testing to insure that they work under real life conditions (Rothman & Thomas, 1994). The group described here is no exception. It has gone through only two stages of pilot testing, so the reader should not view it as a finished product (Meier, 1997b; Meier, 1999). Rather, it is a prototype in mid-development that has been used to find tentative answers to two general questions: How can the Internet best be used to deliver social support? Can online support groups help social workers cope with job stress?

BACKGROUND

Researchers have reported that up to three-quarters of all social workers suffer from moderate to severe psychological and physical strain from work-related stressors (Jayaratne, Chess, & Kunkel, 1986; Poulin & Walker, 1993). Although workers' levels of distress varies across professional specialties, work sites, position in the organizational hierarchy, and length of time in the profession, under persistently stressful conditions, workers often become physically exhausted, emotionally strained, and demoralized. Their professional effectiveness diminishes because chronic stress interferes with their ability to think flexibly and manage complexity. They become less creative in solving their clients' problems and in their responses to other difficulties on the job (Janis, 1993). As social workers become more preoccupied with their own distress, their judgement deteriorates. They are also more likely to make risky treatment decisions or engage in unethical behavior (Grosch & Olsen, 1994). If such conditions are left unchecked within organizations, overall worker productivity decreases, while staff absenteeism and turnover rates increase, further burdening those who remain in their jobs. Clients begin to suffer as organizational functions are disrupted and services deteriorate (Maslach, 1993).

The problem of job stress among professional caregivers first became personally compelling while I was working as an inpatient substance abuse counselor and supervisor in the mid-1980s. During that time, I watched many of my coworkers "burn out." Counselors who had begun their careers highly motivated and dedicated to alleviating their clients' distress became exhausted, alienated from their work, and cynical about the entire "caregiving enterprise" (Pines & Aronson, 1981). After a few years in the field, I was dismayed to find myself feeling the same way. I began to wonder whether this destructive process was unique to addictions counselors, or did others in the helping professions suffer the same kinds of distress? Spurred by these questions and my own distress, I began what has become a decade-long study of professional job stress and burnout (Meier, 1990).

While working as a counselor in private practice and as a consultant, I was able to observe the dynamics of job stress in a variety of human services settings. In 1993, I had the opportunity to pursue doctoral studies at the School of Social Work at the University of North Carolina. There, I was able to investigate these issues more systematically, focussing this time on social workers' experiences with job stress. In all these explorations, I sought to answer four questions: How do institutional policies and procedures create the contexts for workers' job strain? What characteristics of professional roles in the human services create the immediate conditions for job stress? Do the personality characteristics and aspirations of human services professionals predispose them to be vulnerable to work-related stressors? And, finally, what can be done to prevent or alleviate the destructive effects of work-related stress in the human services professions? The online group described in this chapter represents one attempt to answer that last question.

DEVELOPING AN ONLINE GROUP INTERVENTION

I began my dissertation project in 1997 by extensively reviewing the social science literature. To understand the factors contributing to social workers' work-related stress, I examined theory and research in organizational behavior (Hall, 1991), role theory (Hardy & Hardy, 1988), the sociology of the professions (Abbot, 1992), occupational stress (Farber, 1983; French, 1982), and personality and emotional development theories (Fischer, 1983; Hallsten, 1993). To gain insight into social workers' response to technological innovation, I surveyed the literature on diffusion of Innovation Theory (Rogers, 1983), and the changing roles of computers and the Internet in society (Dunlop & Kling, 1991; Pitkow & Recker, 1994). Figure 1 summarizes these factors.

FIGURE 1. Sources of Social Workers' Stress

Environmental Conditions	Stressors
Macro-level changes in social policy (e.g., welfare reform, managed care)	• Cynicism about the value of social services • Increased demand for accountability • Changing funding priorities • Reduced funding • Reductions in publicly-funded services • Increasing proportions of hard-to-serve clients on caseloads
Social workers' professional role definitions	• Role overload • Role conflicts • Ethical dilemmas • Tedium of routines • Frustrated professional aspirations • Work/family role conflicts
Technological innovations in computer and Internet technologies	• Inadequate computer resources and technical support in human services agencies • Inept implementation of computer systems • Inadequate training and practice time • Administrators' unrealistic expectations for the ways computers will improve productivity • Reductions in office support staff
Social workers' reluctance to adopt technologies	• Low status of social workers in the hierarchy of professions • Low salaries restrict personal risk taking and investments in equipment and training • Restricted access to computers and the Internet at work • Competition with other family members for access to home computers and the Internet

Based on this research, I concluded that the causes of the stress that social workers experienced were nested and interactive. Thus, in the context of role overload and role conflict, organizational dysfunction, and rapid institutional and technological change, social workers' personality characteristics and developmental histories could predispose some social workers to become disabled by stress. Therefore, the intervention needed to address stressors at each system level, promote insights into interplay between these factors, and suggest effective ways to cope.

The design of the group discussion format drew upon the research on coping theory (Folkman, Chesney, McKusick, Ironson, & Johnson, 1991), social support (Ganster, Fusilier, & Mayes, 1986; Gottlieb, 1981), and interventions for occupational stress across system levels (Figley, 1995; Firth & Shapiro, 1986; Gibelman & Whiting, 1997). The literature review showed that much more research had been done to describe the sources of professional job stress and their destructive effects than in developing interventions to remedy the problems (Meier, 1997a).[1] Because job stressors are many and complex, researchers have recommended interventions to address problems at various system levels. While interventions at any single level may be helpful under certain conditions, each has significant limitations. Macro-level changes are beyond an individual worker's control and take a long time to implement. Individual therapies and self-management strategies do not address social workers' frustration and professional alienation caused by structural contradictions in social workers' agencies and professional roles. After considering all the alternatives, I concluded that an online support group had the most potential to crosscut micro-, meso- and macro-level systems. Figure 2 summarizes the types of interventions suggested for each system level and the ways that support groups could function as a cross-cutting intervention.

Social support groups can revitalize and enhance members' capacities to adapt to current challenges and cope more effectively with future stressful life events. They can also mobilize to help members advocate for structural changes at their workplaces or for the profession as a whole (Toseland & Rivas, 1995). A support group intervention seemed like an attractive option since social workers' jobs are inherently stressful and most social workers are familiar with the benefits of that kind of intervention. However, social workers usually lead these groups, rather than participate in them. Little research has been done on the use of stress management support groups for social workers, and anecdotal reports suggest that few social workers choose to participate in them voluntarily (Meier, 1995; Meier, 1999). Although social workers will acknowledge that support groups might be beneficial to help them with job stress, they also report that they have neither the time nor energy, nor the desire to go to more meetings outside of work.

To understand how an online support group might work, I also reviewed the research on the evolution of online groups, and particularly online support groups. In the 1970s, Internet developers discovered that they could use the technology to communicate rapidly with groups of people and expedite the development of the entire system (Sterling,

FIGURE 2. Interventions for Social Workers' Job Stress

System Level	Recommended Intervention Strategies	Support Groups as Cross-cutting Interventions
Micro	• Psycho-dynamic psychotherapy to deal with unresolved developmental issues • Cognitive therapy and stress innoculation training • Wholistic self-care strategies • Interpersonal skill development (i.e., assertiveness and self-advocacy strategies)	*Social Support* • Share information • Validate emotions • Reduce feelings of isolation • Reaffirm the value of altruism and the significance of the "helping enterprise" • Encourage persistence in problem solving and stress management activities *Improve Coping* • Supportive challenges of maladaptive appraisals of stressors • Opportunities to practice interpersonal and problem-solving skills • Promote social reengagement with families, coworkers, and clients
Meso	Change organizational structures and processes to reduce role stress	Mobilize workers to improve organizational climate
Macro	*Political advocacy* • Improve social workers' salaries and provide liability protections • Reduce policy conflicts • Increase funding for services	Mobilize social workers and other stakeholders for profession political action to promote professional status and efficacy

1993). Since then, thousands of online groups–including hundreds of support groups–have been formed to offer information, advice and support on an astonishing array of interests and concerns (Harris, 1999; Hensley & Hensley, 1999). Most public online groups are open-ended in duration, allow open membership, and have no official group leaders.

For many social, structural, and economic reasons, however, social workers have been relatively slow in acquiring computer and Internet skills, or adapting these technologies to their professional practice (see Figure 1). These findings made me wonder if there was any way to use the technology "jujitsu-style" to help social workers cope with chronic job stress and enable them to become more comfortable with their computers and the Internet. The research on diffusion of innovation suggested that social workers were likely to be more receptive to the new technology if they knew they could benefit from it personally and professionally (Rogers, 1983). Workers whose lives were already overscheduled might appreciate being able to obtain support without being obliged to leave home to go to another meeting. Such a group would be highly accessible; members could correspond with each other at any time of the day or night, seven days a week. Since members could not see each other, they would not have to worry about appearing presentable. Members could correspond with each other no matter how they were dressed or groomed.

Selecting the group format. There are now many kinds of online groups. In some, members interact using e-mail (text-based communication). In others, members connect with each other through the World Wide Web's graphical interface. Among the e-mail-based groups, there are listserv groups in which members communicate asynchronously. This means they do not all have to be online at the same time to participate in the discussion. There are also "chat groups" in which members are all online at a pre-specified time, and member interactions occur in real time. When the group was designed, however, chat groups were still very new and members had to have specialized software to access the group. In Web-based groups, members' messages are automatically "threaded" so it is easier to follow discussion themes. However, web graphics take longer to download and members of such groups must have fast modems to make the service convenient to use.

Given the factors that have impeded social workers' adoption of new technologies, I decided to be conservative in my assumptions about the Internet technology that members would have available to them. For this reason, I chose to implement the group using listserv technology. In listserv groups, members interact via e-mail–the simplest and most commonly used Internet technology (Graphic Visualization and Usability Center, 1998). Members transmit their messages to a pre-specified address at an Internet service provider's computer (the "listserver") which then automatically distributes those messages to other members of the group. The University of North Carolina's listserver served as the host for the group, using ListSoft's "mailing list" software (L-Soft International, 1999).

E-mail communication is asynchronous. This means that message senders and message receivers do not all have to be online simultaneously to communicate. This characteristic of e-mail offered a number of advantages. When a group member sends a message to the listserver, it appears in other members' onscreen e-mail "inboxes" where the recipients can read and respond to it at their convenience. In face-to-face groups, members are limited in how much time they can talk. When interactions are asynchronous, such time constraints are eliminated. One member's long message does not prevent other members from writing long messages of their own. Because writing is a slower way to communicate than talking, asynchronous communication also appeared to offer members more control over the rate of their interactions. This feature might be attractive to social workers who feel overwhelmed by the number of emotionally charged interactions they have daily with clients and coworkers. Finally, confiding through writing can promote healing self-reflection (Pennebaker, 1990). Group members could benefit from taking time to reflect on their personal and professional values, and reconnect with the reasons why they first chose to become social workers. In this way, an online support group would resemble an intensive journalling group in which members confide their experiences by writing to an audience of sympathetic peers (Pennebaker, 1990; Progoff, 1975).

Research questions. The purpose of the research was to test the feasibility of this kind of intervention for social workers. Since this kind of intervention was new and untested, there were many unanswered questions. Could the Internet could be used to recruit social workers for the group? Would social workers be willing to participate in such a group? How would such a group work? Would social workers find it a satisfying experience? Would it help to reduce their stress levels?

The first pilot study, conducted in the summer of 1997, was a technical feasibility study using a 6-week group composed of six MSW students (Meier, 1997b). The findings from the 1997 study guided the design modifications for the second study, which was completed in the fall of 1998. The latter, a comprehensive feasibility study, is described in detail below. The second study investigated a group that lasted 10 weeks. It was composed of members who were all practicing, masters-level social workers. This group began with 23 members, 19 of whom completed the study.

Data collection. The research design incorporated both quantitative and qualitative methods. To collect the quantitative data, three paper-and-pencil questionnaires were sent to group members using surface mail. A comprehensive survey, developed for this study, was used to obtain background information on each member. This survey contained 79 multiple-choice and Likert-type items about members' sociodemographic characteristics, education and professional training, type of practice and working conditions, relationships and personal caregiving, and computer and Internet experience. Immediately before the group started, members also completed the standardized, 140-item Occupational Stress Inventory

(OSI) to assess their occupational role stress, psychological strain, and coping resourcefulness levels (Osipow & Spokane, 1987). The OSI is composed of 140 Likert-type items that have been compiled into three questionnaires (containing six, four, and four 10-item scales respectively) to measure those three dimensions. After the group ended, members completed another round of the OSI as well as a comprehensive, paper-and-pencil satisfaction survey (75 items). This survey assessed such factors as members' overall satisfaction with: the group as a whole; the amount of discussion on various topics; group structure; the group's informativeness and supportiveness, the Group Leader's role, and their comfort with e-mail communication.

The qualitative data included all the texts of the e-mail that group members posted to the listserv, as well as all their private communications with the Group Leader and with me in my role as technical assistant. The Group Leader and I were in frequent communication to insure that the group was following the research protocol. These exchanges were documented in field notes and e-mail messages. Qualitative data were also collected as part of the satisfaction survey. This data were used to assess what members liked and disliked most about the group, the helpfulness of the group leader, their strategies for tracking the discussions, and their recommendations for ways to improve the group. Members completed these open-ended questions via e-mail to make it easy for them to write as much as they wanted about their experience with the group.

Recruitment strategy. The intervention was designed for MSW-level social workers who were working full time and who could access the Internet from their homes. Participants for the study were recruited via the Internet. I posted announcements about the project to listservs sponsored by NASW and its state chapters, and to listservs that addressed topics of interest to practicing social workers. To insure that people who volunteered for the study met the selection criteria, the first announcement also included six screening questions that volunteers had to answer via e-mail reply to be considered for the study.

Social workers who responded to the announcements, and whose answers to the screening questions satisfied study criteria, were sent a second e-mail message. The second message contained more information about how the group would work as well as the text of the informed consent statement. A paper copy of the consent statement was mailed to each prospective volunteer. The consent statement reviewed the purpose of the study and the participant selection criteria. It specified the expectations for study participants in terms of the number and kinds of surveys they would be asked to complete, the structure and processes of the group, and the group leader's professional qualifications. Prospective participants were told in advance how frequently they would be expected to post messages to the group in order to be considered an active member. They were also informed about the possible risks to confidentiality in their Internet-mediated communication with other group members, and the ways that technology, group norms, and document security procedures would be used to minimize such risks. Finally, participants were assured that they could withdraw from the group whenever they wished and were given the instructions for doing so. Those who returned the signed statement were enrolled in the study as members of the group.

DESCRIPTION OF THE TECHNOLOGY

Goals. The aim of this technology was to provide members with social support to help alleviate their job stress. First, it was designed to provide members with emotional support and validation for their feelings about their work and profession (Schopler & Galinsky, 1993). Second, it aimed to provide members with information about job stressors and alternative ways of coping (Cherniss, 1980). The third goal was to enhance members' coping efficacy by helping them learn to use coping strategies that were most appropriate to different situations (Folkman et al., 1991; Meichenbaum & Cameron, 1983). The fourth goal was to restore members' commitment to the profession by providing them with opportunities to reflect on the reasons they became social workers and affirm their altruistic values (Pines, 1993b).

WHAT IS THE EXPERIENCE OF THE PARTICIPANTS?

Number of participants. We know too little about online groups to say what sizes work best for different formats and purposes. The first pilot study found that groups that are too small are likely not to have enough activity to keep members engaged (Meier, 1997b). On the other hand, large groups can produce a heavy volume of messages that overwhelms members' capacity to read and respond (Meier, 1999). At the end of the recruitment period, 26 people who met study selection criteria were assigned to the intervention group. Of these, all but three completed their pre-group questionnaires and were considered group members. They asked to be dropped from the study before the group started due to schedule conflicts.

E-mail communication created uncertainty about how many people considered themselves to be group members. Members could follow the discussion and not write back regularly. Since the number of participants was small, a liberal definition of membership was used to insure the group's viability. While participants were asked to submit at least one message per week, they were considered part of the study unless they officially asked to be dropped or if they failed to complete the final questionnaires. The group began with 23 members. Of the four others who later officially withdrew, three said that they did not find the discussion topics relevant. The fourth person stopped sending messages by the seventh week and never completed the post-group questionnaires. Six more became inactive as time went on. In two cases, the members reported they had lost interest in the discussion topics. The four others complained that they were too busy to keep up with the discussion or reported that they were too ill and exhausted to correspond with the group. While decreasing participation levels were a concern, they proved to be advantageous for those who remained. In the satisfaction survey, group members reported that they were most satisfied when the number of active members dropped down to around 12.

LISTSERV GROUP PROCESS

Little was known about group process in online groups, so another goal of the research was to explore what members experienced in an online group using a specific intervention protocol. The group format was deliberately designed to resemble a face-to-face stress management support group to enable comparisons between online and face-to-face modalities. As such, it differed from the typical listserv group because it lasted only 10 weeks, had closed membership, and had a professional leader. As time went on, the group diverged somewhat from its original protocol to adapt to members' needs. Details of the intervention protocol will be described here as well as what actually happened when it was implemented.

Orientation. A few days before the start of the group, each member received a detailed e-mail message that reviewed the purpose of the group and described how it would function. In this posting, members were asked to write at least one message to the group each week. If they were going to be traveling or had other obligations that would prevent them from accessing the group, members were asked to notify the group or the Group Leader. They were also informed that the Group Leader would be tracking their participation. She would contact privately any member who had not posted a message within the last week to find out if that person was having personal or technical problems and, where possible, offer support and assistance. Members could withdraw from the study at any time they wished by contacting the Group Leader or the Principal Investigator. Members were also told that they would have the option of continuing as a leaderless group after ten weeks if there were enough members to make a viable group.

Discussion themes. The loosely structured discussion protocol was designed to promote discussions about members' problems with job stress and their coping strategies. While there were focal topics for each week, group members could raise other concerns at any time or revisit topics discussed in previous weeks. During Week 1, members were asked to write messages introducing themselves. They were asked to describe their work settings, previous experiences with support groups, their goals for the group and any concerns they had about how it would function. During the second week, members were asked to describe briefly the four most stressful aspects of their work. The types of stressors members mentioned most frequently were: institutional and policy changes, organizational, and professional role stressors. After further discussion, members agreed to discuss these issues over the next three weeks. In the protocol, Week 5 was designated as an "open topic" session to allow members to revisit issues raised in the previous weeks and to decide which topics to discuss during the latter half of the group.

When participation levels dropped during Week 4, the Group Leader asked members to do a "midterm assessment." She asked for their opinions on whether the group was meeting their needs and if they wanted to change the agenda to make the experience more satisfying. According to the discussion protocol, the discussion had been scheduled to shift from the sources of members' job stress to ways of coping with conflicts between work and personal and family responsibilities. As a result of their midterm assessment, members decided to change the agenda. Most group members decided that they wanted to discuss personal and family problems since they had few other venues in which they felt comfortable doing it. For the next three weeks, members discussed their health, marital and parenting problems, and their struggles to maintain the psychological boundaries between their personal and professional roles. During the final two weeks, the discussion focussed on termination issues. Members described what they liked or disliked about the group, discussed their feelings about the group's ending, and decided whether they wanted to continue as a leaderless group.

The group as a supportive milieu. Support groups work best if members give and receive social support (Schopler & Galinsky, 1993). The protocol was designed to provide members with a private and supportive milieu in which they could recount events that made their jobs stressful and vent painful feelings. In the group, members' perceptions about the sources of their distress were often validated, helping to relieve their feelings of helplessness, loneliness, isolation, and despair (Toseland & Rivas, 1995). Members were encouraged to describe their struggles with the physical and emotional effects of stress but also to give each other recognition for how well they were coping. When members reported that they had discovered new resources that helped them to be more resilient in the face of stress, they were asked to share that information, too.

Social support also can take the form of supportive challenges. In the group, members were encouraged to question respectfully each others' appraisals of the amount of control they had in stressful situations (Folkman et al., 1991). Such inquires were intended to help members use appropriate coping strategies, enabling them to manage or master situations where they had control.

Members could ask for and receive help in problem solving, and get advice about how they could be more assertive or resolve interpersonal conflicts with bosses, co-workers and family members. For example, the group provided encouragement and feedback when a few members decided to try to improve their situations by changing jobs. When others described situations that were clearly beyond their control, the group offered empathy and suggestions to help them to come to terms with their difficult situations.

When subjected to chronic work-related stress, human services professionals often become alienated from the values that originally motivated them to enter their professions (Hallsten, 1993; Pines, 1993a). In their discussions, members were encouraged to recall why they chose to become social workers and the values they tried to express through their work. Group members helped each other reexamine the guilt and shame they felt from perceived professional failures. They discussed how to reframe problems constructively and reminded each other to be realistic about the time and effort needed for significant changes to occur. When some members concluded that their jobs had become intolerable, group members shared information about job opportunities and their experiences with other career paths.

INTERNET-MEDIATED COMMUNICATION AND GROUP PROCESS

Another major goal of this research was to explore how Internet-mediated communication affected group process. Members could comment at any time about how Internet-mediated communication affected their experience with the group. In listserv groups, there is always a high degree of uncertainty about group membership. Since members cannot see each other, members only know who else is part of the group from the messages they receive. Members will be unable to participate fully in an online group if their computer and Internet skills are weak or if they have problems with their computer equipment or access to the Internet. Consequently, for the group to be viable, the technology must be reliable. Internet Service Provider system crashes and disruptions in the telecommunications system may further delay message transmission. In the study, each of these problems occurred to one or more members. It is a testimony to their commitment to the group that even those members who suffered the most technical problems persisted and were able to use the group to get technical assistance.

PARTICIPATION LEVELS

In every group, some members are more active than others (Hare, 1976). Over the ten weeks, members posted a total of 394 messages, but six members sent half of all the messages. While the majority of them *averaged* one message a week, few members complied with the one message per week minimum. However, relying strictly on message counts to assess participation may lead to inaccurate conclusions. As the group went on, many members adopted a timesaving strategy of addressing comments to several different members within the shell of a single message. In these cases, a single message served the function of several messages posted at the same time.

Many factors affected whether or not members posted messages. Many members reported that they appreciated the convenience of being able to participate in the group from home, but sometimes even this level of convenience was insufficient. When members were exhausted with work or ill, their participation levels dropped. Several members lost their access to e-mail when they traveled to conferences or took vacations during the weeks that the group was in session. In the protocol, these variations were anticipated. Members were asked to inform the group when they knew they were going to be unable to access their e-mail for more than a few days. The members who did the most travelling were conscientious about doing this. When they returned, they always read their accumulated messages from the group and sent in their comments, thus reconfirming their commitment to the group.

Discussion content and group dynamics can also affect participation levels. Members' interactions were usually cordial and supportive. Some members wrote in frequently in the first five weeks when discussions addressed job stress. When the group's focus shifted more to members' family and health concerns, however, these members wrote in much less frequently. During Week 4, members openly disagreed with each other about the most appropriate strategy for responding to managed care, and the number of messages dropped off markedly for several days.

Overall, message volume can also affect participation levels in several ways. For online groups to be viable, there must be a continuous flow of messages. However, there are limits. When too many messages are posted in too short a time, members who want to respond to each message may not have enough time to do so. Some may decide to stop writing completely because they feel uncomfortable being forced to decide who most deserves a reply. At the other extreme, members may disengage if there are too few messages. They find spending the time needed to go online to check for messages that never come unrewarding. However, a drop in message volume is not necessarily bad: Some shyer members may find it easier to enter the discussion.

Lurking. In online groups, members who read their e-mail from the group but do not post messages in return are known as "lurkers." They play a role analogous to members in face-to-face groups who rarely say anything but who nonetheless consider themselves members. In the group, members whose participation levels dropped off over the course of the study reported afterward that they continued to read their e-mail regularly and that they appreciated being able to follow other members' stories about their lives. This was especially true for the four members who were quite ill when the group began or had health crises during the group.

The Group Leader sent e-mail messages privately to any member who did not post a message for more than a week to acknowledge their absence and to offer support if anything was wrong. Lurkers were offered opportunities to withdraw from the study if participation had become burdensome. The four members who were the most persistent lurkers also suffered from severe health problems. When offered the opportunity to withdraw from the study, all of them refused. They commented that they appreciated being able to stay connected with their professional peers in the midst of their crises.

What are they meant to be feeling? Members in this kind of online group are meant to feel supported in many different ways. As they share their experiences with job stress and the ways that they cope, members are meant to experience validation and diminished isolation. As they discuss ways to resolve their problems and receive advice from others, members are meant to feel encouraged to make changes. When they report back to the group about the changes they have begun to make and receive recognition for their efforts, they are meant to feel empowered and an enhanced sense of self-efficacy. When situations prove inalterable, members are meant to feel more at peace in tolerating such conditions, knowing that they have done the best they can for the time being.

ROLE OF THE FACILITATOR

Since most online groups do not have formal leaders, another purpose of the study was to explore whether and how a group leader could be helpful in this kind of support group. The Group Leader was a licensed clinical social worker and certified Employee Assistance Counselor. She was also an experienced group leader and Internet user. According to the intervention protocol, the Group Leader was supposed to play an active role for the entire ten weeks of the group. Since the group was short-term, she played an important role in establishing group norms and setting the agenda. Once the listserv was established, she was responsible for posting the initial welcoming message to the group. In this message, she reminded members of the group's norms for confidentiality and mutual respect. She also asked them describe themselves and the type of work they did and invited them to share any concerns they had about how the group would work.

The Group Leader was responsible for helping members see themselves as a group. The group did not have a specified meeting time and members wrote their first messages when it was convenient for them. Consequently, group members were uncertain who was in the group until everyone had posted their first messages. The Group Leader acknowledged the uncertainty, kept track of who had checked in by the end of the first week, and contacted those who had not to remind them that the group had started. At the end of Week 1, the Group Leader summarized members' similarities and differences. She also reviewed ideas on how to make the group a safe "place" for self-disclosure.

While the group was designed to address job stress issues, members decided what aspects of job stress they wanted to discuss. Because asynchronous communication slows decision-making in online groups, the Group Leader helped members to set the agenda in the early weeks (Walther, 1996). At the end of Week 1, she asked members to write about the four most stressful aspects of their work. At the end of Week 2, she performed a content analysis of members' messages, ranked the stressors they described by their frequencies, and then reported the results back to the group.

In the protocol, the Group Leader was responsible for helping to keep the discussion coherent. In listserv groups, multiple discussion themes often develop. Some members found it difficult to keep track of the topical "threads" as they emerged and re-submerged over time. To help members track the various topics under discussion, the Group Leader was supposed to summarize each week's discussion themes, pose follow-up questions, and remind members of the discussion topic for the following week. As it turned out, however, the Group Leader only followed the protocol for the first four weeks.

The Group Leader was authorized to help the group members change the way the group worked so it was most satisfying for them. In this case, members asked the group leader to change the way she interacted with them. In the midterm assessment, members commented that they disliked the follow-up questions because it made them self-conscious and made the group leader seem too different from the group members. In the weeks remaining, the Group Leader stopped posing questions and began to share more of her own experiences as a fellow social worker. When she did raise questions, she also described how they arose out of her own personal and professional experience. In their satisfaction surveys, members reported that they liked having a group leader, but they were more satisfied when she adopted a less active, more egalitarian, facilitation style.

SETTING FOR WHICH THE TECHNOLOGY IS DESIGNED

One advantage of online groups is that they are liberated from the constraints of a specific meeting place. Members can interact with each other via e-mail whether they live in the same building or in different states. Since members only participated in the group when they were sitting in front of their home computers, one could say that this intervention technology was designed for as many different households as there were group members.

There were three reasons for requiring that group members have access to the Internet from home. Given the time constraints of the study and the decision to recruit members nationally, it would be impossible to do any training in Internet skills. Members who had personally invested in home computers and Internet services were more likely to have the basic competencies they needed to participate in such a group. Members were asked to correspond with the group only from home even if they had Internet access at work. This reduced the likelihood of conflicts of interests and protected members' privacy. Finally, members who were corresponding with the group from home would be more comfortable and relaxed, and better able to reflect on their values and the relationship of their work to the rest of their lives.

Populations served. The existence of the group demonstrates that the recruitment strategy did hit its target. It was possible to recruit masters-level social workers for an online support group via the Internet. Sociodemographically, the resulting group was similar to the population of NASW members with masters' degrees (Gibelman & Schervish, 1997). Like their NASW peers, the group was made up mostly of women (84%), almost all of whom were European American (84%). The median age of the group members was 47 years.

In general, group members were seasoned professionals. The median length of time since receiving their degrees was 11.5 years. They represented a range of social work specialties, and they worked in a variety of settings including hospitals (21%) and medical clinics (21%), social services agencies (21%) and private practice (16%). Over three-quarters (76%) of the members worked in privately funded agencies. On average, the group members were better paid than the typical NASW member with similar credentials; nearly three-quarters of them (74%) earned salaries of more than $30,000.

This research aimed to test whether an online support group could help relieve stress caused by computer and Internet technology. However, the members of this group were probably not the best subjects for testing that effect because most of them were already quite technologically sophisticated. Members were asked to rate their own computer and Internet skills in the background information survey and almost all reported that they had excellent skills in both areas. The four members with the most expertise also ran their own online groups.

Needs/problems addressed. The analyses of members' e-mail messages and post-group satisfaction survey data suggest that this kind of online support group can be used to provide three kinds of social support: empathy and validation, encouragement to persist in solving problems, and advice. Here, members benefited in two ways: from the advice they received from other members in response to specific questions and from reading the advice given to others which was applicable to their own situations. Further, when members described how they overcame difficult situations in the past, they nurtured other members' hopes that they too could overcome the challenges they faced. These narratives appeared to serve as cognitive models for effective coping. The discussions about professional roles helped members to clarify their personal and professional values.

The group appears to be less appropriate as a channel for communicating information about resources to improve coping. It also did not work well as a setting in which members could challenge each other's coping strategies. Members used their messages to vent about problems more often than they did to discuss what to do about them. After one instance where two members were in open conflict, others wrote how they did not join the group to participate in arguments. Not surprisingly, the group was ineffective as a way to provide material support for members who were ill or facing financial problems. When members reported that they were struggling with such problems, others in the group were forced to acknowledge the limitations of virtual support. Communicating via e-mail made them feel close emotionally, but their actual geographic separation made it impossible to respond with material comforts, such as casseroles, as they would have for other friends, who lived close by, when they were facing difficulties.

PREDICTED RESISTANCE AND/OR SUPPORT IN TARGET SETTING

Resistance to an online social workers' support group can arise at two levels. Individual social workers may be reluctant to take advantage of this kind of social support. More generally, when human services organizations consider whether to offer online support groups as a new service, staff may raise a variety of legitimate concerns.

Individual level. Social workers who could benefit from this kind of intervention may feel uncomfortable disclosing their vulnerability to their peers. Some may be reluctant to discuss personal issues when they are unable to see their fellow group members. Others may feel unable to articulate their thoughts and feelings adequately in writing. Some may be intimidated by the technology required to participate in the group because they lack the "keyboarding" (i.e., typing), computer, or e-mail management skills needed. Some may worry that they will be distracted by their families' demands if they tried to correspond with the group from home.

Organizational level. Initiating an online group within an agency may spark objections due to all the uncertainty that still surrounds this new, largely untested intervention modality. There has not yet been sufficient research to guide programming decisions about how to integrate online groups into the conventional human services mix. We do not know which clients should be referred to online groups, how to judge the value of the information and support provided by existing groups, or how to choose among possible online group formats to achieve specific therapeutic objectives. If the agency must invest in new computers, Internet services and increased technological support to make the group possible, staff may be concerned about the diversion of resources from other services. To participate in an online support group, consumers must be literate and able to "keyboard," have ready access to the necessary computer equipment and Internet services, and the skills to use them. These conditions may lead staff to object that the agency is investing in services for a privileged group.

Ethical considerations. Social workers may question whether they are competent to lead online groups (Marson et al., 1998). Here again, there are no established protocols for leading online support groups nor programs offering systematic training for leaders. To date, there have been few studies comparing online and face-to-face groups, so we do not know much about how they are similar or different in their developmental processes (Meier, 1999; Phillips, 1996). Thus, even experienced face-to-face group leaders may encounter situations where their practice wisdom is inapplicable. Supervisors who are inexperienced with Internet-mediated communication and the dynamics of online groups may feel awkward advising staff members who lead such groups.

Agencies must also be concerned about how to protect participants' confidentiality and privacy. Due to the large number of online groups, violations of confidentiality by computer hackers are relatively unlikely. However, violations can occur in other ways. For example, non-members may have access to members' computers and their e-mail accounts, or can read information from the screen as they pass by. Alternatively, members may print out message texts and be careless about leaving the printed pages where others can read them. Employers have the right to monitor e-mail posted on or received by their office intranets; group members who send or receive the group's messages at their work places can put their own privacy and confidentiality at risk as well as that of all other members who post messages. Consequently, members must be able to access the Internet from places other than their work sites if they are going to participate in this kind of support group. To reduce the likelihood that members will access the group at work, they must be made aware of these risks in the recruitment stage through informed consents, and again in early stages of the group. Agencies and workers must also be concerned about legal liability when they offer online groups. If agency contacts with online group members occur mostly through e-mail, agency staff may have little information to draw on if a group member goes into crisis and begins to write about suicidal or homicidal thoughts. Further, if group members do not live in the community as the agency hosting the group, it would be much harder to get emergency help to members if they need it.

Testing of software. The major purpose of this study was to test the feasibility of the intervention. It was possible to recruit members and retain most of them for the entire 10 weeks. This outcome demonstrates that the group was technically feasible and that a 10-week, professionally facilitated group composed of social workers could be viable. Member satisfaction was another dimension of intervention feasibility. In their satisfaction surveys, group members reported a high degree of satisfaction with the range of topics discussed. Most were also satisfied with different kinds of social support they received from the group, particularly the opportunities for emotional ventilation. Perhaps the best indicator of member satisfaction is that 13 members of the 19 members who completed the study decided to continue as a leaderless group for an additional ten weeks. Several of those who continued were still in contact with each other nearly two years later.

Group members differed in their opinions about how well various discussion topics had been covered. Members were least satisfied with the amount of discussion on computerization in the human services. They also wished that more attention had been given to identifying resources for stress management, and in problem reframing and problem-solving (Meier, 1999). Most members felt that the group had been too big at the beginning. They reported that the resulting message overload had made it difficult for them to get to know each other and keep track of who had written what. Having a professional facilitator appears to have contributed to member satisfaction. Although members challenged the group leader's assigned role, they appreciated her help in getting the group started, resolving conflicts, and her willingness to facilitate changes in the group's agenda and format.

In general, the low statistical power associated with the study's small sample size made it unlikely that changes would have been detected even if they had occurred. No statistically significant positive changes were found on any of the fourteen OSI subscales. Unexpectedly, the general trend was toward increased stress and diminished coping, although only two subscales showed significant increases. In the Occupational Role Questionnaire, the group as a whole showed significantly increased scores on the Responsibility subscale, which is associated with high degrees of responsibility on the job ($p > .10$).[2] In the Personal Strain Questionnaire, the group as a whole also showed significantly increased scores on the subscale measuring psychological strain ($p > .05$). While these significant increases in stress and strain levels are of concern, they are difficult to interpret. Possibly, such changes reflect the increased stress experienced by several members who changed jobs during the group, or who were struggling to cope with severe health problems–conditions the intervention was not direct or intense enough to overcome.

Accessibility. Listserv groups utilize software that is available through most Internet service providers. Models for running the group, such as the text for the FAQ and detailed lists of the topics discussed, are available by e-mail from the author and can be found on the author's website (*http://ssw.unc.edu/people/biosketch/ameier.html*).

Costs. This online social intervention technology is not a commercially available product. However, practitioners and agencies who are considering the use of online groups need to be realistic about the costs they may incur. The major costs for this kind of online group are: the group leader's fees, his or her computer, modem and Internet fees, and technical support for the Group Leader and members. Although agencies do have to provide the computer, modem, ISP connections and technical support for the Group Leader, they do not have to provide meeting space and the associated facility services. In this group, members bore the costs for their own computers and Internet access fees.

Personnel time represents the most significant costs for the intervention. Although the Internet can expedite message transmission, tracking members' participation, reading their messages, and composing weekly summaries can be very time consuming. In the group, the Group Leader *averaged* 6.5 hours per week, but the amount of time she spent varied from more than 16 hours in the first week to slightly more than two hours in the last week. Investments in supervision and technical assistance were also considerable for this group. Supervision typically took around three hours per week. On average, I also spent about two hours a week communicating with group members about technical problems. In the early weeks, members needed reassurance and advice to cope with system crashes, ISP hassles, and difficulties managing heavy e-mail volume, but requests for this kind of assistance diminished over time.

CONCLUSIONS

The findings from the study suggest that online support groups can be helpful to social workers in coping with psychosocial stressors. However, it remains unclear whether it is an effective means for helping less technologically inclined social workers cope with stress caused by office automation and "Internet-ization."

The online group intervention described here is only one of many possible ways that Internet technology can be used in direct practice. The group described here used relatively primitive, listserv technology. New, web-based discussion forum technology can make it easier for members to track discussion themes and be linked to information sources that address issues raised in their discussions (Hensley & Hensley, 1999). The enthusiastic acceptance of the Internet has opened many possibilities for providing support. To stay socially relevant, social workers must become Internet activists. They must take the lead in exploring how to use the Internet to enhance clinical practice and expand the range of services they can offer to consumers, while weaving stronger networks of support for themselves.

NOTES

1. With a few exceptions, most of these researchers mentioned here had published their work before the full scale entry of personal computers and the Internet into the workplace, so the specific contribution of these technologies to professional work stress were rarely addressed.

2. Significance levels of .10 were used in this study to counteract the low statistical power of the small sample.

REFERENCES

Abbot, A. (1992). Professional work. In Y. Hasenfeld (Ed.), *Human services as complex organizations* (pp. 145-162). Newbury Park, CA: Sage Publications.

Cherniss, C. (1980). *Staff burnout: Job stress in the human services.* Beverly Hills, CA: Sage Publications.

Dunlop, C., & Kling, C. (Eds.). (1991). *Computerization and Controversy: Value Conflicts and Social Choices.* New York City: Academic Press.

Farber, B. A. (Ed.). (1983). *Stress and burnout in the human service professions.* Elmsford, NY: Pergamon.

Figley, C. R. (Ed.). (1995). *Compassion fatigue: Coping with secondary traumatic stress disorder in those who treat the traumatized.* New York: Brunner/Mazel.

Firth, J., & Shapiro, D. A. (1986). An evaluation of psychotherapy for job-related distress. *Journal of Occupational Psychology, 59*, 111-119.

Fischer, H. J. (1983). A psychoanalytic view of burnout. In B. A. Farber (Ed.), *Stress and burnout in the human service professions* (pp. 40-45). New York: Pergamon Press.

Folkman, S., Chesney, M., McKusick, L., Ironson, G., & Johnson, D. S. (1991). Translating coping theory into an intervention. In J. Eckenrode (Ed.), *The social context of coping* (pp. 239-268). New York: Plenum Press.

French, J. R. P., Jr. (1982). *The mechanisms of job stress and strain.* Chichester, UK: John Wiley & Sons.

Ganster, D.C., Fusilier, M. R., & Mayes, B. T. (1986). Role of social support in the experience of stress at work. *Journal of Applied Psychology, 71*(1), 102-110.

Gibelman, M., & Schervish, P. H. (1997). *Who we are: A second look.* Washington, DC: NASW Press.

Gibelman, M., & Whiting, L. (1997). *Social work salaries and what to do about them: A report to the National Association of Social Workers on research gathering and analysis.* Washington, DC: NASW.

Gottlieb, B. H. (1981). Preventive Interventions Involving Social Networks and Social Support. In B. H. Gottlieb (Ed.), *Social Networks and Social Support* (pp. 201-232). Beverly Hills, CA: Sage Publications.

Graphic Visualization and Usability Center. (1998). GVU's 9th WWW User Survey (Vol. 1998): Georgia Institute of Technology [Online].

Grosch, W. N., & Olsen, D. C. (1994). *When helping starts to hurt: A new look at burnout among psychotherapists.* New York City: W.W. Norton & Co.

Hall, R. H. (1991). *Organizations: Structures, processes, and outcomes.* (5th ed.). Englewood Cliffs, NJ: Prentice Hall.

Hallsten, L. (1993). Burning out: A framework. In W. B. Schaufeli, C. Maslach, & T. Marek (Eds.), *Professional burnout: Recent developments in theory and research* (pp. 95-112). Washington, DC: Taylor & Frances.

Hardy, M. E., & Hardy, W. L. (1988). *Role theory: Perspectives for health professionals.* Norwalk, CN: Appleton & Lange.

Hare, A. P. (1976). *Handbook of small group research.* New York: Free Press.

Harris, S. (1999). Emotional support on the Internet. v1.23 (Vol. 1999).

Hensley, A., & Hensley, A. (1999). Support-Group.com: Retrieved April 28, 1999 from the World Wide Web: http://www.Support-Group.com.

Janis, I. L. (1993). Decisionmaking under stress. In L. Goldberger & S. Breznitz (Eds.), *Handbook of stress: Theoretical and clinical aspects* (2nd ed., pp. 56-74). New York: The Free Press.

Jayaratne, S., Chess, W. A., & Kunkel, D. A. (1986). Burnout: Its impact on child welfare workers and their spouses. *Social Work, 31*(1), 448-453.

L-Soft International. (1999). CataListm the official catalog of LISTSERV lists (Vol. 1998): [Online].

Marson, S. M., Vandivort-Warren, R., Boal, L., Edwards, J., Finn, J., Grant, G. B., Grobman, L. M., Meier, A., Reamer, F. G., Schoech, D., & Vernon, R. (1998). Technology and Social Work. A policy statement accepted by the National Association of Social Workers.

Maslach, C. (1993). Burnout: A multidimensional perspective. In W. B. Schaufeli, C. Maslach, & T. Marek (Eds.), *Professional burnout: Recent developments in theory and research* (pp. 19-32). Washington, DC: Taylor & Frances.

Meichenbaum, D., & Cameron, R. (1983). Stress inoculation training: Toward a general paradigm for training coping skills. In D. Meichenbaum & M. E. Jaremko (Eds.), *Stress reduction and prevention* (pp. 115-153). New York: Plenum Press.

Meier, A. (1990). Coping skills for in-patient counselors. *The Counselor, 8*(4), 14-17.

Meier, A. (1997a). Interventions to alleviate burnout in professional caregivers. Unpublished manuscript: University of North Carolina at Chapel Hill, School of Social Work.

Meier, A. (1997b). Inventing new models of social support groups: A feasibility study of an online stress management support group for social workers. *Social Work with Groups, 20*(4), 35-53.

Meier, A. (1999). *A multi-method evaluation of a computer-mediated, stress management support group for social workers: Feasibility, process, and effectiveness.* Unpublished Dissertation, University of North Carolina, Chapel Hill.

Miriam-Webster, Inc. (1984). *Webster's Ninth New Collegiate Dictionary.* Springfield, MA: Miriam-Webster, Inc., Publishers.

Osipow, S. H., & Spokane, A. R. (1987). *Occupational Stress Inventory manual: Research edition.* Odessa, FL: Psychological Assessment Resources, Inc.

Pennebaker, J. W. (1990). *Opening up: The healing power of expressing emotions.* New York: The Guilford Press.

Phillips, W. (1996). A comparison of online, e-mail and in-person self-help groups using Adult Children of Alcoholics as a model (Vol. 1999): Rider University Psychology Department.

Pines, A., & Aronson, E. (1981). *Burnout: From tedium to personal growth.* New York: Free Press.

Pines, A. M. (1993a). Burnout. In L. Goldberger & S. Breznitz (Eds.), *Handbook of stress: Theoretical and clinical aspects* (pp. 386-402). New York: The Free Press.

Pines, A. M. (1993b). Burnout: An existential perspective. In W. B. Schaufeli, C. Maslach, & T. Marek (Eds.), *Professional burnout: Recent developments in theory and research* (pp. 33-51). Washington, DC: Taylor & Frances.

Pitkow, J. E., & Recker, M. M. (1994). Results from the First World-Wide Web User Survey (Vol. 1998): Graphics, Visualization, & Usability Center, Georgia Institute of Technology.

Poulin, J., & Walker, C. (1993). Social worker burnout: A longitudinal study. *Social Work Research & Abstracts*, *29*(4), 5-11.

Progoff, I. (1975). *At a journal workshop: The basic text and guide for using the Intensive Journal process.* New York: Dialogue House Library.

Rogers, E. M. (1983). *Diffusion of innovations.* Glencoe, CA: Free Press.

Rothman, J., & Thomas, E. J. (1994). *Intervention research: Design and development for human service.* New York: The Haworth Press, Inc.

Schopler, J. H., & Galinsky, M. J. (1993). Support groups as open systems: A model for practice and research. *Health and Social Work*, *18*(3), 195-207.

Sterling, B. (1993). Short history of the Internet (Vol. 1999): Internet Society.

Toseland, R. W., & Rivas, R. F. (1995). *An introduction to group work practice.* (2nd ed.). Boston: Allyn and Bacon.

Walther, J. B. (1996). Computer-mediated communication: Impersonal, interpersonal and hyper-personal interaction. *Communication Research*, *23*, 3-43.

Risk Management in Online Human Services Practice

Jerry Finn
Mary Banach

SUMMARY. The growing use of the Internet for human service practice has resulted in ethical and legal issues that have yet to be fully addressed by current professional codes of ethics and the courts. This paper describes issues and risk-management procedures related to online human service practice, including: use of novel and untested services, unclear jurisdiction, equivalence of face-to-face and online practice, duty to warn and to provide emergency services, privacy and security of online transactions, establishment of fiduciary relationships, online assessment, and fees for online services. In addition, risk-management issues related to human service agency Web sites including copyright, ownership of the Web site, posting of staff names, online fundraising, online threats and disruption of services, unsolicited e-mail, and agency e-mail policies are discussed. *[Article copies available for a fee from The Haworth Document Delivery Service: 1-800-HAWORTH. E-mail address: <getinfo@haworthpressinc.com> Website: <http://www.HaworthPress.com> © 2002 by The Haworth Press, Inc. All rights reserved.]*

KEYWORDS. Human service liability, online services, technology, Internet

---

Jerry Finn, PhD, and Mary Banach, DSW, are affiliated with the University of New Hampshire.

[Haworth co-indexing entry note]: "Risk Management in Online Human Services Practice." Finn, Jerry, and Mary Banach. Co-published simultaneously in *Journal of Technology in Human Services* (The Haworth Press, Inc.) Vol. 20, No. 1/2, 2002, pp. 133-153; and: *Human Services Technology: Innovations in Practice and Education* (ed: Hy Resnick, and Phoebe Sade Anderson) The Haworth Press, Inc., 2002, pp. 133-153. Single or multiple copies of this article are available for a fee from The Haworth Document Delivery Service [1-800-HAWORTH, 9:00 a.m. - 5:00 p.m. (EST). E-mail address: getinfo@haworthpressinc.com].

INTRODUCTION

Use of the Internet is growing at an exponential rate, and there is every indication that growth will continue as commerce and education on the Internet become commonplace (Cref, 1997). The Internet is increasingly used as an arena where people turn for interpersonal communication, consumer goods, professional services, and a myriad of information needs, including those related to human services. The primary purposes of agency Web sites thus far have been to promote agency visibility through providing information about agency mission, goals, and services, and to educate the community about related social problems. A small number of human service agencies as well as private practitioners, however, are beginning to turn to the Internet to provide direct services such as brief therapy, counseling, online assessment, social support, and consultation (Finn, 1999; Miller & Gergen, 1998; Graham, 1996). In addition, nonprofit agencies are beginning to successfully use the Internet for fundraising and volunteer recruitment (Allen, Stein, & Warwick; Green, 1998; Hawthorne, 1997; Clark, 1995). The Internet offers a number of advantages to human service practitioners as a vehicle for communication and service delivery (Giffords, 1998; Hannon, 1996; Sampson, Kolodinsky, & Greeno, 1997; Winzelberg, 1997).

- The Internet removes access barriers due to time and distance.
- It is available on a twenty-four hour basis from any computer with Internet access, and thus provides a stable source of support in an increasingly mobile society.
- It is available to those who might not otherwise seek information due to time constraints, care-giving responsibilities, lack of transportation, physical or social isolation, and physical or psychological disabilities.
- With the proper software, the Internet provides a means to anonymously seek information (see for example: *Anonymizer, http://anonymizer.com/guide.shtml* and *Iproxy, http://www.iproxy.com/*).
- It can offer culturally relevant information and services when they may not be available in the local community.
- The information on the Internet can be readily updated so that it can remain current and relevant.

The Internet also presents challenges in service delivery (Childress, 1998; Lee, 1998; Pergament, 1998; Lebow, 1998; Huang & Alessi, 1996). These include:

- lack of empirical research about effective models of online service delivery,
- unclear legal and liability standards surrounding online services,
- threats to privacy, security and confidentiality of online communications,
- potential harassment of Internet users whether these be agencies or consumers,
- presentation of wrong or misleading information by Web sites,
- initial and up-keep costs of Web sites to agencies,
- lack of access by many clients,
- lack of coordination among Web-providing agencies, and,
- technical difficulties inherent in electronic communication.

Given the rapid growth of Internet use, it is not surprising that human service practice on the Internet has developed well ahead of policies, procedures, legal regulation, and evaluation research to guide online practice. This paper presents a review of the issues faced by human service agencies and private practitioners in providing online services and suggests risk-management procedures designed to both protect consumers and agencies from ethical and legal violations that might result in agency liability. These are presented as guidelines only since many issues have yet to be heard and decided by the courts. Given the uncertain and changing nature of online practice issues, legal counsel should be consulted whenever liability issues arise.

DIRECT SERVICES ONLINE

There is limited but growing evidence that online exchanges can provide information, support, and therapeutic interactions for those experiencing a variety of human service problems (Braithwaite, Waldron & Finn, 1999; Karger & Levine, 1998; Gustafson et al., 1998; Graham, 1996). A number of methods have been developed for providing online counseling and support. The most common method is e-mail services in which asynchronous e-mail messages are exchanged between a human service practitioner and a consumer. In addition, providers have offered "chat" (Stofle, 1999) in which a practitioner and consumer exchange messages in real time over the Internet. This may also include use of two-way video as an adjunct to typed messages or videoconferencing services (Holden et al., 1999). Online groups in both asynchronous and chat formats have also been offered on the Internet. Finally, a variety of support and self-help groups are available over the Internet to provide an adjunct to professional services (Ferguson, 1996; Finn & Lavitt, 1994).

Protection for consumers of human services is provided through state licensing laws and professional codes of ethics. Human service professionals are bound by ethical and legal codes whether their practice takes place traditionally or online (Reamer, 1998; Bloom, 1997). Violation of these codes can result in criminal or, more commonly, civil prosecution (Besharov, 1985; Reamer, 1994). Consumers are becoming increasingly litigious, with more than a ten-fold increase in civil suits from 1980 to 1990. The most frequent claims of malpractice against individual social workers from 1969 to 1990 were for breach of confidence/privacy, failure to correctly diagnose a problem, incorrect treatment, and sexual impropriety (Reamer,1994). Those providing online services also face these issues as well as others uniquely related to online transactions.

The Internet has developed faster than the laws that regulate it (Hafner, 1989). In most cases, legal and liability issues are only beginning to be addressed. For example, it is clear that someone may be held sued for libel or defamation over the Internet (Pincus, 1999; Reno v. ACLU, 1997; The Harvard Law Review Association, 1999; Zeran v. America Online, Inc., 1997). In addition, it is illegal to threaten another person or to distribute child pornography over the Internet. Liability issues surrounding agency and private practitioner human services on the Internet, however, are far less clear. For example:

- What if an agency puts information on their Web site (e.g., how to deal with teen suicide) and a parent uses it, and yet the teen later commits suicide, to what extent is the agency liable?
- What if an HIV/AIDS agency receives an unsolicited e-mail message in which someone threatens suicide, must the agency respond?
- What if a client sends an e-mail cry for help and the practitioner doesn't respond in time, is the practitioner liable?

Issues of ethics and liability for human services delivered over the Internet are only beginning to be resolved (Ladd, 1997; Laudon, 1995). The answer in all of the above scenarios is, "It depends." It depends on the actual or implied promises made, the claims and disclaimers associated with the information or service, and, in some cases, on the opinion of a jury. A jury in these cases would utilize standards established by professional organizations (Besharov, 1985). Risk-management refers to practices that should be instituted and others that should be avoided in order to reduce risk of legal liability for violation of legal and ethical codes. This paper outlines possible risks in online practice and suggests risk-management practices based on the guidelines suggested by the American Psychological Association (APA, 1998), the National Association of Social Workers (NASW, 1996), the National Board of Certified Counselors (NBCC, 1987), and the research literature.

Who is the client? Since the client does not physically come to an office for online practice, the practitioner has a more difficult time determining that the client is, in fact, the person who is put forward online. It is common practice in many online forums and groups to assume a "virtual identity." One can never be sure of the age, race, sex, and other demographic characteristics that one presents in their online persona. This is especially problematic since the person seeking services may be underage. It is not difficult to imagine a troubled teenager using a parent's credit card to seek online service under a false identity. There are those who might only participate in mental health services anonymously. However, the dangers in not knowing who is being treated outweigh the potential benefits of anonymous treatment.

> *Practitioners should take steps to verify their client's identity, including gathering address, telephone, work address, a picture, and social security number, and should call clients to verify their identity as much as possible. In cases where a parent or guardian is needed to give consent to online services, the identity of the consenting person should be verified.*

Jurisdiction: Laws differ by state as to who may practice mental health services and at what age someone may seek services without a parent's permission. The practice of health care is also regulated at the state level (Cushman & Detmer, 1997). In some states licensure is required for those offering mental health services. Online human service practice in cyberspace is a complex and yet unresolved issue (Johnson & Post, 1996). Do laws apply to the resident state of the practitioner or the client? Some argue that the laws should apply to the practitioner's state since the client "virtually travels" to their "office," much as a client might drive across state lines to seek in-person services. Some states have begun to grapple with these issues. The state of California, for example, has legislated that anyone providing online counseling services to a California resident must be licensed in California (Stofle, 1999). In order to resolve these issues, the federal government has proposed national licensing standards that would be acceptable across states, but this is only in the preliminary stages.

> *Practitioners should seek legal counsel before providing online services to those in other states.*

Untested methods: Human service professionals are ethically bound to use methods that have theoretical justification, empirical evaluation, and a history of successful practice. While new methods and techniques are continually being developed, professionals must *warn* consumers when unproven methods are being tried and receive consumers' consent to engage in unproven treatments. The efficacy of online practice has yet to be demonstrated. There is still debate as to whether "therapy" can be done online given lack of visual cues, asynchronous communication, transference issues, and differences between computer mediated and face-to-face communications (Holmes, 1997; Bloom, 1998).

> *On their Web site, practitioners should clearly explain the differences between in-person and online services and acknowledge that online services are untested and unproven methods.*

Establishment of treatment relationship: Practitioners are responsible for providing a number of services to clients once a treatment (fiduciary) relationship has been established. For example, practitioners must be available for on-going services and emergency care. A consumer may regard answer to an e-mail as evidence that a relationship has been established. The courts have established that a telephone call advising a prospective patient as to a course of treatment can constitute a fiduciary relationship (Grondahl v. Bullock, 1982; Miller v. Sullivan, 1995; Pergament, 1998). The same may be true of e-mail. A practitioner or agency posting "e-mail for help" may see one e-mail message that provides brief information or advice as the *end* of the relationship, but a client may view it as the beginning. This issue has not yet been clearly resolved by the courts.

> *Practitioners should assume that any answer to a consumer's e-mail may constitute a fiduciary relationship, and should clearly state in their e-mail and Web site that no such relationship is implied if that is the case.*

Appropriate assessment: Professionals must provide appropriate diagnosis and assessment before beginning therapeutic intervention. E-mail tends to be a medium of short messages and quick answers, and there may be a temptation to provide services without proper assessment. Assessment is somewhat limited when clients' physical demeanor, dress, speech patterns, and reactions to questions cannot be directly observed. For example, a practitioner may not be able to observe obvious signs of depression such as lack of care in physical appearance, tearfulness, flat affect, and slumped posture. Online assessment must involve careful and thorough exploration of a client's social history and presenting problem(s). In addition, practitioners must be careful to assess the physical health of their clients since many mental health concerns have an organic basis (Kutchins & Kirk, 1987). They must use valid diagnostic assessment tools. These can be administered though e-mail or online forms at a Web site. This in itself, however, is problematic since the validity of assessment instruments has not been established when they are used online.

> *Online practitioners must use and document their online assessment procedures. In addition, they should inform consumers about the need to get comprehensive medical evaluations to rule out underlying physical problems and to seek additional assessment if warranted.*

Credentials: Practitioners must inform consumers of their credentials and areas of expertise. In addition, they must protect consumers from inappropriate or inadequate services. This creates several difficulties in online practice. First, it is very difficult to verify the authenticity of information on a Web site. Anyone can set up a Web site and offer "counseling." For example, one site, Dr. Schuchocolate (*http://adviceguy.hypermart.net,* May, 1999), was found by searching the Altavista search engine (*http://www.altavista.com*) for the words "online counseling." The site offered "moral advice and therapy." The authors examined the site and found that it offered racist, sexist, and homophobic "advice." In general, there is no systematic means of quality control of the information on the Internet (The Harvard Law Review Association, 1999). Given a lack of community standards on the Internet, it is difficult to identify "false advertising." While this site is not typical of those found in a search of "online counseling," it points to the difficulties consumers face in knowing which online services are offered by trained professionals. Even if a therapist is licensed, a consumer may not know the state in which the practitioner resides, making it harder to report violations (Pergament, 1998). It is also possible for a Web site to send a user to a different page than was initially sought. For example, someone seeking a "mental health" Web site could be immediately sent to a pornographic site upon accessing the "mental health" site (Banks, 1998).

What is needed is a professionally endorsed referral service for human service professionals in which licensed practitioners can be located. This should be easily available to professionals needing to make a referral and to consumers seeking help. One step in this direction has been the development of the "Credentials Check" (*http://www.cmhc.com/check*) Web site. For a small fee, a practitioner can be listed on the Web site. Their credentials, including degree and professional license number, are reviewed and posted on the site. The practitioner is then given a link on their own Web site to the Credentials Check Web site so consumers can verify their legitimacy.

> *Practitioners should post their credentials and areas of expertise on their Web site. They should also provide links to certification bodies and licensure boards to promote consumer protection. In addition, human service professional organizations must work to provide an online mechanism for reviewing and verifying the training and expertise of their members that are involved in online practice.*

Professional skills: Helping professionals are expected to have expertise in their area of practice. Some have argued that there are no "expert" online practitioners because no one has been practicing online long enough to be an expert (Pergamant, 1998), nor has there been enough evaluation of online services to know the extent to which people are being helped by this method of treatment. In addition, a competent in-person practitioner may not be a competent online practitioner since the skills required are not necessarily equivalent (NBCC, 1997). For example, the ability to "tune in" to nonverbal cues and to convey empathy through gesture, facial expression, and eye contact during in-person treatment will not be available online (Holmes, 1999; Stofle, 1999). Rather, an online therapist must be able to accurately convey feelings and thoughts in writing, and be especially careful to check out possible misunderstandings due to the written and asynchronous nature of the communication. Misunderstandings in online communication may be enhanced since online clients may be from different regions or even other countries, increasing the chances of cultural misunderstanding through differences in the meaning of words. In addition, an online practitioner must be aware of any personal bias held against those who may have poor writing skills.

> *Online practitioners should state their areas of expertise as well as the limitations of their services on their Web site. Since misunderstandings are possible, practitioners should follow up serious or ambiguous messages with a phone call when necessary.*

Client records: Human service professionals are both ethically and legally bound to maintain the confidentiality of client records (Gellman & Frawley, 1996). Confidentiality is essential to the establishment of a trusting, therapeutic relationship (Dickson, 1998).

Client records must be kept safe and shared only with the client's consent. Online practice creates new ways in which confidentiality might be breached. E-mail is not a secure medium (Speilberg, 1998). A practitioner's messages can be intercepted in transit by computer hackers. They can also be printed, inadvertently rerouted, and read by others if left on a computer screen in a non-secure environment. Messages can also be read by anyone with access to the client's computer (e.g., a spouse or parent). Finally, it is easy to accidentally send e-mail messages to the wrong party.

Another difference related to client records in online practice is that the entire transcript of sessions is recorded and is stored verbatim. In face to face practice, practitioners generally maintain notes of sessions, but the entire transcript of the session is not written. Should a client or practitioner be involved in a malpractice action, either the client or practitioner could use verbatim transcriptions as evidence. In addition, control is lost over the content of the session. A client may forward a practitioner's verbatim message, for example, to an ex-spouse, as a means to "prove" the marriage couldn't work. Having a concrete and permanent record of the practitioner's statements may cause more anger and resentment in an ex-spouse than if the client simply told the ex-spouse what the practitioner said. Similarly, if a practitioner forwarded a client's message to a colleague for consultation, there is no control over where the colleague might forward the message or how securely it will be handled.

The privacy of online records is also threatened when clients use their work computers to send and receive online health and human service information. Employee challenges to employer access to their e-mail have generally not been successful. The courts have ruled that an employer can read all e-mail residing on computers using the company network as long as workers are informed that company policy permits it (Pergament, 1998).

> *Online practitioners should institute measures to protect the confidentiality and security of online messages. E-mail should be treated as formally as other client documentation. Practitioners should take steps to prevent unauthorized access to their electronic records through using password protection of their computer and maintaining storage of back-up files in a secure place. In addition, encryption software programs should be used to prevent messages from being read by anyone but the intended receiver. Clients should be informed if and for how long their messages are being preserved as part of their file, and practitioners should obtain signed informed consent before any materials are forwarded to another party. There should be appropriate electronic and/or hard copy back-up of all e-mail messages. Online practitioners should also provide materials that educate their clients about security risks of online communication and legal issues related to the use of e-mail at the workplace. Finally, human service agencies and private practitioners should establish written polices that establish how e-mail is to be used, by whom, and what the sanctions are for violation of those policies.*

Duty to third parties and vulnerable populations: Helping professionals are ethically and legally bound to warn others if a client presents a danger to themselves or to others, although the "duty to warn" statutes vary across the states (Kagle & Kopels, 1994). Practitioners can be held accountable if actions are not taken should a consumer issue threats against themselves or others. In addition, professionals must report child abuse in all states and elder abuse in many states (Reamer, 1994). In instances in which the practitioner and the consumer of services reside in different states, the appropriate and necessary actions are unclear (Johnson & Post, 1996).

Fulfilling the duty to warn requirements may be more difficult in online practice. Given the potential for relative anonymity of cyberspace communication, a practitioner confronted with a potentially dangerous or suicidal client would have greater difficulty in facilitating needed help. This is compounded with the difficulties of accurate online assessments in this arena and associated problems of locating the intended victim and authorities in a geographical location in which the client (but not the practitioner) resides. The difficulties in notifying intended victims and authorities leaves the practitioner who has been told of an intended or actual action by a client vulnerable to future malpractice claims by victims or family members of the client (Kagle & Kopels, 1994).

> *Practitioners should avoid taking online clients who have a risk of being dangerous to themselves or to others. These clients, as well as clients who become potentially dangerous during online treatment, should be referred to in-person services. Practitioners should know the duty to warn laws in their own state and in all states and countries in which their online clients reside. Finally, as previously suggested, practitioners must take steps to establish the identity and whereabouts of their online clients.*

Duty to be available: Practitioners must be reasonably available to their clients for both on-going and emergency services. Similar to issues involving the duty to warn, given geographic distance and lack of knowledge of local resources, an online practitioner may have greater difficulty providing services in an emergency situation.

> *Practitioners should discuss with clients the procedures to be used to contact the practitioner when they are not online. They should post an emergency phone number where they can be reached, and should locate emergency helping resources in the geographic areas in which their clients reside. Finally, online practitioners should be aware that an Internet service provider may delay e-mail messages for up to several days, so practitioners should not use e-mail to convey urgent or important information.*

With regard to on-going services, clients must be clear about how often they may write, what is expected of their writing, and how long they will have to wait for a response. In addition, the technology itself poses a risk to the continuity of services. Internet service providers break down or go out of business, electrical storms may cause power outages, hard disks crash, and modems malfunction.

> *Online practitioners should have a clear contract with their clients about the nature of their services that includes the type of ser-*

vices offered, how often they will communicate, the expected time between receiving and responding to communications, and emergency procedures. In addition, online practitioners should seek an established and reliable Internet service provider for their Web site and have a back-up system that can function in case of technological breakdown of their primary system.

Information and referral: Human service practitioners are ethically and legally bound to provide appropriate referral for their clients when they are unable to provide the requested services. This may take place because the service is outside of the practitioner's area of expertise. In-person practitioners generally are knowledgeable about local resources for making appropriate referrals. In addition, they can refer clients to local "back-up" practitioners who can be called upon in emergencies, while the practitioner is on vacation or at a conference, or if the practitioner goes out of business. The online practitioner, separated by geography, may not be aware of local resources in the client's geographic area.

Online practitioners will need to become adept at locating local resources in the areas in which their clients reside. In addition, they must insure that appropriate back-up personnel, either in the local community or online, are available in case the practitioner is unable to provide services.

Online practitioners may also be tempted to refer clients to other online resources. For example, there are thousands of online self-help groups and tens of thousands of online human service information sites on the Internet that may provide clients with supplemental support and psycho-education (Ferguson, 1996). Referral to other Internet sites may be problematic because the content of the sites often changes frequently. The membership, mission, and degree of support offered by an online self-help group may also change over time. Referral to online sites may raise liability issues. For example, if a practitioner refers a client to an online self-help group and the client is psychologically injured as a result of participation in the group, is the referring practitioner liable? Or, if a client is referred to a psycho-educational or health-related site and receives inaccurate or harmful information, is the referring practitioner liable? The answers to these questions will be decided by future court cases.

Practitioners should be cautious about referral to online sites and self-help groups with which they are not thoroughly knowledgeable. In general, risk management procedures should include referring a client to a general rather than a specific category of online help. For example, a client might be referred to the national Mental Health Association Web site rather than to a specific online depression-related self-help group. Additionally, Web site disclaimers should include language indicating that the consumer agrees to hold harmless the practitioner for any adverse effects incurred as a result of these referrals.

Avoiding inappropriate relationships: Sexual misconduct is one of the most common reasons that a human service professional is sued for malpractice (Reamer, 1995). The risk of inappropriate sexual relationships also exists online. There is some research to suggest that communication may be disinhibited in online communication due to the lack of social status cues available to participants (Sproul & Kiesler, 1986). This may encourage an online sexual encounter. In addition, given only written cues, it may be easier to misunderstand messages as being seductive or flirtatious. Finally, there is a considerable culture of sex online. There have been anecdotal reports of people falling in love and eventually marrying, having online "affairs" and "compusex" (similar to phone sex), and getting divorced as a result of online relationships (Wiggins, 1995). In addition, people have met online and later agreed to meet in-person for a sexual relationship. Given that a verbatim transcript of all messages will exist, the potential for a successful malpractice suit in this area against an online practitioner is great. Finally, a chance encounter with a client whose physical appearance is unknown is also possible.

Human service professionals are also ethically and legally bound to avoid relationships with other persons that are detrimental to a client or former client. This is made more difficult in cyberspace where pseudonyms are common and where one does not know the physical appearance or social circle of the client.

Online practitioners must take care to maintain their ethical standards regarding sexual relationships in their online practice, and should be aware of the potential for sexual misunderstanding in online communication. Obtaining a recent picture of the client might also be useful in avoiding inadvertent relationships.

Fees: Practitioners must be clear about their services, schedules, fees, and billing practices. In-person practice is generally charged on a per-session rate with a fixed length of session. There is no agreed upon standard of charges for online human service practice. Online practice complicates the fee arrangements. How will a practitioner charge for services: by the message? the page? a specific period of time? reading time? typing time? Will a client be limited to a certain number of words or pages? Adding to the complication, third party reimbursement policies for online practice have generally not been established.

Online practitioners should have a clear description of their fee structure posted on their Web site and discuss fee expectations with their clients.

HUMAN SERVICE AGENCY WEB SITE ISSUES

The above issues related to online direct practice are applicable to human service agencies that seek to provide therapeutic services. Only a small proportion of all human service agencies that offer a Web site seek to provide online direct services. Many agencies provide a Web site in order to promote agency visibility, provide community education, engage in online advocacy, and solicit funds, goods, and services. Human service agencies also face risk-management issues related to these other aspects of their Web site.

Who owns the Web site? A recent study found that almost one-half of nonprofit agencies used volunteers to develop their Web site (Finn, 1999). Unless there is an employee relationship or an agreement to the contrary, the creation of the Web site is not a "work for hire" under copyright laws, and the creator is likely to be the author and copyright holder (Blaustein, 1997). Legally, a volunteer who worked independently to create an agency Web site could simply move or delete the site because the agency may have no legal ownership of the site.

Human service agencies should have clear written contract with the developer of their Web site, whether it is a consultant or a volunteer, stating that ownership of the Web site resides with the agency.

Copyright: Many agency Web sites are designed to provide community education about issues such as domestic violence, HIV/AIDS, teen pregnancy, and mental health issues. In the service of community education, agencies may publish materials on their site that they did not create. Many educational publications and materials are copyrighted, as are design aspects of Web sites. The risk of using copyright materials is increased when volunteers or agency staff who are not familiar with copyright laws are involved in developing and maintaining the online materials.

Agencies must insure that content on their Web site does not infringe on copyrights or trademark. Staff and volunteers should be trained to be sensitive to copyright issues and to ask permission when using other's written or Web-based materials.

Threats and disruption: Human service agencies, especially those involved in controversial issues or working with potentially dangerous clients, may be the target of e-mail threats or online disruption of their services. Given the hostility some agencies such as gay rights and family planning organizations face from certain segments of society, agencies must be prepared to encounter attempts to disrupt their Web site. Agencies are vulnerable to disruption through flooding the e-mail account with thousands of unwanted messages (spam), attaching viruses and worms to other programs, sending provocative or threatening messages to staff, and e-mailing false requests for help (Johnson, 1994).

Human service organizations should provide training to staff and volunteers about the range of messages that they may receive and use e-mail filters and virus protection software. Organizations should maintain a copy of any threatening message and contact the police when threats are received.

Posting names and personal information: Human service agencies use their Web site to provide information about many aspects of agency functioning. Some agencies post the names and e-mail address of staff and/or others who work with the agency. An agency might post the names of Board members, new volunteers, or donors. Posting names and other demographic information on a Web site may, however, be viewed as a violation of privacy. Others may target these individuals found on the Internet to receive unwanted business or personal messages. The posting of names may even be dangerous for those working in agencies that may be targeted by militant groups. For example, family planning, domestic violence, and HIV/AIDS organizations have all been the recipients of threats and violence.

> *Agencies should carefully consider whether it is safe to post names of agency personnel on the Internet and should obtain written permission before posting an individual's name on their Web site.*

Unsolicited e-mail: While many human service agencies and private practitioners seek to provide services online, others intend only to offer information. Agencies may, however, receive e-mail requests for help because their e-mail address is posted on their Web site or someone found the e-mail address of the agency or employee through an Internet e-mail search engine. A recent study of unsolicited e-mail sent to dermatology health care providers found that half of the sites responded to unsolicited e-mail and there was great variation in the provider's response to unsolicited e-mail (Eysenback & Thomas, 1998). Some providers returned a diagnosis and advice, others suggested in-person consultation, and still others replied that they do not respond to unsolicited e-mail. As stated previously, an e-mail response by agencies may be assumed to be the beginning of a fiduciary relationship, whether or not the agency intends to provide follow-up services. A quick reply involving advice about a course of action may also leave the agency vulnerable to charges of inappropriate diagnosis.

> *Human service agencies and practitioners should have written policies and staff training about how to handle unsolicited e-mail. Practitioners and agencies offering Web sites should also have carefully worded disclaimers outlining the parameters of their online services.*

Agency e-mail policy: Agencies that provide e-mail and Internet access for staff and volunteers may face internal issues related to the privacy and personal use. It is assumed that agency computer resources should be used for agency-related business. Staff may construe some e-mail discussions with their colleagues that may appear personal, such as discussion of social and family events, as important in building and maintaining a working relationship. In addition, agency staff may be tempted to use their e-mail or Internet connections for personal reasons during lunch or after work hours. As stated earlier, the courts have ruled that an employer can read all e-mail residing on computers using the company network as long as workers are informed that company policy permits it.

> *Agencies should have written policies about appropriate use of e-mail and the Internet, and should have documentation signed by staff that they are aware of the agency policy regarding online communications.*

Fundraising: A number of nonprofit agencies are using their Web site to secure resourccs including funds, goods, and services. Online fundraising efforts range from sophisticated online appeals with secure credit card transactions to simple online requests for donations to be mailed to the agency (Mercer, 1998; Clark, 1995). A recent study of nonprofits (Finn, 1999) found that online fundraising was rated as an important goal by one-third of nonprofit agencies with a Web site. Online fundraising raises jurisdictional questions. Many states require that an agency be licensed in that state and pay registration fees in order to receive donations. The fees and the staff time needed for proper registration nationwide could conceivably cost an agency several thousand dollars (Mercer, 1998). Organizations ignoring these responsibilities or employing other organizations, such as an auction house that neglects regulations, could face legal liabilities (Williams, 1998).

> *Human service agencies that solicit funds online should seek legal counsel and review the state laws regulating nonprofit contributions in each state from which funds may be received.*

CONCLUSION

We are entering an information age in which geography and the delivery of health and human services need no longer be linked. This opens the possibility of educational, supportive, and therapeutic services to an ever-increasing number of people. In the near future we will see the deployment of fiber optic networks promoting the merger of television, telephone, and computers in an interactive system permitting two-way real-time video and audio transmission. These will no doubt also be used in the delivery of human services. Online services may provide supplementary services to those already in traditional services or, for some, especially those now growing up with the Internet in their homes and schools, may be a preferred delivery system. While the promise of online services is great, they have developed faster than the evaluation research, policies, and ethical practices necessary to insure quality services to consumers and protection from legal action for human service agencies and practitioners. There are many situations in which the current professional codes of ethics in social work, counseling, and psychology offer guidelines that should also be followed in online practice. There are other issues, especially those related to jurisdiction, fiduciary relationships, and the appropriateness of online treatment that remain unclear. They are likely to be sorted out only when cases have been tested in the courts. In the meantime, human service agencies and practitioners must be aware of what the issues are when they provide services through the Internet and take appropriate risk-management steps to limit both ethical violations and legal liability.

REFERENCES

Allen, N., M. Stein, and M. Warwick, eds. (1996). *Fundraising on the Internet: Recruiting and renewing donors online*. Berkeley: Strathmoor Press.

American Psychological Association. (1998). Services by Telephone, Teleconferencing, and Internet. Statement of the Ethics Committee of the APA. Online: August 1998, *http://www.apa.org/ethics/stmnt01.html.*

Banks, M.A. (1998). Web psychos, stalkers, and pranksters: How to protect yourself in cyberspace. Online: *http://w3.one.net/~banks/psycho.htm.*

Besharov, D. (1985). The vulnerable social worker. Silver Spring, MD: National Association of Social Workers.

Blaustein, S. (1997). Internet Law. Online July 21, 1998, *http://www.patent plus.com/Webaudit.html.*

Bloom, J. (1998). The ethical practice of Webcounseling. *British Journal of Guidance and Counseling*, *26*(1), 53-60.

Bloom, J. (1997). NBCC WebCounseling standards. *Counseling Today,* Nov., pp. 6, 8, 12. Online August, 1998: *http://www.counseling.org/ctonline/news/nbcc_standards.htm.*

Braithwaite, D., V. Waldron, and J. Finn (1999). Communication of Social Support in Computer Mediated Self Help Groups. *Health Communication*, *11*(2), 123-151.

Childress, C. (1998). Potential Risks and Benefits of Online Psychotherapeutic Interventions. International Society for Mental Health Online. Online, February 17, *http://www.ismho.org/issues/9801.htm.*

Clark, J.P. (1995). Non-profits in cyberspace: The fund raiser's guide. *Fund Raising Management*, *26*, 28-32.

Cref, V.G. (1997). When they're everywhere. In P.J. Denning and R.M. Metcalfe, *Beyond calculation: The next fifty years of computing*. Springer-Verlag: New York. pp. 33-42.

Cushman, R. and Detmer, D. (1997). Information policy for the U.S. health sector: Engineering, political economy, and ethics. *The Milbank Quarterly: A Journal of Public Health and Health Care Policy.* [Online]. Available: *http://www.med. harvard.edu/ publication.Milbank/art/index.html.*

Dickson, D. (1998). *Confidentiality and privacy in social work.* New York: The Free Press.

Eysenback, G. and Diegpen, T.L. (1998). Responses to unsolicited patient e-mail requests for medical advice on the World Wide Web. *Journal of the American Medical Association, 280* (15), 1333-1335.

Ferguson, T. (1996). *Health Online*. Reading, MA: Addison-Wesley.

Finn, J. (1999). Seeking Volunteers and Contributions: An exploratory study of nonprofit agencies on the Internet. *Journal of Technology in Human Services, 15*(4) 39-56.

Finn, J. and Lavitt, M. (1994). Computer-based self-help groups for sexual abuse survivors. *Social Work with Groups, 17* (1/2), pp. 21-45.

Gellman, R. and Frawley, K. (1996). The need to know versus the right to privacy. In T. Trabin (Ed.), *The Computerization of Behavioral Health Care,* San Francisco, CA: Jossey-Bass.

Giffords, E.D. (1998). Social Work on the Internet: An Introduction. *Social Work, 43* (3), 243-251.

Graham, M.A. (1996). Telepsychiatry in Appalachia. *American Behavioral Scientist, 39* (5), 602-615.

Green, M. (1998). Fundraising in Cyberspace. The Grantsmanship Center. Online: July 9. *http://www.tgci.com/publications/fall95mag/cyberled.htm.*

Grondahl v. Bullock, 318 N.W. 2d 240 (1982).

Gustafson, D.H., McTavish, F., Hawkins, R., Pingree, S., and Neeraj, A. (1998). Computer support for elderly women with breast cancer. *Journal of the American Medical Association, 280* (15), 1305.

Hafner, A.W. (1989). Computers and the Legal Standard of Care. *Archives of Ophthalmology, 107*(7), 966.

Hannon, K. (1996). Upset? Try cybertherapy. *U.S. News & World Report, 120*(9), 81-82.

Hawthorne, N. (1997). The history and development of Internet resources for volunteer programs. *Journal of Volunteer Administration, 16* (Fall), 28-33.

Holden, G., Bearison, D., Rode, D., Rosenberg, G., and Fishman, M. (1999). The impact of a virtual environment on hospitalized children: A pilot study with aggregation of results of replicated single system designs via meta-analysis. *Research on Social Work Practice, 9*, 365-382.

Holmes, L. (1997). You can't do psychotherapy on the net, yet. Paper presented at the American Psychological Association Annual Convention, August, 1997. Online: February, 1999, *http://mentalhealth.miningco.com/library/aa010499.htm?/pid= 2791&cob=home.*

Huang, M. and Alessi, N. (1996). The Internet and the future of psychiatry. *American Journal of Psychiatry, 153* (7), 861-869.

Johnson, D.G. (1994). Crime, abuse, and hacker ethics. In *Computer Ethics*. (pp. 40-55), Englewood Cliffs, NJ: Prentice-Hall, Inc.

Johnson, D. and Post, D. (1996). Law and borders: The rise of law in cyberspace. *48 Stanford Law Review,* 1367.

Kagle, J. and Kopels, S. (1994). Confidentiality after Tarasoff. *Health & Social Work, 19,* 217-222.

Karger, H.J. and Levine, J. (1999). *The Internet and technology for the human services.* New York: Addison Wesley Longman.

Kutchins, H. and Kirk, S. (1987). DSM-III and social work malpractice. *Social Work,* May-June, 205-211.

Ladd, J. (1997). Ethics and the computer world: A new challenge for philosophers. *Computers and Society, 27* (3), 8-13.

Laudon, K.C. (1995). Ethical concepts and information technology. *Communications of the ACM, 38* (12), 33-39.

Lebow, J. (1998). Not just talk, maybe some risk: The therapeutic potentials and pitfalls of computer-mediated conversation. *Journal of Marital and Family Therapy, 24,* 203-206.

Lee, C. (1998). Counseling and the challenges of cyberspace. *Counseling Today Online.* Online, April 28: *http://www.counseling.org/ctonline/sr598/lee498.htm.*

Mercer, E. (1998). How Can We Use the Internet for Fundraising? Online, February: *http://www.nonprofit-info.org/misc/981027em.html.*

Miller, J.K., and Gergen, K.J. (1998). Life on the line: The therapeutic potentials of computer-mediated conversation. *Journal of Marital and Family Therapy, 24,* 189-202.

Miller v. Sullivan, 625 N.Y.S. 2d 102 (1995).

National Association of Social Workers (1996). *The National Association of Social Workers Code of Ethics.* Washington, DC: NASW Press.

National Board of Certified Counselors, Inc. (1998). Standards for the Ethical Practice of Web Counseling. Online, April: *http://www.nbcc.org/wcstaandards.htm.*

Pergament, D. (1998). Internet psychotherapy: Current status and future regulation. *Journal of Law Medicine, 8* (2), 233-280.

Pincus, W. (1999). The Internet paradox: Libel, slander & the First Amendment in cyberspace. 2 Green Bag 2d 279.

Reamer, F.G. (1998). *Ethical Standards in Social Work: A Critical Review of the NASW Code of Ethics,* Washington, DC: NASW Press.

Reamer, F.G. (1994). *Social work malpractice and liability.* New York: Columbia University Press.

Sampson, J.P., Kolodinsky, R. and Greeno, B. (1997). Counseling on the Information Highway: Future possibilities and potential problems. *Journal of Counseling and Development, 75,* 203-212.

Speilberg, A. (1998). On call and online. *Journal of the American Medical Association, 280* (15), 1353-1359.

Sproul, L. and Kiesler, S. (1986). Reducing social context cues: Electronic mail in organizational communication. *Management Science, 32,* 1492-1512.

Stofle, G.S. (1999). Thoughts about online psychotherapy: Ethical and practical considerations. Online, February, 1999: *http://members.aol.com/stofle/onlinepsych.htm.*

The Harvard Law Review Association. (1999). 112 *Harvard Law Review* 1610.

Wiggins, R.W. (1995). *The Internet for everyone.* New York, NY: McGraw-Hill, Inc.

Williams, G. (1998, December 3). Court upholds registration of fund-raising consultants. *The Chronicle of Philanthropy*, p. 30.

Winzelberg, A. (1997). The analysis of an electronic support group for individuals with eating disorders. *Computers in Human Behavior, 13*(3), 393-407.

Zeran v. America Online, Inc., 958F. Supp. 1124, 1127 n.3 (E.D. Va. 1997).

Computer-Supported Distance Art Therapy: A Focus on Traumatic Illness

Kate Collie
Davor Čubranić

SUMMARY. We propose *computer-supported distance art therapy* as an innovative and inexpensive form of telehealth, and present a rationale for developing distance art therapy services for people with traumatic illnesses. The rationale is based on four current trends: (a) the aging of the population, (b) a shift in focus in the field of telehealth, (c) an increase in

---

Kate Collie, MA, MFA, formerly with the Department of Counselling Psychology, University of British Columbia, is now at the Institute of Health Promotion Research, University of British Columbia.

Davor Čubranić, MSC, is with the Department of Computer Science, University of British Columbia.

Address correspondence to: Kate Collie, Institute of Health Promotion Research, University of British Columbia, 2206 East Mall, Room 324, Vancouver, British Columbia, Canada, V6T 1Z3 (E-mail: kcollie@interchange.ubc.ca).

In this paper, the authors describe an ongoing cross-disciplinary research project that they undertook as equal collaborators. Portions of the material contained herein have appeared in conference proceedings, in Kate Collie's master's thesis, in Davor Čubranić's master's essay, and in *Art Therapy: Journal of the American Art Therapy Association*.

Partial funding for the project was provided by the Webster Foundation, the TeleLearning Network of Centres of Excellence under Theme 3, and the University of British Columbia.

The authors would like to acknowledge the assistance of Dr. Bonita Long, Dr. Kellogg Booth and Dr. Shauna Butterwick, the 10 members of the participatory design team, our two research assistants, and the many volunteers who helped us test the concept and the communication system.

[Haworth co-indexing entry note]: "Computer-Supported Distance Art Therapy: A Focus on Traumatic Illness." Collie, Kate, and Davor Čubranić. Co-published simultaneously in *Journal of Technology in Human Services* (The Haworth Press, Inc.) Vol. 20, No. 1/2, 2002, pp. 155-171; and: *Human Services Technology: Innovations in Practice and Education* (ed: Hy Resnick, and Phoebe Sade Anderson) The Haworth Press, Inc., 2002, pp. 155-171. Single or multiple copies of this article are available for a fee from The Haworth Document Delivery Service [1-800-HAWORTH, 9:00 a.m. - 5:00 p.m. (EST). E-mail address: getinfo@haworthpressinc.com].

psychosocial treatments for people with traumatic physical illnesses, and (d) the recent burgeoning of the art and healing movement. Forms of telehealth such as computer-supported distance art therapy have both a technical and a human dimension, which need to be developed in parallel. Our process of participatory development and initial feasibility assessment was part of a cross-disciplinary collaboration involving the two authors (an artist/counselor and a computer scientist) and a participatory design team of ten others.

KEYWORDS. Art therapy, telehealth, telepsychiatry, traumatic illness

This paper contains a description of the preliminary stages of the development by the two authors of a computer system and basic communication procedures for *computer-supported distance art therapy*. We discuss this innovative form of telehealth within the context of psychosocial care for people with traumatic illnesses, particularly cancer. The paper includes a rationale for developing distance art therapy services for people who have traumatic illnesses, a general description of computer-supported distance art therapy, and a technical description of the computer system we have created.

In this paper, the term *art therapy* is used inclusively to mean therapeutic art, art as therapy, or any kind of therapeutic activity during which the client makes art images. We use the term *traumatic illness* to refer to illness that is either life-threatening or is chronic in that it cannot be cured, significantly influences everyday life, and necessitates assistance or treatment by others (Reid, 1984).

The first author (KC) is an artist and a counselor with a special interest in art groups for adults with traumatic illnesses. The second author (DC) is a computer scientist with a specialty in human-computer interaction and background experience in the area of computer technologies for people with disabilities. By working together, we were able to invent an art-based form of telehealth that is relatively inexpensive and is congruent with current social trends.

Computer-supported distance art therapy makes it possible for art therapy sessions to take place when the client(s) and the therapist are in different places. The computer system that mediates this supports communication by speech and shareable hand-painted images. Although the system has both audio and visual dimensions and therefore has more scope than telephone or e-mail services, it can be handled by the current generation of home computers with modem access to the Internet.

Clients would learn about computer-supported distance art therapy either by visiting a web site where the service would be described, by receiving a referral from a health care professional, or by picking up a flyer. They would then contact the therapist by e-mail or by telephone to receive more information. For those clients who choose to go ahead, an initial intake interview would be conducted by telephone if possible, or by e-mail or online chat.

The rationale for developing a computer-supported distance art therapy service for people with traumatic illnesses relates to KC's clinical interests and is in accordance with a preliminary evaluation of computer-supported distance art therapy (Collie, 1998; Collie & Čubranić, 1999). The evaluation showed that computer-supported distance art therapy has great potential for people who have mobility limitations–as many people with traumatic illnesses do–or who prefer to have extra privacy.

The use of art as therapy in medical settings can be traced back at least to the 1930s (Rosner David & Ilusorio, 1995). Currently, therapeutic art activities are used in the care of people with cancer and other traumatic illnesses both in North America and elsewhere (e.g., Breslow, 1993; Hiltebrand, 1999; Pinchover, 1998) and are thought to have both preventative and curative influences (Taylor, 1999). Many ideas have been put forward as to why art-making may be beneficial for people with physical illnesses. Aldridge (1993) claims that expressive arts therapies are useful for integrating the physiological, psychological, social, and spiritual domains during traumatic illness and for restoring hope. Piccirillo (1995) argues that art-making facilitates crucial nonlinear processing of "the complex constellation of thoughts, feelings, and conflicts" (p. 25) that accompany major illness.

A patient's sense of control is known to be an important factor in adjustment to illness (Helgeson, 1992; Reid, 1984). Reid has shown that for people experiencing chronic illness, a destabilizing sense of a loss of control in one area can be compensated for by developing a sense of control in another area. Art therapy can be useful for generating a sense of control during illness (Breslow, 1993). Clients have control over the art materials and the art images, they experience their own creative power, and they have control over their creative production. When art images contain difficult emotional material, this material can also be experienced as controllable by being contained within the art work.

CURRENT TRENDS

Our rationale is further derived from four current trends: (a) the aging of the North American population, (b) a shift of focus in the field of telehealth, (c) an increase in psychosocial treatments for people with traumatic physical illnesses, and (d) the recent burgeoning of the art and healing movement.

An aging population. As the "baby boom" generation moves into retirement and old age, the average age of people in North America will increase steadily (US Bureau of the Census, 1997). The likelihood of becoming seriously ill increases with age, and therefore a higher percentage of the population will need medical care that ever before. Concurrently, the ratio of physicians per capita will decrease as baby boom physicians retire. This decrease in the number of physicians per capita has already begun and is especially noticeable in rural areas (Watanabe, Jennett & Watson, 1999). As this trend continues, new approaches to health care will be required, particularly approaches that emphasize self-care.

Telehealth. Telehealth is being promoted as a solution to the problems just described (Watanabe, Jennett & Watson, 1999). Telehealth refers to the use of telecommunications technologies to increase availability of health care by making it possible to have access to services from a distance. People living in rural or remote areas are expected to benefit from telehealth services, as are the elderly, people who are home-based or home-bound, people outside the cultural mainstream, people in lower socio-economic groups, and people with disabilities or disabling illnesses (Brauer, 1992; Sampson, Kolodinsky, & Greeno, 1997).

Telephones and radios have been used for many years to aid in the delivery of health care (Cervinskas, 1984). Recently, the advent of the Internet has caused a renewed interest in distance health care and has been a catalyst for rapid growth in this area (Lugg, 1998). Videoconferencing, e-mail, and interactive websites are some of the forms of distance delivery currently being explored as ways of making both physical and mental health services more readily available.

As telehealth has expanded in the last decade, expensive technologies–such as high-bandwidth lines, satellites, and powerful computers–have been used to reach toward the goal of full-speed two-way video communication for distance delivery of health care services. Although preliminary studies of distance mental health programs that have employed complex technologies have shown promising results (e.g., Doze, Simpson, Hailey & Jacobs, 1999; Mielonen, Ohinmaa, Moring & Isohanni, 1998), it is not clear that high-tech telehealth can be cost-effective (Whitten, Kingsley, & Grigsby, 2000). Attention is shifting to less technologically complex methods of telehealth delivery (Della Mea, 1999; Grigsby & Sanders, 1998).

Psychosocial medical care. Cancer is one of the most common traumatic illnesses in North America and is currently the second most common cause of death in the US (Maguire, 1999). Therefore, trends in the treatment of cancer may give some indication of overall trends in care for people with traumatic illnesses. Psychosocial treatments are starting to be a regular part of care for people with cancer, as the benefits of preventative behavior change are being recognized and as increased attention is given to the quality of life of cancer patients, cancer survivors, and their families (Maguire, 1999). Psychosocial care for people with cancer typically takes the form of education and group support, as well as counseling to help with such things as decisions about treatment options, management of pain, side effects of medications, and the chronic stress a life-threatening illness can cause (Baum, 1999). These types of psychosocial interventions, that focus on education, adjustment, and coping, translate readily into self-care.

The Art and Healing movement. The belief that art-making can be healing and life-enhancing is one of the fundamental tenets of the art therapy profession. Recently, the idea that art can be used to promote wellness and ameliorate illness has also been embraced by artists and health care practitioners (Malchiodi, 1998). The Society for the Arts in Healthcare, The International Arts Medicine Association and The Arts and Healing Network are examples of organizations that have recently been formed to promote the arts as an integral component of health care.

Arts programs are being established in hospitals and other medical care settings. In some cases, the purpose of these programs is simply to use art and music to create comforting environments (Kaye & Blee, 1997). There are also artist-in-residence programs, such as the Arts and Healing Program at the Palmetto Richland Memorial Hospital in Columbia, South Carolina, that are designed to make art activities available to staff and families as well as to patients. The Healing and the Arts program at Dartmouth Medical Center is an example of a comprehensive hospital arts program in which art activities are used to build more effective doctor-patient relationships, support the healing process, enhance medical education, and promote good health habits (Malchiodi, 1998).

Computer-supported distance art therapy fits with the four trends described above. It is a low-tech form of telehealth that can be used to expand access to services that are usually only available in urban centers. It fills an obvious niche as a form of psychosocial care for people with traumatic illnesses, for whom the costs and strain of traveling to receive care can significantly limit the benefits–making distance delivery especially important.

DEVELOPMENT OF COMPUTER-SUPPORTED DISTANCE ART THERAPY

The computer system and the communication procedures we have been developing are suitable for either individual or group art therapy sessions. However, we focused primarily on group art therapy out of consideration for the isolation that can be a consequence of traumatic illness. We wanted to make it possible for someone with mobility limitations to be able to access psychosocial treatment–in this case art therapy–and to have contact with other people having similar experiences.

There were two main development tasks. One was to design a communication system that permits a group of people in different places to talk with each other through their computers and make computer paintings that the other people can see on their screens. This is human-human interaction using computers, with a human-computer interaction component that is deliberately minimized so that the human interaction can be maximized. The project required a user-friendly computer system that could support audio and graphic group communication, and that would be suitable for standard home computers with dial-in access to the Internet. The other main development task was to generate appropriate communication procedures for conducting distance art therapy sessions. We drew on literature about telephone therapy (e.g., Haas, Benedict & Kobos, 1996; Rittner & Hammonds, 1992), computer-supported collaborative work (Grudin, 1994), e-mail therapy (e.g., Murphy & Mitchell, 1998), computers in art therapy (Canter, 1989) and computer-mediated communication (Chesebro & Bonsall, 1989) for guidance in our development decisions.

We used as a template the face-to-face format KC uses for therapeutic group art activities with people with traumatic illnesses. The configuration is one in which a group of clients and a therapist sit around a table with pastels, markers, crayons, and watercolor paints within easy reach–simple art materials that favor directness and immediacy, and require no training to use. The first session of a six-week group begins with a warm-up activity designed to build group cohesion and foster confidence about art making. An example is "pass-the-painting," an activity in which each person begins a painting, then after a minute passes it to someone else who continues painting, and so on until everyone has contributed something to each image. In subsequent sessions, the art therapist/facilitator guides the group through more complex art activities that are done individually. The therapist/facilitator talks intermittently throughout the activities and glances around to see how things are going–without looking closely at what people are making (allowing some privacy). Group members are aware of other people making images, and typically feel supported and encouraged by the group. They can also glance around without interrupting anyone and speak if they wish to. At the end of each activity, the group looks at what the others have done by standing up and walking around the table. When it is time for the group to discuss the art images together, the images are either put up on a wall or laid out on the floor in sequence.

Participatory Design

The initial stages of the development process were structured as *participatory design* (Clement & Van den Besselaar, 1993), a broad set of design practices that all have in common direct user participation in system development activities and decisions. The focus of participatory design is not only the improvement of the information system, but also the empowerment of future users so they can co-determine the development of the system and of their workplace (Clement & Van den Besselaar, 1993). Two themes govern practical implementation of participatory design principles (Floyd, Mehl, Reisen, Schmidt, & Wolf, 1989). The first theme is mutual reciprocal learning, in which users and designers teach one another about (respectively) work practices and technical possibilities through joint experiences. The second theme is design by doing, in which interactive experimentation, modeling, and testing support "hands-on design" and "learning by doing."

There were three phases to our participatory design process. The first was the preliminary collaboration between the two authors, when we learned the possibilities and limitations of each other's field and determined initial parameters for computer-supported distance art therapy. When we had a usable prototype and a general sense of how distance art therapy might be conducted, we worked with groups of volunteer testers to discover what kinds of communication the system could support (the technical dimension) and to determine what communication guidelines and social protocols would be necessary (the human dimension).

During the final stage of the participatory design process, a team of 10 potential users experienced simulated distance art therapy using the system. In two groups of five, they took the role of clients for mock group art therapy sessions led by KC. There were two sessions for each group. Geographic distance was simulated by using a closed network of computers in different rooms of the same building. Using the computer software, everybody could hear KC as she led the sessions and they could respond to her, for example, to get clarification of the instructions she gave throughout each activity, or to report a technical problem. They could also speak to each other, which they needed to do during the group-building activities at the beginning and at the end of each 15-minute painting activity when it was time to look at the paintings each person had made. Typically, a few people would make comments during the painting activities, just as would be expected if the group were sitting around a table together. At the completion of each hour-long session there was a round-table discussion about the possibilities and problems of computer-supported distance art therapy (and related forms of distance psychosocial care).

The 10 people on the team were artists, counselors, art therapists, and educators, each with at least one area of personal or professional experience directly related to computer-supported distance art therapy. These included computer science, ethics of Internet counseling, distance art therapy, computer art, rehabilitation counseling, e-mail therapy, and support services for people with cancer. At least three of the 10 have lived with life-threatening illnesses and two use wheelchairs.

The group discussions were audiotaped and the transcriptions analyzed to identify key issues that were raised. The purpose was to lay a conceptual foundation for this and other similar forms of telehealth. Suggestions made by the team were used to improve the system between sessions and to refine the communication procedures we were using. For a detailed discussion of the issues that were explored by the participatory design team, see Collie (1998) and Collie and Čubranić (1999).

System Implementation Details

The system provides support for five tasks: speaking within the group, painting, passing paintings, maintaining awareness of other group members' activities, and showing paintings to the rest of the group. DC achieved this by creating an art program specifically for art therapy and combining it with a pre-existing communication program.

The system described here was developed on Silicon Graphics' Indy workstations, but runs on any machine running a Unix operating system. An affordable and widely available hardware platform would be a PC with Linux.

Audio communication. Our system had to support two modes of communication: verbal and visual. Distance verbal communication in our case required conference call-like audio connection between the participants. In practice, if clients' dial-in lines turn out to have too small a bandwidth, this could be done by telephone, although it would require the addition of a second phone line to their location.

In this instance, since the workstations were already networked via a local area network to transmit visual information, it made sense to use the network to transport the audio as well, especially since there was more than sufficient bandwidth available. This scenario is likely to be feasible even in the real world, with the constant improvements in the speed of communication lines available to a home customer; besides, modern audio streaming programs such as RealAudio can run comfortably even in today's conditions. There are numerous programs that have network audio conferencing capability, and we decided to use Silicon Graphics' InPerson, which was pre-installed on our development platform and offered everything we needed.

The paint program. Visual communication at the minimum required some sort of painting surfaces that can be viewed by all the participants. Group painting programs are quite common groupware applications; however, despite several such programs being available both for free and commercially (including a component of *InPerson*), none of them quite suited our needs and the special requirements of art therapy. Typically, those programs–for example *NetMeeting*–are designed for making diagrams and business presentations rather than expressive art, and consequently have a limited range of colors and tools for freehand painting. Therefore, we decided to write our own, based on *XPaint*, a publicly available single-user paint program for UNIX and the X Window System platform (Martinsen, 2000). DC followed KC's specifications and made a program that is simple, naturalistic, and aesthetically pleasing. The program supports freehand painting with a wide range of colors and is maximally simplified for intuitive use (see Figure 1).

The user interface. A major goal in the program's design was to keep it intuitive and easy to use. We wanted to augment the enhanced feelings of control that therapeutic art activities can bring by making it easy for clients to experience a sense of mastery and control over the computer. For this reason, the user interface has no complex commands or arcane features, and all the available operations are immediately visible. Similarly to standard paint programs, there is a small "toolbox" (brush, marker, pastel, spray paint, eraser, color-matcher, and pointer) at the side, and a large painting space filling most of the computer screen (see Figure 1). A new painting space can be created at any time with one mouse click, which is one of the ways in which the paint program is more straightforward than traditional art materials; the ease of "mixing" colors is another.

The system is very responsive to hand-painted marks and can show a great deal of artistic nuance, and yet it does not require a high level of manual or cognitive functioning. It is usable by someone with limited dexterity or by someone who is fatigued or dulled by medication. The painting can be done with whatever input device (mouse, track ball, stylus) that the person prefers.

System architecture. The system was implemented as a fully replicated architecture with the paint and audio-conferencing programs running on every participating workstation. As a person paints, the information that makes that picture is transmitted to all the other computers in the group. This information is transmitted as individual user actions, such as mouse clicks and strokes, rather than as whole images, so that the required network bandwidth can be kept relatively low. The system is composed of participating computers running the paint program, which in general correspond to a therapist and clients in a therapy session. The therapist's program starts first and accepts connections from other participants. It also serves as a sequencer of painting events in the system. All participants' events are relayed to it and then broadcast to the rest of the system, ensuring the same sequence of events on all computers. Thus, participants' programs do not usually communicate directly with each other at all, although each one knows who the others are. This is useful in the event of the failure of the sequencer, in which case a simple software re-election algorithm determines a new sequencer among the remaining participants. Late-comers, and participants who were dropped out of the session because of a network or software failure, can (re)join a session in progress, in which case the

FIGURE 1. A Screen Shot Showing the Simplicity of the Paint Program User Interface.

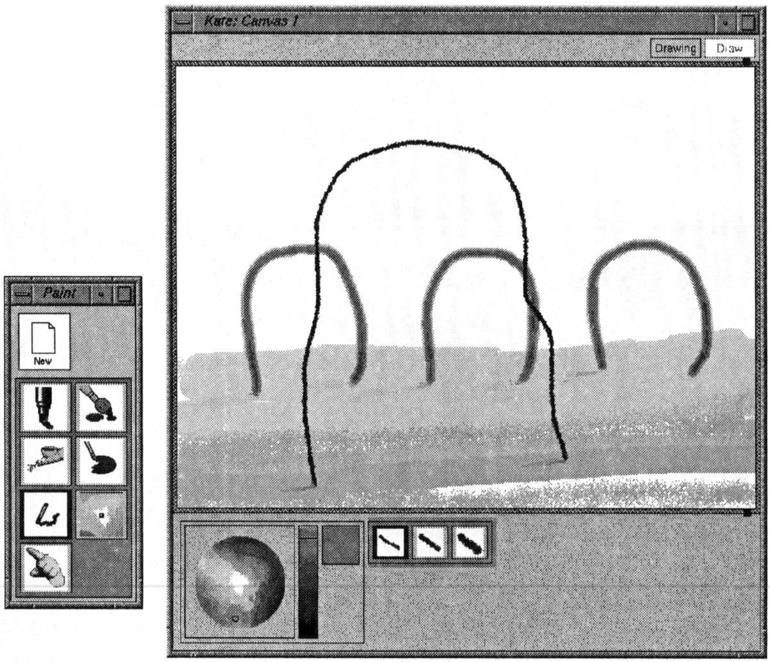

sequencer automatically takes care of notifying the rest of the participants and sends out requests to the controller of each open canvas to bring the newcomer's state up to date with the rest of the system.

The paint program itself consists of two concurrently running processes: a communication module and a paint module. The reason for this is to keep the painting component of the program as unaware of session management and information broadcasting details as possible. All it needs to do when it wants to notify other session participants is to pass the information packet to the communication module, which then takes care of the rest. The communication module also takes care of session management issues: late-joins, drop-outs, re-election, etc., and only sends to the paint module the information that it really needs (for example, names of the participants, because they are displayed in window titles).

Commonly, group painting programs (Bly & Minneman, 1990; Greenberg & Bohnet, 1991) are conceptual equivalents of a shared whiteboard where users most often work together on a single painting. In group art therapy situations, however, each participant paints on his or her own "canvas." For this reason, this system does not implement simultaneous painters in a single canvas; while everybody may look and "point" at a canvas at any time, there is only one controller who may paint in it. However, each canvas is displayed in a window on each participant's screen, and control of a canvas can be passed to somebody else, as, for example, in a "pass-the-painting" exercise.

Awareness support. Existing groupware systems often present a miniature view of other participants' windows to maintain a sense of workspace awareness. In our case, because we needed to accommodate focused individual work as well as group interaction, we found that constantly seeing others' work underway in the background was distractive. We sought a way to maintain a sense of group activity, but minimize distraction, and found that having canvases opened by others lined up as icons along the top of the screen, together with the spoken dialog on the audio channel, was sufficient for this purpose. On the therapist's workstation, however, the images by default remain fully visible so that the therapist can see them as they are being made. When it is time to discuss everyone's images together, the iconized images can be opened with a single click.

We eventually decided not to include small video images of the therapist/facilitator and group members on each person's screen because this would surpass the capabilities of most home computers. Although there is evidence that at least some video contact could be helpful (Rocco, 1998), it is not clear that it is necessary or that it would always be beneficial. Stein, Rothman and Nakanishi (1993) found that members of a telephone group for people with multiple sclerosis were opposed to exchanging photos of each other and put high value on remaining unseen. Our decision not to include video is supported by research indicating that people using computer networks to do collaborative work adjust their communication according to the medium, by focusing on what is most important when there are fewer channels of communication (Vera, Kvan, West, & Lai, 1998).

Art Activities for Distance Art Therapy

Although we designed the system to support a wide range of therapeutic art activities, those that worked best were ones that allow, or require, the therapist/facilitator to talk during the art activities and to elicit some spoken responses from the group. We discovered that it was important to limit periods of silence, as awareness of the group and group connectedness hinge largely on speaking. The participants reported feeling uncomfortable during periods of silence, and during silences it was hard to know if the connections between the computers were intact. KC found it worked best to talk intermittently and steadily to the whole group during the art activities and to talk occasionally with individuals as well, to confirm their presence and to reinforce the inclusion of all group members. For a more detailed discussion of procedures and communication guidelines, see Collie and Čubranić (1999).

As a counselor using art in therapeutic groups for people with major illnesses, KC works within a narrative therapy framework (Freedman & Combs, 1996; White & Epston, 1990). The art activities we used during the simulated sessions were based on the narrative therapy ideas of increasing a client's sense of personal agency (i.e., a belief in one's capacity to exert positive influence) and enhancing awareness of personal resources. Two examples are: (a) an "empowerment" activity in which people are asked to imagine feeling the kind of personal strength they like to feel and to use this as a starting point for creating an image; and (b) an intuitive painting activity that is followed by questions about the images that are answered privately. The empowerment activity is designed to build confidence and to demonstrate that a sense of competence and agency can be accessed deliberately. The intuitive painting with questions lets people see themselves as creative and capable of making original and meaningful images, and lets them experience their problems as manageable and solvable.

DISCUSSION

When we started this project, we thought the impersonal nature of computers and the lack of face-to-face contact might make computer-supported distance art therapy impractical or impossible. However, our experiences during these first stages of development have shown us that computer-supported distance art therapy is feasible. The people involved in the initial participatory development reported that the system was engaging and easy to use. Once they were using it, typically they would not want to stop! During the round-table discussions, the participatory design team discussed a range of applications for computer-supported distance art therapy and easily came up with solutions to almost all the problems and potential problems they identified (see Collie, 1998).

The process of simultaneously developing the technical and the human dimensions of a new form of telehealth is complex. It has been suggested (e.g., Sanders & Rosenfield, 1998) that cross-disciplinary collaborations, such as this one, that allow mental health clinicians and computer systems developers to work together are necessary for the development of computer-mediated telehealth services, and that the success of telehealth services depends on human factors more than technological factors (e.g., Stamm, 1998; Yellowlees & Kennedy, 1996). However, examples of this approach to development are hard to find. There is no literature to refer to about this, just as there is no literature about distance art therapy. Therefore, we are moving cautiously and using a participatory process that allows us to draw on the expertise of many people.

As we move forward, we will continue a parallel development of the system and of procedures for conducting computer-supported distance art therapy. Two of the priorities for the software development will be keeping the user interface simple and adapting the program to a range of computer systems, so that when computer-supported distance art therapy services are offered, they can be widely available to people at home. The continuing development of the human side of computer-supported distance art therapy will involve not only refining communication procedures for this type of distance group interaction, but adapting art therapy methods to a distance format and perhaps developing new methods.

The next phase of this project will again be based on simulated therapeutic situations–this time using the Internet–and will involve a participatory design team of medical art therapists and cancer survivors who have experienced face-to-face art therapy. Later, we will conduct pilot studies with actual art therapy clients.

Ultimately, the development process will result in a software package designed to accompany a clinical manual written in consultation with a group of art therapists. As new communication software appears on the market, it may be that a program will become available that will be better than ours at handling the types of nuanced audio and visual communication required for distance art therapy. In this case, we will concentrate entirely on the human dimension.

REFERENCES

Aldridge, D. (1993). Hope, meaning and the creative arts therapies in the treatment of AIDS. *The Arts in Psychotherapy, 20*, 285-297.

Baum, A. (1999). Opportunities, problems for cancer research and practice. *APA Monitor, 30(6)*, 19.

Bly, S. A., & Minneman, S. L. (1990). Commune: A shared drawing surface. In *Proceedings of the Conference on Office Information Systems* (pp. 184-192). Boston, MA: ACM Press.

Brauer, G. W. (1992). Telehealth: The delayed revolution in health care. *Medical Progress Through Technology, 18*, 151-163.

Breslow, D. M. (1993). Creative arts for hospitals: The UCLA experiment. *Patient Education and Counseling, 21*, 101-110.

Canter, D. S. (1989). Art therapy and computers. In H. Wadeson, J. Durkin, & D. Perach (Eds.), *Advances in art therapy* (pp. 296-316). New York: John Wiley & Sons.

Cervinskas, J. (1984). *Telehealth: Telecommunications technology in health care and health education in Canada.* Ottawa, Canada: Canadian Commission for UNESCO.

Chesebro, J. W., & Bonsall, D. G. (1989). *Computer-mediated communication: Human relationships in a computerized world.* Tuscaloosa, AL: University of Alabama Press.

Clement, A., & Van den Besselaar, P. (1993). A retrospective look at participatory design projects. *Communications of the ACM, 36(4)*, 29-37.

Collie, K. (1998). *Art therapy on-line: A participatory action study of distance counselling issues.* Unpublished master's thesis, University of British Columbia, Vancouver, Canada.

Collie, K., & Čubranić, D. (1999). An art therapy solution to a telehealth problem. *Art Therapy: Journal of the American Art Therapy Association, 16(4)*, 186-193.

Della Mea, V. (1999). Internet electronic mail: A tool for low-cost telemedicine. *Journal of Telemedicine and Telecare, 5*, 84-89.

Doze, S., Simpson, J., Hailey, D., & Jacobs, P. (1999). Evaluation of a telepsychiatry pilot project. *Journal of Telemedicine and Telecare, 5*, 38-46.

Floyd, C., Mehl, W. M., Reisen, F. M., Schmidt, G., & Wolf, G. (1989). Out of Scandinavia: Alternative approaches to software design and system development. *Human-Computer Interaction, 4(4)*, 253-350.

Freedman, J., & Combs, G. (1996). *Narrative therapy: The social construction of preferred realities.* New York: Norton.

Greenberg, S., & Bohnet, R. (1991). Groupsketch: A multi-user sketchpad for geographically-distributed small groups. In *Proceedings of Graphic Interface '91* (pp. 207-215), Calgary, Canada: Canadian Information Processing Society.

Grigsby, J., & Sanders, J. H. (1998). Telemedicine: Where it is and where it's going. *Annals of Internal Medicine, 129(2)*, 123-127.

Grudin, J. (1994). Groupware and social dynamics: Eight challenges for developers. *Communications of the ACM, 37(1)*, 92-105.

Haas, L. J., Benedict, J. G., & Kobos, J. C. (1996). Psychotherapy by telephone: Risks and benefits for psychologists and consumers. *Professional Psychology: Research and Practice, 27*, 154-160.

Helgeson, V. (1992). Moderators of the relation between perceived control and adjustment to chronic illness. *Journal of Personality and Social Psychology, 63*, 656-666.

Hiltebrand, E. U. (1999). Coping with cancer through image manipulation. In C. Malchiodi (Ed.) *Medical art therapy with adults* (pp. 113-135). London: Jessica Kingsley.

Kaye, C., & Blee, T. (Eds.) (1997). *The arts in health care: A palette of possibilities.* London: Jessica Kingsley.

Maguire, P. (1999). Psychology and medicine connecting in war on cancer. *APA Monitor, 30(6)*, 8-9.

Malchiodi, C. A. (1998). Art as Healing, Art in Healthcare and Arts Medicine: New names for Art Therapy? *Art Therapy: Journal of the American Art Therapy Association, 15(3)*, 154-155.

Martinsen, T. (2000). home.worldonline.dk/~torsten/xpaint/

Mielonen, M., Ohinmaa, A., Moring, J., & Isohanni, M. (1998). The use of videoconferencing for telepsychiatry in Finland. *The Journal of Telemedicine and Telecare, 4*, 125-131.

Murphy, L. J., & Mitchell, D. L. (1998). When writing helps to heal: E-mail as therapy. *British Journal of Guidance and Counselling, 26*, 21-31.

Piccirillo, E. (1995). Taking inventory in the age of AIDS. *Art Therapy: Journal of the American Art Therapy Association, 12(1)*, 62-66.

Pinchover, E. (1998). Art therapy for hospitalized children inspired by Elizabeth Kuebler-Ross' approach. *Harefuah, 135(7-8)*, 256-262.

Reid, D. W. (1984). Participatory control and the chronic-illness adjustment process. In H. Lefcourt (Ed.), *Research with the locus of control construct: Extensions and limitations* (Vol. 3, pp. 361-389). New York: Academic Press.

Rittner, B., & Hammons, K. (1992). Telephone group work with end stage AIDS. *Social Work with Groups, 15*, 59-72.

Rocco, E. (1998). Trust breaks down in electronic context but can be repaired by some initial face-to-face contact. In *Proceedings of CHI'98* (pp. 496-502). Los Angeles, CA: ACM Press.

Rosner David, I., & Ilusorio, S. (1995). Tuberculosis: Art therapy with patients in isolation. *Art Therapy: Journal of the American Art Therapy Association, 12(1)*, 24-31.

Sampson, J. P., Kolodinsky, R. W., & Greeno, B. P. (1997). Counseling on the information highway: Future possibilities and potential problems. *Journal of Counseling and Development, 75*, 203-212.

Sanders, P., & Rosenfield, M. (1998). Counselling at a distance: Challenges and new initiatives. *British Journal of Guidance and Counselling, 26*, 5-10.

Stamm, B. (1998). Clinical applications of telehealth in mental health care. *Professional Psychology: Research and Practice, 29(6)*, 536-542.

Stein, L., Rothman, B., & Nakanishi, M. (1993). The telephone group: Accessing group service to the homebound. *Social Work with Groups, 16*, 203-215.

Taylor, D. B. (1999). The arts and public health (editorial). *The International Journal of Arts Medicine, 6(1)*, 3.

US Bureau of the Census. (1997). Population profile of the United States (USBC Series P23-194). Washington, DC: U.S. Government Printing Office.

Vera, A. H., Kvan, T., West, R. L., & Lai, S. (1998). Expertise, collaboration, and bandwidth. In *Proceedings of CHI'98* (pp. 503-510). Los Angeles, CA: ACM Press.

Watanabe, M., Jennett, P., & Watson, M. (1999). The effect of information technology on the physician workforce and health care in isolated communities: The Canadian picture. *Journal of Telemedicine and Telecare, 5(Suppl. 2)*, 11-19.

White, M., & Epston, D. (1990). *Narrative means to therapeutic ends*. New York: Norton.

Whitten, P., Kingsley, C., & Grigsby, J. (2000). Results of a meta-analysis of cost-benefit research: Is this a question worth asking? *Journal of Telemedicine and Telecare, 6(Suppl. 1)*, 4-6.

Yellowlees, P., & Kennedy, C. (1996). Telemedicine applications in an integrated mental health service based at a teaching hospital. *Journal of Telemedicine and Telecare, 2*, 205-209.

Electronic Technology for Social Work Education and Practice: The Application of Telephone Technology to Counseling

Maxine Rosenfield

SUMMARY. The author in this article argues for the legitimization of the telephone in one-on-one and group professional practice in social work. She contrasts telephone hotline work and face-to-face counseling with her view of telephone counseling. *[Article copies available for a fee from The Haworth Document Delivery Service: 1-800-HAWORTH. E-mail address: <getinfo@haworthpressinc.com> Website: <http://www.HaworthPress.com>* © *2002 by The Haworth Press, Inc. All rights reserved.]*

KEYWORDS. Telephone therapy/counseling, telephone hotline practice, counseling, professional standards

---

Maxine Rosenfield, DCR(T), DipCouns, is an experienced counselor, trainer, and management consultant who, since 1991, has specialized in the use of the telephone for counseling rather than for hotline services, the latter being the more common practice. Rosenfield has pioneered both one-on-one and group telephone counseling in the United Kingdom, with particular emphasis on teleconferencing. In addition, she has guided the U.K.'s telephone hotline "industry" in developing and monitoring quality standards both through her work as the first chairwoman of the Telephone Helplines Association and as manager of the Telephone Training and Consultancy Service for Broadcasting Support Services (1994-1999). Currently residing in Australia, Rosenfield continues to work with telephone hotlines, and she is developing a private telephone and internet counseling practice.

[Haworth co-indexing entry note]: "Electronic Technology for Social Work Education and Practice: The Application of Telephone Technology to Counseling." Rosenfield, Maxine. Co-published simultaneously in *Journal of Technology in Human Services* (The Haworth Press, Inc.) Vol. 20, No. 1/2, 2002, pp. 173-181; and: *Human Services Technology: Innovations in Practice and Education* (ed: Hy Resnick, and Phoebe Sade Anderson) The Haworth Press, Inc., 2002, pp. 173-181. Single or multiple copies of this article are available for a fee from The Haworth Document Delivery Service [1-800-HAWORTH, 9:00 a.m. - 5:00 p.m. (EST). E-mail address: getinfo@haworthpressinc.com].

INTRODUCTION

The following article argues for the legitimization of the telephone as a valid means by which to deliver counseling. While in the United States telephone counseling has been practiced for some time, in the United Kingdom, Europe, and Australia, it is far more of a recent occurrence, although telephone hotlines have existed in the U.K. for more than 45 years. Indeed, the British Association for Counselling, the regulatory body for all practicing counselors in the U.K., only acknowledged that counseling could be carried out by telephone in the late 1990s. This is the context in which this article is presented.

To dispel misconceptions of what telephone counseling entails, this paper will contrast it with both telephone hotline and face-to-face counseling services, with which it is often confused. To aid in the acceptance of telephone counseling among mental health care professionals, recommendations for best practices will follow, with an emphasis on adequate training, support, and supervision in the field. Finally, avenues for future research in this area will be offered, since formal inquiry into the effectiveness of telephone counseling has been slow to be valued and supported by traditional counseling establishments. As the discipline is gradually accepted, related areas, such as Internet counseling, may soon be accepted.

Telephone counseling does not simply involve having a telephone and good will; it requires professionalism. Many counselors will say that they occasionally work by telephone with any given client, but this is not the same as conducting an entire relationship by telephone, with no face-to-face contact. It is this process of building a balanced, trusting client-counselor relationship while working with no visual aids that makes telephone counseling so challenging and exciting.

Perhaps one of the most valuable side effects of telephone counseling is that it encourages practitioners to adopt a broad and flexible approach to their work. That has to be positive for anyone in the profession and, of course, for our clients.

DEFINITION OF TELEPHONE COUNSELING

Telephone Counseling versus Telephone Hotline Services

In order to legitimize the telephone as a medium for counseling, it is essential to distinguish telephone counseling from telephone hotline services. While both involve the use of active listening skills, the former is delivered by credentialed professionals, the latter, most commonly, by trained volunteers. The lack of the kind of legal standards which govern counseling in the United States has perhaps contributed to the suspicion with which mental health practitioners in the United Kingdom regard the telephone as a valid means of counseling. Many U.K. based agencies lend hotline services status by labeling them as "counseling," despite the fact that they have hired laypeople rather than trained mental health care professionals to answer calls.

Furthermore, what many refer to as "counseling" is simply skilled, supportive listening. A hotline service's goals can be to give callers information (often in the form of a mail or e-mail follow-up), to work with callers to create action plans, or to help callers reach an understanding of an issue. Calls to telephone hotlines are usually "one-offs" (single calls) and can be productive whether they last for five minutes or an hour. A telephone counselor, in contrast, sets out to explore issues in greater depth and over a longer period of time in regular, pre-arranged sessions. Anyone with good communication skills and training, plus ongoing support via debriefing sessions, can work for a telephone hotline service. In contrast, only a credentialed mental health professional can deliver telephone counseling. The professional engages in a contract with the client and receives regular, clinical supervision.

Telephone Counseling versus Face-to-Face Counseling

While both telephone and face-to-face counseling are delivered by credentialed mental health care professionals, important distinctions exist between the two. First, in telephone counseling, the client holds the ultimate power, while power is more balanced between counselor and client in a face-to-face scenario: Hanging up is much easier to do than leaving a counselor's office. Telephone counseling affords the client greater privacy for the simple reason that her or his gestures and facial expressions are hidden. Disclosure can be made when it feels "safe" to the client.

In addition, telephone counseling is more accessible to a greater number of people than is face-to-face counseling. It can be far more practical and affordable for a client to "attend" telephone sessions than to travel to face-to-face sessions. Those who are ill, physically disabled, geographically isolated, and/or financially restricted can enjoy access to counseling via the telephone. The telephone opens up a greater array of choice to clients in that they can go out of their immediate areas to find a counselor who is the best match. Thus, those who would identify best with a gay or lesbian counselor, or with a counselor possessing a particular religious or ethnic background, or a particular disability can find the ideal fit. Finally, it is important to note that telephone counseling occurs exclusively via the telephone. While counselors who usually hold face-to-face sessions may occasionally hold telephone sessions out of necessity, they are not practicing telephone counseling.

RECOMMENDATIONS FOR BEST PRACTICE

The Counselor

Not all counselors are meant to use the telephone counseling strategy. However, those who do may find that the experience encourages them to take a more broad, flexible approach to their work. First, the counselor must be capable of using accent and vocal tone to make the client feel comfortable, while being aware that accents seem more pronounced via the telephone than they do in face-to-face communication. Second, the counselor must be able to work without the client's gestures and facial expressions as a guide, and again, to put the client at ease without the aid of body language. Finally, perhaps one of the most exciting aspects of telephone counseling (and one that many traditional mental health professionals find difficult to accept) is that the telephone balances the power relationship between client and counselor. Thus, the counselor must operate with the awareness that the client may be inclined to simply hang up the phone. Moreover, the client has greater freedom to paint any picture she or he chooses over the telephone than in person: The counselor must learn to read the client's deeper feelings when *what* is said and the *manner* in which it is said do not dovetail.

Training, Support, and Supervision

Of course, a counselor who is skilled in the face-to-face setting will most likely make a gradual transition in her acquisition of the above skills. Adequate professional support is key to this process. Interestingly, burnout had long been common among telephone hotline volunteers before the advent of adequate training and support programs.

McCarthy and Reese (1990) sought to explore why volunteers did not continue to work by telephone after training in a particular agency. They found that the most common reasons cited for stress were lack of knowledge and skills linked to the complexity of the problem presented by the client.

Ideally, supervision of telephone counselors should be carried out by telephone, so that any nuances or issues that are medium related can be better addressed. This may not be appropriate in the case of psychologists, social workers, or nurses working out of the same hospital or office, but it should be considered for at least some sessions. For two telephone counselors/facilitators involved in ongoing group work, a monthly teleconference with a supervisor is appropriate. For experienced facilitators, co-supervision after each session may be adequate, with referral to a supervisor only if an issue is difficult to resolve, or if a key juncture has been reached, as when a group's work has ended.

Training, support, and supervision should emphasize the development of the telephone counselor's intuition, since all counselors work from intuition as well as from fact, and telephone counseling is no exception to this rule. Transference and counter transference can be thought of as projections or unconscious emotional bonds that exist between two people in a therapeutic relationship (Jacoby 1984). It takes training and practice for a counselor to consciously utilize them. This is one reason why counselors who are inexperienced and lack confidence in face-to-face work may not be ideal candidates for telephone work. For example, telephone counselors must deal with silence on the part of a client in ways not immediate apparent to a beginner: It may be necessary to break a silence on the telephone that would not be broken in a face-to-face session. A ten-second silence can feel more like a minute during a telephone session. With supervision, telephone counselors can develop strategies to handle silence, such as talking with the client about what the silence feels like or what it is about, or deciding not to break a silence for a maximum of seven seconds. A silence longer than this can become a "game" of "who will give in first" and the counselor could find herself being manipulated by the client in this context. It is, of course, common for there to be silence at the start of a telephone session, while the client looks for "safe ground" to begin talking. The client will look for some verbal response from the counselor following a disclosure, as a sign of encouragement or acceptance. A counselor's ability to handle silence intuitively is closely related to her ability to assess a client's needs.

Assessment skills are a key component of successful telephone counseling. Research conducted in the early 1990s (McLennan et al.) demonstrates that a large gap can exist between counselors' and clients' perceptions of how accurately the practitioner assesses callers' problems. The studies asked clients to rate their counselor's ability to accurately detect any underlying issues as well as the overt presenting problem. The counselors, in turn, were asked to pinpoint their client's problems, to explain what was behind them, and to outline how the person might be helped. The counselors often rated themselves as more successful at accurately detecting the clients' concerns than the clients expressed. The differences were particularly acute where the counselors were new to telephone work. Any training of telephone training counselors must, therefore, include instruction on how telephone assessment differs from face-to-face assessment.

In addressing clients' problems, the telephone counselor should be encouraged to develop an eclectic style. Experienced telephone counselors must be flexible and possess sharp cognitive skills in order to be able to gain and maintain the clients' trust. Cognitive-behavioral, cognitive-analytic, and person centered techniques work well on the telephone. What is applicable to individual clients is also relevant to groups. It can be difficult to convince clients to participate in teleconferencing, but telephone counselors/facilitators can assist by preparing fact sheets in a question/answer format, describing how groups are constructed and run. Teleconference facilitators are generally trained to work in pairs, and groups are limited to five members, so that all the clients have a chance to speak. Sessions last for one hour and run for six to eight weeks before a review is held. The two facilitators may be in the same or different locations, but whatever the case, they should debrief immediately post-session. In particular, facilitators need training and support in helping groups to form during the first session. For example, participants can be prompted to introduce themselves by describing their immediate surroundings. Skillful facilitators will lend teleconferences structure, guiding groups as they develop their norms. Early telephone groups in the U.K. focused on people who had phobias and on people who had cancer, who were usually unable or unwilling to go to traditional self-help groups. The cancer teleconference groups were held to bring together those who had specific types of cancer or where geographical barriers existed or illness prevented travel

(Rosenfield and Urben 1994; George, 1998; Rosenfield and Smillie 1998).

The Contract

The acceptance of common guidelines in drawing up counselor-client contracts will also help to legitimize telephone counseling among mental health care professionals. As with a face-to-face approach, the telephone counselor should make her or his policies clear to clients at the outset. Any strong feelings regarding language or ethical issues such as suicide or abortion should be disclosed. If both parties are willing to work together at the end of a telephone assessment session, a contract may be negotiated. Although an agreement can be made on the spot, most counselors prefer to wait a week after this session for both parties to reflect. Some will mail a copy of the tentative contract and at the start of the first session, this can be acknowledged and, if necessary, adapted and finalized. As with face-to-face counseling, the telephone counseling contract should include the timing and duration of sessions. Fee negotiation and method of payment, where the counselor and client will be during sessions, and how the client's privacy will be protected must also be outlined. For example, if the counselor must call the client outside of the usual, agreed upon times, what should the counselor say if someone other than the client answers the phone? Or, what message should the counselor leave on an answering machine? If the counselor is working with an adolescent or a referral from a medical or police source, what, if anything, might necessitate disclosure to a third party, and would the client's permission be sought first? At what point should the counselor intervene when a client talks of suicide? And how? How should the counselor handle note taking during telephone sessions, to both facilitate the conversation and ensure confidentiality? Will the counselor and client both takes notes? During or after the session? Who will have access to them? All of these questions should be considered during the contract negotiation process. With open ended telephone counseling, an initial contract commonly specifies six hour-long sessions to be held on a weekly basis, followed by a review session intended for both parties to consider if the work is effective and should continue further.

The Technology

Best practices in terms of the technology used in telephone counseling point to land lines as the best in terms of both sound quality and privacy. However, exciting developments are on the horizon, opening up avenues for future research.

RECOMMENDATIONS FOR FUTURE RESEARCH

Technology

Rapid development in the realm of communications technology has opened up new avenues to counselors who are experimenting with media. For example:

- The Internet is an increasingly popular medium for counseling. It is possible to set up "net meetings" between counselor and client in "real time," which is similar to teleconferencing and better than e-mail, which involves delays in transmission.
- Text phones can be used by counselors working with deaf clients. This medium requires the counselor to be familiar with the language of text phone users.

Effectiveness

Anecdotally, when practitioners who have experience with both face-to-face and telephone counseling are asked to compare their effectiveness, they describe telephone counseling as more intense, saying that clients reach disclosure and openness more quickly via the telephone than via face-to-face sessions. Waters and Finn (1995) make reference to this, but the scope for research into this area is great. It is easy to speculate that the anonymity the telephone affords the client would be a factor in making it safer for the client to disclose more quickly. This principle certainly exists in telephone hotline scenarios, where most calls are "one offs" and training and operating practices are focused on this (Telephone Helplines Association 1999). In teleconferencing, for example, clients tend to open up at around the week three session. Cancer groups were most effective at discussing more intimate issues when they were single gender groups. For other groups, the topic of the group can make a single gender more comfortable than mixed gender, participants preferring to talk about sexual problems with their own gender, for example.

CONCLUSION

Telephone counseling is a growing discipline and one for which there is a lack of effective, specialized training and supervision amongst professional counselors. All too frequently it is a single lecture as part of a training course for face to face counselors. In fact, it requires specific training for counselors who already have some experience (and confidence) in face to face work. The increased use of technology, such as the growth of therapeutic work by e-mail, should have a positive impact on telephone counseling since both challenge pre-existing attitudes and assumptions about the viability and efficacy of counseling in non-visual contexts.

REFERENCES

George, D.S. (1998) "Teleconferencing support: Women with secondary breast cancer." *International Journal of Palliative Nursing 4*(3):115-119.

Jacoby, Mario (1984) "The Analytic Encounter–transference and the human relationship." Toronto: Inner City Books.

McCarthy, Patricia R. and Reese, Robin G. (1990) "Crisis intervener perceptions of the stressfulness of caller problems." Paper delivered at the Annual Convention of the American Psychological Association, August.

McLennan, J. (1990) "Client's perceptions of counsellors: A brief measure for use in counselor research, evaluation and training." *Australian Psychologist, 25*:133-44

McLennan, J., Culkin, K. and Courtney, P. (1994) "Telephone counsellors' conceptualizing abilities and counseling skills." *British Journal of Guidance and Counseling, 22*(2): 183-96.

McLeod, J. (1993) "An introduction to counselling." Buckingham: Open University Press.

McLeod, J. (1994) "Doing counselling research." London: Sage.

Rosenfield, M. (1997) "Counselling by Telephone." London: Sage.

Rosenfield, M. and Smillie, E. (1998) "Group Counselling by Telephone." *British Journal of Guidance and Counseling 26*(1): 11-19.

Rosenfield, M. and Urben, L. (1994) "Running a telephone cancer support group–evaluation of a short-term project." London: Cancerlink.

Telephone Helplines Association (1999) "Guidelines for Good Practice." Third Edition, London: Telephone Helplines Association.

Videoconferencing in Telepsychiatry

Marja-Leena Mielonen
Arto Ohinmaa
Juha Moring
Matti Isohanni

SUMMARY. Interactive videoconferencing is an easy, fast, and relatively inexpensive method of providing psychiatric services over long distances. The experiences of telepsychiatry practitioners have been promising in Finland, Norway, the United Kingdom, the USA, Canada, and Australia.

The first practical telepsychiatry experiments in Finland were carried out at the Department of Psychiatry of the University of Oulu, where videoconferencing has been used for family therapy, psychiatric supervision, consultation, patient negotiations, and teaching. During 1998, out of a total of 400 hours, 35% of the online time was used for teaching, 24% for occupational counseling, 21% for consultations and patient negotiations, and 20% for methodological development and other activities (mainly testing the connections). The costs of inpatient negotiations via teleconferencing is half those of conventional negotiations. In general, cost analyses have also shown that telepsychiatric services are economi-

Marja-Leena Mielonen, PhD, Juha Moring, MD, and Matti Isohanni, MD, PhD, are affiliated with the Department of Psychiatry, Oulu University Hospital, Finland.

Arto Ohinmaa, PhD, is affiliated with the Department of Economics, University of Oulu, Finland.

Address correspondence to: Marja-Leena Mielonen, Department of Psychiatry, Oulu University Hospital, Peltolantie 5, 90210 Oulu, Finland (E-mail: marjaleena.mielonen@ppshp.fi).

[Haworth co-indexing entry note]: "Videoconferencing in Telepsychiatry." Mielonen et al. Co-published simultaneously in *Journal of Technology in Human Services* (The Haworth Press, Inc.) Vol. 20, No. 1/2, 2002, pp. 183-199; and: *Human Services Technology: Innovations in Practice and Education* (ed: Hy Resnick, and Phoebe Sade Anderson) The Haworth Press, Inc., 2002, pp. 183-199. Single or multiple copies of this article are available for a fee from The Haworth Document Delivery Service [1-800-HAWORTH, 9:00 a.m. - 5:00 p.m. (EST). E-mail address: getinfo@haworthpressinc.com].

cally cost-effective in most European countries and in Australia, where a relatively small number of connections exists, while in the USA and Canada, high telecommunications costs make telemedicine more prohibitive compared to conventional care.

KEYWORDS. Psychiatry, mental illness, telepsychiatry, videoconferencing

INTRODUCTION

The first experiments in telepsychiatry were made as early as 1959 (Benshoter et al. 1965, Wittson & Benshoter 1972), and the studies published up until now have mostly been research reports of pilot studies. The countries to explore telepsychiatry early on were the USA (Preston et al. 1992), Canada (Dongier et al. 1986), England (McLaren et al. 1995), Australia (Yellowlees 1996), Norway (Pedersen & Harviksen 1994), and Finland (Mielonen et al. 1998). What all these countries have in common is that long distances separate their communities, and that they envision telemedicine as one possible way to bring psychiatric services to remote primary health care centers. In this article, the main aspects of the technology of clinical applications and costs of telemedicine will be described, with special reference to telepsychiatry. In Finland and other western countries, the need for networking between primary and secondary care and the other fields of social and health care services has increased. Videoconferencing may provide an easy and inexpensive way to network between authorities located at remote sites or in different parts of the country.

WHAT ARE TELEMEDICINE, TELEPSYCHIATRY, AND VIDEOCONFERENCING?

Stanberry (1998) defined the etymology of the basic concept of telemedicine in the following way: "Telemedicine," a phrase first coined in the 1970s by Thomas Bird, refers to health care delivery whereby physicians examine distant patients through the use of telecommunications technology. The term derives from the Greek, "tele," meaning "at a distance," and the current word, "medicine," which itself derives from the Latin, "mederi," meaning "healing."

Telepsychiatry consists of psychiatric communication at a distance, normally over a network, enabling at least two parties to be in real-time audiovisual contact. It is used for clinical negotiations with people in remote areas instead of conventional, face-to-face negotiations at the ward. A good example is patient care planning negotiations, which can be arranged via videoconferencing between the psychiatric primary staff and the patient's relatives. About three to ten people at a time usually participate in patient care planning negotiations.

The central part of telepsychiatry is the videoconference. Videoconferencing is an audiovisual real-time connection between two or more participants via multi-point connection in the gateway. One of the advantages of using videoconferencing is that expert knowledge can be obtained when and where it is needed. In this way, it is possible to improve the regional distribution of psychiatric services. Another possibility is to improve the treatment and consultations provided by medical staff through supervision and teaching at a distance. A third goal is to save resources and to reduce costs.

HISTORICAL DEVELOPMENT OF VIDEOCONFERENCING

The use of videoconferencing in medicine began in the 1950s. The experiments conducted in Nebraska in 1959 were among the first to be published. Experimentation continued in different parts of Canada and the USA. Before videoconferencing equipment became generally available, a picture telephone was developed in the USA in 1964. It was first used experimentally to transmit video within a hospital, and for surveillance.

In the 1990s, the cost of videoconferencing decreased substantially, owing to the development of low-cost, PC-based equipment and reductions in the cost of telecommunication. At the same time, the quality of both sound and picture improved. Videoconferencing has subsequently been employed successfully for many purposes in telepsychiatry.

With videoconferencing equipment, contact between distant, hard-to-reach, and peripheral health care centers and the expert consultation available in large central hospitals has been facilitated, aiding in the treatment of many serious illnesses. The next generation of videoconferencing equipment may be desktop PC equipment linked by ISDN or, increasingly, the Internet. These technologies, together with other innovations, will reduce costs and may increase the use of videoconferencing.

VIDEOCONFERENCING IN PSYCHIATRY

Reports of the experimental use of interactive videoconferencing systems in psychiatric treatment have been published since the beginning of the 1960s, but little scientific research has been conducted on this topic. In the first telepsychiatry reports published in the 1950s, the suitability of video techniques for consultations and clinical teaching was described (Wittson & Benshoter 1977). Videoconferences have been in experimental use for a long time for emergency examination and treatment, and especially for follow-up in the USA, Australia, and New Zealand (Dwyer 1973, Preston 1995, Yellowlees 1992).

In Australia, Yellowlees and Hemming (1992) and co-workers used videoconferencing in their extensive psychiatric research and development project on the learning of new working practices by medical staff, patients, and local cooperative networks. The results indicated, for example, that the patients were less afraid of their doctor in videoconferencing than in conventional, face-to-face consultation. The concept of being on television is not foreign to patients. The staff undergoing training found that their isolation decreased. In order to develop successful telemedicine systems, clinical leaders are needed to champion the systems, to demonstrate their use, and to encourage other clinicians to use them.

Vinikoor and Perrault (1980) studied the suitability of videoconferencing for the follow-up care of alcoholics in the USA. Information was collected on the experiences of the patients, who participated in the experiment for a month. Forty of the 42 patients (95%) found the situation easier than a traditional meeting in a hospital, and 23 (55%) wished to continue their treatment through videoconferencing.

Dongier et al. (1986) experimented in Canada with different psychiatric patient groups using both videoconferencing interviews and face-to-face interviews. The assessments given by the patients on these two interviewing techniques differed only slightly from each other. Nor did the assessments given by the consultants on the disadvantages and results of the different interview techniques differ from each other. Based on previous studies, the researchers recommended further development of the use of videoconferencing in admission and emergency consultations. In the researchers' opinion, videoconferencing was a limited approach, but one which aided staff development.

McLaren et al. (1995) studied the use of videoconferencing in an acute intensive-care unit of a psychiatric clinic in a London hospital. They used a qualitative method to examine the interaction between patients and staff. There were 105 clinical interactions over four months. The study demonstrated the potential of interactive television to support many of the communication tasks necessary in a dispersed psychiatric service and of telepsychiatry to become a major method of service provision. Although the researchers had certain reservations, the technology was deemed to have the capacity to develop in such a way as to improve user attitudes towards videoconferencing.

Many authors see telepsychiatry as an innovation in clinical practice, although its origin can be traced back 40 years. The videoconferencing technique is well known in psychiatry, but the system whereby it is used has been studied very little. The development of telepsychiatry should be seen as a process that will continue. The improvement of the quality of psychiatric care and the requirement to keep the costs low have led to experimentation with information and communication technologies.

OUR PRACTICAL AND CLINICAL EXPERIENCES

Videoconferencing in Finland

Finland is the most sparsely populated country in northern Europe. The population of northern Finland is about 730,000. The Oulu University Hospital provides services to the whole region. The distance to Utsjoki, which is the most remote municipality of the catchment area, is over 600 km (see Figure 1). The long distances and high travel costs were the most important reasons for starting our telemedicine project. The aims of the project were to provide expert assistance quickly, to reduce travel expenses, and to produce innovations for the social and health care multidisciplinary networks and educational service at a low cost. During five years, the usability of telepsychiatry has been generalized in our networks to cover the entire country.

The Northern Ostrobothnia Hospital District has three hospitals, Oulu University Hospital, Oulaskangas Hospital, and Visala Hospital, which are responsible for the specialized medical care of a population of approximately 370,000 and for the demanding specialized medical

FIGURE 1. Telepsychiatric Connections Between Department of Psychiatry in Oulu University Hospital and Its Partners.

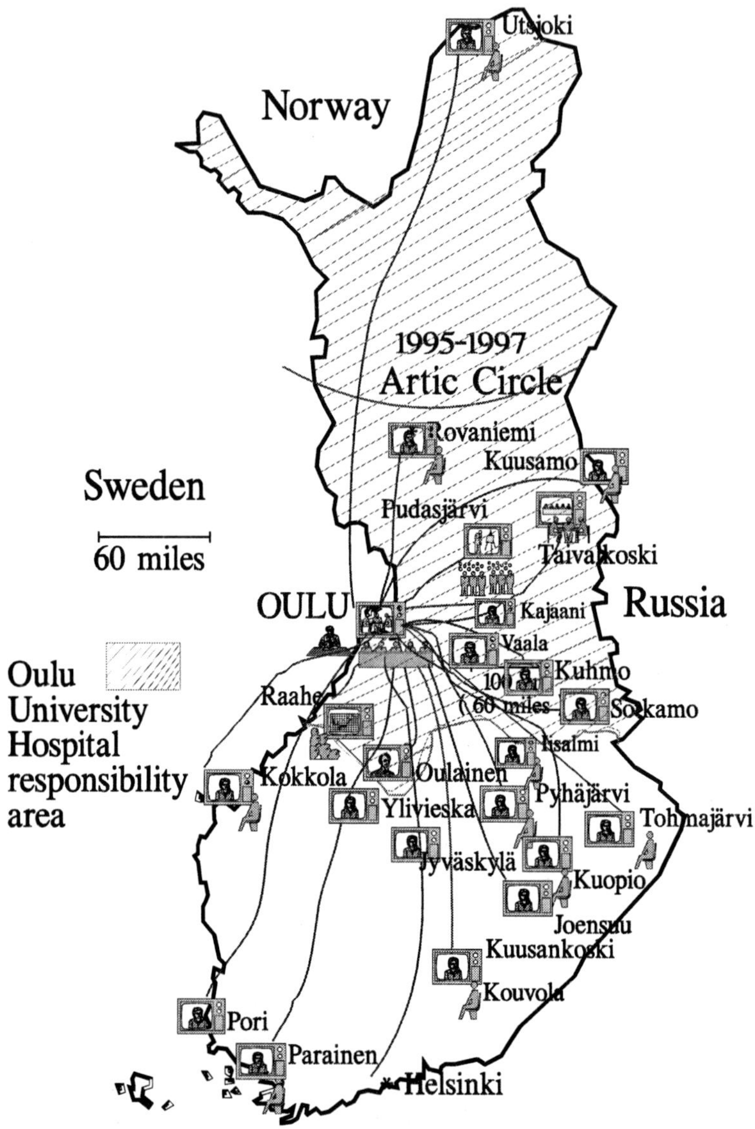

treatment of a population of 720,000, covering the whole of northern Finland (Figure 1).

The first clinical connections in telepsychiatry (videoconferences) were made to the Kuusamo primary care center in 1995, after which cooperation via telepsychiatry was started with several primary care centers in northern Finland (Mielonen et al. 1996). Videoconferencing is used in numerous psychiatric services. At the Department of Psychiatry in the Oulu University Hospital, it has been used for patient care planning negotiations, family therapy, counseling, consultation, and teaching. During this time, most patients have been satisfied with their "visits" via a video connection (Mielonen et al. 1998). In 1996, a large assessment study of telemedicine was started at the University Hospital in Oulu with financial support from the Finnish Office for Health Care Technology Assessment (FinOHTA). The project developed a technology assessment model for five specialties, including telepsychiatry (Ohinmaa, Reponen et al. 1997).

Patient and Staff Reactions to Videoconferencing

During 1998, out of a total of 400 hours, 35% of the online time was used for teaching, 24% for occupational supervision, 21% for consultations and patient negotiations, and 20% for training and other activities (mainly testing the connections). The overall number of consultations had not increased in this region, but a greater proportion of the consultations and discussions were done by videoconferencing. In Northern Ostrobothnia, the demand for psychiatric community services has increased markedly at the expense of in-hospital treatment. The supervision and training that the health care staff needed were mostly obtained from Oulu. Primary care workers have been interested in obtaining these services via videoconferencing. The availability of videoconferencing may also increase the use of consultation services, but we do not yet know whether this will happen.

The experiences in patient care have been positive. The patients and their families have been less negative about videoconferencing than expected. The attitudes of the staff have become more positive along with the increase in participation and user experience. The workers who carried out family therapy sessions and supervision pointed out, among other things, that the participants have to take turns to speak in a videoconference and cannot speak simultaneously, as is normal in a family session. This helps to structure the interaction. Participants in family therapy and supervision generally want to continue with videoconferences.

It is important to identify the possible shortcomings of videoconferencing that may affect treatment. Usual physical contact is lacking in a videoconference, such as shaking hands and touching. It is not possible to sense smell, for example. The significance of these factors has not been properly evaluated yet.

In patient work, the participants in a videoconference should meet each other beforehand. At the beginning of the videoconference, the content of the meeting should be explained, especially to first-time patients and relatives. The doctor or other specialist always needs to assess the suitability, acceptability, and legality of the decisions concerning a patient reached via videoconferencing.

The treatment sessions carried out by videoconferencing are entered in the patients' case records. Written consent for treatment is recommended. The current Finnish legislation does not recognize the use of videoconference systems in treatment. Legally, videoconferencing is equated to conventional telephone consultation, and the legal responsibility is therefore at the site where the patient is. Other legal questions abound, such as, can we equate a videoconference with a face-to-face consultation? For example, how does one estimate the patient's suicide risk on the basis of a videoconference, if one must settle the (legal) responsibility issues? Cases have been reported from Australia in which a specialist working through telepsychiatry has, under the requirements of a mental health act, performed an assessment of a patient who has been confirmed to be mentally ill by a magistrate. The personnel, patient, relatives, and other social and health care staff who had participated in videoconferences were given a user survey questionnaire after the sessions. The participants were satisfied with the quality of the audio and video, and with the general quality of the videoconferencing interaction. The participants were seldom unhappy after videoconference negotiations. Technically, the connections were successfully made every time.

Quality Treatment and Savings Offered by Videoconferencing

The price range of the videoconferencing equipment available in Finland is wide. In 1999, the prices varied within 15,000-60,0000 euros (1 euro = 1.3 US$). Depending on the number of ISDN lines, the installation costs were about 300-350 euros per ISDN line. The lease for one ISDN line was about 20 euros per month. The cost of a videoconference was six times the cost of a telephone call. The lease for the gateway needed for a multi-point conference (i.e., a conference connecting more than two sites) varied (1-3 ISDN) from 40 to 60 euros per site when it was used for district or domestic calls. In practice, videoconferencing required an initial investment of about 17,000 euros. In the Oulu University Hospital's Department of Psychiatry, the cost of the PC-based videoconferencing equipment and ISDN lines was approximately 15,000 euros. The health care centers used similar equipment.

If a doctor from a health center in Kuusamo travels to a psychiatric meeting in the Oulu University Hospital (Figure 1), the journey takes an entire working day. For this doctor, therefore, the cost of a meeting lasting for one and a half hours is about 300 euros. A comparison of the traveling and teleconferencing alternatives shows that the videoconference is economically feasible between Kuusamo and Oulu. This difference is already obvious after a relatively small number of meetings (25-30) per year, assuming that 30% of the transmissions from the Department of Psychiatry and 60% of those from the health center are between these sites. However, efficient use of the videoconferencing equipment lowers the fixed costs per transmission, and then the only significant cost of telepsychiatry in videoconferencing is the salary costs of the participants. In Canada and the USA, ISDN lines are more expensive than in most European countries and Australia. For example, the annual rent for a single ISDN line may be about $60,0000 in the USA (Werner & Anderson 1998) and the rent for three ISDN lines about C$54,000 in Canada. The variation in the cost of other videoconferencing equipment is not so great. The significant differences in the costs of telecommunication lines point to why telepsychiatry can be cost saving in Europe and economically almost unfeasible in some other areas (USA and Canada). Because of the expense of ISDN lines, Internet technology is frequently used to transmit videoconferences in the USA.

Telepsychiatry can be used for clinical negotiations with people in remote areas instead of the conventional face-to-face negotiations at the ward. At the Department of Psychiatry, Oulu University Hospital, patient care planning negotiations are arranged with the psychiatric personnel of the primary care units and the relatives in the municipality. The aim of the study was to assess the feasibility and costs of videoconferencing (see appendix).

The data were collected by questionnaires presented to the medical staff, relatives, and patients after patient care planning, either through videoconferencing or in a conventional negotiation. The videoconferencing data included 97 staff members from psychiatric wards and primary care, 14 patients and 13 relatives. Of the 47 conventional negotiation respondents, 29 were staff, nine patients, and nine relatives.

The cost of videoconferencing was half of the cost of conventional negotiations. Over half of the primary care staff would have been unable to participate in conventional negotiations at a psychiatric ward due to the long distances. The most important reason for the primary care personnel to arrange the negotiation by videoconferencing was financial. Of the respondents, 90% were satisfied with the quality of the communication via videoconferencing. Videoconferencing can improve the quality of psychiatric care and increase co-operation between primary and secondary care units.

Technology Used for Videoconferencing

In a videoconference, the signals for image and sound are commonly transmitted along ISDN lines between the conference sites. The video is digitized and compressed before transmission to reduce the bandwidth (i.e., the number or capacity of lines) required. The equipment necessary for transmitting the image and sound is a codec (compression-decompression unit), which compresses and digitizes the video signal. The spatial resolution and frame rate of the image and the quality of the sound are all-important factors in telemedicine. The equipment consists of a video-codec, a controllable camera and audio unit, a control unit, a microphone, a monitor, and a device to prevent echo. The ISDN lines allow conferences to take place between two or more participants. It is also possible to connect a second camera if, in the conference, it is desirable to have an overview of the room or a close-up of the doctor, the patient, a part of the body, or a document. The ISDN network covers the whole of Finland, and this digital communication medium allows for the transmission of images between all municipalities. We have used commercial videoconferencing equipment (Videra, VCS H.320) connected by one to three ISDN lines. Most connections with the Videra equipment have used three ISDN lines (i.e., 384 kbit/s), but the connections with the equipment of other manufacturers have used mainly one or two lines (i.e., 128 or 256 kbit/s). In our system, all the other health care centers used Videra equipment except that at Utsjoki, where schools have been made with Philips or PictureTel equipment. High-quality connections require at least three ISDN, but the ATM allows a wider bandwidth and otherwise even better quality sound and image transmission.

The preparation of the room, the patient and the psychiatrist is important. The room should have adequate lighting and be as soundproof as possible. We have a background of light-blue walls with curtains. In the videoconference, the quality of image and sound was found to be considerably better with three ISDN lines than with one. Most participants found the options of an adjustable camera, zooming, and the possibility of switching the image between pre-set camera positions to be important. In addition, people appreciated the remote control and being able to see the small "outgoing" screen. In general, the staff became accustomed to the use of the conference communication guidance in discussions and has, at the same time, developed good command of the control devices and especially the camera, which was found to improve the progress and fluency of the conference.

Many detailed corrections have been made to the communication and technical devices. We believe that the technical realization of videoconferencing may, in the future, take place without auxiliary personnel. The equipment can be moved to new surroundings without a new telephone extension by using cables, additional cameras, and microphones. For example, it will be possible to connect the equipment from a videoconference room to a video projector situated in a lecture hall and to hold the meeting there, so that one can follow the discussion in both places. On the basis of our experiences, the technical requirements may be summarized in Table 1.

STAFF TRAINING

We always assess the use of videoconferencing in psychiatry from the point of view of different user parties, focusing on questions of operation, productivity, and acceptability, as well as effectiveness. In our experience, when videoconferencing is started, it is necessary to provide staff with both written instructions and training. The goal is to make each professional able to act independently in an online situation. Beginners make many mistakes but acquire skills with experience. The participants' practice with videoconferencing increases the likelihood of success. Each situation should be planned beforehand, and the special features possibly involved should be borne in mind.

TABLE 1. Practical Requirements in Videoconferencing

- A special videoconference room or other space should be provided.
- The sound quality is important; picture and sound must be integrated.
- A clear picture is important; in practice, three ISDN lines (i.e., 384 kbit/s) are necessary.
- A zoom function on the camera is recommended.
- The ability to control the camera is required at both ends.
- A document camera is necessary to show text or figures, or a PC can be used for slide shows, which is especially important for teaching purposes.

Preparing for a Videoconference

It is important to highlight the basic elements that improve the quality of videoconferencing. Using a checklist, health care staff can avoid making mistakes with technical situations, consultation, therapy, and healing (see Table 2).

User training will be necessary for staff, because videoconferencing is a fairly demanding technique. People who only use the equipment occasionally tend to forget the instructions quickly. The equipment should also be tested well before the beginning of the conference. Communication and interaction via videoconferencing involve certain limitations, which is why it is important to give attention to nonverbal communication and interaction.

Communication Skills Necessary for Videoconferencing

The videoconference consists of many different key points that are often forgotten (see Table 3). Verbal and nonverbal communications are both very important, but staff should keep in mind that most communication is nonverbal. The patient or some other partner may send practitioners a hidden message, and it is therefore important to hone skills in this area.

The Staff Viewpoint: Strengths and Limitations of Videoconferencing

Videoconferencing is one method of communication with patients and one way to provide mental health services. If the videoconferencing connection is bad, it will project a poor image of practitioners' organization and skills. Table 4 shows the strengths and problems of videoconferencing from the viewpoint of staff members.

TABLE 2. Checklist for a Videoconference

- Send the invitations to attend the videoconference in time
- Be personally interested
- Prepare an implementation plan
- Have somebody chair the group discussion
- Introduce the participants
- Ask people to take turns speaking

TABLE 3. Nonverbal Communication and Interaction

- Wear light colored, not dark, clothing.
- Look at the camera.
- Greet the viewers.
- Tell the viewers what is going to happen: Communicate the structure of the session.

TABLE 4. Strengths and Limitations of Videoconferencing

Strengths	Problems/Limitations
Saves time and travel costs	Time may still not be used wisely
A quick way to get expert help	Dependence on the availability of communication lines
Transfer of information instead of patients	Need to create new operating routines
More versatile information sharing than over the telephone	People largely unaware of telepsychiatric services
Inspires people to be innovative	Rapid technological development may discourage innovation
New technologies facilitate work	High acquisition costs of technology prohibit use
Improves the quality of psychiatric services	User interface is not yet user friendly
A seamless chain of treatment and services	Scarcity of telemedical evidence
Networked and multiprofessional cooperation	Fears and prejudices may discourage cooperation
Development of communication methods among the staff	Staff may experience stress of change
Facilitates contacts with colleagues working in health care centers	Requires planning and preparation
Reduces patients' fears more quickly due to promptness of service	Distance work may detract from social relations inherent in normal work
Better than no treatment	Excessive expectations may be applied to videoconferencing
Multiple-point negotiations	Problems with patients' privacy and information protection

CONCLUSION

Oulu was the first site in Finland to make extensive use of videoconferencing for psychiatric treatment, supervision, and consultation. Although our experience extends only over five years, this experimentation with videoconferencing has confirmed its suitability for psychiatric work. Videoconferencing offers much more information to the participants than does a telephone conference, and it is suitable for interactive communication of various kinds. Our rough cost estimates have also shown that videoconferencing with PC-based equipment is economical in telepsychiatry between primary and special-care units, even with a relatively low level of utilization (about once every two weeks), when the distances are long and the costs of the loss of working time are high. Similar savings have also been reported in Australia.

In normal clinical practice, the need to consult experts in psychiatry may arise suddenly. In a videoconference, the patient and the family have access to expert help and can easily participate in the consultation at the same time. Financial savings in equipment and telecommunication costs, as well as in new ways of working, may be substantial as telepsychiatry becomes more common.

Municipalities in Finland are very interested in developing their health care services by investing in telemedicine equipment, the goal being to improve health care and reduce costs. Telemedicine is considered part of the overall health care process. Since videoconferencing equipment is still relatively new and expensive, the assessment of modern technology has become more and more important in medicine. Telepsychiatry is one of the four fields of telemedicine in Oulu being assessed in a technology assessment study. The other fields are surgery, opthamology, and radiology. This study is supported by FinOHTA (Finnish Office for Health Care Technology Assessment) and aims to measure the cost effectiveness of videoconferences in psychiatry.

REFERENCES

Benshoter, R.A., Wittson, C.L. & Ingham, C.G. (1965). Teaching and consultation by television. *Hospital and Community Psychiatry, 16*, 99-100.

Dongier, M., Tempier, R. & Lalinec-Michaud, M. et al. (1986). Telepsychiatry: Psychiatric consultation through two-way television: A controlled study. *Canadian Journal of Psychiatry, 31*, 32-34.

Dwyer, T.F. (1973). Telepsychiatry: Psychiatric consultation by interactive television. *American Journal of Psychiatry, 130,* 865-869.

McLaren, P., Ball, C.J., Summerfield, A.B., Watson, J. & Lipsedge, M. (1995). An evaluation of the use of interactive television in an acute psychiatry service. *Journal of Telemedicine and Telecare, 1*, 79-85.

Mielonen, M.L., Ohinmaa, A., Morning, J. & Isohanni, M. (1998). The use of videoconferencing for telepsychiatry in Finland. *Journal of Telemedicine and Telecare, 4*, 125-131.

Ohinmaa, A., Reponen, J. & Working Group. (1997). A model for the assessment of telemedicine and a plan for testing of the model within five specialties. *FinOHTA Report, 5*. Helsinki.

Preston, J., Brown, F.W. & Hartley, B. (1992). Using telemedicine to improve health care in distant areas. *Hospital and Community Psychiatry, 43*, 25-32.

Stanberry, B. (1998). The legal and ethical aspects of telemedicine. In Richard Wootton (Ed.). *Research Associate & Associate Lecture Seafarers International Research Centre*. Cardiff University, UK: RSM Press.

Trott, P., & Blignault, I. (1998). Cost evaluation of a telepsychiatry service in northern Queensland. *Journal of Telemedicine and Telecare, 4*(1), 66-68.

Werner, A., & Anderson, L.E. (1998). Rural telepsychiatry is economically unsupportable: The concorde crashes in a cornfield. *Psychiatric Services, 49*(10), 1287-1290.

Yellowlees, P. (1997). The use of telemedicine to perform psychiatric assessments under the Mental Health Act. *Journal of Telemedicine and Telecare, 3*, 224-226.

APPENDIX

The following is a model of the questionnaire given to study participants.

Kindly answer the following background questions by writing your answer on the line or circling one alternative reply to each question.

1. Date and time of the videoconference: __________1997, at __________.
2. Sex: 1 male 2 female
3. How old are you now? ________Years.
4. Where are you employed?
   1 in the Clinic of Psychiatry
   2 in a health center
   3 elsewhere
5. In what municipality are you employed? ________________________.
6. What is your current job?
   1 doctor or psychologist
   2 nurse or therapist
   3 other, what: ______________
7. What is your basic education?
   1 primary school or less
   2 junior secondary school
   3 senior secondary school
8. What is your professional education?
   1 no professional education
   2 one or more professional courses
   3 lower post secondary degree (e.g., commercial school)
   4 higher post secondary degree (e.g., technical college)
   5 academic degree

9. Have you participated in a videoconference before?
    1 No
    2 Yes
10. According to your own estimate, how many hours did you use for the videoconference, including traveling time?
    ________ Hours
11. If this had been an ordinary meeting in the Clinic of Psychiatry in Oulu, would you have been able to attend?
    1 No
    2 Yes
12. If you need to participate in another meeting, how would you like it to be arranged?
    1 as a videoconference
    2 as a normal meeting in the Clinic of Psychiatry in Oulu
13. If you chose videoconference in the above item, was your choice affected by the following factors?

	No	Yes
a. saving of time	1	2
b. saving of costs	1	2
c. less need to travel	1	2
d. difficulty to come to OYS	1	2
e. less need to make arrangements	1	2
f. other reasons		

14. If you chose a normal meeting in Oulu Clinic of Psychiatry in item 12, what were the reasons for your choice: ____

____

15. Compared to a conventional therapy meeting, how would you describe the therapy meeting (or other meeting) arranged as a videoconference?
    1 It was better than a conventional therapy meeting.
    2 It was similar to a conventional therapy meeting.
    3 It was poorer than a conventional therapy meeting.
    4 It was much poorer than a conventional therapy meeting.

Could you also give your opinion about how successful you found this meeting. Kindly circle the most suitable reply to each of the following questions. The reply alternatives are:

1 = very good / very well
2 = good / well
3 = moderate / moderately
4 = poor / poorly
5 = very poor / very poorly
6 = I cannot say, or the question is not relevant.

Traveling to the meeting:
How well did you find time for the meeting?
How well were you able to make the traveling arrangements?

Contents of the meeting and interpersonal interaction:
How was the purpose of the conference explained to you? How was the progress of the conference ensured?

How well were you able to express your own views?
How well were the participants able to cooperate?

Outcome of the meeting:
How useful did you find this meeting?
How content were you with the outcome?

Meeting room:
How well was the meeting room suited to this purpose?
How well were peace and lack of disturbance attained?

Also evaluate the following four points:
How well were you able to follow the speech of the persons on the screen?
What was image quality like?
How well were people able to use the video equipment?
How would you describe the technical quality of the videoconference?

Write here any other thoughts or ideas that you may have about the videoconference:

Thank you for answering!

Applying Group Support Systems in Social Work Education and Practice

L. Floyd Lewis
Joseph E. Garcia
Ann L. Hallock

SUMMARY. This article describes an electronic tool or process called *Meeting Works*™, which supports and arguably improves human service staff meetings. *Meeting Works*™ has been shown to be effective with action planning, focus groups, project planning, quality initiatives, and a number of other activities associated with the human services. *[Article copies available for a fee from The Haworth Document Delivery Service: 1-800-HAWORTH. E-mail address: <getinfo@haworthpressinc.com> Website: <http://www.HaworthPress.com> © 2002 by The Haworth Press, Inc. All rights reserved.]*

KEYWORDS. Meetings, staff meetings, focus groups, project planning

---

L. Floyd Lewis, PhD, is Professor of Information Systems, and Joseph E. Garcia, PhD, is Professor of Management, College of Business & Economics, Western Washington University.

Ann L. Hallock, ACSW, is affiliated with the Student Health Center, Western Washington University.

[Haworth co-indexing entry note]: "Applying Group Support Systems in Social Work Education and Practice." Lewis, L. Floyd, Joseph E. Garcia, and Ann L. Hallock. Co-published simultaneously in *Journal of Technology in Human Services* (The Haworth Press, Inc.) Vol. 20, No. 1/2, 2002, pp. 201-225; and: *Human Services Technology: Innovations in Practice and Education* (ed: Hy Resnick, and Phoebe Sade Anderson) The Haworth Press, Inc., 2002, pp. 201-225. Single or multiple copies of this article are available for a fee from The Haworth Document Delivery Service [1-800-HAWORTH, 9:00 a.m. - 5:00 p.m. (EST). E-mail address: getinfo@haworthpressinc.com].

INTRODUCTION

This article is intended to give the reader a better understanding of a fascinating new application of information technologies for the support of task-oriented group activities such as meetings. Social workers, like professionals in many other fields, frequently conduct important work in groups. So, everyone benefits if ways are found to improve the efficiency and effectiveness of task-oriented groups. This article describes Group Support Systems (GSS), which have been created in an attempt to use information technologies to improve task-oriented group activities. In this discussion of GSS software, the focus will shift from a general concern with GSS to a specific focus on a representative GSS product: *MeetingWorks*™.

Growing Importance of Group Activities

The nature of work life in the modern organization is changing. Management structures are flattening, with fewer levels and greater autonomy for workers on the lower levels. Problems are becoming more complex, and there is less time to solve them. Increasingly, new constituents are demanding to be involved in the decisionmaking process, and there is a reduced willingness to simply defer to authority. As a result, many organizations are depending more on workgroups and teams to make decisions, solve problems, and carry out the basic activities necessary to meet organizational goals. Some experts believe workgroups are a fundamental part of an emerging organizational structure that will become dominant in the 21st century (Orsburn, Moran, Musselwhite, & Zenger, 1990). For example, Peters (1988, p. 297) advises that "the self-managing team should become the basic organizational building block." As teams and groups become more important, meetings will become even more frequent.

Common Problems in Meetings

Groups have encountered many well-documented difficulties in trying to have people work together to solve problems and make decisions. For example, there may be an overemphasis on social-emotional rather than task activities (Delbecq, Van de Ven, & Gustafson, 1975). Another difficulty occurs when groups fail to adequately define a problem before rushing to judgment (Maier & Hoffman, 1960). It is not uncommon for meeting participants to feel pressures for conformity that can reduce creativity and result in "group-think" (Chung & Ferris, 1971; Janis, 1981). Latane, Williams and Harkins (1979) found that some participants feel they don't have to contribute to the work of a group, and they will engage in "social loafing," where they let the other members do the hard work. Mosvick and Nelson (1987) identified even more problems reported with typical meetings, such as:

- Getting off the subject
- Too lengthy
- Inconclusive
- Starting late
- Time wasted during meeting
- Disorganized
- No goals or agenda
- No pre-meeting orientation
- No published results or follow-up actions
- Poor or inadequate preparation
- Individuals dominate / aggrandize discussion
- Irrelevance of information discussed
- Not effective for making decisions
- Interruptions from within and without
- Rambling, redundant, or digressive discussion
- Ineffective leadership / lack of control

Techniques to Improve Meetings

With so many problems, it may seem surprising that anybody tries to get anything done in a group. However, there are solid reasons that organizations continue to use the group approach. One model of small group functioning based on ideas from Steiner (1972) and Shaw (1976) proposes:

Group Effectiveness = (Individual Contributions) + (Synergistic Effects)–(Process Losses)

The individual contributions are based on the skills, experience, knowledge, and judgment of each of the participants. These resources that participants bring to a problem are the same whether they are in a group or not. Synergy describes a relationship where the whole is greater than the sum of the parts. For example, a symphony orchestra is somehow more than just a collection of the individual instruments and musicians. The hope is that the effectiveness of a task-oriented group will be greater than the sum of the individual contributions. The possible synergistic effects in a group include such factors as the ability to learn from and build on each others' information and ideas, an increased level of commitment to solving the problem due to a sense of *esprit de corps,* a more objective evaluation of ideas, and so on. Process losses include the kinds of problems discussed in the preceding section, and other factors such as competition for air time, production blocking, increased costs of communication and coordination, and so on.

The evolution of Group Support Systems really depended on research and developments in three broad fields over a period of time. Behavioral Sciences have contributed much to our understanding of small group process and to the development of useful techniques for facilitating and improving the process of group problem solving and decision making. The Decision Sciences have contributed valuable knowledge about the nature and formal structure of decisions, as well as quantitative techniques for decision making. Information Systems contributed knowledge about how to support management decision making, tools and techniques for the design and development of information systems such as DSS and GSS, as well as the actual PC and network hardware. Group support systems could only be developed when there was a sufficient critical mass of knowledge in all three areas to serve as a solid foundation.

The specific GSS we will discuss, *MeetingWorks*™, began as a PhD project at the University of Louisville in the early 1980s (Lewis, 1983). It went through a process of rapid evolution as various design approaches were tried and abandoned. At Western Washington University, the authors (along with Dr. Kenneth Keleman) have worked together to improve the software for over 15 years. In 1993, the software rights were sold to a private company, Enterprise Solutions, Inc., who now distribute the software.

Typical GSS Applications

Most available GSS software is flexible and general purpose, so that it can be adapted for a wide variety of task-oriented group processes. A representative list of actual GSS applications would include:

- Action Planning
- Annual Business Meeting
- Choosing By Advantages
- Competitive Analysis
- Control Self-Assessment
- Focus Groups
- Idea Generation
- Joint Application Design
- Market Analysis
- Monthly Update Meeting
- Organizational Design
- Portfolio Review
- Process Reengineering
- Project Implementation Planning
- Project Planning
- Project Prioritization
- Quality Initiatives
- Software Development Project Reviews
- Strategic Option Analysis
- Strategic Planning
- Team Development
- Values Analysis
- Vendor / Product Selection
- Visioning

Social workers are frequently involved with meetings, often for administrative purposes. A GSS may be helpful in improving administrative meetings and helping groups increase their effectiveness. Examples of some social work tasks that might be supported by GSS include (but are not limited to): multi-disciplinary team (MDT) planning sessions in hospital settings, educational planning and placement (EPP) meetings in school settings, casework planning in community child welfare settings, and casework planning and evaluations as part of social service networks. Personnel evaluations, hiring decisions, planning and impact prioritization analysis could also be enhanced by GSS.

Untried as yet, but with the growing number of people and families familiar with computer usage, there lies the potential to develop a GSS model for family therapy. Think of the possibilities for busy families (traveling parents, reluctant teenagers, etc.) if they could join the family therapy session by adding confidential comments (when appropriate), dialog with each other, and always be included by GSS when family sessions are held. The task of identifying family problems and bringing them out in the open could be facilitated by the confidential nature of data entry within the group, as well as prioritizing family needs and tasks. GSS could also keep particular family members from dominating a session, or rambling and digressing for long periods. There are many possibilities yet to be explored in the use of this new technology for social work.

GSS are already being used by a wide variety of organizations in a wide variety of settings. Much of our own work has been in an academic setting with students and faculty, community groups, and state government agencies. The use of GSS in social work settings is still new; however; consulting firms that use *MeetingWorks*™ have worked with a variety of public and private organizations, as shown in the following list:

- Boeing
- IBM
- BP
- Weyerhaeuser
- Mitre
- Sedgwick
- Washington State Department of Agriculture
- Best Consulting
- CIBER
- National Park Service
- Microserv
- Regence BCBSO
- Casey Family Programs
- Independent consultants
- Over 50 Universities use it for teaching, research, & consulting

GSS RESEARCH RESULTS

By 1999, research in GSS was almost 20 years old, and over 200 papers had been written reporting on various aspects of GSS research. What has been learned about GSS from all this activity? The following section will review the major findings in GSS research so far. The first four variables discussed concern the *outcome* of the meeting (user satisfaction, meeting effectiveness, meeting efficiency, quality of decision); the second set of five variables concern the meeting *process* itself (equality of participation, parallel production, anonymity, structure, and group size).

User Satisfaction

The typical way that user satisfaction with GSS has been measured is by questionnaires that ask participants for their level of satisfaction with the GSS process, the outcome of the session, or overall satisfaction. Pervan (1994) has summarized the results of 37 lab and field studies that measured user satisfaction in this way. He found that the results for lab studies were quite mixed. Across the three types of satisfaction, nine out of 16 lab studies showed no difference between user satisfaction for GSS or non-GSS, while four were more positive for GSS and three were less positive. However, the results of field studies of real applications of GSS are dramatically different. Nineteen out of twenty-one field studies showed user satisfaction to be higher for GSS, and in the other two cases there was no significant difference. In no case was user satisfaction lower for GSS.

Meeting Effectiveness

Effectiveness has to do with how well the meeting meets it goal(s). Did the group actually accomplish what it set out to do? Pervan (1994) summarizes seventeen studies that measured perceived effectiveness, where sixteen studies were in the field and one in the lab. Effectiveness was measured by questionnaires, case evidence, formal interviews, informal comments, and general case observation. Of these seventeen studies, fifteen reported greater effectiveness for GSS meetings, while two showed no significant difference. No study reported lower effectiveness for GSS sessions.

Meeting Efficiency

Meeting efficiency is concerned with time and cost savings that might accrue from the use of a GSS. This has been measured by having participants estimate the cost and/or time typically required for a manual session that addressed the same problem, and then comparing it to the time and cost of the GSS session, or by measuring the perceptions of the group regarding efficiency by using a Likert scale. All ten of the studies that measured efficiency concluded that GSS groups were more efficient than non-GSS groups (Pervan, 1994).

Quality of Decision

The quality of the decision the group makes has been measured by Likert scale ratings, interviews, independent judges' assessments, and closeness to a "correct" answer. As has been true for several other variables, the results are different for field and lab studies. Of sixteen lab studies, most showed no significant difference (ten of the sixteen), while five showed GSS to result in a better decision, and one showed the manual method to result in a better decision. This is only slightly positive for the GSS approach. However, the field results are much more encouraging. In seven out of eight studies, GSS groups produced better decisions than manual groups, and in the eighth case, there was no significant difference (Pervan, 1994).

Equality of Participation

One of the supposed impacts of GSS use is that more of the participants will actually contribute to the meeting, and that it is less likely that the meeting will be dominated by a few members. This has been measured by asking participants for their perceptions of participation using questionnaires, and by actually counting the number of comments made by each participant. Of the six studies that compared GSS to manual meetings on this dimension, four reported greater equality of participation in GSS sessions, while two reported no significant difference (Pervan, 1994).

Parallel Production

One of the basic features of almost all GSS's is the ability for participants to enter information in parallel, or simultaneously through their individual PCs. A participant does not have to wait for the last speaker to finish, or for a facilitator to write the ideas on a flipchart, in order to contribute an idea. There seems to be a clear indication from several studies that this is a significant benefit from the use of a GSS (Dennis, 1991; Gallupe et al., 1990; Gallupe et al., 1991; Gallupe & Cooper, 1991). The most common result is a greater number of ideas generated, for example, in a brainstorm activity. As a side benefit, participants are assured that the ideas are worded exactly as they intend, and not as interpreted or summarized by some third party, like a facilitator.

Anonymity

Most GSS emphasize the availability of anonymity in the generation of ideas, and in the evaluation of ideas. No one knows who contributes a particular idea, and no one knows how particular participants rate ideas. The rationale for this is that anonymity is supposed to protect shy or hesitant members, and increase their willingness to contribute. It is supposed to result in participants being more candid in their evaluations, since anonymity protects them from retaliation. The usefulness of anonymity may depend on the level of trust and openness in a group, and the amount of hierarchical structure (Dennis, 1991). Peer groups may not find anonymity as important as groups where several layers of a hierarchy are present. Likewise, groups that have established a good working relationship with mutual trust may not need the anonymity feature. Some studies have found that groups using the anonymity feature are more critical and probing in their comments, which can lead to higher quality decisions (Jessup, Connolly, & Galegher, 1990; Connolly, Jessup, & Valacich, 1990).

Structure

A GSS can provide a good deal of structure to the problem solving process through the use of specific tools, techniques, and agendas or meeting agendas (Keleman, Lewis, & Garcia, 1994). Many studies have looked at the impact of providing such structure, and generally found positive effects. For example, structure has been found to improve group consensus (DeSanctis et al., 1989; Sambamurthy & DeSanctis, 1989), result in higher quality decisions (Sambamurthy & DeSanctis, 1989; Easton, Vogel & Nunamaker, 1989; Venkatesh & Wynne, 1991), and the generation of more ideas (Easton, Vogel & Nunamaker, 1989; Dennis, 1991).

Group Size

Several studies on the effects of group size seem to indicate that quite large groups (12-18 members) can successfully use GSS and that they will generate more ideas and often experience greater satisfaction than smaller groups (Dennis, Valacich, & Nunamaker, 1990; Gallupe et al.,

1991; Fellers, 1989). Interestingly, studies also seem to show that groups using GSS outperform individuals working separately in the generation of ideas (Dennis, 1991; Dennis & Valacich, 1991).

GSS FRAMEWORK

One of the best ways to guide learning in a new field is through the development of conceptual frameworks and models that provide structure to the process. Early on, DeSanctis and Gallup (1987) developed a useful framework to describe the possible types of GSS based on two dimensions: time and place. When participants interact at the same time in the same place, the type of GSS facility can be referred to as a Decision Room. The advantages of meeting face-to-face include the ability to read body language and tone of voice, easier coordination of activities, the ability to have verbal discussions when appropriate, easier to build a sense of group identity, perhaps a higher sense of commitment, among other aspects. So far, this has been the most common configuration for GSS research and applications.

If participants are meeting at the same time, but some of the members are not in the same place, it is now possible for the remote participants to link into the meeting using a *Live Internet* version of the GSS software, possibly supplemented with some form of *Video Conference*. Telephone conference calls can also be used for this purpose. Since many third party vendors are offering ever more powerful and less expensive systems for video conferencing, this may become a common form of meeting in the future. At the moment, it is generally still too technically complex (and often too expensive) to be widely used.

When participants are in the same place, but do not interact at the same time (for example, in the case of shift work in a group home), they might use a *Local GSS Network* to send messages, exchange files, and schedule projects. It is also possible to design GSS's to support group interactions in an asynchronous format. For example, a brainstorming step could be started, and participants informed that they have a set time (24 hours, for example) to enter their ideas. Participants could drop by a decision room and add their input at any time during that period. The group might need to come together for a discussion, but could be de-coupled again for an evaluation step.

If participants are separated by both time and space, the appropriate type of support might be an *Distributed Internet GSS* session. These systems allow participants to sign-in at any time from any place with a standard web browser, and take part in a GSS group process. As a participant, you can contribute ideas and evaluations at your own convenience. Reports summarizing group results can be placed on a web site for viewing by participants. While preliminary results appear positive, much work remains to be done to develop the effectiveness of this approach.

MeetingWorks™ provides support for all combinations of time and place. The Internet-Edition now supports meeting processes where participants can log into a web site at different times from different places using a standard web browser. This could be appropriate, for example, when participants are asked to contribute a list of ideas for later discussion, or to rate a set of ideas that they have previously discussed. Another new version of *MeetingWorks*™ (Connect) can be used when some participants are unable to attend a live meeting, but they may be able to connect via the Internet during the meeting. They can then contribute material, evaluate ideas, and even see the summary results of the meeting in real time using a standard web browser. Teleconferencing may be especially useful in supplementing this mode. These distributed GSS approaches are especially useful for supporting virtual teams that may be geographically dispersed. Figure 1 shows how various *MeetingWorks*™ versions can be mapped into the time/space matrix.

FACILITATION IN A GSS ENVIRONMENT

One of the ways organizations have sought to improve the process of group decision making and problem solving has been to use the services of trained group facilitators. As described by Schwarz (1994), "group facilitation is a process in which a person who is acceptable to all members of the group, substantively neutral, and has no decision-making authority intervenes to help a group improve the way it identifies and solves problems and makes decisions, in order to increase the group's effectiveness." Facilitators may be primarily concerned with helping a group effectively solve a single problem, or they may be trying to improve the group's long-term effectiveness by helping them learn to diagnose and correct their own behavior.

Importance of Facilitation for GSS

The use of a GSS does not mean that a facilitator is not needed. Indeed, it could be argued that a GSS is primarily a set of tools for helping

FIGURE 1. *MeetingWorks*™ Support for Time/Place Combinations

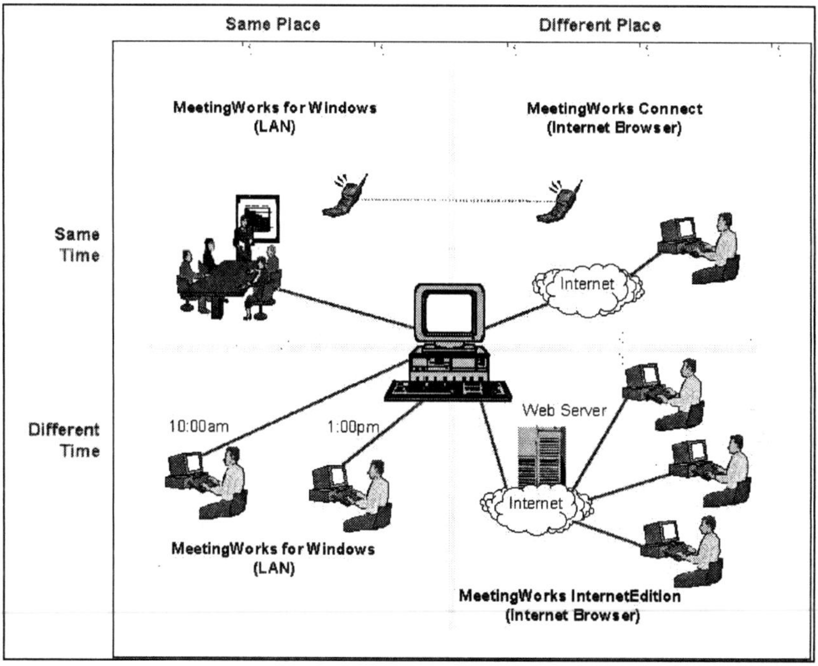

facilitators do a better job. The use of a GSS does, however, change the nature of the job a facilitator does. Some of the features built in to a GSS may replace or modify certain techniques a facilitator might use in a manual setting. Even a person experienced in facilitating manual meetings will need additional training in how to facilitate electronically-supported meetings. For example, when using a GSS tool to support idea generation, since every participant can enter ideas directly without competing with others for "air time," a facilitator does not have to worry as much about drawing out the quieter members. On the other hand, a facilitator must be more explicit about the GSS process when planning a session. This requires that facilitators be more personally disciplined about how they design meeting sessions.

Many GSS researchers are becoming convinced of the critical impact the facilitator has on a GSS meeting. Dennis, Nunamaker, and Vogel (1991) reported in an integrative study that, while *none* of the lab studies they reviewed used a process facilitator, *all* of the field cases they reviewed found a facilitator necessary. Grohowski et al. (1990) first identified facilitation as a key aspect in the success of GSS use at IBM. This was later confirmed by McGoff and Ambrose (1991) in their study of 900 IBM group sessions. They reported that "the quality of the group session is predominantly dependent on the facilitator." Bostrom and Anson (1992) have come to the same conclusion in their studies.

Facilitation Teams

Some GSS researchers and practitioners recommend using a facilitation team: one member to manage group process, and one for the technical aspects of running the hardware and software. For example, the developers of *MeetingWorks*™ recommend the use of a *chauffeur,* who is a technical facilitator versed in the details of running this particular GSS software (Lewis & Whiteley, 1992). A two-person team is not required in all situations. As group sessions becomes more complex and challenging, the utility of a team approach increases. While a single person can play the facilitator/chauffeur role in a simple session, this person can become overwhelmed in more complex settings. The relationship between the facilitator and chauffeur is itself complex and evolves over time (Whiteley & Garcia, 1996).

Special Considerations for Facilitating Distributed GSS Meetings

Distributed GSS meetings are not the same as face-to-face meetings–they have their own unique advantages and challenges. In a different time/different place meeting where all participants are dispersed, it is more important but also more difficult to communicate clearly about what is needed in each step of the process. A facilitator tries to do this with clear written instructions, but handling the inevitable questions by e-mail and phone is not as satisfactory as immediate verbal interaction in a face-to-face setting. If the group has never met face-to-face, it may be hard to provide for social interactions that can help the group develop a sense of identity and shared purpose. It may be easier for some members to "drop out" in a distributed meeting, especially if they do not feel a sense of connection. The facilitator may have to work harder to encourage participation. If the group will be using audio and/or video conferencing, the management of these additional technologies add to the complexity of the process, and may tax the ability and energy of the facilitator. Developing new techniques for facilitating distributed meetings should be a high priority in the near term. On the other hand, the psychological distance that the Internet provides may enable otherwise reticent participants to contribute to the meeting or therapy session.

GSS FACILITY DESIGN

Face-to-face GSS meetings (the decision room approach) require some sort of facility to support the meetings. While there have been quite a number of approaches tried, from quite simple and inexpensive, to rather elaborate and very costly, they tend to have several features in common.

The most popular configuration for a decision room tends to be some variation on a U shape (see Figure 2). This may be the best configuration to use when some part of the meeting will involve oral discussions, since it allows the participants to see each other. The open end of the U generally faces one or more large display screens, and is often where the facilitator with be positioned. Many facilities like this are designed for approximately 10-15 participants, but when a facility is designed to support a large number of participants, it is common to use a series of nested U shapes, in an amphitheater design.

The furniture that has been used in GSS facilities ranges from standard tables and chairs found in almost any organization, to specially designed modules that house the computer equipment and cables in an elegant and unobtrusive format. Installations have been built where the furniture is all permanently installed in place, while others have used units that can be easily moved and re-configured as necessary.

A GSS facility must include the ability to project at least one large computer display to the front of the room. Some rooms have two or even three displays. There are now many high-quality and inexpensive video projectors available–some of them quite light and portable. Projectors can be permanently installed in the ceiling, or used on a table or cart. The computer images are generally projected onto standard movie screens, or onto plain light-colored walls. Proper lighting is critical to the usability of a GSS decision room. It may be important to be able to dim some lights so the screen is not washed out.

A basic issue for GSS facility design deals with the question of whether to have a permanent facility that is used exclusively for GSS sessions, or whether to try an approach where a GSS meeting can be set up in almost any standard conference room at short notice. In general, it is easier to manage a facility that is in place and is dedicated to GSS use. Once it has been installed and configured, the need for technical support greatly diminishes. However, one drawback is that everyone has to travel to the

FIGURE 2. Typical GSS Room Configuration

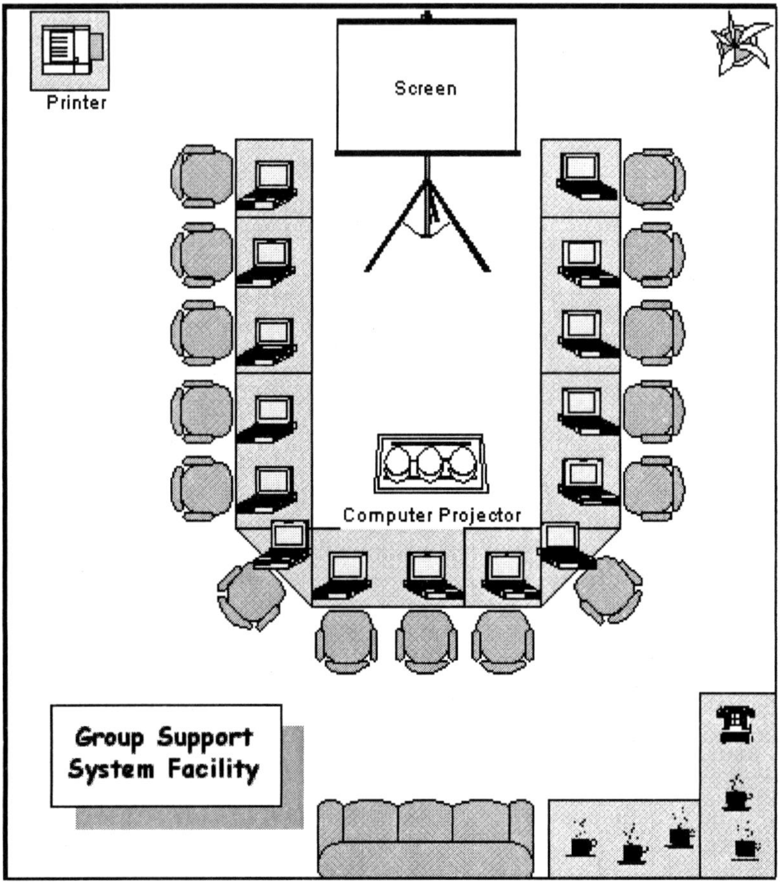

special room, no matter how inconvenient. And, it can be difficult in many organizations to find an extra room that can be dedicated to GSS, especially when GSS use is still new and unproved to many.

HARDWARE CONSIDERATIONS

A variety of issues arise in connection with the hardware requirements of a GSS facility related to the computers, networks, printers, and large screen video displays.

Computers

Most GSS facilities are designed so that each participant will have the use of their own PC, and most commercial GSS's are designed for use on PCs running Microsoft Windows, although some have been designed for UNIX and Macintosh systems as well. Typically, the stations used by participants can be standard machines without any unusual requirements. For example, when using *MeetingWorks*™, almost any PC capable of running Microsoft Windows would be satisfactory.

Some GSS's distinguish between the stations used by participants, and a special station used by the chauffeur or facilitator. For example, the *MeetingWorks*™ chauffeur station always runs through the Windows environment and often acts as a network server. This station should be as powerful as possible, using a fast CPU, additional RAM, a large and fast hard drive, and a high quality display. The speed is needed because this station collects all the information from the participants and creates summary display tables and graphs.

The computers used in a GSS facility can either be standard desktop models, or laptop PCs. The primary advantage of a desktop model is the lower price when compared to a laptop with equivalent features. However, there are several reasons why many GSS facilities are turning to the laptop approach, including the possibility of taking the laptops to different locations to run GSS sessions where the client prefers.

It is very difficult to move a set of GSS equipment based on standard desktop PCs that require multiple power cords and network cables for all the participant workstations. However, the growing availability of relatively inexpensive laptop PCs that can run on batteries for 6 or more hours, along with wireless network adapters, and lightweight video projectors are making a portable GSS capability truly feasible for the first time. Laptops have the advantage of being much more unobtrusive than desktop PCs with their large monitors. When laptops are closed, they virtually disappear in the meeting, while the need to peer around a large monitor can create a "bunker mentality" when using desktop systems. The experience of interpersonal distance between group members is greatly reduced with the notebook configuration.

Networks

In order for the participants to communicate through their computers, they need to be connected in a Local Area Network (LAN). The most common way to do this is to use a network adapter card, like an Ethernet card, for example. In the last few years, vendors have begun providing wireless network devices that use infrared or radio frequencies for transmission of data. Some of these are designed to be used with laptop PCs, using just the internal power supply, which raises the possibility for installations that are almost completely without wires or cables of any kind.

Printers

One of the real advantages of using a GSS is the capability of producing useful reports during the meeting and handing them out to the participants. Since multiple copies will usually be needed, speed can be an important consideration. A fast laser printer is ideal. Some GSS software will also provide various color graphs and charts. A color inkjet printer is a good solution for this situation.

SOFTWARE CONSIDERATIONS

There are three areas of concern related to software for GSS: the operating system or environment, the network operating system, and the actual GSS software.

Operating System/Environment

As mentioned earlier, most GSS's run on IBM PC-compatible PCs, and Windows is now the most common operating system. *MeetingWorks*™ is primarily designed for Windows, though some versions make use of Internet web browsers that might run on other operating systems.

Network Software

Most GSS facilities will use a Local Area Network (LAN) and will need software to manage this network. *MeetingWorks*™ has been designed to work with all the major network operating systems such as Novell, Lantastic, Banyan Vines, and so on. Windows has some network support built in, and that is sufficient for *MeetingWorks*™. Not all GSS software is compatible with all network software, so be sure to check carefully with the vendor.

Group Support System Software

The heart of any GSS facility is the special purpose software that is used during the meeting. While there are significant differences between the available GSS software packages (like there are differences between the major spreadsheet packages), they also share many key features (as most spreadsheet packages do). Packages may differ in the specific modules included, the design of the user interface, the ability to create and use meeting agendas, the relative emphasis on oral discussion, and several other aspects. In the following section, some common GSS software modules will be described, and in order to get a more specific idea of what a typical module is like, the *MeetingWorks*™ package will be described in some detail. For more thorough descriptions of other GSS packages, see Bostrom, Watson, and Kinney (1992), and Jessup and Valacich (1993).

Meeting Management: A GSS package needs tools to prepare for and manage meetings. This might include support for defining the meeting procedures including choosing the tool modules and their contents, and defining data file and report names. Also, there must be a way to control execution of these tools during a meeting, and a way to manage information about meeting participants, such as their names and what computer they are using. *AgendaWriter* is the component of the *MeetingWorks*™ system used to create and maintain meeting agendas. Agenda writing is the general process of translating problem-solving requirements or organizational processes into an ordered set of steps which are supported by *MeetingWorks*™. The *Chauffeur* module is used by the chauffeur to run a meeting using an existing agenda. This module also includes the participant registration function. Finally, the *Chauffeur* module maintains a detailed "session log" that records information about the events that occur in a meeting session.

For example, here is a hypothetical agenda for a meeting organized by a social worker where a Multi-disciplinary Team in a research hospital (e.g., doctors, physiotherapist, speech pathologist, psychologist, social worker, pediatric nurse) will decide on the treatment options for a child brought in for evaluation of developmental delays:

MEETING AGENDA:	
1.	Generate a list of findings by discipline
2.	Discuss and organize the list of findings
3.	Generate a list of potential diagnoses

4.	Discuss and organize the list of potential diagnoses
5.	Select the most appropriate diagnosis
6.	Generate a list of treatment options
7.	Discuss & organize the treatment options
8.	Rate the treatment options

Idea Generation: One of the features that users seem to appreciate most about a GSS is the ease with which groups can create lists of ideas or comments. These tools generally allow for simultaneous and anonymous generation of written text. This avoids the bottleneck of having one person write down ideas on a flipchart as they are orally contributed. It also protects participants from personal attacks, since no one knows who contributed an idea.

In *MeetingWorks*™, this is accomplished through the use of the *Generate* module, which is designed to collect, display, and do some preliminary organizing of text lists created by the participants. Typically, as participants enter ideas at their workstations and send these through the network to the chauffeur station, the ideas are collected on a list by *Generate* and then displayed at the front of the room through a video projector of some kind. *Generate* maintains the anonymity of the authors of ideas and comments to increase the likelihood that participants will be creative in their generation of ideas and candid in their evaluation comments meetings. *Generate* can set a limit on the number of ideas contributed by each participant, or allow an unlimited number when appropriate.

For our example case, the group might use *Generate* to build a list of findings as shown below:

RELEVANT FINDINGS:

1. Child has no coherent speech at 28 months of age
2. Child seldom sleeps through the night
3. Family is intact, parents gainfully employed
4. There is no history of mental illness or retardation in family
5. Child relates well to sibling
6. Child makes repetitive sounds and gestures
7. Birth trauma involved inhaled fecal material from amniotic fluid
8. Mother was in motor vehicle accident during 6th month of pregnancy
9. Child has had frequent ear infections and tonsillitis
10. Mother suffers from migraine headaches
11. Maternal grandmother is Holocaust survivor

Idea Organization: Perhaps the greatest challenge a group will face is how to take a raw list of ideas and discuss, edit, and organize these ideas to create a coherent result. Each of these steps is itself a complex task.

In *MeetingWorks*™, the *Organize* module provides a group with valuable support for these difficult but necessary tasks. *Organize* will help the group systematically process raw lists of ideas, typically those created during a *Generate* step. Participants will be able to set a time budget, and *Organize* will help them stay on track. The facilitator can make sure that each idea on the list will be considered, and understood by the participants. *Organize* makes it easy to edit and re-word ideas as they are discussed. Finally, *Organize* will give the group support in structuring a list using an outline approach. A chauffeur can use multiple methods to group ideas together, change their order or sequence, and place them at different levels of an outline. The result of an *Organize* session is a clearly worded structured outline of the group's ideas.

Idea Evaluation: Many tasks that groups are asked to perform involve some type of evaluation, like selecting the best product features, choosing the superior candidate for a position, or ranking a set of strategic options. These are often complex and critical decisions that can have a major impact on the success of the organization. Yet, many times groups will use simplistic and inappropriate evaluation methods that can lead to the wrong decision. This may occur because the participants do not know any methods more sophisticated than "let's see a show of hands for option A." Or, perhaps it happens because they don't have the time and resources to use a more sophisticated approach. In *MeetingWorks*™, there are three software modules concerned with idea evaluation: *Evaluate, Cross-Impact,* and *Multiple Criteria.*

The *Evaluate* module offers voting, selecting, ranking, and rating using various numeric scales. One of the important features of *Evaluate* is the preservation of participant anonymity. While the group will see detailed summaries of the results of an evaluation, the author of any specific rating or comment is not disclosed. This can result in more candid evaluations representing the true feelings of the group members.

Multiple Criteria is the most sophisticated of the *MeetingWorks*™ evaluation tools. Many decisions involve choosing between several alternatives–groups commonly consider multiple alternatives when making a decision. However, most decisions also involve more than one factor, or decision criteria, that must be considered when making the decision. This GSS tool allows the group to evaluate several alternatives at a time using multiple criteria. The software integrates individual evaluations into a master table that summarizes the results, using the mean of the groups' individual scores. Since this report contains such a wealth of detailed information, a set of graphics displays is available as an aid to analysis.

In our example, suppose the group had built the following list of treatment alternatives using *Generate:*

TREATMENT ALTERNATIVES:

1. Exceptional Development Program
2. Surgery to remedy physical problem
3. Speech Therapy
4. Intensive rehab
5. Referral for headache evaluation for mother
6. Family counseling
7. Legal referral related to accident claim

They might then agree to apply a set of criteria to evaluate these alternatives. Criteria might include: Cost of Treatment, Effectiveness of Treatment, Acceptability to Client, Travel Requirements, Reliability, etc. The *Multiple Criteria* module would then allow the group to apply these criteria to the set of alternatives to identify the best choice(s) for treatment.

External Linking: While many GSS tools are extremely flexible and adaptable to many different group tasks, they cannot necessarily do everything that the group might need. The *External Program* module allows other non-*MeetingWorks*™ programs to be directly entered into a agenda and executed at the appropriate time during a GSS session. So, an agenda step might consist of starting the EXCEL spreadsheet program, and loading in the file with the department budget for discussion. Virtually any program that can run under Windows (including those that run in a DOS session) can be included as part of a *MeetingWorks*™ agenda.

Internet Versions: The Internet versions of *MeetingWorks*™ (Connect and InternetEdition) make use of standard web browsers as the participant interface. If a group decides to hold distributed sessions through the Internet, they would use the browser to log into a site for the meeting. No software installation is required at the participant station beyond the standard web browser.

SOFTWARE AVAILABILITY

MeetingWorks™ is a commercially available product distributed by *meetingworks.com*. There are a number of versions with separate pricing structures. Additional details about product features and pricing are available from the authors or from the following web site: <*www/ meetingworks.com*>

A free version of *MeetingWorks*™ limited to 8 participants can be downloaded from this web site for trial use. An educational version suitable for teaching and research can be obtained from the authors.

CONCLUSION

Group Support Systems have evolved and improved greatly over their nearly twenty year life span. GSS can support a wide variety of group tasks, and under the right circumstances, they can improve the effectiveness and efficiency of group processes. There is evidence that the appropriate use of GSS can also increase participation and user satisfaction. New versions now allow groups to break the limitations of time and place by conducting some meeting processes over the Internet, with participants interacting at any time from any place.

Social workers are frequently involved with meetings, often for administrative purposes. A GSS may be helpful in improving administrative meetings and in helping groups increase their effectiveness. Distributed GSS may be especially helpful when team members travel frequently and it is difficult to schedule face-to-face meetings. There may also be useful applications of GSS to treatment, such as family therapy. Further work is needed to ascertain the efficacy of GSS in this regard.

REFERENCES

Alter, S. (1980). *Decision Support Systems: Current Practice and Continuing Challenges*. New York: Addison-Wesley.

Bostrom, R., & Anson, R. (1992). "The Face-to-Face Meeting: A Tutorial." In R. Bostrom, R. Watson, & S. Kinney (Eds.), *Computer Augmented Teamwork: A Guided Tour*. New York: Von Nostrand Reinhold.

Bostrom, R., Watson, R., & Kinney, S. (Eds.) (1992). *Computer Augmented Teamwork: A Guided Tour*. New York: Von Nostrand Reinhold.

Bui, T., Jelassi, T., & Shakun, M. (1992). "Negotiation Support Systems." *Proceedings of the Twenty-fifth Hawaii International Conference on Systems Science*, Vol. IV, p. 152.

Carlson, E. (1977). "Decision Support Systems: Personal Computing Services for Managers." *Management Review, 66(1),* 4-11.

Chung, K., & Ferris, M. (1981). "An Inquiry of the Nominal Group Process." *Academy of Management Journal, 55*, 520-524.

Clawson, V., Bostrom, B., & Anson, R. (1993). "The Role of the Facilitator in Computer Supported Meetings," *Small Group Research*, Vol. 24, No. 4, p. 547-565.

Connolly, T., Jessup, L., & Valacich, J. (1990). "Effects of Anonymity and Evaluative Tone on Idea Generation in Computer-Mediated Groups." *Management Science, 36*(6), 689-703.

Delbecq, A., Van de Ven, A., & Gustafson, D. (1975). *Group Techniques for Program Planning*. Glenview, IL: Scott-Foresman.

Dennis, A. (1991). *Parallelism, Anonymity, Structure, and Group Size in Electronic Meetings*. Unpublished doctoral dissertation, University of Arizona, Tucson.

Dennis, A., George, J., Jessup, L., & Nunamaker, J. (1988). "Information Technology to Support Electronic Meetings." *MIS Quarterly*, 12(4), 591-624.

Dennis, A., & Valacich, J. (1991). "Electronic versus Nominal Group Brainstorming." Working paper, University of Arizona, Tucson.

Dennis, A., Valacich, J., & Nunamaker, J. (1990). "An Experimental Investigation of the Effects of Group Size in an Electronic Meeting Environment." *IEEE System, Man, and Cybernetics*, 25, 1049-1057.

DeSanctis, G., D'Onofrio, M., Sambamurthy, V., & Poole, M. (1989). "Comprehensiveness and Restriction in Group Decision Heuristics: Effects of Computer Support on Consensus Decision Making." *Proceedings of the Tenth International Conference on Information Systems*, 131-140.

DeSanctis, G., & Gallupe, B. (1987). "A Foundation for the Study of Group Decision Support Systems." *Management Science*, 33(5), 589-609.

Diener, E. (1980). "Deindividuation: The Absence of Self-Awareness and Self-Regulation in Group Members." In P. B. Paulus (Ed.), *Psychology of Group Influence*. Hillsdale, NJ: Erlbaum.

Dufner, D., Hiltz, S., & Turoff, M. (1994). "Distributed Group Support: A Preliminary Analysis of the Effects of the Use of Voting Tools and Sequential Procedures." In J. Nunamaker & R. Sprague (Eds.) *Proceedings of the Twenty-Seventh Annual Hawaii International Conference on System Science,* Vol. 4, 114-123.

Easton, A., Vogel, D., & Nunamaker, J. (1989). "Stakeholder Identification and Assumption Surfacing in Small Groups: An Experimental Study." In J. Nunamaker (Ed.) *Proceedings of the Twenty-Second Annual Hawaii International Conference on System Science,* Vol. 3, 344-352.

Eden, C. (1989). "Strategic Options Development and Analysis (SODA)." In J. Rosenhead (Ed.) *Rational Analysis in a Problematic World.* Chichester: Wiley.

Fellers, J. (1989). "The Effect of Group Size and Computer Support on Group Idea Generation for Creativity Tasks: An Experimental Evaluation Using a Repeated Measures Design." Unpublished doctoral thesis, Indiana University, Bloomington.

Fjermestad, J., & Hiltz, S. R. (1999). "An Assessment of Group Support Systems Experimental Research: Methodology and Results." *Journal of Management Information Systems, 15(3),* 7-149.

Gallupe, B., Bastianutti, L., & Cooper, W. (1991). "Unblocking Brainstorms." *Journal of Applied Psychology*, 76(1), 137-142.

Gray, P. (1999). "New Directions for GDSS." *Group Decision and Negotiation*, 8(1), 77-83.

Greif, I. (Ed.). (1988). *Computer-Supported Cooperative Work: A Book of Readings.* San Mateo: Morgan Kaufmann.

Grohowski, R., McGoff, C., Vogel, D., Martz, B., & Nunamaker, J. (1990). "Implementing Electronic Meetings at IBM: Lessons Learned and Success Factors." *MIS Quarterly*, 14(4), 369-383.

Hackathorn, R., & Keen, P. (1981). "Organizational Strategies for Personal Computing in Decision Support Systems." *MIS Quarterly*, 5(3), 21-28.

Hayne, S., Rice, R., & Licker, P. (1994). "Social Cues and Anonymous Group Interaction Using Group Support Systems." In J. Nunamaker & R. Sprague (Eds.) *Proceedings of the Twenty-Seventh Annual Hawaii International Conference on System Science,* Vol. 4, 73-81.

Huber, G. (1984). "Issues in the Design of Group Decision Support Systems." *MIS Quarterly*, 8(3), 195-204.

Janis, I. (1981). *Groupthink.* Boston: Houghton-Mifflin.

Jessup, L., Connolly, T., & Galegher, J. (1990). "The Effects of Anonymity on Group Process in an Idea-Generating Task." *MIS Quarterly*, 14(3), 313-321.

Jessup, L., & Valacich, J. (Eds.) (1993). *Group Support Systems: New Perspectives.* New York: Macmillan Publishing Company.

Keen, P., & Morton, M. (1978). *Decision Support Systems: An Organizational Perspective.* Reading, MA: Addison-Wesley.

Keeney, F., & Sicherman, A. (1976). "Assessing and Analyzing Preferences Concerning Multiple Objectives: An Interactive Computer Program." *Behavioral Science*, 21, 173-182.

Keleman, K., Lewis, L. F., & Garcia, J. (1993). "Agenda Management: A Link Between Group Support Systems and Organizational Learning," *Small Group Research*, 24(4), 566-582.

Latane, B., Williams, K., & Harkins, S. (1979). "Many Hands Make Light the Work: The Causes and Consequences of Social Loafing." *Journal of Personality and Social Psychology*, 37, 822-832.

Lewis, L. F. (1998). "Using Group Support Systems for Program Evaluation in a State Agency." *Proceedings of the XXXI Hawaii International Conference on Systems Science,* January.

Lewis, L. F. (1996). "Special Issue on Facilitation in Computer-Supported Meetings." *Group Decision and Negotiation,* Vol. 5(1).

Lewis, L. F. (1995). "Using Group Support Systems (GSS) in the Teaching of International Business." *Journal of Teaching in International Business,* Vol. 7(4), 1995.

Lewis, L. F. (1987). "A Decision Support System for Face-to-Face Groups." *Journal of Information Science,* Vol. 13, 211-219.

Lewis, L. F. (1983). "FACILITATOR: A microcomputer decision support system for small groups." PhD Dissertation, University of Louisville.

Lewis, L. F., Garcia, J., & Keleman, K. (1997). "Possible Barriers and Challenges to the Adoption of Group Support Systems." *Group Decision and Negotiation,* Vol. 6(2).

Lewis, L. F. & Shakun, M. (1996). "Using MeetingWorks for Windows Group Support System to Implement Evolutionary Systems Design." *Group Decision and Negotiation,* Vol. 5(5).

Lewis, L. F., & Shakun, M. (1994). "A MeetingWorks Agenda based on Evolutionary Systems Design for Policy Making/Negotiation." Presented at the TIMS/ORSA, National Meeting. Boston, April 24-27.

Lewis, L. F. & Spich, R. (1996). "Principled Negotiation, Evolutionary Systems Design, and Group Support Systems: A Suggested Integration of Three Approaches to Improving Negotiations." *Proceedings of the XXIX Hawaii International Conference on Systems Science,* January.

Lewis, L. F., & Whiteley, A. (1992). "Initial Perceptions of Professional Facilitators Regarding GDSS Impacts: A Study Using the Grounded-Theory Approach." In J. Nunamaker & R. Sprague (Eds.) *Proceedings of the Twenty-Fifth Annual Hawaii International Conference on System Science,* Vol. 4, 80-89.

Maier, N. R. F., & Hoffman, L. (1960). "Quality of First and Second Solution in Group Problem Solving." *Journal of Applied Psychology*, 44, 278-283.

McGoff, C., & Ambrose, L. (1991). "Empirical Information from the Field: A Practioner's View of Using GDSS in Business." In J. Nunamaker (Ed.) *Proceedings of the Twenty-Fourth Annual Hawaii International Conference on System Science,* Vol. 3, 805-811.

McGrath, J., & Hollingshead, A. (1993). "Putting the 'Group' Back in Group Support Systems: Some Theoretical Issues about Dynamic Processes in Groups with Technological Enhancements." In L. Jessup, & J. Valacich (Eds.) *Group Support Systems: New Perspectives.* New York: Macmillan Publishing Company.

Mintzberg, H. (1971). "Managerial Work: Analysis from Observation." *Management Science*, 18B, 97-110.

Mosvick, R., & Nelson, R. (1987). *We've Got to Start Meeting Like This: A Guide to Successful Business Meeting Management.* Glenview, IL: Scott, Foreman.

Nunamaker, J., Dennis, A., Valacich, J., Vogel, D., & George, J. (1993). "Group Support Systems Research: Experience from the Lab and Field." In L. Jessup, & J. Valacich (Eds.) *Group Support Systems: New Perspectives.* New York: Macmillan Publishing Company.

Osborne, A. (1963). *Applied Imagination.* New York: Scribners.

Orsburn, J., Moran, L., Musselwhite, E., & Zenger, J. (1990). *Self-Directed Work Teams: The New American Challenge.* Homewood, IL: Business One Irwin.

Pervan, G. (1994). "The Measurement of GSS Effectiveness: A Meta-Analysis of the Literature and Recommendations for Future GSS Research." In J. Nunamaker & R. Sprague (Eds.) *Proceedings of the Twenty-Seventh Annual Hawaii International Conference on System Science,* Vol. 4, 562-571.

Peters, T. (1988). *Thriving on Chaos.* New York: Alfred A. Knopf.

Phillips, L. (1988). "Decision analysis for group decision support." In C. Eden & J. Radford (Eds.) *Proceedings of the International Symposium of Future Directions in Decision Management*. London, UK: Sage Publications.

Pollard, C. (1994). *Organizational Assimilation of Group Support Systems: A Case Study of OptionFinder, a Keypad-Based GSS*. Unpublished doctoral dissertation; University of Pittsburgh.

Poole, M., & Jackson, M. (1993). "Communication Theory and Group Support Systems." In L. Jessup, & J. Valacich (Eds.) *Group Support Systems: New Perspectives*. New York: Macmillan Publishing Company.

Raiffa, H. (1970). *Decision Analysis*. Reading, MA: Addison-Wesley.

Rokeach, M. (1973). *The Nature of Human Values*. New York: Free Press.

Sage, A. (1977). *Methodology for Large-Scale Systems*. New York: McGraw-Hill.

Sambamurthy, V., & DeSanctis, G. (1989). "An Experimental Evaluation of GDSS Effects on Group Performance During Stakeholder Analysis." In R. Blanning & D. King (Eds.) *Proceedings of the Twenty-Third Annual Hawaii International Conference on System Science,* Vol. 3, 79-88.

Schoderbek, P., Kefalas, A., & Schoderbek, C. (1975). *Management Systems: Conceptual Considerations*. Dallas: Business Publications, Inc.

Schwarz, R. (1994). *The Skilled Facilitator*. New York: Macmillan.

Shakun, M. (1988). *Evolutionary Systems Design: Policy Making Under Complexity and Group Decision Support Systems*. Oakland, CA: Holden-Day.

Shaw, M. (1976). *Group Dynamics: The Psychology of Small Group Behavior* (*2nd Edition*). New York: McGraw-Hill.

Steiner, I. (1972). *Group Process and Productivity*. New York: Academic Press.

Van De Ven, A. (1973). "An Applied Experimental Test of Alternative Decision Making Processes." Kent, OH: Kent State University.

Van Gigch, J. (1974). *Applied General Systems Theory*. New York: Harper & Row.

Van Gundy, A. (1981). *Techniques of Structured Problem Solving*. New York: Von Nostrand Reinhold.

Vemuri, V. (1978). *Modeling of Complex Systems*. New York: Academic Press.

Venkatesh, M., & Wynne, B. (1991). "Effects of Problem Formulation and Process Structures on Performance and Perceptions in a GDSS Environment: An Experiment." In J. Nunamaker (Ed.) *Proceedings of the Twenty-Fourth Annual Hawaii International Conference on System Science,* Vol. 3, 564-572.

Whiteley, A., & Garcia, J. (1996). "The facilitator and chauffeur in GSS: Explorations in forging a relationship." *Group Decision and Negotiation*. 5(1), 31-50.

Introduction to Technology in Education

Hy Resnick

INTRODUCTION

This section contains eight articles which describe how electronic technology is increasingly being utilized in the human service education class and workshop setting.

There are a number of ways to use electronic technology to support or enhance human service instructional work, only three of which will be included in this edition: (1) Web-Based Courses, (2) Distance Learning,[1] and (3) CD-ROM/Videodisc.

Web-Based Courses and *Distance Learning* are similar modes of electronic technology, and share many of the same characterizations or requirements:

- a computer with sufficient power,
- a connection to the Internet,
- a course curriculum from an educational institute, and
- an instructor to manage the curriculum (suggest reading or web sites, help students navigate the Internet, problem solve communication and technical problems that inevitably come up, be accessible/available).

[Haworth co-indexing entry note]: "Introduction to Technology in Education." Resnick, Hy. Co-published simultaneously in *Journal of Technology in Human Services* (The Haworth Press, Inc.) Vol. 20, No. 3/4, 2002, pp. 227-230; and: *Human Services Technology: Innovations in Practice and Education* (ed: Hy Resnick, and Phoebe Sade Anderson) The Haworth Press, Inc., 2002, pp. 227-230. Single or multiple copies of this article are available for a fee from The Haworth Document Delivery Service [1-800-HAWORTH, 9:00 a.m. - 5:00 p.m. (EST). E-mail address: getinfo@haworthpressinc.com].

The main difference between Web-based instruction and Distance Learning is that the former is often used to augment an existing traditional, face-to-face classroom, both in reinforcing the day's instruction and in encouraging further discussion via electronic mode. In this volume, the web-based courses, illustrated by Brett A. Seabury's "COW: Conferencing on the Web," Jack A. Cummings and Curtis J. Bonk's "Facilitating Interactions Among Students and Faculty via Web-Based Conferencing Systems," act as enhancements and additions to regularly scheduled and attended face-to-face classroom sessions. The benefit of the additional web-based course is that the student can access, at any time, the day's lessons, including PowerPoint presentations; the discussion from class can be continued asynchronously between students and with the professor; and learning can extend beyond the traditional setting.

In his article "COW: Conferencing on the Web," Seabury, a University of Michigan social work educator with a distinguished record of scholarly work in social work education and electronic technology, provides "case" illustrations from his practice classes of how COW can be used to facilitate learning with a special emphasis on the value of student-student communication and faculty to learning. COW, as employed by Seabury, is different from earlier conference systems because it can send and receive images, sound, video as well as text. It can be used as a home page where instructors can post syllabi, assignments, class notes, links to course resources and even digital pictures of students in the class. A useful feature of this article is Seabury's thorough evaluation of his conferencing system.

The next article by Cummings and Bonk describes a Web-based course offered in an education psychology department in a large mid-western university where the focus is also on students learning from each other as well as from the instructor. "Too often when we thing of teaching opportunities we only consider what teachers can do for students." Building on the importance and utility of a two way communication system in this design of this Web-based course, Cummings and Bonk develop a three by three framework which the authors use to understand–and increase–communication not only between students and faculty but with practitioner experts as well. Thus, they indicate the potential of electronic technology to reduce the *town-gown gap* and at the same time improve education and practice in the human services.

Distance Learning, on the other hand, is utilized to convey instruction and information across distances, especially useful in rural areas where there are no formal educational institutes. The Distance Learning model of instruction, which will be illustrated by Steven Hick in his article "Connecting Aboriginal Learners in Remote Communities: An

Online Social Work Course," and Robert J. McFadden, Sarah Maiter and Gary C. Dumbrill's "High Tech and High Touch: The Human Face of Online Education," utilizes all of the technological characteristics that web-based courses do, but there are no face-to-face classes. As a result, the distance learning courses are often considerably more comprehensive and detailed and involve both asynchronous communication via a newsgroup and synchronous communication through designated meeting times in a chatroom system. All communication with the professor is online and possibly via telephone, but depending on where the students are, they may meet for groupwork.

Hick, a Canadian social work educator whose article "Connecting Aboriginal Learners in Remote Communities: An Online Social Work Course," describes a distance learning course designed to provide social work instruction to First Nation students living in remote areas.

A second article, entitled "High Tech and High Touch: The Human Face of Online Education," introduces a topic rarely addressed in the small but growing literature of this field and that is the subjective experience of the learner and the teacher. In this thoughtful and perhaps seminal examination of this issue, MacFadden and his colleagues (Canadian social work educators and doctoral students) look into the human experience of the participants in online education in the human service professions.

The third mode of electronic technology discussed in this collection is *CD-ROM/Videodisc* based learning as illustrated by Harold B. Engen and Robert David Dawson's "Counseling Simulations: An Interactive CD-ROM Approach," Forrest C. Bud Hansen, Hy Resnick, and Jerry Galea's article "Better Listening: Paraphrasing and Perception Checking," Alan D. Bookhagen, David P. Wegenast, and Richard J. McCowan's "Multimedia Interactive Training Development," and A. Elizabeth Cauble and Janice M. Dinkel's "The Development of a Multimedia Training Project." This mode of educational technology is typically developed by a team of content and computer technology specialists who create a multi media learning vehicle usually focused on a specific body of information, e.g., poor laws in England, social welfare system in Japan, etc., or less frequently, focused on a set of skills required in the human service professions. These multimedia programs are properly sequenced, usually modular based, and designed to be used as a supplement to classroom instruction. Occasionally, they can function as a stand-alone program.

A compact disk based program is available as a resource for courses offered on the World Wide Web. It was recorded first on videotape, then converted onto videodisc, and finally in a shorter version, transferred onto a CD-ROM. It is described in this section by Engen and Dawson, two education psychologists from the University of Indiana. Despite changing electronic techniques, the authors, who are also the developers of this program, continue the use of the simulation as the major teaching/learning vehicle in all three electronic technological versions.

A multimedia program utilizing technologies, one or another version of which will most likely be the technology of the 21st century for educators, was developed by Hansen, Resnick and Galea. Their article describes a listening skills training program for human and health service students and practitioners and then describes a study conducted in Canada to evaluate its effectiveness with two groups of undergraduate social work students.

"Multimedia Interactive Training Development–*Journey: Discovering Social Services* CD-ROM," by Bookhagen, Wegenast, and McCowan, describes a compressive and creative distance training program designed to orient new staff into the complexities of a public agency. After a needs assessment study revealed that new workers were not using an existing orientation manual, the authors developed a self instructional, interactive program that makes use of a variety of media to provide for the new worker an interesting and informative training program.

Cauble and Dinkel's article, "The Development of a Multimedia Training Project," describes a major project they developed and administered to produce a multimedia training curriculum for staff in a public agency. At the time of the development of the program, Interactive Video Disk (IVD) technology, which they used to deliver the curriculum, was seen as state of the art. This article is included in this section not only because it captures a technology which unfortunately became obsolescent in the 90s but because of its respectful and participatory approach to development. Their strategy was simple–involve the end user (social workers) early in a focus group planning process and thereby increase utilization and effectiveness.

NOTE

1. There are at least three distance learning models in use in human service education today. Interactive Compressed video which is the most efficient (and probably the most effective) offers a two-way audio and video system which allows students and instructors at different locations to see and hear each other. Videotapes, a second distance learning method, typically involved instructors taping their own lectures and making those tapes available to students at different sites. Communication, other than through telephone or e-mail, is asynchronous. Satellites, a third distance learning method, are mainly commercially-owned networks which transmit "canned" educational programming to students at various sites. It is more expensive than the other two and sending and receiving sites may have uplink and downlink capabilities.

COW: Conferencing on the Web

Brett A. Seabury

SUMMARY. This article describes a Web-based social work practice course which provides instruction in text, sound, images, and video and allows students and faculty to communicate with each other asynchronistically. *[Article copies available for a fee from The Haworth Document Delivery Service: 1-800-HAWORTH. E-mail address: <getinfo@ haworthpressinc.com> Website: <http://www.HaworthPress.com> © 2002 by The Haworth Press, Inc. All rights reserved.]*

KEYWORDS. Web-based education, asynchronistic and synchronistic communication, social work education, technology, online instruction

Brett A. Seabury, DSW, ACSW, is affiliated with the University of Michigan, School of Social Work.

[Haworth co-indexing entry note]: "COW: Conferencing on the Web." Seabury, Brett A. Co-published simultaneously in *Journal of Technology in Human Services* (The Haworth Press, Inc.) Vol. 20, No. 3/4, 2002, pp. 231-244; and: *Human Services Technology: Innovations in Practice and Education* (ed: Hy Resnick, and Phoebe Sade Anderson) The Haworth Press, Inc., 2002, pp. 231-244. Single or multiple copies of this article are available for a fee from The Haworth Document Delivery Service [1-800-HAWORTH, 9:00 a.m. - 5:00 p.m. (EST). E-mail address: getinfo@haworthpressinc.com].

INTRODUCTION

Although conferencing on the Internet has been around for decades (Zinn, 1977), there are many computer mediated ways that conferencing is used today. The two most common ways of conferencing over the Internet involve "chat technology" in which people communicate with each other synchronistically (online at the same time) or asynchronistically (people leave messages or responses to others' messages that can be accessed, read, and responded to at a later point in time).

Social work practitioners have employed various forms of conferencing technology from e-mail groups, to Internet conferencing groups, to contemporary web based "chat" software. For example, conferencing has been effectively used to create self-help and support groups online (Finn, 1995; Finn, 1996; Kurtz, 1997, pp. 186-195; Madara, 1990). These computer mediated groups have expanded to encompass almost every kind of face-to-face self help group found in geographical communities (e.g., twelve step groups, groups for individuals with mental and physical impairments, loss/grief groups, etc.).

Over the past three years, various kinds of software programs and tools have been developed that can be used in higher education to organize and deliver courses over the Internet. There are commercial web sites (such as *www.Blackboard.com* or *www.WebCT.com*) as well as University based tools (such as *www.Prometheus.com* or *https://coursetools.ummu.umich.edu*) that allow faculty members to develop on line courses. This paper will focus on an asynchronistic conferencing program (COW) that is user friendly and can be employed by faculty to organize an Internet course.

WHAT IS COW?

COW (Conferencing on the Web) is a web-based conferencing system that was designed by Eric Klavens at San Francisco State University, and later refined at the University of Michigan. COW can be accessed at the University of Michigan through the World Wide Web at *http://calypso.rs.itd.umich.edu/COW/*. COW is different from earlier conferencing systems because it is graphical and icon based and does not require users to remember a series of letters and words to move around inside the conference. COW is much more user friendly, and in my experience with it in classes, it is much easier for students to learn. Earlier conferences were text based and could not receive images, sound, video, etc., the way COW can over the Web. COW uses html (the language of the web) so that information in almost any form can be posted or linked to COW conferences. Some faculty use COW conferences as a substitute for "home pages." Faculty can post syllabi and class notes, *PowerPoint*™ presentations, course assignments, links to course resources, images such as a digital pictures of students in the class or streamed video sequences, as well as streamed audio of class discussions.

OVERVIEW OF COW

When an individual signs onto COW, the entry level to COW is the individual's Personal Conference Page. The list of conferences on an individual's Personal Conference Page are called (in COWese) a "HotList." It is at this level that a participant organizes the various COW conferences that she wants to join. A participant's HotList can be easily modified. Each time the participant enters her HotList, the number of new responses that have been added to conferences are listed. See Figure 1 as an example of my HotList for May 2, 2000.

Listed on my HotList are the last five courses that I have taught that use COW as a conferencing system. The buttons on the bottom of the Personal Conference Page are there to search; move around within; to modify the Personal Conference Page in various ways; or to exit from the COW program. It is from this Personal Conference Page that various class conferences are accessed and entered. This paper will not discuss all of the functions that are available in COW, but will focus on how COW can be used to deliver a course with Internet resources.

There are three levels to a conference in COW, as indicated in Figure 2. The first level of organization in each conference is a series of "*Topics*." These topics represent the highest level of organization in a conference and are created by the conference organizer. For each topic in the conference, there may develop a number of "*Conversations*" (i.e., next level of organization) that are initiated by the participants or conference organizer. These conversations are titled, organized chronologically, and represent various inputs to that particular topic that have been generated by members of the conference. The final level of a COW conference represents the "*Responses*" that members can enter under a particular conversation. These responses may be comments or reactions to the conversation or they may be responses to other responses that individual members have generated to the conversation. It is at this level that the

FIGURE 1. Example of a Personal Conference Page or HotList

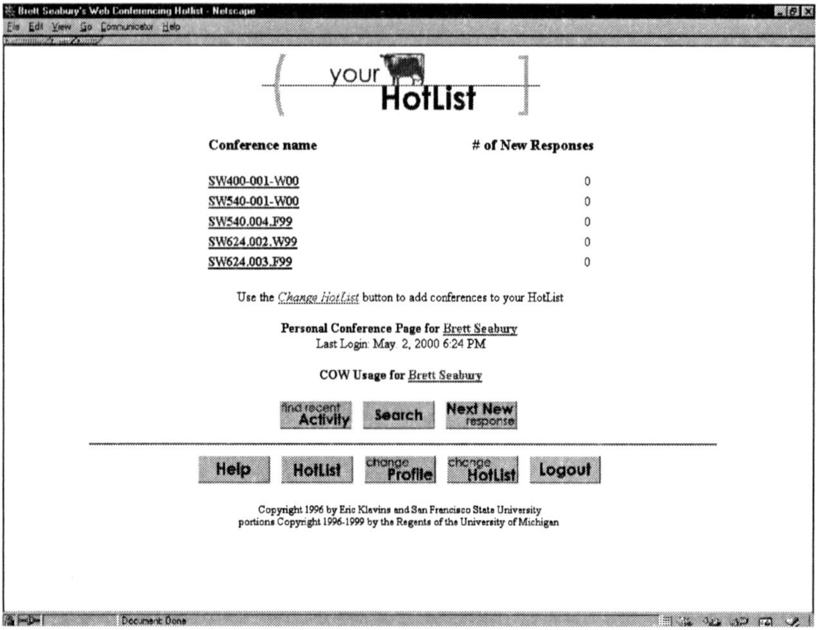

interactivity of COW takes place with many member to member exchanges about responses, conversations, or the topic itself.

EXAMPLE OF TOPICAL LEVEL ORGANIZATION

Though there are many ways that an organizer can use the topics and conversations in a conference, I will describe how I have employed COW in my classes over the past three years. Basically I have three kinds of topics in my class conferences. Many of the topics correspond to the written assignments for each of the major course topics (e.g., topics 1-14). Another large group of topics covers each of the class sessions of the course (e.g., topics 17-30). The third kind of topic covers miscellaneous and system maintenance topics such as the class photo with student names, instruction how to copy and paste word documents into COW (e.g., topics 15 and 16). Figure 3 shows how these various topics were arranged in a graduate methods course (i.e., SW 540–Introduction to Interpersonal Practice) that I taught in the Winter, 2000 term.

FIGURE 2. Structure of a COW Conference

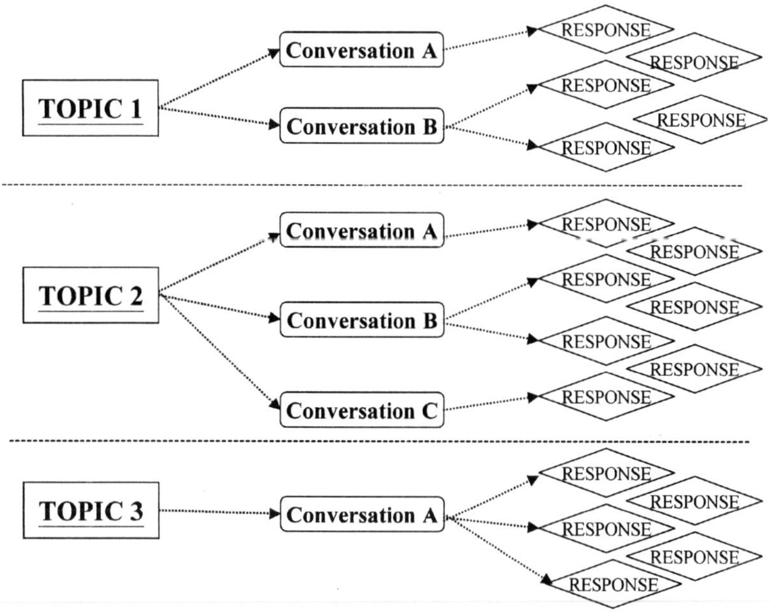

Before the first class session, I generated topics 1 through 16, and the other 14 topics were created on a weekly basis as the class progressed during the winter semester. There is a lot of summary information contained on this page. Under the term "New" is a list of any new activity (e.g., conversations or responses) that has occurred in the conference since the last time the participant may have signed on. In this particular example, the class is over, and I have accessed all conversations and responses for this class conference so a column of zeros appears. During the course of the semester, this page would look very different with numbers appearing in various topics with new conversations or responses that have not yet been accessed. From this page in COW, a participant can access any topic by simply clicking on that topic.

CONVERSATIONAL LEVEL OF COW

In order to demonstrate how the conversational level in COW is used in my courses, I will demonstrate how conversations are developed around

FIGURE 3. Example of Topics in SW 540

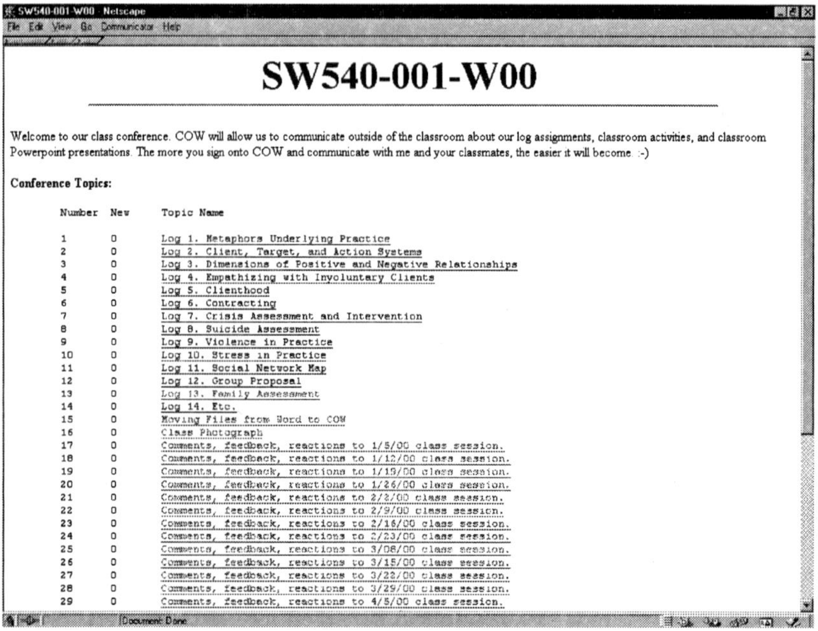

each of the class sessions and each of the course assignments. When I have completed a class session in one of my courses, I will create a new topic that describes what we have covered in class (see Figure 4–Example of 2/2/00 Class Session in SW 540). This example from SW 540 shows that there were three conversations generated under this class session. The first conversation is a link to my *PowerPoint* presentation for that class session. The second conversation, which I also generated, is a copy of the case examples I used during our class session. Students who have attended class and those who have missed class can access both the *PowerPoint* presentation and the case example later at their own convenience.

The third conversation under this class session was generated by a student who wanted to comment on an exercise that we did in class to sensitize students to multicultural issues in interpersonal practice. This conversation generated 24 responses from fellow classmates and me. It is at this level–the response level to conversations–that much of the interaction takes place within COW. In order to maintain the confidentiality of my students, I will summarize these responses and describe the basic themes that emerged and were generated by this conversation and topic area of the class. The exercise

FIGURE 4. Example of 2/2/00 Class Session in SW 540

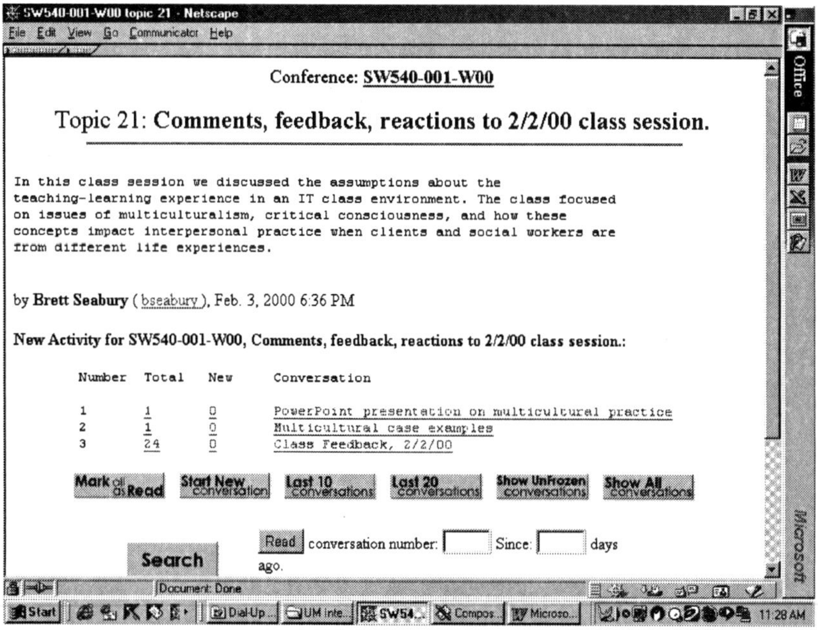

I used in class was a small group exercise in which each student is confronted about how different clients will perceive him or her in an initial encounter.

Nine students out of a class of 19 students participated in this conversation about diversity issues in interpersonal practice. I generated three responses scattered throughout this discussion (in order to keep the conversation going), and the students generated the other 21 responses. Two students responded only once and the other seven students responded two or three times.

A number of important practice themes were played out in these responses. The conversation began with a discussion about how hard it is to realize that clients may be responding to any number of our identities in an initial contact–i.e., gender, age, ethnicity, etc. The responses then went on to a discussion of the importance of appearances and how to look "professional" to various clients by the way we dress and the way we speak. Students then began to discuss situations in which they were in a professional situation (as teachers) with children who were from a different racial/ethnic group, and how this made them feel. Two students then discussed the initial discomfort they felt in their practice setting because the staff and clients were from another ethnic group. The dialogue then turned to the discomfort that participants felt when they were an "outsider" in an interpersonal situation. The responses then focused on issues of age and how with some clients age can be an asset or a liability. Students felt comfortable working with children and teens but rather uncomfortable when they had to work with older adults. The responses then shifted to "titles," and how we should refer to our clients and how we should have clients refer to us. One student, who grew up in the South where African Americans were called by their first names as a sign of disrespect, concluded that we should all be very careful to call oppressed clients by a formal title (Mr. or Mrs.) unless the client requested otherwise. Finally, these responses turned to issues of identity and whether we should try to hide our various identities from clients. A lesbian student, who was reminded by her partner that they should not hold hands in public for fear of recriminations, sparked this conversation. This summary reflects the "meandering way" that responses unfold and also demonstrates how the sharing and interaction among students and instructor inside COW can contribute to the educational experience of the course.

EXAMPLES OF RESPONSES TO WRITTEN ASSIGNMENTS SUBMITTED BY STUDENTS

In order to demonstrate how COW is used to generate student responses to students' written work, I will use as my example another graduate social work course (SW 624–Social Work with Groups) that I taught in the Fall, 1999 term. Students are expected to choose four assignments from a list of ten possible assignments and submit a 2-3 page paper into COW: These mini-papers are designed to connect the course concepts with groups that students have experienced in the past, or groups the students are running in their field placements.

Log 1. CURATIVE OR THERAPEUTIC FACTORS
Log 2. EFFECTIVENESS OF INTERNET SUPPORT GROUPS
Log 3. ROOTS OF GROUP WORK
Log 4. PLANNING FOR A GROUP -- THE GROUP PROPOSAL
Log 5. TEAMS
Log 6. GROUP COMPOSITION
Log 7. GROUP DEVELOPMENT
Log 8. PROGRAM ACTIVITIES
Log 9. GROUP GEOGRAPHY
Log 10. ETC

All of the students' written work is submitted into the class conference so that all students have a chance to read and respond to the work of all students in the class.

In Figure 5, which describes this assignment as a "Group Proposal," ten students opted to complete this assignment (out of a class of 28 students). This conference page shows that many different kinds of groups were being proposed by students in their field placements: groups for children, adults, siblings, parents, etc., which focused on many different kinds of issues–e.g., mental illness, grief, sexual abuse, foster care, social skills, etc. These ten assignments generated 101 responses from classmates and me. The value of submitting these assignments for all students to see is that students get to look at a wide range of examples of groups that their social work colleagues are interested in leading. The students who submitted this assignment also get support from their classmates to follow through with the proposal in their agencies, and many of the groups become realities that are then used as examples in other written assignments in the class.

FIGURE 5. Example of Students' Written Work

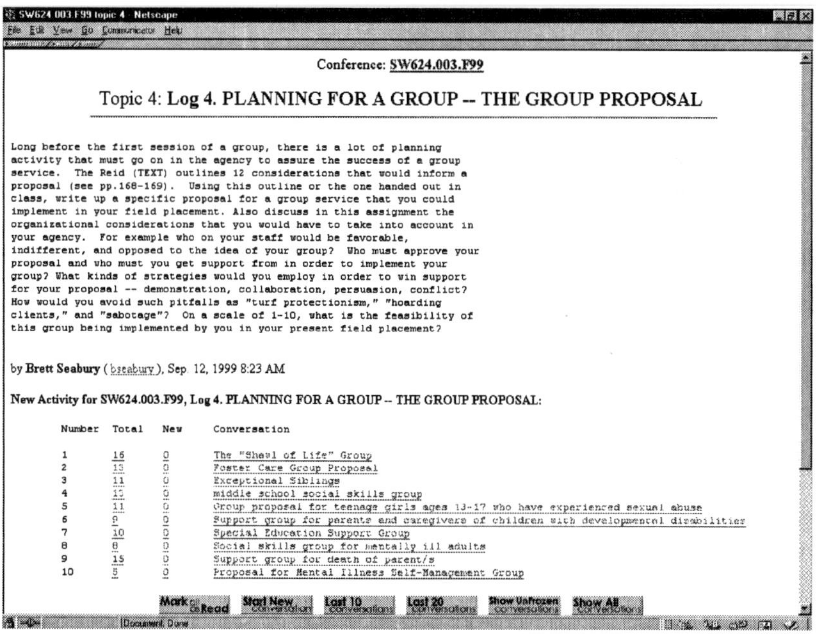

These examples from these two classes clearly demonstrate how COW can function as a tool to increase interactivity in a given class. Not only does the instructor get feedback about class presentation and exercises, but also every student gets a chance to see the written work of other students and to give feedback. There is an exponential increase in the teaching/learning process, which in other class situations may only go from individual student to instructor. In this class everyone is both teaching and learning from each other. Another benefit that is particular to COW is that assignments are not consuming paper and trees–an environmentally friendly process.

RESPONSES OF STUDENTS TO COW

In the last four classes in which COW was part of the educational structure of the class, I asked students to evaluate COW at the end of the course. I also asked them to tell me how many times they actually responded to the items in COW. The evaluation was structured with seven statements about COW and the students were asked to respond on the scale–SA strongly agree, A agree, N neutral, D disagree, and SD strongly disagree.

In general, the overall response to COW was very positive and over 80% of the students participated in the COW part of the course. This high participation rate in COW is much greater than in previous classes with conferencing tools when participation was optional (about 60% of students participated), because participation in COW now represents 10% of the students' course grade. Many of my colleagues have a class participation requirement, but I have found that a COW participation requirement is much more fair and objective because COW has a statistical function that calculates student participation.

The results of these surveys show that over 90% of the students felt that COW contributes to the educational experience of the course. Over 95% felt that COW exposed them to the varied practice experiences of their classmates, and 74% felt that the feedback they received on their written assignments was useful and instructive. All of the students felt that they had little difficulty learning how to use COW.

There were, however, some aspects of COW that were problematic for a small percentage of the students. About one fifth of the students were concerned about how much time they spent on COW. One student responded in the open ended part of the survey: "I find it to be very time consuming and unfair for those of us who are only on campus twice a week and don't have access to COW at home." As more and more of our classes are developed with Internet resources, this has become a real strain for commuter students who do not own their own computer or do not have a modem at home. About a quarter of the students were not comfortable with the idea that their classmates would be able to see and respond to their written work. I have had this feedback for many years, especially from students who have poor writing skills, but it is interesting that the public nature of these assignments has improved their written quality. Because a lot of social work involves written communication, I am not so sympathetic to students who complain about this element of COW.

The final item on the evaluation form concerned the students' overall impression of COW as a learning experience and whether it should continue to be used in courses: 84% of students agreed with this statement. A quote from one student best sums up the general reaction of students to COW: "I have to admit that I was not fond of COW initially, but I have become a supporter of the method. I think it was beneficial to be able to read other students' reactions and experiences and to have the opportunity to make comments and have positive and negative feedback. Keep COW!"

IMPLICATIONS AND LIMITATIONS OF COW

COW is presented in this paper as a positive add-on to the teaching/learning process in social work classes. COW enhances the educational experience of these particular classes in four ways:

1. Because the interaction among students increased, COW contributed to the building of group cohesion in these methods classes. For experiential classes, group cohesion is a critical dimension to effectiveness.
2. COW is a forum for class assignments. In a usual class, it is only the instructor who sees written assignments, but here COW provides the structure and opportunity for all students in the class to read and respond to each other's written assignments. Not all students like this idea, especially if they have trouble expressing themselves in writing, but COW pushes these students to do a better job of writing up their experiences. COW also gives students an opportunity to practice giving classmates effective feedback, which is an important practice skill that must be learned and exported into practice when collaborating with colleagues and other professionals.
3. COW becomes an effective forum for debriefing and commenting on class sessions, especially class sessions that generated a lot of anxiety in the experiential exercises that were employed by the instructor. Even though time was set aside at the end of class to de-

brief exercises, much more debriefing will go on after class in COW. As students developed group cohesion, they were able to give the instructor feedback and comments about what they liked and disliked about class sessions. This kind of on-going feedback is critical to effective teaching. (See, for example, Angelo & Cross, 1993.)

4. The final value is an anomaly that I have noticed in all conferences that I have run for classes over the past seven years. The most active members of conferences are often the least active members in the classroom. Some of the students who are most reserved and will make no comments or raise no questions in the classroom will become the most responsive, motivated, and active members of the class conference. Conferencing for these reserved students is a way to really get them to open up to their classmates and for their classmates to open up to them. I have had many students comment that they have had several classes with reserved students, but only got to really know them through the class conference. This can be seen in the comments of one student on the evaluation form: "COW provides a forum for discussion for people who are less likely to talk/participate in class. It was valuable for me, especially when I had supportive comments to my assignments."

What are the downsides of COW and using conferences in classes? The biggest downside is time spent teaching students how to use COW and dealing with all of the issues that arise as students finally get on-line and start submitting written assignments. The web is not a perfect communication medium, and some browsers have trouble accessing COW's encrypted interface. COW works best with Netscape Communicator™ 3.0 or higher, and it also works with Internet Explorer™. The web can be very slow at certain times of the day when Internet traffic is at its peak and even slower when it is accessed from a home phone with a slow modem. Middle aged students who are re-entering school have the biggest struggle with COW. They are often overwhelmed by the information technology that is used in their courses and least familiar with using the computer as a tool. Some even have strong biases against computer technology and would prefer to learn from books, articles, and other written artifacts. There are also times when the university server goes down or needs repair, and this seems to happen at inopportune times–when assignments are due at the end of the month.

Another major downside is the instructor's time spent on the computer. In these classes used as illustrations in this paper, there were over 1000 conversations and responses generated in each of these class conferences by students. I not only read all of them, but I also responded over 200 times. That is a lot of time on the computer reading assignments and responses. In the modern academic setting, this kind of commitment of time and effort to students may not get an instructor promoted or a salary increase. This kind of process activity with students does not count the way papers and research proposals do in a faculty member's annual review.

CONCLUSIONS

This paper has illustrated how COW can be used as a computer-mediated conferencing system in graduate social work classes. COW can be used in other ways to bring a group of participants together. Its big advantage is that it is a Web-based technology and can be used to bring people together over great distances. COW can be applied in distance learning courses to bring students together between classes. In the past computer-mediated conferencing has been used to bring scholars together from all over the world in an electronic symposium (Ferguson, 1977; Spelt, 1977), and COW can be used to bring students together from all over the world in a distance learning course. COW can even be used to deliver entire courses over the web because it allows instructors to post on COW their *PowerPoint*™ presentations, the accompanying audio lectures, images, graphics and even streamed, digitized video (Burton & Seabury, 1999). Hopefully as more and more people experiment with this new technology, more and more ways of using COW will be developed, and more and more social work faculty will begin to use COW and other information technology tools to deliver courses with Internet resources.

REFERENCES

Anderson, M. (1996). Using computer-mediated conferencing to facilitate group projects in an educational psychology class. *Behavior Research Methods, Instruments & Computers*, *28*(2), 351-353.

Angelo, T., & Cross, K. P. (1993). Minute Paper. In *Classroom Assessment Techniques* (pp. 148-153). San Francisco, CA: Jossey Bass.

Burton, D., & Seabury, B. (1999, August). *The "Virtual" Social Work Course: Promises and Pitfalls*. Paper presented at HUSITA-V Conference, Budapest, Hungary.

Dobos, J. A. (1996). Collaborative learning: Effects of student expectations and communication apprehension on student motivation. *Communication Education, 45*(2), 118-134.

Ferguson, J. A. (1977). PLANET: A computer conferencing system and its evaluation through a case study. *Behavioral Research Methods, Instruments & Computers, 9*(2), 92-95.

Finn, J. (1995). Computer-based self-help groups: A new resource to supplement support groups. *Social Work with Groups, 18*(1), 109-117.

Finn, J. (1996). Computer-based self-help groups: On-line recovery for addictions. *Computers in Human Services, 13*(1), 21-41.

Hiltz, S. R. (1982). The impact of a computerized conferencing system on the productivity of scientific research communities. *Behavior and Information Technology, 1*(2), 185-195.

Hiltz, S. R. (1992). The virtual classroom: Software for collaborative learning. In Barrett, Edward (ed.), *Sociomedia: Multimedia, Hypermedia, and the Social Construction of Knowledge* (pp. 347-368). Cambridge, MA: MIT Press.

Hiltz, S. R. (1986). The "virtual classroom": Using computer-mediated communication for university teaching. *Journal of Communication, 36*(2), 95-104.

Kurtz, L. (1997). *Self-Help and Support Groups*. Thousand Oaks, CA: Sage Publications.

Madara, E. (1990). Maximizing the potential for community self-help through clearinghouse approaches. *Prevention in Human Services, 7*(2), 109-138.

Schnase, J. L. & Cunnius, E. L. (1995). In J. L. Schnase & E. L. Cunnius (Eds.), *Proceedings of CSCL '95: The First International Conference on Computer Support for Collaborative Learning*. Mahwah, NJ: Lawrence Erlbaum Associates.

Spelt, P. F. (1977). Evaluation of a continuing computer conference on simulation. *Behavior Research Methods, Instruments & Computers, 9*(2), 87-91.

Velayo, R. (1994). Computer conferencing as an instructional tool: Exploring student perceptions of use, cognitive and motivational characteristics, and frequency of interaction. *Dissertation Abstracts International Section A: Humanities and Social Sciences, 54* (LL-A).

Zinn, K. L. (1977). Computer facilitation of communication within professional communities. *Behavior Research Methods, Instruments & Computers, 9*(2), 96-107.

Facilitating Interactions Among Students and Faculty via Web-Based Conferencing Systems

Jack A. Cummings
Curtis J. Bonk

SUMMARY. The authors describe a Web-based conferencing system for graduate and undergraduate students in educational psychology which illustrates the wide range of communication possibilities of such a system. Students, faculty, and practitioners experience increased and beneficial communication by using this system. *[Article copies available for a fee from The Haworth Document Delivery Service: 1-800-HAWORTH. E-mail address: <getinfo@haworthpressinc.com> Website: <http://www.HaworthPress.com> © 2002 by The Haworth Press, Inc. All rights reserved.]*

KEYWORDS. Technology in higher education, Web-based education, online instruction, case method

The potential of Web-based electronic conferencing to facilitate interactions between and among groups of graduate students, faculty, and practitioners is limitless. What follows are approaches we have used at Indiana University with graduate classes of school psychology and

---

Jack A. Cummings, PhD, and Curtis J. Bonk, PhD, are affiliated with the Department of Counseling and Educational Psychology, Indiana University.

[Haworth co-indexing entry note]: "Facilitating Interactions Among Students and Faculty via Web-Based Conferencing Systems." Cummings, Jack A., and Curtis J. Bonk. Co-published simultaneously in *Journal of Technology in Human Services* (The Haworth Press, Inc.) Vol. 20, No. 3/4, 2002, pp. 245-265; and: *Human Services Technology: Innovations in Practice and Education* (ed: Hy Resnick, and Phoebe Sade Anderson) The Haworth Press, Inc., 2002, pp. 245-265. Single or multiple copies of this article are available for a fee from The Haworth Document Delivery Service [1-800-HAWORTH, 9:00 a.m. - 5:00 p.m. (EST). E-mail address: getinfo@haworthpressinc.com].

counseling psychology students as well as with undergraduate teacher education majors. Student feedback on our Web-based instructional practices has allowed us to consider the merits of various ways communication takes place within the digital domain. Too often when we think of teaching opportunities, we only consider what teachers can do for students. However, the electronic environment of the Internet allows rapid information flow from the instructor to students as well as students to the instructor, and students to other students. Extending this framework a step further, it becomes possible to grasp how electronic information flow can also take place to and from practitioners. This article, therefore, is an attempt to clarify such communication possibilities while illustrating the dynamic nature of electronic learning via the Web.

A FRAMEWORK FOR WEB INTERACTION

To conceptualize the avenues for facilitating students' movement toward higher levels of expertise via the Web, it is useful to have an overarching framework. Based on a review of the literature in instructional technology journals, an analysis of Web-based syllabi in the World Lecture Hall, and our own personal reflections of our use of the Web in graduate and undergraduate courses, we (Cummings, Bonk, & Jacobs, 1999) created a 3 × 3 matrix for categorizing components of Web-based instructional activities. The three levels of instructor, students, and practitioner/researchers were crossed with each other to form the matrix. Table 1 provides a matrix of possible Web interactions between and among instructors, students, and practitioners.

As alluded to above, Table 1 reveals multidirectional information flow: from the instructor to students; from students to the instructor; from student(s) to other student(s). Two features of communication in the Internet/Web medium should be noted. Those communicating need not be in the same place nor present at the same time. Thus, communication is neither place-based nor contingent on the participants being available simultaneously. Since participants have more time to reflect on their ideas and consult available references, asynchronous communication allows participants to be more reflective in their responses. This changes the dynamics of the classroom discussion as well as the entire teaching-learning environment. Individuals who are silent in conventional face-to-face class sessions have no option but to speak in electronic conferences; otherwise, they would not be counted as having "attended" the electronic class session. By communicating clear expec-

TABLE 1. Communication Flow Among Instructors, Students and Practitioners/Experts

	To Students	To Other Instructors	To Practitioners/ Experts
From Instructor	assignment schedule lecture notes assignment feedback web links to local and worldwide resources instructor profile assignment clarifications	listservs World Wide Lecture Hall Textbook web electronic forums Lecture notes/ activities	learning communities listservs electronic conferences research articles
From Students	exemplary models of past students' work intra-course discussions in listservs or electronic conferences extra-course discussions virtual debates sharing links	Journal reflections Online quizzes/tests Pre-class session balloting Reflective electronic minute Session evaluations	Web pages resumes on the Web
From Practitioners/ Experts	teleapprenticeships announcements of jobs and internships virtual field trips	listservs	virtual professional development communities listservs

tations for assignments and grading students' contributions, the normally quiet students in the conventional class are forced into active online participation in the class discussion. Our online students have admitted to us, they cannot coast through an online discussion as they can in a conventional college class lecture since they must read all prior posts in order to coherently contribute to the class.

A computer and a connection to the Internet from any type of dwelling, climate, or time zone is all one needs to successfully participate. No longer must participants gather in one centralized location as in the conventional face-to-face classroom or a computer lab. This means that participants can be located literally anywhere on the planet or docking station above and still be actively involved in class discussion. Our focus for this article will be on the use of asynchronous electronic forums. We have experimented with Allair Forums, Conferencing on the Web (COW) and SiteScape (and its previous version, Alta Vista Forums) in our efforts to explore the capabilities of electronic conferencing forums that are Web-based. In the chapter we will not address the use of synchronous "chat" functions. For a more comprehensive discussion of uses of the web in higher education, see Bonk, Cummings, Hara, Fischler, and Lee (2000).

Three approaches we have used to facilitate student interaction in our Web-based classes will be covered. Actual examples generated by our students will illustrate responses to the three approaches. The first approach provides a way for the instructor and students to introduce themselves. By having the instructor model an introduction, it sets a tone for other interactions and serves as a foundation for the electronic classroom climate. The second and third approaches exemplify the two ends of the continuum from highly structured to open-ended unstructured assignments. In the virtual debate, the directions for the assignment help script the expectations for the student interaction while providing indicators of where and when instructor feedback on such interactions may occur. After we discuss the virtual debate, we present a less structured procedure where students from three different continents bring case situations to an open discussion conference. In the final section, we describe how we will use electronic conferencing to address weaknesses in our graduate program in school psychology.

ESTABLISHING A CLIMATE FOR DISCUSSION VIA THE WEB

In the primarily Web-based version of an entry-level educational psychology course for teacher education majors as well as in a graduate seminar in academic assessment and intervention for graduate students in school psychology, introductions were accomplished by a Web-based eight-noun exercise. Students were asked to enter a Web-based forum and go to the "Introduce yourself" thread. The first message in the thread read, "Post a message and introduce yourself. Use eight nouns to describe yourself." The instructor also did the assignment and for each noun provided a paragraph to explain why the noun applied. One of the eight nouns was as follows:

> Cyclist: I have enjoyed riding bicycles since my parents bought a bike that was way too big for me when I was about five. I had to stand on an overturned bucket to even get on it. My feet only reached the pedals for about half a revolution. Now, riding through the hills of southern Indiana keeps me sane. My goal is to ride 3 to 5 times a week. On a good week, I sometimes get in three rides. The piles of paper in my office keep me chained to the desk.

At the conclusion to the instructor's eight nouns with corresponding paragraphs, a caution was given.

> While writing this, I realized that this statement is much more revealing than my normal disclosure to classes at the start of the semester. Typically, I will tell the class about my kids, cycling, and research interests. My introduction is relatively brief because it is necessary to leave time for the class members to introduce themselves.
>
> This illustrates a couple of differences for the virtual classroom v. the traditional face to face classroom. The virtual classroom permits a higher level of participation by the whole class. In the traditional class, people toward the end usually have to rush through their introduction because the bell is about to ring. Another difference is that classroom participation is not whatever rolls off the tip of your tongue but rather the product of more deliberate reflection.
>
> Unlike the traditional classroom, your words will not evaporate. For instance, if you wanted to refresh your memory on someone in the class you could return to the CoffeeHouse Forum and look at their introduction. The same idea applies to ed. psych. concepts we will discuss. Unlike a traditional class, you may return to text from previous discussions.
>
> A caution: When composing your assignment, reveal only those details about yourself that you feel comfortable sharing. If you have a personal question or evaluative comment, please e-mail me (cummings@indiana.edu).

Most of the students started the exercise by stating that it was quite challenging to come up with eight nouns to describe themselves. Four of the first six who posted mentioned that it was difficult. Typical nouns they used to describe themselves were; student, brother, sister, friend, daughter, son, musician, and Christian. While the instructor did not provide a religious affiliation, the first individual who completed the assignment used the term Christian to describe herself. Most of the other students followed suit by identifying their religious affiliation. In using electronic forums during this undergraduate Web class, it became increasingly clear that early postings affected the content of those posting subsequent messages, thereby highlighting the critical role of the instructor in providing guidance to students by commenting on the early postings. This is not surprising, since research in student online case conferencing confirms that the first posts or reactions have a significant impact of later posts as well as the depth of discussion (Bonk, Malikowski, Angeli, & Supplee, 1998; Daytner, Daytner, Dennen, & Malikowski, 1999). If the title or the first response is not interesting, then other students are typically not drawn into the discussion. This perhaps points toward the need for a confederate or devil's advocate within these conferences who provokes student discussion and debate. To understand the role of such role play and debate, online learning instructors need to continue to experiment with their pedagogy in order to achieve quality results.

The careful selection of instructional method in this class significantly extended the personal nature and depth of information revealed by the majority of class members. See Table 2 for a sample of the nouns and corresponding paragraphs. The quotes were selected to illustrate how individuals opened up during the first "virtual" class.

Comments from students at the end of the semester indicated the eight-noun introduction assignment was important in establishing a climate within the virtual classroom. From reading the eight-noun postings of students in the class, one could become acquainted with them as individuals much more quickly than occurs in the conventional classroom. In conventional classes, personal information emerges from a series of classes. By mid-semester in a typical class, the instructor knows a comparable level of information about some of the more vocal students; however, those more reticent tend not to share much about themselves, or even to talk much in class. Class participation in the conventional classroom for the quiet student is either non-existent or takes places within the confines of internal self-dialogue. As a consequence, the instructor knows little about the student. Simply put, the quiet student cannot hide in an electronic classroom.

VIRTUAL DEBATE AS A VEHICLE TO PROMOTE CRITICAL ANALYSIS AND PERSONAL REFLECTION

Debate is a time-honored approach for stimulating discussion and critical thinking (Baird, 1928; Pearson, 1909). In structuring an electronic or "virtual" debate, the general topic, "cultural test bias," was divided into subtopics (Cummings, 1998). For the debate, the subtopics were content bias, predictive validity bias, construct validity bias, mean score differences, efficacy of special education for children with mild

TABLE 2. Selected Quotes Illustrating the Personal Nature of Information Revealed by Students Responding to the Eight Noun Introduction Assignment

Student - This noun comes to mind first because of the context of this assignment as a class assignment. As a student I interact with others in classes in both a learning and a social environment. It can be a challenge to do this since I am so much older than the majority of the students, but I still enjoy it. There are sometimes people that are such fun to talk to and who add so much to my life with their experiences and insights that we no longer think of the age difference.

Chris Farley fan - I have always had a crush on this guy for some reason. I believe that even though he is a huge man, he is extremely graceful and athletic. The way he can do a dead fall on a coffee table takes my breath away.

Ankle twister - Ever since I was a child, I have been falling on concrete, tripping on carpet, falling off my bike, and slipping on the ice. I am a very clumsy person by nature and I've sprained my ankle every year of my life. Attractive?. . . Many see this quality as simply irresistible. . . . . . And I'm the pope's mother.

Quote-collector - I have a friend studying in Germany who sends me two quotes every day. I underline two sentences at a time and write other things on index cards. From Bible verses to cartoon soothsayers' sayings, I love a good quote. Although, I'm not much on the drippy Hallmark inspirational ones.

People-person - You wouldn't think that I'm a people person since I'm taking this course on the web, eh? No, it's true. Ask Mary or Tom. I really come alive in the middle of a crowd of people, sometimes to the point of obnoxiousness. I have a loud voice and I use it very much. I can usually draw a crowd and repulse them just as fast, at least I think I can.

Athlete - I enjoy sports and the outdoors!!! I love to run and go hiking. Hawaii has some really beautiful trails, so if any of you are interested in knowing them when you plan your next vacation feel free to email me.:) I also enjoy entering races with my family. I have completed several triathlons and did the Honolulu marathon once (and will remain that way). I enjoy playing racquetball, volleyball, basketball...most sports.:)

Wife - This noun is one of my two favorites. I have been very happily married for eight years now to a man who never stops surprising me both in his personality and his abilities. Just when I think I know him, another facet is revealed. The old cynical view of the "spark" being gone after a few years of marriage is baloney. My day still brightens and my heart still sings when he walks into a room. We are very opposite in many ways, and I think that helps us to not take each other for granted.

mental disabilities, and the impact of special education labels. Pairs of students were assigned to each subtopic. For example, one student was assigned to play the role of criticizing tests on the basis of predictive validity bias and another defended tests by finding arguments and evidence that were supportive.

There were three parts to the web-based debate assignment; posting an initial position statement, rebuttal, and personal reflection. Each student was assigned to be either a critic or defender of intelligence testing. Half the students were placed in the role of critic, while the other half defended the use of intelligence testing. Whereas in a conventional face-to-face debate one side goes first and then the next, using an electronic forum avoided the problem of who spoke first, and who was able to say the last word. In the electronic debate, the critic and defender simultaneously posted initial position statements. Two separate electronic forums were constructed so that defenders for the various subtopics could see the initial position statements posted by fellow defenders, but not until a pre-specified date and time were they able to cross into the critics forum. Likewise, during the formative stage of the initial position statements, the critics could not see the work of the defenders but could see the work of the critics. At a set time, the forums were opened such that those on the opposite side could view the work of their opponents and offer rebuttals. The student who was assigned the role of critic on the topic of predictive validity crossed to the defenders' forum and was required to reply to the initial position statement by critiquing and rebutting the defender's initial position statement on predictive validity bias. The other student in the pair crossed to the critics' forum and wrote a rebuttal to the original position statement of the critic on the subtopic of predictive validity. As should be clear by now, while online learning offers unique and rich learning opportunities, it also mandates greater task structuring on the part of the instructor.

The goal of the rebuttal was to expose inconsistencies, false analogies, irrelevant arguments, errors of logic, and inaccurate causal relationships (Pfau, Thomas, & Ulrich, 1987). To the degree possible, the rebuttal was to offer plausible alternative arguments. It is important to point out that a common problem with oral refutation is that most students fail to go beyond a restatement of the evidence presented in the initial position. This lack of justified reasoning and lack of depth of processing, however, is more prevalent in online discussions among undergraduate students (Bonk, Malikowski, Supplee, & Angeli, 1998) than graduate students (Hara, Bonk, & Angeli, in press). In this particular study of graduate students, an effective rebuttal was both offensive (destroying others' arguments) and defensive (buttressing and strengthening one's own arguments).

The final and third part of the assignment was to review the entire set of position statements and rebuttals and to construct a personal reflection on the broad topic of intelligence testing with minority children. Each student posted his or her personal statement in a private forum. In the private forum, only that particular student and the instructor could read and write messages. Students were unable to view their peers' private forums.

Students' reports of time associated with phases of the assignment. At the time of the initial assignment, students were given self-monitoring sheets and asked to keep a record of the time they spent on the various phases of the electronic debate. See Figure 1 for the mean times for phases of the debate reported by the graduate students. Students spent most time preparing the initial position statement. The position statement took an average of 7.3 hours to research and compose. Reading others' initial statements took 1.4 hours, with preparation of the rebuttal accounting for 3.9 hours. Transferring their responses to the Web via Allaire Forums took an average of 37 minutes the first time. The second transfer for submitting the rebuttal and third for submitting the personal reflection were quicker, 21 minutes and 23 minutes, respectively. The use of the conferencing software did not prove to be a distraction from the content goals of the exercise. The total transfer time averaged 1 hour and 21 minutes, compared with more than 25 hours spent in library research, analysis of articles, and composing statements and rebuttals.

Graduate students' reactions. The feedback from graduate students was highly positive. Among the unsolicited comments were general observations about enjoying the electronic forum as a tool for debate. In an unsolicited e-mail to the instructor, one student commented "I absolutely love this format of idea exchange–should be a standard tool for our dept." See Table 3 for representative comments from students in the class. It should be noted that feedback was anonymous and solicited via

FIGURE 1. Mean Student Time Allocated to Phases of Debate

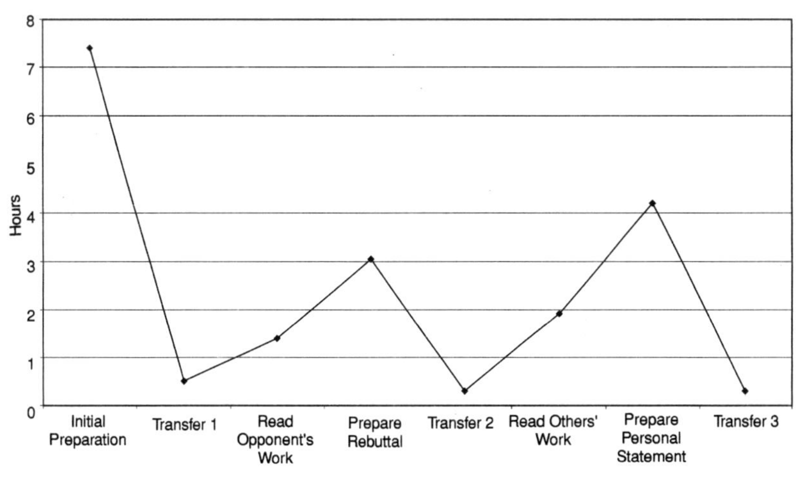

TABLE 3. Perceptions of Strengths and Weaknesses of the Electronic Debate

Strengths	Weaknesses
format eliminated the anxiety that would have been present in a traditional face-to-face format	the other side (did not) answer some questions I had for them, in a face-to-face debate, I would have had an opportunity to ask them questions about some of their points
less inhibiting, had time to formulate my thoughts and then time to think about my opponent's position and then rethink and develop another argument	during the initial debate you really weren't sure which angle to take; therefore, the critic and defender may have been debating different issues
overall it was not a difficult process (referring to electronic transfer of statements)	the interactive, oral, spontaneous aspect of traditional debates was missing and could have added to the excitement
enjoyed this much more, my concern would have been if somebody became more aggressive in the debate because the interaction was not face-to-face . . . However that did not occur	face-to-face formats force us to think on our toes, think quickly, etc.
great critical thinking assignment	
the ability to exchange ideas with others, we need more of this	
being able to do the final in complete isolation, having the opportunity to interact with someone else in the class, it made what I said seem real and relevant because I knew someone was not only going to read what I wrote but reply to it	
liked the novel approach to debating; what a tumultuous project!	

QuizSite (*http://www.best.indiana.edu/*), a web-based assessment program developed by the staff of the Bureau of Evaluative Studies and testing at Indiana University.

In the 3 × 3 matrix, mentioned earlier, the debate would be classified as a student to student activity; however, with minor modifications it could be expanded to other forms of interaction. For instance, practitioners might enter such a debate at a prearranged time and in a manner chosen by the instructor. Practitioners, or researchers with expertise in the area, might pose counter arguments or alternative scenarios. They might also sympathize or support one side of the debate over the other. Or, alternatively, experts might pose the original case or controversial issue to be solved by small groups with an award awaiting the highest quality response or most creative solution. While the debate described previously was held within a single class, future debates will invite classes from other universities as well as researchers and practitioners to comment on the merits of various arguments. The next debate could be intercollegiate with teams drawn from different universities, or teams composed so as to have team members collaborating across institutions.

FACILITATING INTERNATIONAL CONVERSATIONS

Use of online learning tools such as Conferencing on the Web (COW) allows for students and instructors an opportunity to discuss important personal issues on the Web as well as receive advice from peers and mentors around the globe. To motivate student learning, it is vital to have these discussions concern meaningful, authentic, and representative situations. For the preservice and in-service teachers we have been teaching on the Web the past five years, case situations often have shown students how similar their problems are whether they are in Korea, Finland, or one of various universities around the United States. This international component within the COW conferences has not only expanded the volume of cases students can discuss and debate, it has markedly elevated the level of case discussion and debate. Students in the US were amazed at the depth of discussion and degree of research backing in the posts from the Finnish students. And while they were anxious about writing in their second language, the students from Finland were planning to teach English as a second language. As a result, they fared quite well in the COW environment.

There were some interesting trends in COW. From a quantitative standpoint, each semester the depth of student discussion increased as the words per post elevated from slightly more than 100 words per post in the spring of 1997 to nearly 200 words per post in the spring of 1999. This increase was likely due to better training, easier conference configurations, and the added international component. At the same time, the number of responses per case posted was reduced from around six responses per post in 1997 to three in 1999. So, students increased the depth of discussion but did not respond in as many discussions. While most of the hundreds of cases submitted in COW each semester entail relatively minor problems related to classroom management and motivation, there are usually cases that involve major issues related to drugs, suicide, and school violence.

Table 4 provides an example of a discussion started by a Finnish college student about a potential student suicide. It is interesting to note that peer, instructor, and practitioner advice commenced in less than an hour after the original posting and did not end until more than two months later. A total of 20 responses were made with numerous suggestions for how to handle the situation. To a degree, the instructor plays

TABLE 4. Conversation on Student Suicide (Note: All names of students have been changed)

Conference: Finland_Cases
Topic: 202. Big Global Problems

---

1. **Author: Nina Velkonen** (nvelkone)
Date: Feb. 20 6:11 AM 1998
I don't know whether this case is a major global problem but at least there are similar problems all over the world, I believe. Tell me if you have had similar experiences or have any solutions to the following situation: you've just finished a class and the school day ends. All the children joyfully pack their backpacks and rush out of the door. You notice that one of the shyest pupils is taking his time and seems kind of nervous. It's obvious that the child has something on his mind: "I'm planning to commit suicide tonight...", he says. This really happened to me when I was working as a substitute teacher! Now give me some ideas: what are you supposed to do? What I did (whether I acted in the right way or not, I do not know) was that I tried to help the student by talking to him and asking him questions and so on. The reason he had lost hope was that he did not want to go home. His parents were alcoholics and aggressive toward each other. This boy's older brother had committed suicide some years earlier. I told him that I would become awfully sad if he did it and that it's not a solution to the problem.

Then I spent a sleepless night thinking about the situation and blaming myself about not contacting any authorities...Luckily the boy came to school the next day. I love teaching and especially the responsibility the teacher has in education but situations like this really make you puzzled.

---

2. **Author: Kirsi Rarva** (krarve)
Date: Feb. 20 7:01 AM 1998
Hello Nina, I used to have a student as well as a friend who were both considering committing a suicide. They would talk to me about it and I would just listen about their problems. In addition to listening and asking questions about their problems I invited them to meet me and some of my friends when we were doing something fun (playing volley ball, sledging...). I think they finally got more friends and found motivation to live on. I think that a person with such difficulties or who is so depressed needs to know that someone is willing to go through the difficulties with them, but that that someone not just stays in that misery with them but shows them some positive things in life that they could cling to.
In your case, how old was the boy? Some of my friends are surrogate mothers to children with unstable home backgrounds. If the child is young and the situation at home very bad I think the teacher should contact a social worker. It's moving to see how these children enjoy their new homes. Anyway, I think that in this kind of situation the teacher should not stay alone but contact other teachers and authorities in order to help the child.

---

3. **Author: Sheila Barney** (sbarney)
Date: Feb. 24 5:39 PM 1998
I agree with Kirsi that the authorities should be contacted. The child is obviously in danger, either from his parents or himself. And it is also good to give them good things to live for, so that they know that life can be better, and it will be better one day. I think you were right to talk to him and try to talk him out of it, but he also needs help from more than one person. It is important to have a network of people you can count on. Since he could not count on his parents, he needs even more people to fill

in that gap. I think the best thing would be to take the boy down to the guidance office, or to call someone to come help him (we have child services in the US who do that, I don't know if you have that in Finland). But of course when you are faced with a problem like that, one that you never would have planned for, it's hard to know what to do. I think that you did a good job, and I'm glad things worked out for the best.

---

9. **Author: Jordan Ferret** (jferret)
Date: Mar. 5 11:08 AM 1998
Nina,

As I read everyone else's responses, I agree that you should talk with the student and try to get involved in his life, but you also need to remember that he has two alcoholic parents who are obviously neglecting him. I would have called the authorities sooner, only because you don't know what could be going on at home, and someone with more authority than you should check it out. I don't disagree how you handled the situation, but you could have done more to protect that child. Obviously he was hitting rock bottom, and sometimes just talking to a child isn't enough. Next time, everyone should be more ready to handle these kind of situations. You are talking about a child's life, you're lucky he came back the next day.

---

20. Author: Ryan Itkus (ritkus)
Date: Apr. 6 2:31 PM 1998
To me most suicide cases could have been prevented if there was a friend involved. We as educators must wear many faces and one of them is a friend to the students. In this situation you were lucky. I do believe someone else should have been contacted. After individually talking to the student you should have been able to identify a problem, and perhaps contacted the school counselor, then I would have taken all precautions before releasing the child to go home. Perhaps involve the administration. I wouldn't have left the child until I became almost positive that he would be there the next day.
Throughout the years children develop and learn the limits of peer pressure, and helps to have others around to support their self-esteem.

Hide/Unhide Response

the same role in the electronic discussion as in the conventional face-to-face classroom. He or she must account for participants, ask questions, provide task structuring, push students to explore, model responses, and offer needed information when asked. Such tasks should increase both the sense of complexity and intrigue within the teaching profession.

Whereas the role of online instructors may appear quite different, there are similarities to conventional face-to-face instruction. The online instructor has to decide when to intervene in the electronic discussion. Decisions about whether to query, provide a partial answer, or to directly answer a question are comparable across teaching formats. How to redirect the discussion when it is off track is another instructional decision that is faced. In addition, the online instructor must decide whether to provide public or private feedback to the student submitting the case. Posting in a Web forum means all students see the feedback. Such decisions about feedback increase in complexity when the student seems particularly troubled by the events described. For instance, the student submitting the original case listed in Table 4, reentered the discussion at two different points to reflect on the advice she received and to note the happy ending that ensued. Web conferencing simultaneously opens up a New World for educational assistance and confrontation. It is clearly a place for professional mentoring, inquiry, debate, personal reflection, collegiality, and shared knowledge.

Table 5 illustrates an international conversation on a lighter topic, the appropriateness of male teachers with pierced ears. The responses of the American, Korean, and Finnish students clearly reveal the role culture plays in how one views body piercing. For some it is culturally acceptable, for others it is repulsive, and for still others, one must reflect on the commonly accepted and viable professional practices of the school community before piercing portions of the male anatomy. As with the previous approaches described in this chapter, the procedure of having students submit case problems allows for substantial student to student interactions. Here, students can test their views on issues like body piercing and suicide prevention as well as obtain advice on what to do. Such explicit discussion is much rarer in the traditional classroom.

Of course, as alluded to earlier, the instructor still plays a vital role in the electronic conference. He or she might point out similar issues faced during his or her career as well as some of the decisions that were made. Additionally, the instructor can seek outside parties to inform the discussion. These outside participants can bring the perspectives of researchers and practitioners.

OUR NEXT STEPS

Due to how quickly innovative ideas can be implemented and tested, we have found using the medium of the Web to be an invigorating experience. In designing activities for the Web, we have been mindful of the learner-centered principles developed by a task force of the American Psychological Association (*http://www.apa.org/ed/lcp.html*). Using these principles as a framework, we devised a dozen recommendations for placing students at the center of their learning (Bonk & Cummings, 1998). The Web provides a potent vehicle to shift the focus of learning. Table 6 provides a summary of our learner-centered recommendations.

TABLE 5. Conversation on Males and Earrings (Note: All names of students have been changed)

Conference: Indiana_Cases_Fall98
Topic: 100. Big Global Problems
Conversation 1
All posts and replies

---

1. Author: Gregory Flees (gflees)
Date: Nov. 24 10:13 AM 1998
The teaching profession is relatively conservative in their attire. But as more males start to get their ears pierced I wonder how this is going to go over in the education system. I personally do have my ears pierced and I know that when interviewing and in other situations such as that earrings in males have no place. But what about after being hired? Is it appropriate for males to have earrings when teaching in the normal classroom environment? As it becomes more common for males to have earrings should men have the ability to walk into a classroom (and someday interviews) wearing earrings just like a female and not have social stigma attached to them?

---

2. Author: Hanyuk Lee (hlee)
Date: Nov. 27 11:54 AM 1998
I read your article very considerly.
I'm a Korean student. In my country, males also have gotten their
ears pierced since about three years ago. We are negative to males wearing earrings, especially to adults. Also I dislike it. I think that earrings are just for women to make more beautiful. why man wears earrings? for the beauty. or for the self-satisfaction. Though man wears earring for that reasons, I don't understand.

---

3. Author: Hunsook Kang (hkang)
Date: Nov. 29 9:59 PM 1998
I 'm also a Korean student. I sometimes saw a male wearing earring and met somebody who will wear same earrings with her boyfriend. At first, I was really surprised a man who wore earrings. I was also surprised to see a student who pierced ear or wore earring because it was prohibited in Korea middle school and high school. In Korea it is very rare to see a male student who pierces his ear because our prejudice that wearing earrings is just for women (even a female student should not wear earring in class according to school's rule), and there were somebody even a lady should not wear earrings.

In Korea we have many regulation that prohibited student's behavior like smoking, wearing earrings and necklace, growing hair, etc. They just think the prohibition helps student's sound spirit and his concentration of studying. You agree with this? Some degree I agree with this but I think for the expression of student's character some prohibition should be disappear.

---

4. **Author: Liisa Pelkonen** (lpelkon)
Date: Nov. 30 6:15 AM 1998
This appears to be an issue that reveals some vast cultural
differences between the so called western and oriental cultures.

Body piercing became a new fashion trend in Finland about a year
ago, and it's fairly common to see young people wearing earrings
in their nostrils, eyelids and tongues or lips, not to mention the body areas that aren't visible to all...

I don't want to criticize the Korean school regulations, but as a Finn I see this problem from a totally different perspective. I believe that in Finland the first men started wearing earrings in public in the late 1960's and 1970's so we are fairly used to them by now.
I've never heard of a man not hired for a job because of an earring. Although last winter I heard of a girl who took off her tongue-earring when she applied for a shop assistant's post and who then put it back on when she got the job. I think that cowardly. If you try to be a rebel, do it properly. I think she should wear it all the time if she's for it, not just when she feels it's safe. . .

I personally feel that earrings don't look good on every guy, but I don't have anything against male teachers' wearing them.

---

6. Author: Dedra Nobrowski (dnobrows)
Date: Dec. 2 5:07 PM 1998
I have a friend that works in an after school daycare associated with the school corporation. She recently added an eyebrow ring to her four other earrings. My question is that if women are allowed bodypiercing, why shouldn't the men be allowed? Personally, I believe that men with earrings and women with many sets of earrings would be accepted in a larger, urban, liberal community and that smaller, more conservative communities might reject it. I guess that it depends on where you want to teach.

---

11. Author: Jerry Smith (jsmith)
Date: Dec. 17 10:33 PM 1998
Special note about earrings and other jewelry: The High School Athletic Rules does not permit jewelry no matter the sex in any sport!! As for earrings etc for teachers–do as the school district you are looking for a job in!!!!

Hide/Unhide Response

... next new post >>

Your Reply:

Check here to have your post interpreted as HTML

submit reply | preview reply | clear typing

TABLE 6. A Dozen Recommendations for Using the Web to Place Students at the Center of Their Learning[1]

1. Establish a safe environment and a sense of community by allowing participants to introduce themselves.
2. Exploit the potential of the medium for deeper student engagement by considering the unique environment offered by the Web and by avoiding the temptation to transfer conventional face-to-face activities without significant reconceptualization.
3. Let there be choice by allowing students freedom to select discussions they wish to join, thus capitalizing on their interest areas and strengths.
4. Facilitate, do not dictate. The opportunity is to be "a guide on the side" as opposed to "a sage on the stage."
5. Use both public and private forms of feedback to students. Posting feedback to a student's submission where all can see allows the instructor to guide the discussion. E-mail directed to a single student allows private feedback on grades.
6. Vary the forms of electronic mentoring and apprenticeship by using feedback from peers, more advanced students, other faculty, and practicing professionals.
7. Employ recursive assignments that build from personal knowledge. Sequential assignments that revisit students' earlier submissions avoid the feeling that the work may be forgotten after its initial submission.
8. Vary the forms of electronic writing, reflection, and other pedagogical activities.
9. Encourage students to explore the Web and bring back material that enhances course content.
10. Provide clear expectations and prompt task feedback.
11. Plan strategies for evaluation prior to giving assignments and recognize that individual feedback is time consuming; also, score student work dimensionally where possible.
12. Look for ways to personalize the web experience.

[1]Elaboration on the recommendations may be obtained from Bonk, C. J. & Cummings, J. A. (1998). A dozen recommendations for placing the student at the centre of Web-based learning. *Educational Media International*, *5*(2), 82-89.

Our experiences experimenting with the Web have revealed the use of electronic conferences can be time consuming and laborious in the amount of student feedback and task structuring required. To save time, the instructor should use a combination of feedback to the entire group and judicious use of feedback to individuals. Again, see Bonk and Cummings (1998).

In order to talk about our future use of the Web as an electronic conferencing tool in the graduate program in school psychology at Indiana University, it is appropriate to consider some of our instructional goals. As a function of a recent student/faculty evaluation of our program, we identified the following goals: to increase the quality of interactions across beginning and advanced students; to increase the frequency of interactions among geographically dispersed interns; and to expose our students to multicultural aspects of clinical practice. Our experience has been that students within cohorts develop close relationships, i.e., first year students know each other well but associate infrequently with more advanced students. As a consequence, knowledge transfer is limited across cohort levels and student apprenticeship into a community of practice is limited (Rogoff, 1990, 1995). The problem is exacerbated by interns whose sites are spread across the country, making frequent face-to-face interactions prohibitively expensive. Introducing diversity into the curriculum is a goal of the faculty that is shared by others preparing professional psychologists (Fowers & Richardson, 1996; Sue Bingham, Porche-Burke, & Vasquez, 1999).

To accomplish these goals we asked our interns to post genuine cases in a password protected Web forum. During the 1999-2000 academic year, the interns were geographically dispersed in urban locations like Cleveland and Dallas, and in suburban and rural areas across Indiana. Multicultural cases were requested. Interns submitted detailed problems with as much context as possible. Interns were encouraged to modify the background information so as to protect the confidentiality of the individual student, the student's family and the school setting. Interns submitted the background information and assessment data to a Web-based electronic forum that could be accessed by all the current interns, advanced pre-internship students, first year students, and one primary faculty member.

Teams of two to three first-year students in a seminar on academic assessment and intervention selected their cases from those posted by interns. Each team summarized critical aspects of the case and performed a literature review to determine potential interventions with empirical evidence to support their use. While the primary participants in the case discussions were the interns and their peers who are still in the course work phase of their programs, other faculty of the Indiana University-Bloomington have been invited to participate in selected portions of the discourse. While faculty members might bring years of practical experience as well as a wealth of theoretical knowledge to the cases, they also benefit from exposure to geographically and culturally diverse cases. Such interactions will help keep university faculty in touch with the dilemmas of schools in different parts of the country, thus providing exposure to critical topics in the field as well as to the needs of interns and future students.

Students and faculty are not the only possible players here. In fact, since the forum is Web-based, researchers and practitioners with special expertise and experience will also be asked to enter the conference forum and comment on specific aspects of the case, including the adequacy of the assessment procedures, treatment design, and treatment acceptability, as well as any of a host of practical and theoretical issues that may relate to the case.

Naturally, a key goal here is to relate theory to practice in an stimulating and efficient manner. By discussing authentic case situations, the students in the field will be reconnected to experts at Indiana University while those still taking classes have a taste of the real world, and concurrently increasing the bond they feel with peers. Hopefully through such shared knowledge and teleapprenticeship will foster lifelong bonds among students, and between student mentee and instructor are forged. Worries that online learning will depersonalize learning and reduce social contact seem to be unfounded. In fact, just the opposite seems to be occurring in successful computer conferencing situations.

For us, exploring the instructional uses of the Web is a work in progress. Depending when you read this article, the planned use of the Web with interns may be in its first trial or may have gone through multiple iterations and improved significantly by adding many. We invite you to check the status of our project by visiting *http://www.indiana.edu/~schpsy/*. Your participation in its success is just a few keystrokes away. See you online!

REFERENCES

Baird, A. C. (1928). *Public discussion and debate.* Boston: Ginn & Co.

Bonk, C. J., & Cummings, J. A. (1998). A dozen recommendations for placing the student at the center of Web-based learning. *Educational Media International, 35(2)*, 82-89.

Bonk, C. J., Cummings, J. A., Hara, N., Fischler, R. B., & Lee, S. M. (2000). A ten-level integration Web continuum for higher education. In B. Abbey (Ed.) *Instructional and Cognitive Impacts of Web-based education* (pp. 56-77). Hershey, PA: Idea Group Publishing.

Bonk, C. J., & King, K. S. (1998). Computer conferencing and collaborative writing tools: Starting a dialogue about student dialogue. In C. J. Bonk, & K. S. King (Eds.), *Electronic collaborators: Learner-centered technologies for literacy, apprenticeship, and discourse* (pp. 3-23). Mahwah, NJ: Erlbaum.

Bonk, C. J., Daytner, K., Daytner, G., Dennen, V., & Malikowski, S. (1999, April). *Online Mentoring of Preservice Teachers with Web-Based Cases, Conversations, and Collaborations: Two Years in Review.* Paper presented at the American Educational Research Association (AERA) annual convention, Montreal.

Bonk, C. J., Malikowski, S., Angeli, C., & East, J. (1998). Case-based conferencing for preservice teacher education: Electronic discourse from the field. *Journal of Educational Computing Research, 19*(3), 267-304.

Bonk, C. J., Malikowski, S., Supplee, L., & Angeli, C. (1998, April). *Holy COW: Scaffolding case-based "Conferencing on the Web" with preservice teachers.* Paper presented at the American Educational Research Association (AERA) annual convention, San Diego, CA.

Bonk, C. J., & Reynolds, T. H. (1997). Learner-centered web instruction for higher-order thinking, teamwork, and apprenticeship. In B. H. Khan (Ed.) *Web-based instruction.* Englewood Cliffs, NJ: Educational Technology Publications.

Cummings, J. A. (1998, April). *Promoting academic discourse with the web.* Paper presented at the American Educational Research Association annual convention, San Diego, CA.

Cummings, J. A., Bonk, C. J., & Jacobs, B. (1999). *Twenty-first century syllabi: Dynamic tools for promoting interactivity.* Manuscript submitted for publication.

Fowers, B. J. & Richardson, F. C. (1996). Why is multiculturalism good? *American Psychologist, 51(6),* 609-621.

Hara, N., Bonk, C. J., & Angeli, C. (in press). Content analyses of on-line discussion in an applied educational psychology course. *Instructional Science.*

Pearson, P. M. (1909). *Intercollegiate debates.* New York: Hinds, Noble & Eldredge.

Pfau, M., Thomas, D. A. & Ulrich, W. (1987). *Debate and argument: A systems approach to advocacy.* Glenview, IL: Scott, Foresman & Co.

Rogoff, B. (1990). *Apprenticeship in thinking: Cognitive development in social context.* New York: Oxford.

Rogoff, B. (1995). Observing sociocultural activity: Participatory appropriation, guided participation, and apprenticeship. In J. V. Wertsch, P. D. Rio, & A. Alvarez (Eds.). *Sociocultural studies of mind* (pp. 139-164). New York: Cambridge University Press.

Sue, D. W., Bingham, R. P., Porche-Burke, L., & Vasquez, M. (1999). The diversification of psychology: A multicultural revolution. *American Psychologist, 54(12),* 1061-1069.

AUTHOR NOTE

Independently and as a team, we have been seduced by technology for the majority of our professional careers. In 1981, Cummings quickly became enamoured with the first Apple II that was delivered to the Institute for Child Study at Indiana University. Since the early days of learning new word processors on what seemed like a monthly cycle, he has directed technology projects funded by AT&T, and the Office of Special Education and Rehabilitative Services of the U.S. Department of Education. In the late 1980s, he explored the potential of interactive video to assist trainees to improve their interviewing skills. In 1993, his interest turned to the Web as a vehicle to facilitate communication. Initially, his attention was on the development of static Web pages for the School Psychology program and the Department of Counseling and Educational Psychology at Indiana University. In the spring of 1997, he began exploring more dynamic uses of Web conferencing systems and offered the first undergraduate teacher education course delivered solely over the Web from Indiana University-Bloomington.

Bonk has been interested in the world of computer technology since computerizing financial and accounting systems for various companies in the early 1980s. His work at a high technology company in the circuit board industry led him to his graduate studies in educational psychology and instructional technology at the University of Wisconsin. Here, Bonk researched how to utilize technology tools for critical and creative thinking as well as for fostering student reflection and higher-order thinking in writing. His research on writing soon evolved to a focus on collaborative writing and online learning. As one who considered the Internet a gigantic writing tool, this was a logical path for him. In further journeying down this path, he is interested in pedagogical techniques for the Web as well as videoconferencing. He recently edited *Electronic Collaborators: Learner-Centered Technologies for Literacy, Apprenticeship, and Discourse* published by Erlbaum (Bonk & King, 1998) and was also the technology contributor for the 9th edition of Houghton Mifflin's educational psychology textbook, *Psychology Applied to Teaching* by Jack Snowman and Robert Biehler. In following Cummings' lead, Bonk has been offering a preservice teacher education course in introductory educational psychology via the Web since the fall of 1997. And this work continues to evolve as Bonk is currently creating one of the first electronic readers in educational psychology.

Connecting Aboriginal Learners in Remote Communities: An Online Social Work Course

Steven Hick

SUMMARY. This article describes an Internet mediated first year social work course for First Nation participants. It was developed to meet the needs of several remote communities in Canada for distance education in social work. *[Article copies available for a fee from The Haworth Document Delivery Service: 1-800-HAWORTH. E-mail address: <getinfo@haworthpressinc.com> Website: <http://www.HaworthPress.com> © 2002 by The Haworth Press, Inc. All rights reserved.]*

KEYWORDS. Rural social work, First Nation social work students, Web-based education, distance education, focus groups, Aboriginal culture

Steven Hick, PhD, is with the School of Social Work, Carleton University (course Web address: *http://ia1.carleton.ca/52100/home.html)*.

[Haworth co-indexing entry note]: "Connecting Aboriginal Learners in Remote Communities: An Online Social Work Course." Hick, Steven. Co-published simultaneously in *Journal of Technology in Human Services* (The Haworth Press, Inc.) Vol. 20, No. 3/4, 2002, pp. 267-281; and: *Human Services Technology: Innovations in Practice and Education* (ed: Hy Resnick, and Phoebe Sade Anderson) The Haworth Press, Inc., 2002, pp. 267-281. Single or multiple copies of this article are available for a fee from The Haworth Document Delivery Service [1-800-HAWORTH, 9:00 a.m. - 5:00 p.m. (EST). E-mail address: getinfo@haworthpressinc.com].

INTRODUCTION

This article provides a description of an Internet-mediated first year introductory social work course, and the results of an evaluation study with First Nation course participants. The course description discusses the course structure and instructional design, and presents how the author came to the decision to develop such a course. An evaluation comprised of a focus group with 20 First Nation course participants from remote communities in Canada is also presented. The online course was part of a larger study to develop an innovative learning model for remote Aboriginal communities in Canada. This arose due to an expressed need by several communities for distance education to educate social workers from their culture and community. This, they believe, will enable them to obtain a higher degree while staying connected to their local community. A major concern in remote Native communities is that social workers in the community are unfamiliar with Aboriginal culture and local conditions.

The full-year introductory course was delivered with 20 Anishinaabeg or Ojibway First Nation students in Northern Ontario (Canada) in 1999. Completion of the course was followed by a focus group. The focus group intended to identify aspects of the online course which they "liked" and "disliked," as well as any barriers which may impede their success in an online course.

WHY AN ONLINE SOCIAL WORK COURSE?

The decision to develop an online course for social work arose from the experiences of faculty at Carleton University (School of Social Work, Ottawa, Canada) teaching an introductory social work course over five years, and a widespread need displayed by leaders in a variety of communities for social work educational opportunities using advanced information and communication technology (ICT) to locally train social workers who are from their community and culture.

The School of Social Work at Carleton University has offered an outreach program providing the courses necessary for a Bachelor of Social Work degree in remote communities, with a special emphasis on Aboriginal communities. Demand for the program has exceeded expectations. Part of the degree program is an introductory course entitled "Introduction to Social Work and Social Welfare." This course, usually offered over two terms, builds the foundation for future studies. Historically, delivery of the course off-campus entailed an instructor traveling to a town near the students' location for three or four separate 4-day sessions. Given that the students are living in remote communities, the travel time and cost for both the students and the instructor is high, frequently more than that for a trip to Europe. As well, this model attempted to deliver too much material in a short time span.

After experiencing the limitations of off-campus course delivery, as described above, it was concluded that analysis was required to determine how computer-based learning using the Internet could improve the course. Also, such analysis was seen as important due to the widespread need expressed by adult learners in remote communities for innovative learning models that utilize the high levels of technology available in their communities. I proceeded to develop the course into an online course and ultimately, a request from an Aboriginal educational institute to take the online course was received.

BACKGROUND OF COURSE DEVELOPER

The author (Steven Hick) has been a professor at Carleton University for 10 years. The opportunity to explore online learning combined my interests in innovative and effective teaching, teaching and learning with Aboriginal communities, and information and communication technology. While teaching the first year introductory social work course to 550 students, 400 of which watched the course on television, I concluded that the course would be improved (at least over the television model) by delivering it over the Internet. As I investigated the possibilities, I quickly realized that it would not be the technology that improved the course, but rather the instructional design. I, therefore, stepped back and began investigating how the course should be framed and organized for effectual online delivery.

My interests, both in technology and Aboriginal peoples, arose from my experience as a human rights worker in the Philippines for 2 years (1985-87). I worked closely with several Native communities collecting data on human rights abuses suffered under the Marcos regime. Challenged with smuggling the information out of the Philippines to various international human rights organizations, we resorted to Internet communications. It was in this work of compiling a computerized database of human rights abuses, encrypting the information and sending it through a 300 baud coupler modem, that my familiarity with technology began.

DESCRIPTION OF THE ONLINE COURSE

The development of the course began with interviews with the target learners. From this a learning model was designed that combined elements from several teaching strategies including: didactic learning, reflective learning and experiential learning. The First Nation students believed that elements from all three models were required for a first year online social work course being delivered in remote native communities. Instructional or learning models prescribe how combinations of instructional strategy components should be integrated to produce a course of instruction.

The eventual model combined elements of three teaching strategies in the context of developing an online course:

1. didactic learning
2. experiential learning
3. reflective learning

With the didactic learning mode facts are presented in a manner that is similar to what is used in a well-illustrated text (even though in the case of the multimedia tutorial, the text is electronic). The tutorial incorporates additional detail which might be similar to footnotes or appendices. It also includes visuals such as graphics, still and/or full motion video and may include sound.

The experiential learning mode is characterised by presenting the content in such a manner as to foster decision-making. The learner is expected to be able to apply the knowledge gained to scenarios or case studies and make appropriate decisions.

The reflective learning mode takes the student to a higher level of application of knowledge than does experiential learning. In this mode the learner is presented with extended cases to help gain knowledge through insights and actively applying concepts and information to the situation under consideration. The navigation patterns must support the teaching strategy being used.

The course also included elements of various collaborative learning models whereby learners and the instructor work together to understand, make decisions and apply the knowledge from the course.

The operational components of the learning model include:

- use of practice;
- methods for communication between learners and between instructor and learners;

- methods to collaborate on assignments and learning in general;
- use of multiple examples;
- variations in feedback;
- sequencing strategies, and;
- use of advanced organizers.

Models for instructional design provide procedural frameworks for the systematic production of instruction. The models incorporate fundamental elements of the instructional design process including analysis of the intended audience or determining goals and objectives. Models may be used in different contexts. One model can be used for an entire course of instruction or elements from multiple models can be combined.

In the model developed for this course each piece of learning must have its own learning goals or purposes, and the education strategy of the learning will differ depending on the goal or desired skill level.

The course was developed using dynamic HTML, JavaScript and Active Server Pages, and more recently XML. No template based development tool was used due to the imposed instructional design dictated by such software. Our survey of the "easy-to-use" development tools such as *Toolbook*™, *ICON Author*™ and *Authorware*™ found that each contains an underlying instructional model or models which must be followed in order to use the templates. None of these tools would allow us to develop the course using the model developed in consultation with the target users.

Our initial review (in 1997) of general web development tools such as *Frontpage*™ and *PageMill*™ found that while they are flexible concerning instructional design, they limit the navigational and display options available. It is important to note that since this project began, these development tools have advanced and probably do provide a viable option. For example, *Frontpage*™ now allows fairly advanced options such a XML, which enables the advanced features required by the learning model. The main disadvantage of our initial option was that it required extensive programming expertise and development time, and therefore may be too expensive for many academic applications. The flexibility to design the course to best meet learning needs was the primary advantage of our approach.

The course encompassed the features and elements identified in the model development consultations. The elements include:

- easy to navigate;
- self-test of key concepts;
- use of different media (video, audio, text, images);

- different levels (depth) of material coverage;
- a glossary of key terms;
- an advanced search capability;
- advanced communication and collaboration tools, and;
- simulations and interactive exercises.

The course contained the elements identified above integrated with the combined learning model. It took a team of three people approximately 2000 hours to develop. It contains 300 images, 38 video and audio clips, and 72,000 words of text.

One of the key elements in the design of the online course was the ability to examine course material at different levels or depth of coverage. For example, when a learner enters a new topic, basic information is displayed (didactic learning) along with options to explore the topic further. Each additional selection provides the learner an opportunity to go deeper into the topic (experiential and reflective learning). A "More Notes" button provides deeper information where the concept is applied to a particular context. As well, audio, video and illustrated audio options are sometimes presented to show how the concept applies. For example, a role-play of a social work counselling session is used to illustrate how structural social work differs from generalist social work. Finally, the topic page may also present the learner with an exercise that allows them to try out what they have just learned in a case or scenario.

Another key design element is the ability to communicate with other students and the instructor. A conferencing system (newsgroup) connects the instructor and all students asynchronously, and a "chat system" connects everyone synchronously at scheduled times. Allarie forums was used for conferencing and ICQ for real-time chat. The discussion groups asynchronously enable learners to go online whenever they chose and read messages posted by other members of the class. Learners can post their own messages or reply to the messages of others. Allarie Forums has several advanced features that enable learners to attach files, HTML content and to be notified by e-mail whenever another person replies to a particular posting.

The conferencing system had several threads or discussion areas: "Chit-chat Café" for general conversation, "Administrative Questions" for administrative questions for the instructor, and "Topic Discussion" to discuss specific topics. The "Topic Discussion" discussion group was a key aspect of the online course. Every Friday morning I left a discussion question specific to a topic for that week. Students are required to leave at least two replies to each weekly question. Twenty percent of their grade is based on the number and quality of the replies.

EVALUATION RESULTS

Analysis of the experience of delivering the course with 20 learners from remote communities in Canada was completed using a focus group. Learners were asked three questions to elicit discussion: What did you like most about the online course? What did you like least about the online course? and, What were the major barriers inhibiting your success in the course? These three questions elicited discussion about a variety of topics with emphasis on what aspects of the online course assisted them in their learning, and what aspects hindered their learning. The three-hour focus group included all students who were registered in the course and was completed at the end of the course.

The learners consisted of 17 Aboriginal students and three non-Aboriginal students who work in remote communities with Aboriginal people. All but three of the learners were employed full-time as social workers. Most were mature students with anywhere from 5-20 years of direct practice experience. Several of the learners were managers and directors of agencies in their communities. All the students were from remote communities: 500 km from the closest university or college.

The "Summary of Findings" chart (see Table 1) captures the main ideas discussed in the focus group. Overall, the learners were very positive about the experience, but did have concrete recommendations and critiques. Perhaps the most significant conclusion was that the group positively received the suggestion that another future course in the BSW program be taught as an online course.

"WHAT ASPECTS OF THE COURSE DID YOU LIKE THE MOST?"

The group voiced numerous aspects of the course which they liked or that they believed helped them in their learning. Two items stood out as factors that all students appreciated. First, they liked that they learned about the computer and the Internet. For example, one learner stated, "I like the idea that I am learning the operation of the computer–how to use e-mail, send an attachment, send files from home to work–this is stuff that I wouldn't have learned otherwise." Learners also appreciated the convenience and flexibility of the online course. The course enabled them to learn anytime and anywhere. Since they had full-time employment and families, they found convenience to be very important. The ability to learn at a distance from both other students and the instructor

TABLE 1. Summary of Findings

Aspects of Course Liked	Aspects of Course Disliked	Barriers to Success
Online test helped see if I retained material	Too much reading on screen	Scary
Online discussion helped confirm that you understand	Too many readings	I really got discouraged
Online discussion helps to connect with other students	No idea how long it would take me to get through the material	I did not think that I was learning anything
I enjoyed the online discussion	I learn better by having you in a class	Not everyone has a computer out here
I liked that I learnt the operation of the computer & Internet	More examples to explain concepts would have helped me understand better	It is hard to get to the centre to access a computer
I liked that you had objectives and summaries for each module	You left too much time between questions on the discussion group	Not enough time with other students to learn from one another
The glossary really helped me understand all those University-type words	No one told me before the course that it was online	Face-to-face time is important in a 1st year course
I like the layout and look of the online course	I lost interest in the discussion group when people didn't respond to my question	I didn't have any computer skills when I started
Others didn't have to wait for me to understand something	Smaller online study groups would have helped	Did not know about browsers or e-mail
I could log on and learn anytime I wanted		
You really had to motivate and discipline yourself		
I liked that we did not have to meet as often since we are busy and it is hard to travel to classroom		

was appreciated. Foregoing the need to travel from their remote communities to a central location was seen as a major benefit. Learners also found that the online nature of the course enabled them to learn at their own pace. "The online course gave me the time I need to understand something–people didn't have to wait for me, and I could learn anytime I wanted."

The convenience and flexibility aspects of the course also had spin-off benefits that were identified by learners. Several students found that because they could learn at their own pace and anytime, that it took commitment and dedication to motivate them to learn. One student summarized this view: "I was able to see where my dedication and commitment to the course was at. If I wasn't that committed it may have been different. You really had to motivate yourself and discipline yourself–I thought that was good." A few students believed at the beginning of the course that they would not make it–that they would not have the discipline to do the course on their own. They were pleasantly surprised and this helped increase their confidence in their own ability to learn on their own and continue with the BSW program. The majority of learners also stated that they learned more than they thought they would at the outset.

Beyond the general favourable aspects of the course, learners discussed specific components or features of the course that they thought helped them learn better. Specific features that learners found particularly beneficial include: online self-tests after each module; weekly discussion groups; the online glossary of terms; the modular layout of the course, and the organization of the modules with objective and summaries.

Learners found they gained significant benefits from the online tests. The tests were simple multiple choice and true/false questions which corresponded to the material and concepts for each module. Students went as far as saying that the simplicity of the tests was one of its major benefits. They found it useful to have a simple test of their comprehension of the module. As one student summarized the discussion: "I liked the online test to see where I was and if I was retaining the material. It tells you if you are on the right track. Things fall into place." Students felt that a more complicated testing function would have been less effective. "If you made it more complicated it would have just been scary. I liked that I could take a quick quiz and see where I needed to review or go back." The feedback from learners on this aspect of the course was contrary to my expectations. I expected criticism of the online test as being simplistic and lacking detail. In fact, the tests existed as simple multiple-choice quizzes mostly because of development time and costs constraints. It was surprising, therefore, to find that the simplicity of the quizzes was what students liked the most.

The weekly online discussion groups were also appreciated as a major beneficial element of the course. This was supplemented with synchronous (at the same time) CHAT capabilities that was used by only a few students. The asynchronous (at any time) discussion groups were organized such that each student was required to leave at least two messages per week for a grade allotment of 10%. Students believed that the grade allotment motivated them to get going with the group, but in the end they did it because they enjoyed it and found it useful. In particular, students said they used the online discussion to "talk" with other students about the course content and "just to get to know them." As well, they found it useful to confirm their understanding of the course material. Several learners stated that with the online course they were frequently concerned that they did not comprehend the material and concepts, and the discussion group was a way for them to test their understanding and confirm comprehension.

Three distinct discussion groups were established: an administrative questions area, a chit-chat area for casual discussion between students, and a content discussion area where I was vigilant about stopping non-content related discussion. The students especially enjoyed the chit-chat area. Although this feature was a last-minute addition, the learners found it to be an essential component of the course. They believed that it facilitated a connection with others and the development of a sense of community or group cohesion.

The course participants were employed in various social service agencies, but were isolated from other social work colleagues. The course provided their first exposure to online discussion groups or conferencing. The realization that they could connect and discuss issues with similar people in other communities had an extremely positive impact, beyond their experience in the course.

The quality of the writing in the online discussion was excellent. Learners, generally, expressed concerns that their writing skills were lacking, because they had been out of school so long and writing skills were not emphasized in their Aboriginal communities. The online conference gave the learners an opportunity to practice writing, and obtain feedback from other students and the instructor. Perhaps because of the oral tradition of Aboriginal people the students had excellent oral presentation skills, but were less confident about their writing skills. The necessity of having to write their conversations in the online conference group enhanced their writing skills. Many students also appreciated the way in which online discussion groups created a learning environment in which students learned from each other.

The synchronous chat facility was not widely used. Only a few learners have used it, and mostly to get in contact with the instructor. Work schedules and family commitments meant that many learners went online at odd hours of the night or early morning. This made it difficult to schedule any time that everyone could have an online chat at the same time.

One feature that was overwhelmingly appreciated by learners was the glossary of terms. Students found that if they did not understand something the first step would be to go to the glossary and see if definitions of the key concepts in the material would help. The focus group research found that of all the features in the course the online glossary is most essential for a first year level course.

Learners also believed that the modular structure of the course was necessary to facilitate their learning. This was accomplished in two ways. First, the concepts and material for each week was presented in a sequential manner which ensured that all the necessary ideas were learned before a new concept was presented. As well, the material followed a week-by-week progression. This, the learners believed, ensured that they stayed on track. Stepping them through the material week by week was seen as a key structural element for a beginning level course. Several learners stated that they are more non-linear in their approach to learning and at first they thought the course structure would impede their learning. Eventually, they found that the course allowed them to follow the course ideas in an organized way, and also enabled them to explore and discover the material in a non-linear way, if they desired. This was facilitated by a detailed "site map" or table of contents. With the site map students could pick an idea or concept and easily explore it further. This study indicates that having a sequential structure in conjunction with a detailed course map may empower students with different learning styles to learn effectively. We also found that learners may use different learning styles for different material so no one approach is always better. The key for this course appears to be its flexibility.

Finally, learners appreciated the presentation of module objectives at the beginning of each module and module summaries at the end. They said that they wished all courses used this approach, including classroom-based courses. One student summarized the discussion by stating: "The summaries and objectives helped me know what I was getting into and let me know if I learned what I was supposed to learn." Again, the notion that learners need features to confirm that they were learning what was intended was emphasized.

One course element that was not mentioned as being "liked" was the advanced search capability. This was a facility which enabled the learners to search the course using Boolean search parameters or simple key words either by module or for the entire course. The facility used the Microsoft Index server and was one of the most time consuming and costly functions to develop. Given that few students neither used the search nor understood its capability, I would consider foregoing the expense–as least for this particular course. It is possible that the learning model and course layout did not necessitate such a function. For example, the layout made it easy to find materials and the model brought learners through the material step-by-step. For other types of courses the search function may be a necessary and useful function.

"WHAT ASPECTS OF THE COURSE DID YOU DISLIKE THE MOST?"

Learners were immediately vocal on their belief that the course had too much text. They stated that there were too many online readings, and that it was difficult to read text on the computer screen. One student found that she "learned better when you sent printed material. It is better to have it in my hands. You can see ahead, you know where you are and how far you have to go." These comments raise several important design considerations for online courses. First, I assumed that students would print many of the readings and read them from paper copies. This assumption was incorrect, as at least one-half of the students did not have access to a printer. This is an important consideration for education with learners in social work and for learners in remote communities who may not have access to, or the income for, a printer. Secondly, the abundance and ease of access to online readings encouraged me to select too many readings per week. This was anticipated to an extent and I labelled the readings as either "required readings" or "additional suggested readings." This did not elevate the problem as many learners felt that they still need to read everything.

This finding raises important design and structural questions that need to be seriously addressed in online courses. First, for online courses that have an abundance of readings it may be preferable to mail print copies. Students were not adverse to the notion of purchasing a printed course reader, much like they would purchase a textbook. Further, with online readings it may be relatively straightforward to address copyright issues. Finally, an extremely clear method should be used to inform students that they do not have to read everything referred to in the Web site. My future online courses will have separate sections for required and supplemental readings, with clearer instructions.

Several criticisms of the course centered on the facilitation of the online discussion groups. This is a key aspect of the course, as indicated by the focus group discussion. While this is an easy feature to add to an online course, it is clearly a difficult feature to facilitate and administer properly. Learners had two primary criticisms, and a suggestion for a new type of online discussion group. The learners felt that too much time elapsed before the instructor posted new discussion questions. This meant that the students would logon looking for new items upon which to comment and nothing new would be there. Learners also believed that all the questions should be answered whether posted by the instructor or another student. As one learner stated, "I lost interest in the discussion group at times and I hoped that people would participate . . . I wondered if my responses were relevant, but no one said anything . . . anyway my kids really motivated me to keep going back."

Two considerations emerged from these findings. First Nation learners place a high importance on the online discussion group in a social work course, and it is difficult to meet the expectations. Commenting on student responses and facilitating the discussion is a large task for an instructor that consumes considerable amounts of time. One of two approaches could address the learner concerns. Either more instructor time would be required or the learner expectations for instructor facilitation and comments would need to be lowered and specified. In the case of a first year course comprised of First Nation learners from remote communities, it would seem that an increased amount of facilitation and instructor time is required. In other situations a different approach may suffice. At any rate, the importance of the online discussion groups should not be under-estimated, nor the time and skill required by the instructor to adequately facilitate.

The students had a clear desire to connect with other students. Perhaps this was more accentuated, as this was their first of many courses together. Several learners suggested that smaller online study groups would have helped lessen the expectations of the discussion groups, and would have helped in further exploring interesting ideas, as well as help confirm that they were understanding the course. This is an item that should be considered for online courses.

BARRIERS TO SUCCESS

The barriers to success of the course were envisioned as: lack of access to computer equipment and Internet connections in remote communities; lack of knowledge of learners on how to use e-mail, conferencing and Internet browsers; and motivating learners to consistently go to the course on their own time and on a consistent basis. As it turned out the students did have access to the required equipment. The more important barrier was the lack of knowledge and skills in using the computer and web software. A significant amount of time was spent with several students teaching them how to use the necessary software.

The course began with a 3-day meeting of the class in a face-to-face format. I believed that an initial meeting was required for several reasons. First, this online course was to be the first course taken by this particular cohort of students. Although the group will spend the next 5 years together in the BSW program, most had never met each other. I thought that it was important for the students to meet, establish personal contact, and to discuss the BSW program overall. At the initial meeting frustration was expressed by several students concerning the difficulties they envisioned in getting their computer to work properly. Other expressed concerns about not having more face-to-face meetings, given that it was a new program for them. In the end, I assured the group that if they had technical difficulties, I would print and mail them the pages from the web site.[1]

The second reason for an initial face-to-face meeting was that 4-5 students lacked the necessary computer skills to take the online course. The meeting was also used, therefore, to discuss the feasibility and perceptions around taking a social work course online. The meeting was a success in that all participants voiced a desire to "give it a whirl" and see how the online course would work. The learners displayed incredible enthusiasm in learning how to use the Internet software. At the end of the second day, which was largely used to go through the online course, the students did not want to leave at the end of the scheduled time. They were not only exploring the course, but were also discovering the vast resources which were available on the Internet that could help them in their social work practice. For example, one learner described a research assignment that he was given at work in the area of child welfare. When he discovered the vast resources on the Internet, he was surprised and startled. Given the lack of material and library resources in remote communities, the Internet provided access to materials never envisioned. With this experience I concluded that providing an online course to these students not only provided a course of accessible learning, but also opened the doors to learn about the Internet and computer skills in general.

A few students were quite adamant that face-to-face time is critical for a social work course. They found that they got discouraged and bored "just sitting at the computer." They would prefer a course that has a combination of both online learning and classroom learning. When other students asked them about travel time, the desire for classroom time quickly fell. In the end, two meetings were seen as adequate. Overall, the barriers to success of the course hinged on the lack of computer skills and the desire for increased amounts of face-to-face discussion, particularly because it was their first course as a group.

CONCLUSION

The design, development, delivery and evaluation of the online social work course has raised numerous questions and issues. Some faculty were concerned that online learning takes away from the face-to-face interaction that is necessary for a proper social work education. As well, some were concerned that online courses would be used to replace faculty in higher education. Students, on the other hand, were more concerned with how to make online learning better. They enjoyed the experience and found both the method of learning and the computer skills gained to be useful.

The geographic size of Canada and the numerous remote communities of Aboriginal peoples who desire distance social work education necessitate further exploration of the potential of online learning. The experience and evaluation detailed in this chapter illustrates the need to further explore how the Internet can be used to make quality education available to remote Aboriginal learners in their communities. Social service agencies, community organizations and the learners themselves are requesting online educational opportunities, so it is incumbent upon those of us attempting to meet their educational needs to explore the potential of new technologies. Online social work education is not the panacea to address the needs of remote Aboriginal learners, and it could pose significant dangers and limitations. It does, however, provide another method with potential positive impacts and effects.

NOTE

1. This is not an ideal solution as the web site has numerous exercises, audio and video that cannot be printed.

REFERENCE

Hick, S. (1999). Learning to Care on the Internet: Evaluating an online introductory social work course. *New Technology in the Human Services*, 11(4) CHST.

High Tech and High Touch: The Human Face of Online Education

Robert J. MacFadden
Sarah Maiter
Gary C. Dumbrill

SUMMARY. This article decribes and evaluates a Web-based course in cultural competency. The evaluation focused not only on course content but also on the experiences of both the learners and instructors in a relatively new Internet environment of an online course for social work students and faculty. *[Article copies available for a fee from The Haworth Document Delivery Service: 1-800-HAWORTH. E-mail address: <getinfo@haworthpressinc.com> Website: <http://www.HaworthPress.com> © 2002 by The Haworth Press, Inc. All rights reserved.]*

KEYWORDS. Web-based education, online courses, cultural diversity, synchronous communication, instructional technology

THE FORGOTTEN PARTNER: THE LEARNER

Much of the discussion in the literature concerning online education focuses on two major dimensions: technology and pedagogy. The at-

Robert J. MacFadden, PhD, RSW, is Associate Professor, University of Toronto.
Sarah Maiter, MSW, is Lecturer, Faculty of Social Work, Wilfrid Laurier University.
Gary C. Dumbrill, MSW, is Doctoral Candidate, Faculty of Social Work, University of Toronto.

[Haworth co-indexing entry note]: "High Tech and High Touch: The Human Face of Online Education." MacFadden, Robert J., Sarah Maiter, and Gary C. Dumbrill. Co-published simultaneously in *Journal of Technology in Human Services* (The Haworth Press, Inc.) Vol. 20, No. 3/4, 2002, pp. 283-300; and: *Human Services Technology: Innovations in Practice and Education* (ed: Hy Resnick, and Phoebe Sade Anderson) The Haworth Press, Inc., 2002, pp. 283-300. Single or multiple copies of this article are available for a fee from The Haworth Document Delivery Service [1-800-HAWORTH, 9:00 a.m. - 5:00 p.m. (EST). E-mail address: getinfo@haworthpressinc.com].

traction of powerful technologies and new opportunities is usually accompanied by equally interesting discussions on the instructional models and modifications required to deliver online education. Rarely is there any significant focus on the subjective experience of the most important partner in this new educational process–the learner. The literature on online education is largely promotional in nature (Hara & Kling, 2000) omitting references to negative and personal experiences. This chapter explores the human face of online education through an examination of the subjective experiences of both the learner and course facilitator, including the emotional and perceptual changes that impact learners and facilitators in this new educational experience.

As facilitators and evaluators of a recent online course designed to enhance cultural competency (Cultural Competency Course) among human service professionals (MacFadden, Dumbrill, & Maiter, in press), we became concerned that the human issues involved in this new approach to learning needed to be addressed. We were aware, for instance, that our learners experienced a changing emotional topography with both anxiety and excitement peaking in the early stages and as a result, we deliberately scheduled assignments that were more difficult when the anxiety levels were lower.

This six week, Web-based, online course offered individual and group level activities and was designed to encourage learners to explore the issues of cultural competency, their perceptions and practice, and to learn together in an environment that maximized use of the Internet. Results for the nineteen learners who completed the course indicated that they had gained in multicultural skills and awareness and on the Multicultural Counseling Inventory (Sodowsky & Impara, 1996) as a whole. Information was also gathered on the experiences of both the learners and facilitators within this course and will be incorporated below as quotations within square brackets. The course was conducted within the framework of a research evaluation and included an ethics committee review and an informed consent process. Note that many of the comments within this chapter and especially the recommendations at the end relate particularly to Web-based, online courses where interactivity and connection with others is emphasized. More structured, individualized and non-collaborative forms of online education may raise some different issues and result in different experiences.

READING, WRITING AND THE WEB: A NEW PARADIGM FOR LEARNING

Online education is quite new to human service workers. Although various forms of distance education have been around for decades, it is only recently that Web-based, online education has become an option for professionals in human service sectors.

Consequently, both the technology and the pedagogy of online education can be new experiences for both learners and facilitators. Technologically, using a computer to participate in course work, requires both existing and novel technological knowledge and skills. The e-mail component to online courses, as an example, is likely to be familiar to many learners. Other components such as audio, video, presentation programs (e.g., PowerPoint), network or telephone connectivity, whiteboards (i.e., common areas where comments are made on a virtual board and learners can see the comments together and quickly add points) and chat rooms may demand new knowledge, skills and resources for most learners. Several studies report students' frustrations with these technological demands, but do not thoroughly examine this (Burge, 1994; Gregor & Cuskelly, 1994).

Additionally, online courses can vary considerably from traditional or onground courses. Usually there is no face-to-face contact in the online format, and most communication occurs via e-mail or listservs (i.e., digitally). Much communication occurs asynchronously (i.e., messages are read later and responded to after some thought) and there is considerable opportunity in online courses to explore other topics, and surf the Web. In comparing traditional, onground courses with online courses pedagogically, online courses typically involve more interaction with facilitators and students, and more learner control including time and place (Khan, 1997). The online experience is more constructivist for the learner with the teacher becoming a facilitator or "guide on the side" rather than "sage on the stage" (Reeves & Reeves, 1997). The new demands of this online environment can be exciting and challenging but can also create considerable frustration and anxiety if problems arise.

Each section below will be discussed from the perspectives of the learner and facilitator.

EMOTIONS AND ONLINE LEARNING

Learner

Learning can been conceived, generally, as a process that assists in reducing learner anxiety through providing knowledge and insight into issues or problems that the learner wishes to address. This new medium can foster additional emotions associated with new technological and pedagogical demands described above.

Some authors suggest that almost half of the population has some degree of technophobia (Brosnan, 1998) which is defined as a ". . . negative affective and attitudinal response to technology which the technophobe acknowledges to be irrational" (Kirkup, 1999, p. 279). Brosnan associates technophobia with anxiety, prior experience, confidence, self-efficacy, cognitive style, and persistence.

In an article on designing instructional technology from an emotional perspective, the authors recommend addressing the emotional dimensions of learning (Astleitner & Leutner, 2000). Increasing positive and decreasing negative emotions is recommended when creating instructional technology. The negative emotions of fear, envy, and anger should be minimized through a variety of instructional strategies such as being critical but positive, providing consistent and transparent methods of evaluation, encouraging constructive anger, and creating a relaxed learning situation. Positive emotions such as sympathy and pleasure are increased through strategies such as establishing co-operative learning structures, peer helping, intensifying relationships, establishing open learning opportunities, humor and play-like activities. Rather than focus solely on the cognitive and motivational processes, these authors emphasize the importance of a sound emotional experience to learning.

With the new demands of the online pedagogy and technology, learners can become anxious, frustrated, confused, hostile, lonely and feel disoriented, disenfranchised, disempowered, and passive. Conversely, with success, learners can also feel empowered, engaged, connected, competent, knowledgeable, intelligent and active.

In a recent book entitled *Teaching Online*, the author provides the following advice to the new online learner:

> You will experience many feelings when you begin to learn online . . . these feelings won't necessarily be positive. You will feel confused, frustrated, irritated, unappreciated, lonely. You will not feel satisfied at the end of the online experience. (Draves, 1999, p. 30)

Draves notes that online learning is still in the primitive stage and has a whole different set of feelings and emotions to it than does the traditional in-person lecture/presentation.

One recent qualitative study of a Web-based course found that students' distress that included confusion, anxiety and frustration continued throughout the course and that the instructor did not appreciate the duration of these experiences (Hara & Kling, 2000). Students may have had difficulty in expressing these concerns throughout the course because of the power differential between instructor and student.

An added emotional dimension for learners within our course related to the subject matter–cultural competency. Typically, online courses focus on facts and procedures, whereas this course related much more to an exploration of personal attitudes and values. Generally, onground courses on cultural competence are emotionally charged because they require reflection on personal attitudes and values with the additional expectation of personal growth. The struggle experienced in onground courses in this subject matter was also evident in this online course. The online medium, however, may have provided additional opportunities for self-exploration and self-reflection. Many students discussed their own dilemmas while others read about these and added additional comments [it was good to see the struggle to identify one's own culture and the lectures allowed a process of learning to unfold]. There was time to deliberate between messages and to reflect more on personal experience and how this related to comments from other learners. Our preliminary experience suggests that online courses that encourage collaboration and group interaction can be appropriate ways to process emotionally challenging topics.

Facilitator

Many of the emotions experienced by learners may also be mirrored by the course facilitators.

A primary goal for facilitators in the authors' Web-based course was to create a safe learning environment for participants, but it was not clear to the facilitators how safe the environment was for them. Both facilitators had considerable experience in delivering cross-cultural and anti-racist training and education, but no experience in either taking or delivering an online course. How would participants react to the facilitators' material in a virtual environment? How are the conflicts and tensions that cross-cultural training usually evokes managed online? What do they look like online?

The facilitators felt a mix of apprehension and excitement about the challenge of testing their skills in an online setting [Designing this online course has been extremely exciting, although challenging at times; . . . this online environment is completely new to me. So if at times I seem a little lost, it is probably because I am :)]

The facilitators suspected that given the virtual environment was new to both themselves and to the learners, that the constructivist educational principles of being "guides" and "co-learners" with participants would apply more online than it did in their onground teaching. Yet the question of *how* to guide in a completely virtual setting caused the facilitators to worry whether they would become disoriented, disempowered and perhaps be unable to guide with their normal proficiency.

Indeed, in onground settings the participants respect and look to the facilitators for guidance because of the personal presence the facilitators establish and because participants soon learn that the facilitators have a wealth of information and experience in the subject area being taught. Would the facilitators credibility be affected by the difficulties they too would experience with the technology? Would the facilitators be undermined by the mistakes and tensions associated with the new technology? The facilitators wondered whether Draves' (1999) advice to the new online learner about what they might feel would also apply to them as educators; that they too should expect to feel "confused, frustrated, irritated, unappreciated [and] lonely" (p. 30).

Additionally, in our Cultural Competency Course, learners presented with two major goals: eighty-one percent wanted to improve their cultural competency knowledge and skills, and seventy-five percent wanted to acquire skills and knowledge about technology. [My interest in this course is twofold–to become more sensitive and competent in working with diverse populations and to acquire some skills around the use of the Internet; . . . I am struggling mightily to keep on top of this new technology; hence my involvement in this course]. This dual focus generated considerable anxiety for the facilitators. Could both goals be achieved well? Would problems in one area (e.g., technology) seriously impact goal attainment in the other area?

PERSONAL TRANSFORMATIONS IN THE ONLINE ENVIRONMENT

Learner

Given that many human services professionals have not received direct education in computers within their educational experience, some professionals may have forged a self-image that does not include a feeling of competency with technology. Transformative comments such as "Wow, I can't believe I finally figured this thing out! I am not a computer specialist by far" (MacFadden et al., in press) and [I'm looking forward to something new and becoming less of a technopeasant], reflects this redefinition of self and its impact.

Experiencing a successful online course can promote positive changes in the self-definition of the learner [I don't feel quite so much like . . . baying at the moon or into cyberspace]. For some learners, this transformation is like a voyage [I boldly go where no group 3 member has gone before; I am just having fun with this postmodern cyberworld so far so good; I'm fairly comfortable using the Internet and e-mail, so I'm quite excited about the new learning experience I'm embarking on].

Depending on how the online course is structured, a virtual course can promote a very unusual educational experience where the normal identity markers such as age, appearance, race, culture, and gender are not immediately available to participants. For some learners and educational purposes, this can be positive in that prejudice and stereotyping are not as likely to occur and experimentation with self and others' perceptions can occur. Conversely, some learners may be more guarded in their communication and the quality of the interaction impacted without this information. In a course on diversity in social work that employed technology, the instructors noted that the electronic medium allows students to interact with others through the written word and move above the stereotypical responses in face-to-face interaction (Huff & Edwards, 1999). In another study, Latting (1994, p. 37) reports about an online student who wrote, ". . . for me, the whole medium is new. We send letters in a void, and get answers back. We're dealing with people we've never met, and have to learn without labels, which is a great experience for social worker wannabes."

Several studies of computer attitudes and performance in educational contexts have identified women as likely to be more technophobic than men (Brosnan, 1998). Given that the majority of human service professionals are female, this is an important assertion. Brosnan argues a gender schema perspective that suggests that individuals have a perception of themselves as masculine or feminine to different extents and activities within the environment can be identified as masculine or feminine. He suggests that many women perceive using computers as masculine and themselves as feminine and therefore have anxiety and lack confidence in the use of computers. Brosnan contends that this gender inappropriateness strongly influences a woman's sense of self-efficacy with computers. If Brosnan's arguments have validity, then gender may be an important factor in how online education is perceived and experienced. Indeed, one might not only wonder about the extent the pedagogy of online education is gendered, but the extent it is also racially and culturally bound. The focus on individualistic efforts and a separation of emotion from learning and "rational" decision making has been associated with European male thinking (Kincheloe, 1999). In addition, the unstructured exploratory active learning design of online education is not a learning style that rests equally well with all cultures (Wong & Law, 1999).

Facilitators were sensitive to the danger of the online environment isolating learners from each other and fostering individualistic learning divorced from emotion and social context. Weekly assignments, therefore, were centered on both individual and group exercises and co-operation and connection among learners was emphasized.

The facilitators also wanted to avoid fostering gendered thinking. Since one of the facilitators was female and the other male, this provided an opportunity to reinforce non-stereotypical thinking through a deliberate avoidance of only the male facilitator responding to technological issues and avoiding other gendered positioning. Modeling equal gender competence was intended to promote changes in self-definition and self-efficacy among the learners.

Facilitator

As with students, facilitators of online courses have a wide range of direct education in, and comfort level and expertise with computers. Given that many instructors of online courses are relatively new to this teaching medium (Besser & Donahue, 1996; Rahm & Reed, 1998) a considerable level of anxiety can be present for facilitators. Students' frustration with technical problems and anxiety about communication approaches and standards (Dede, 1996; Feenberg, 1987) are reflective of the experience of facilitators. Even if facilitators are comfortable with the technology and the course material, anxiety around the teaching medium can still be present. Indeed, becoming familiar with the technical aspect of the course is probably the lesser concern because of both its concreteness and the option of practice ahead of the course start date while familiarity with communication norms largely occurs during the course itself. In preparation for our course we read much material and engaged in discussions with each other regarding aspects of online communication, but still many surprises occurred during the course. For instance, we learned that giving written directions to students is much more complicated than simply telling them. Just as individuals become frustrated with reading an instruction manual or in trying to follow the "help" of a computer program, participants can also become frustrated by not understanding the text of the instructions given when help is sought from facilitators. It can be extremely difficult to be totally clear and encompassing in explaining a task in a written instruction. There is an assumption that the text of instruction is easily followed by the reader, yet it is not always the case (Hara & Kling, 2000).

Despite the challenges and frustrations, facilitators also gain a sense of achievement not unlike that experienced by participants. Gaining comfort with the technology and learning to solve problems by using the technical support during the development stage of the course can contribute to a greater sense of control and achievement. Facilitators can also feel that they are exploring new frontiers with the attendant risks. Throughout the course, the sense of mastery and achievement gained by facilitators can be tenuous. At times there is a sense that one has helped participants with technical issues or that strides are being made in the learning, yet this sense can change quickly as new issues emerge. Feeling competent is a relative sensation that does not mean that the technology is mastered. Rather, some skills have been gained and one's sense of discomfort is reduced.

Personal transformation and identity redefinition for the facilitator can be influenced by external sources. Mentioning to colleagues that one has taught an online course results in mixed reactions ranging from "Wow, you are a computer whiz" to "That's really a cold way to teach." Yet much of the collegial feedback has been positive reinforcing a desire to experiment, once again, with this medium.

LOST IN SPACE

Learner

A common experience for new online users is the sense of not knowing where one is in the online learning process. There is a distinct risk of becoming lost and not realizing the learning objectives (Khan, 1997). Technologically, navigating through a series of windows within the areas of the course can create a type of dizziness and disorientation not knowing whether one should go up or down to find the appropriate screen. In a sense, there can be a "loss of gravity" for learners in online education [I lost three messages yesterday, somewhere in cyberspace].

Pedagogically, with all the tempting hot links to related resources, it is easy to explore and lose focus and momentum. Some authors have reported how easily students using the Internet become distracted from the task at hand (Faux & Black-Hughes, 2000). Even within each course module, sometimes knowing what level (e.g., individual assignments versus group assignments) the learner is at can be difficult and disorienting. Part of this disorientation can relate to structure. Even though clear structure is critical in online education, learners can still become confused or uncertain what to do next. As an example, learners can choose when to sign on to do the work. Some learners find this freedom liberating while others do not like the "looseness." [Could some of the discussion be more structured–i.e., have a specific group available to chat with the facilitator–to discuss a specific lecture, or a specific issue?].

In addition, learners also report confusion and anxiety from the lack of physical cues in communicating with others. One learner stated,

> I agree with her, but I am not sure if I should send a message saying, "I agree." That's the problem with this e-mail. If this is a classroom, you just nod your head to show your agreement. (Hara & Kling, 2000, p. 11)

This lack of cues reflects problems with feedback for learners in online education. Prompt feedback is important and particularly in Web-based courses (Bonk & Cummings, 1998). Emotional reactions such as anxiety and confusion are also related to the limited social cues, including facial expressions and gestures (McIsaac & Gunawardena, 1996) and this has been referred to as "communication anxiety" (Feenberg, 1987).

Facilitator

While learners can be "lost in space" during the course, facilitators run the risk of becoming disoriented while developing and conducting the course. Use of technical support prior to the start of the course and navigating and familiarizing oneself with the many windows of the course is essential, not only to ensure that the windows link in a logical way, but also to be able to relate to students' feelings when they are moving from window to window.

A greater challenge for facilitators is the absence of normal referents that are lost by the virtual learning environment removing learners from the traditional context of a face-to-face setting. "Some students are found to be impacted by such separation in terms of motivation, retention, and achievement" (Lockee, Burton & Cross, 1999, p. 40). However, little reference is made in the literature of the impact that the lack of a face-to-face setting has for the facilitator. In the traditional onsite classroom instructors are highly aware of students and their nonverbal behaviour. It is fairly easy to read cues from students about their interest level in each presentation and to adjust the material when necessary. Although some cues are verbal, often many are just as likely to be nonverbal. Facilitators use strategies such as scanning the room, noticing eye contact and nods of agreement or disagreement to ascertain the level of interest of participants. These cues contribute to the processing of information resulting in the information becoming meaningful to participants and contributing to their learning (Brindel & Levesque, 2000; Salancik & Peffer, 1978). Not having these reference points can make facilitators feel quite disempowered and feel as though they are functioning within a vacuum. In some online systems, when logging on to the site, the facilitator is not certain whether anyone else from the course is online at the same time or how long ago a message was posted. Some online course structures do provide ways to find out whether someone else from the course is online, but there is a sense of uncertainty whether the participant wants to be working on their own. Facilitators are challenged to find cues that will provide them feedback that helps to assess availability, level of interest of the student and whether learning is taking place.

Facilitators grapple with issues such as: What does bored look like online? How do theories of group dynamics apply to an online group? What does "acting-out" look like online and how do we respond to acting out students without curbing constructive discussion? When has group process become stagnant requiring more intervention from the facilitators? Remaining active in the course by asking questions, making comments, providing encouragement, and connecting people to others in the group can increase the interaction in the virtual setting providing instructors with some indication of students' level of engagement.

It is important for facilitators to find ways to anchor themselves within the course, to gain direction, maintain momentum, seek feedback and adopt strategies that will enhance their sense of orientation and stability. If the facilitator becomes disoriented at any time, there is a good chance this will also happen to the online learners.

NEW ROLES: THE CYBERLEARNER AND CYBERFACILITATOR

Learner

Online education emphasizes particular features of the learner role. Generally, learners are viewed as needing to be more active, more exploratory, and having more responsibility for when, how and what is learned. This increases the learner-centeredness and places more demands on the learner. Some learners may enjoy this centeredness and other learners may experience difficulties. Schoech (2000) notes that the instructor as "sage on the stage" becomes a "guide at the side" and students become more responsible for their learning while instructors become curriculum designers, guides and monitors. [This is certainly a new and different (at least for me) way of learning and interacting.]

Facilitator

While the "guide at the side" role of the online facilitator is emphasized in the literature, facilitators may have mixed reactions. Some may dislike this more indirect role while others may be challenged by the new learning required.

Facilitators in an on-ground course may be accustomed to students not coming to class and have developed strategies for addressing such issues. In an online course, reasons for students not participating may be unclear for facilitators. Reaching out to students more intensely at the early stage of the course seemed to increase their level of engagement. Additionally, as the course progressed, students participated more in discussions with group members and had less interaction with facilitators.

Although students appeared to require less interaction with the facilitator, feedback from participants suggests that it may not be that they required less interaction, but the type of interaction required was different. They required less interaction around the technology and the new medium but more around the actual work being completed. Indeed, Web-based instruction (WBI) may demand a higher level of interaction with students. Stock and Freddolino (1998) found in their comparative study of a Web-delivered course in human services with an onground course that student performance was comparable for onground and online courses. However, even though Internet students enjoyed the flexibility of WBI, they found the lack of face-to-face interaction to be a negative factor. Furthermore, WBI is not labour saving but is a way to take social work education to a wider audience. Schoech (2000) found that even with a very small class size (8-10 students) more time is required of the instructor in developing and delivering a Web-based course. Additional time is also required in preparation for class presentations as Internet technology limits flexibility. In his course, Schoech used the chat forum to deliver the class and to engage in discussions thereafter. He notes:

> You cannot "wing it" very easily on the Web. Class content needed to be thoroughly planned so that the instructor could guide the interaction in the chat room rather than become immersed in the hot topics usually under discussion. (p. 472)

ONLINE AND ONGOING: LEARNER AND FACILITATOR SUPPORT

Learner

As with traditional education, online education also features support from fellow students (Khan, 1997). This support can be especially critical when novel skills and knowledge are required. In a recent study of a social work online course, the author notes the importance of chat on the overall satisfaction for the user and the need to build mechanisms for informal learning. In traditional courses, much support occurs before and after class to validate perceptions, share emotions and explore new ideas. In online courses, unless some interaction like this is structured in, there is more isolation. The author recommends having netmeetings, advanced e-mailed agendas, or telephone conference calls as possibilities (Schoech, 2000).

The facilitators of our Cultural Competency Course encouraged participants to connect and work with each other through "chat" sessions, but participants were unable to schedule mutually convenient times for these sessions to take place and pressure to do so frustrated learners. Some participants, however, replaced online peer support with "live" support by colleagues in their own work settings, as one participant noted [my co-worker kept encouraging me (re: technical problems) and this made the difference].

As mentioned above, Hara and Kling (2000) report a reluctance of learners to persist in indicating to facilitators the difficulties they face with online technology because they feel "stupid." Such reluctance to seek help occurred in the Cultural Competency Course. A participant who stopped signing onto the course and was contacted by facilitators explained:

> Technical difficulties have me on a holding pattern. I have called [online support] and did not find the gentleman very helpful. I am unable to access chat, I get an error message. I can and do get the readings. I can't seem to make audio work but can download file. I feel rather inept.

Other learners did not feel their difficulties had anything to do with their own ineptness and had no problems voicing their complaints. A learner annoyed with the time it was taking to navigate the course structure complained to the facilitator about [the bullshit you have to go through to access the information to begin to assess your information that would lead to actually doing what your requesting]. Although blunt, these comments were constructive because they indicate the degree of frustration some learners were facing. Such directness prevents the danger Hara and Kling (2000) noted occurring, of facilitators failing to recognize the extent or duration of student distress and anxiety.

Facilitator

Just as isolating online learners needs to be avoided, isolating online facilitators also needs to be avoided. The course facilitator's perceptions and new ideas about the course direction and content need to be scrutinized and validated. Participants can provide the facilitator with essential feedback but relying on learner support alone is inadequate and inappropriate.

Facilitator support was achieved in the Cultural Competency Course through use of a three-person team comprised of two facilitators and a course coordinator. It may not always be practical to have two facilitators but facilitator access to at least one other support person outside the facilitator-learner dynamic is essential, particularly when the facilitator is new to providing online education. Typical aspects of this team support in the development stages were e-mails asking [I have made considerable changes to the case examples for week 2, could you read them to see whether they are okay?]. A member of the development team checked every online item for clarity and accessibility. Throughout the course, the team shared their perceptions and feelings that provided an important aspect of support.

Support for the facilitators is particularly important regarding dealing with participant distress. The discrepancy between the immensity of learner distress and the expression of this distress (Hara & Kling, 2000) needs to be bridged. Yet learner comments of frustration could easily leave facilitators feeling "stupid" or "inept" themselves and leave a facilitator feeling hopeless about responding effectively to learners. By working as a team, facilitators in our Cultural Competency Course managed to avoid demoralization and to accept rather than react to blunt feedback and worked to remedy the problems and distress, rather than let this remain dormant.

Finally, facilitators need excellent technology support to ensure that the course runs as smoothly as possible. This support needs to be available anytime and delivered by staff who can understand questions and respond with clear instructions. While some authors suggest that technological competence is not required of online facilitators (Draves, 1999), our experience is that the more one understands technology, the easier it is to comprehend the technology support staff and to communicate, problem-solve and empathize with learners.

CONCLUSION AND SUGGESTIONS

Drop-out rates among distance education and online courses are reputed to be significantly higher than for onground courses (Noble, 1999). Part of the reason for this may relate to the subjective experience of learners, many of whom are struggling with several novel features at once and yet are responsible for completing assignments on time.

Designers, developers and facilitators need to be aware of these subjective experiences and address the issues they raise. Based on the literature and our experience, we offer several suggestions that might be useful in promoting a positive, challenging experience for learners and facilitators. These suggestions are essentially hypotheses and need to be tested empirically.

1. Designers need to consider the emotional topography of online courses, especially for new users, and construct the courses to build early successes, feelings of competency and connections with others. This may mean delaying assignments that are more difficult until the technology has been mastered and personal connections made with others. Creating dovetailing structures (e.g., low emotional intensity, high assignment difficulty, high emotional intensity, low assignment difficulty) may provide more control for the learners and avoid early frustration and possibly premature drop-out.
2. Emphasize the personal connection in the early stages with bios and assignments involving increased communication with other

learners and facilitators. Face-to-face introductory sessions, when possible, may facilitate early connection. This early connection can provide emotional, informational and appraisal support and help the learners cope with some negative experiences and remain engaged with the learning.

3. Facilitators should emphasize early and frequent positive reinforcement of achievements and support for different experiences. Other learners should be encouraged to provide this support and encouragement as a normal part of this new learning culture. Scheduled chat times and regular office hours are additional ways to structure in communication and connection with others.
4. A system should be developed to enable transmission of emotions with the ideas and content. This may take the form of emoticons or feeling images ☺ and/or emotional bracketing (e.g., I'm nervous that you may not understand this technical term) (Collie, Mitchell, & Murphy, 2000). This enriches the exchanges and adds an important level of communication that is usually missing in online courses.
5. Learners should be encouraged to provide regular feedback to the facilitators as part of the overall learning contract for the course. Facilitators should deliberately seek and clarify experiences, being sensitive to meanings of words, capitalizations (i.e., SHOUTING), extended periods of silence, etc.). Formal feedback should be sought at least twice: mid-course and at the end. Facilitators can use this as another source of information regarding their effectiveness and if received early, can modify some of the course process.
6. The course evaluation should include dimensions related to the subjective experience of the learners, including changes in self-perceptions, and self-efficacy. These experiences should be examined as they relate to performance in the course.
7. Designers and facilitators need to be aware of the disorientation and loss of "gravity" element to online instruction and deliberately develop structures and processes that will serve to provide more stability to the learners. Such strategies might include: simple, clear identification of where the learner is at every screen within the course and how to get to other locations through a mouse click; repeated checks by facilitators when learners go "missing"; use of familiar metaphors to provide comfortable reference points (e.g., lounge, café, front-porch).

REFERENCES

Astleitner, H., & Leutner, D. (2000). Designing instructional technology from an emotional perspective. *Journal of Research on Computing in Education*, 32(4), 497-510.

Besser, H., & Donahue, S. (1996). Introduction and overview. *Journal of the American Society for Information Science*, 47 (11), 801-814.

Bonk, C., & Cummings, J. (1998). A dozen recommendations for placing the student at the center of web-based learning. *Educational Media International*, 35 (2), 82-89.

Brindel, M. & Levesque, L. (2000). Bridging the gap: Challenges and prescriptions for interactive distance education. *Journal of Management Education*, 24 (4), 445-457.

Brosnan, M. (1998). *Technophobia: The psychological impact of information technology*. London: Routledge.

Burge, E. J. (1994). Learning in computer conferenced contexts: The learners' perspective. *Journal of Distance Education*, 9 (1), 19-43.

Collie, K. R., Mitchell, D., & Murphy, L. (2000). *Skills for online counseling: Maximum impact at minimum bandwidth*. In J. W. Bloom & G.R. Walz (Eds.), Cybercounseling and cyberlearning: Strategies and resources for the millennium (pp. 219-236). Alexandria, VA: American Counseling Association.

Dede, C. (1996). Emerging technologies in distance education for business. *Journal of Education for Business*, 71 (4), 197-205.

Draves, W. A. (1999). *Teaching online*. WI: Learning Resources Network.

Faux, T. & Black-Hughes, C. (2000). A comparison of using the Internet versus lectures to teach Social Work history. *Research on Social Work Practice*, 10 (4), 454-466.

Feenberg, A. (1987). Computer conferencing and the humanities. *Instructional Science*, 6 (2), 169-186.

Gregor, S.D. & Cuskelly, E. (1994). Computer mediated communication in distance education. *Journal of Computer Assisted Learning*, 10, 168-181.

Hara, N., & Kling, R. (2000). Students' distress with a web-based distance education course. Retrieved September 27, 2000 from the World Wide Web: *http://www.slis.indiana.edu/CSI/wp00-01.html.*

Huff, M., & Edwards, S. (1999). *Using technology in a Social Work diversity course*. Retrieved September 27, 2000 from the World Wide Web: *http://www.cc.utah.edu/~jy1415/techconf/Docs/papers/Huff.htm.*

Johnson, G. R. (1995). *First steps to excellence in college teaching* (*3rd ed.*). Madison, WI: Magna Publications, Inc.

Khan, B. (Ed.). (1997). *Web-based instruction*. Englewood Cliffs, NJ: Educational Technology Publications, Inc.

Kincheloe, J. L. (1999). The struggle to define and reinvent whiteness: A pedagogical analysis. *College Literature*, 26 (3), 162-194.

Kirkup, G. (1999). Technophobia: The psychological impact of information technology. [Review]. *Computers & Education*, 323, 279-280.

Latting, J. K. (1994). Diffusion of computer-mediated communication in a graduate social work class: Lessons from the "class from hell." *Computers in Human Services*, 10 (3), 21-45.

Lockee, B. B., Burton, J. K., & Cross, L. H. (1999). No comparison: Distance education finds a new use for 'no significant difference.' *ETR&D*, 47 (3), 33-42.

MacFadden, R. J., Dumbrill, G., & Maiter, S. (in press). Web-based education in a graduate faculty of Social Work: Crossing the new frontier. *New Technology in the Human Services.*

McIsaac, M., & Gunawardena, C. (1996). *Distance education.* In D. Johnassen (Ed.), Handbook of research for educational communications and technology. (pp. 15-38). New York: Praeger.

Noble, D. F. (1999). Digital diploma mills, Part IV, Rehearsal for the revolution. Retrieved September 27, 2000, from the World Wide Web: *http://www-rcf.usc.edu/~ics/ed/ddm4.html*.

Rahm, D., & Reed, B. (1998). Tangled webs in public administration: Organizational issues in distance learning. *Public Administration and Management: An Interactive Journal*, 3(1). Retrieved September 27, 2000 from the World Wide Web: *http:www.pamij.com/rahm.html.*

Reeves, T., & Reeves, P. (1997). *Effective dimensions of interactive learning on the World Wide Web.* In B. Khan (Ed.). Web-based instruction (pp. 59-66). Englewood Cliffs, NJ: Educational Technology Publications, Inc.

Salanik, G.R., & Pfeffer, J. (1978). A social information processing approach to job attitudes and task design. *Administrative Science Quarterly*, 23, 224-253.

Schoech, D. (2000). Teaching over the Internet: Results of one doctoral course. *Research on Social Work Practice*, 10 (4), 467-486.

Sodowsky, G., & Impara, J. (Eds.). (1996) *Multicultural assessment in counseling and clinical psychology.* Lincoln, NE: Buros Institute of Mental Measurements.

Stock, J. T. & Freddolino, P. (2000). Enhancing computer-mediated teaching through interactivity: The second iteration of a World Wide Web-Based graduate Social Work Course. *Research on Social Work Practice*, 10 (4), 505-518.

Wong, Y., & Law, C. K. (1999). Learning social work online: A WebCT course on policy issues among Chinese. *New Technology in Human Services*, 11 (4), 18-24.

Counseling Simulations: An Interactive CD-ROM Approach

Harold B. Engen
Robert David Dawson

SUMMARY. The Microcounseling Skills Simulation Program uses interactive CD-ROM technology to provide realistic situations to which students can learn and evaluate their microcounseling skills. The contents of the CD-ROM contain simulated counseling sessions first recorded on videotape and videodisc. The initial products consisted of four simulated counseling sessions, documentation consisting of an instructor manual, student worksheets, and scripts of the counseling sessions. This article will relate the process of creating a Microcounseling Skills Simulation Program and its conversion of the videodisc to a CD-ROM. This CD-ROM will include only one of the simulated counseling sessions. (The CD-ROM is being used as a resource activity for a Guided Correspondence Course currently offered on the World Wide Web.) *[Article copies available for a fee from The Haworth Document Delivery Service: 1-800-HAWORTH. E-mail ad-*

Harold B. Engen, PhD, is Professor Emeritus, Division of Counselor Education.
Robert David Dawson, PhD, recently received his doctoral degree in Rehabilitation Counseling at The University of Iowa, Iowa City, IA.

[Haworth co-indexing entry note]: "Counseling Simulations: An Interactive CD-ROM Approach." Engen, Harold B., and Robert David Dawson. Co-published simultaneously in *Journal of Technology in Human Services* (The Haworth Press, Inc.) Vol. 20, No. 3/4, 2002, pp. 301-316; and: *Human Services Technology: Innovations in Practice and Education* (ed: Hy Resnick, and Phoebe Sade Anderson) The Haworth Press, Inc., 2002, pp. 301-316. Single or multiple copies of this article are available for a fee from The Haworth Document Delivery Service [1-800-HAWORTH, 9:00 a.m. - 5:00 p.m. (EST). E-mail address: getinfo@haworthpressinc.com].

KEYWORDS. Simulations, microcounseling, interactive, computer-based instruction, CD-ROM

(Figure 1 above shows the first scene of the CD-ROM with the trainer in the center, the client on the left and the counselor on the right.)

INTRODUCTION

The past 15 years have demonstrated an explosion in the advancement of technology that has lead to an increase of multiple formats for instructional media. In the late 80s the videodisc was used extensively for multimedia instruction. The videodisc was able to interact with a computer allowing the user to have control, and allowed for audio and visual media on both sides of the platter. The cost of the laser disc and the media it utilized presented problems. The increases in technology have led to improved current formats and have rendered the videodisc obsolete. Currently the CD-ROM offers the advantage of speed, storage capabilities, and an industrial norm for computer systems. Computer programs that were developed for videodisc and then advanced to match CD-ROM technology have evolved to incorporate the technology of the Internet. Online tutorials and programs available via the Internet offer a global application for informational databases and training. These applications can range from text-based information sites, multimedia tutorials, and simulations.

As history has shown it is difficult to predict the future concerning changes in technology related to instruction. The development of the *Microcounseling Simulation Computer Program* reflects not only how technology has changed but how we must match this evolving technology as a tool for learning. From videodisc to the use of the Internet and distance learning, the media changed, but the basic format remained constant. It is the task of educators to continue to improve instruction in training counselors and other helping professionals. In addition, it is necessary to keep informed of the technological advances, and to work toward integrating an essentially technological resource into an interpersonal process (Sampson,1986). The development of a computer assisted instructional CD-ROM has led to new opportunities with its application to education. Traditional classroom paradigms are enhanced through integration of computer applications. Simulations take information from classes and integrate it into computer programs allowing students to practice those skills.

Engen (1994) states a computer program such as the *Microcounseling Skills Simulation* offers the following advantages and disadvantages in training persons in the helping professions:

ADVANTAGES OF COMPUTER SIMULATION

(a) simulation assists the learner in actively participating in the instructional process; (b) ability to pace and schedule instruction to the needs; (c) the instruction is impartial, patient, objective, and relatively fast paced; (d) feedback can immediately follow each action by the learner; (e) learner performance can be summarized and changes in future instruction can be on performance records; (f) the capacity to control external audio-video media, (g) the all important capacity to simulate real life situations; which (h) provides a common experience for all class members as a basis for Discussion; and (i) can readily repeat segments to reconsider what happens.

DISADVANTAGES OF COMPUTER SIMULATION

There are some disadvantages: (a) the counseling sessions are scripted instead of being actual counseling sessions; (b) providing student access to the necessary hardware adds complexity; (c) projection system is needed to use in large classes; (d) relatively expensive development cost, (e) making copies is expensive; (f) time-consuming to produce a quality product (Engen, 1994).

The Co-Director, Professor Engen, was granted a one-semester developmental leave assignment to work on this project. The University Video Production Fund awarded a grant to assist in the video-taping of the counseling simulations and mastering the tape for the video-discs. Academic Affairs and the College of Education contributed funds to the cost of creating the videodisc masters. The Instructional Computing Award Program is an annual competition that provides selected University of Iowa faculty with the resources necessary to successfully complete instructional projects employing computer technology. These funds provide software development and instructional design support and provide the hardware necessary for the development and delivery of the final products.

THEORIES USED

Microcounseling is a training process developed by Allen Ivey (1971, 1983, 1988) which demystifies the counseling process by breaking counseling into single skills. Ivey based his Microcounseling concept on Allen's (1967) Microteaching paradigm and utilized several of his important principles: (a) focusing on teaching specific skills while gradually integrating them; (b) use of modeling to modify existing behaviors or bring about acquisition of new behaviors; (c) practice and rehearsal that causes self-observation and confrontation and leads to behavior change; (d) feedback as reinforcement, which facilitates learning; and (e) microcounseling sessions that in their simulated realism often resemble a counseling relationship (Ivey, 1971). Computer simulation to train students in Microcounseling skills goes beyond the traditional direct instruction by allowing the student self exploration and practice of their Microcounseling skills.

DEVELOPMENTAL PROCESS OF INSTRUCTIONAL SOFTWARE

Principles of software engineering have been utilized for years in producing high quality, state-of-the-art software. The process is an involved stepwise approach to creating the many tangible things that make up a software package. It employs a series of steps akin to those in any engineering process, bridge-building, for example (Spector, 1986). Also, the steps emphasize the earlier planning and design phases, which must be done with great care to ensure that later phases go smoothly and that the end product is successful. In fact, a project is typically two-fifths to three-fifths design. Furthermore, as in bridge building, it is often necessary to construct a smaller model of a finished system to make sure the end product will work as planned. This is what is referred to as a "prototype" or "prototyping" (Lantz, 1987).

The process of creating a computer program is a developmental process. (See Figure 2.)

Each step in the process builds upon the other until a final product is reached. Throughout the process, a team is created consisting of people working together with appropriate experience to accomplish the necessary tasks during the software design. The expertise included: a Manager of the Instructional Software Development Group, two Instructional Design Specialists, a Software Developer, a Video Media Specialist, and the Co-Directors of the project, a doctoral student and the Professor in Counselor Education. First, discussions focused upon the design of the software and the feasibility of developing counseling simulations and its utilization.

Following an examination and definition of the goals and objectives of the instructional software, the co-directors designed appropriate software. Other interactive projects that had been developed on campus and were currently operational were reviewed. In addition the professor co-director also visited the University of Indiana's School Psychology Program where instructional interviewing programs were operational. After reviewing instructional programs and the goals and objectives of the *Microcounseling Simulation Program*, the design team was able to set the requirements needed (i.e., target audience, and hardware requirements needed for the final product such as videodisc player, computer, and CD-ROM). In addition the design team addressed how the software external design would look and act from the user's perspective. In developing the software, an understanding of instructional design and educational psychology were essential. Prototypes were

FIGURE 2

Flow Chart 2
Developmental process of instructional software

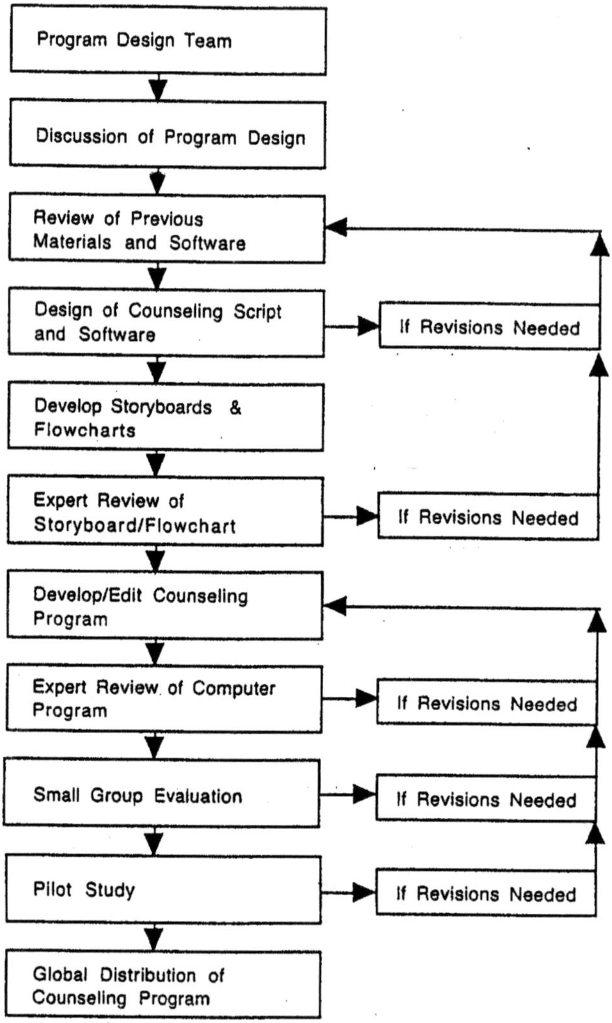

developed of the proposed simulation activities and it was determined that the video component would (1) consist of a trainer's introduction to the counselor session, a counseling session with client and counselor thoughts, summaries by the client, counselor, and trainer of the counseling session, and trainer feedback for meaning responses, (2) be organized so those classroom presentations used only the computer, and (3) emphasize all of the Microcounseling skills.

Storyboarding the computer program allowed for the design of how the software activities would look and act inside the computer and the physical layout of the program subsequent to writing the program. Storyboarding a program might be compared to a blueprint, a flowchart in which the structural design and user interactions are developed, tested and transferred to the development of the computer program. The results of these four scripts were written and reviewed by counseling professionals along with the identification of the four instructional software activities and their general look and feel. During the program's development, the counseling sessions were filmed, edited, placed on videodiscs, and later on a CD-ROM. The software was created to the requirements identified in the earlier phases. Finally, the software was tested and evaluated using students enrolled in the Microcounseling class taught by Professor Engen, Project Co-Director. Revisions to the software activities were made based on feedback from the students.

COMPUTER PROGRAM DEVELOPMENT

The original version of the microcounseling program was on videodisc using a program called Hypercard to link Macintosh computers with videodisc technology. Due to the advancement of technology and the need to make a program be cross platform (Macintosh and Windows based systems), the program was converted to CD-ROM and a different program interface was used. The transition of the counseling simulation from the videodisc to a CD-ROM was achieved by using an authoring program called *Authorware*. This program allows for the combining of several medias (text, video, pictures) into a linear interactive program. The program development was divided into stages: review of the material used for the videodisc, design of the program and creation of a storyboard, production of the program (this included coding, integration of movies, graphics, and debugging the program), and finally evaluation of the program. Much of the program development time was devoted to the coding of the *Authorware* program from the format of a hypertext media. The program was truly a gestalt in which the program itself was no more than a sum of its part in that if any part of the program would not function correctly the whole program would be affected. Most of the program development time was spent debugging the program to ensure that all sections of the program were working together.

A flowchart mapped the flow of the users' interactions throughout the program. Use of the flow chart aided in creating a layout that delineated user paths that would not conflict with other actions in the program. Storyboarding was created, offering a rough sketch of the information layouts. The storyboard offered a graphic example of the layout of the graphics and text in the program. They were useful in redesigning and editing some of the videodisc program paths.

The content language was designed for persons who were beginning counselors and familiar with some Microcounseling ideas and functions. Editing of the language and grammar was ongoing in this program. Each reviewer aided in correction of the language or editing of the program. Corrections to language and grammar were performed after each reviewer observed the program and made corrective comments. Spelling was officially checked by use of a word processing spelling tool.

The graphics and the videos were gathered from the original videodisc. Pictures were edited using *Photoshop 3.0*. Video presented in the simulation was developed in the University of Iowa television studio. All video was encoded into Quicktime movies and later edited and compressed using *Adobe Premier*.

SIMULATION OBJECTIVES AND DEVELOPMENT

The general objective of this project was to use interactive computer technology to provide realistic situations to which students could react as they dealt with the Microcounseling skills for helping professionals. Four simulated counseling experiences were developed to achieve these objectives. Learning activities, implemented using an authoring program (*HyperCard* and later *Authorware*), provided opportunities for students to observe, identify, practice, and evaluate a variety of microcounseling skills. The final product consists of four simulated counseling sessions and four instructional software activities which interact with two simulated counseling sessions. Documentation consisted of an instructor manual, student worksheets, and scripts of the counseling sessions.

SIMULATED COUNSELING SESSIONS

The four simulated counseling sessions were designed to allow the user to practice their Microcounseling skills in a real life scenario. One of the four simulated counseling sessions is a simulated client named Sheryl. Figure 3 is an opening scene of the client Sheryl, with the counselor.

This session involves Sheryl, a 24-year-old female involved with John, an alcoholic. The counselor and the client have met three times prior to this meeting. It has become evident to the counselor that Sheryl has been enabling John's drinking and has demonstrated characteristics common in co-dependent people. The counselor's plan was to assist Sheryl in realizing she needed to work through her previous parental abuse and her current enabling of her boyfriend. The referral to an Adult Children of Alcoholics (ACOA) group for continued therapy is the end result.

INSTRUCTIONAL SOFTWARE ACTIVITIES

In order for the person using the program to learn and practice basic Microcounseling skills, four instructional activities were developed to interact with Sheryl's simulated counseling sessions. These activities are: Guided Practice in the Identification and Use of Microcounseling, Coding for Focus, Identifying the Use of Eliciting and Reflecting Meaning, and Skills Coding for Basic Listening Skills.

Guided Practice in the Identification and Use of Microcounseling Skills

This activity is the primary objective of the instructional package. This activity has been tested several times using students registered in the Microcounseling Skills class. The purpose is to provide students with guided practice in the identification and use of the skills of eliciting and reflecting meaning while considering the developmental level of the client. Students are required to write a rationale for each preferred choice from a list of possible counselor statements at designated points in the counseling interview. As the activity begins, the learner watches the trainer's summary of previous interviews and the counselor's plan for the session. The video interview then plays to a choice point and pauses. At this point, the learner, as the counselor, creates a response he/she would make and provides a rationale. Five alternative counselor

FIGURE 3

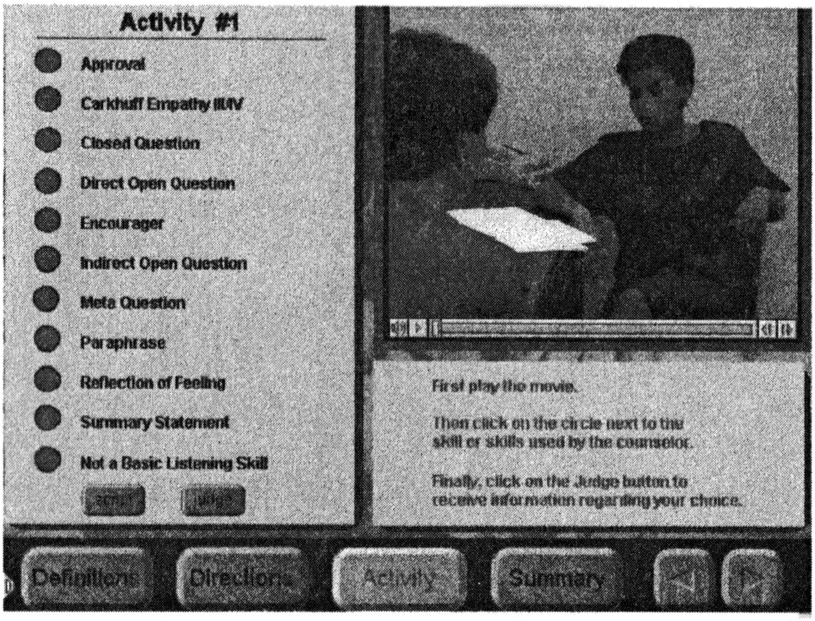

responses are presented and the learner selects the one he/she would most likely make, based on a consideration of meaning issues and the client's developmental level. A rationale for the selection is typed. A possible outcome of the selected response is then shown on the videodisc, including the counselor's thoughts (available when the learner selects a counselor response designated by the trainer), the counselor's response, the client's thoughts and response, and the trainer's rationale. The learner is encouraged to compare his/her rationales with the trainers. All five alternatives are presented again and the learner is encouraged to explore other choices. The sequence (the counseling session stops and the learner takes the role of the counselor) is repeated four more times. At the end of the session, the learner sees the counselor, and the client and trainer summarize their thoughts regarding the interview.

Coding for Focus

Coding for focus lets the learner practice coding various dimensions of responses by the counselor and client, thereby making it possible for counselors to expand the perspectives of the client and the counselor. There are three groups of client/counselor interactions. The objective is to identify the dimensions of focus by the speaker. For each group of interactions, the learner is able to observe patterns of change in the focus. Feedback on the change in patterns is provided by the trainer. A recent test of these activities has led us to encourage students to work in small groups as they go through the exercise.

Identifying the Use of Eliciting and Reflecting Meaning

For this activity, segments of the counseling session are played. The learner specifies whether the counselor made a meaning response, i.e., one eliciting or reflecting meaning. If the learner replies yes, then he/she identifies the specific meaning response. Feedback is in the form of identification of the Microcounseling skill the counselor used. If no meaning response occurs and the student implies "No," the program moves on to the next segment.

Coding for Basic Listening Skills

This allows the learner to practice identifying counselor statements according to the specific behaviors, such as, encouragers, closed questions, direct and indirect open questions, meta questions, paraphrase, summary, reflection of feelings and various levels of Carkhuff empathy. At any point, students can review the definitions for these behaviors. The final activity is one that requires overall knowledge in order to participate in the development of counselor responses and rationales. (See the Basic Listening Skills glossary of definitions in Figure 4.)

The learner steps through the interview seeing consecutive pairs of client and counselor responses and codes the counselor's responses. There may be more than one code for a response. At the end of the practice session a summary of how well the learner did is presented. The learner then can obtain a printout of his/her results which may be handed in as a homework assignment. In addition a complete summary of all learner responses is saved for the instructor. In the process of converting the microcounseling simulation from videodisc to CD-ROM, the Basic Listening Skills were the first to be converted. This program was set as the base for the CD-ROM.

FIGURE 4

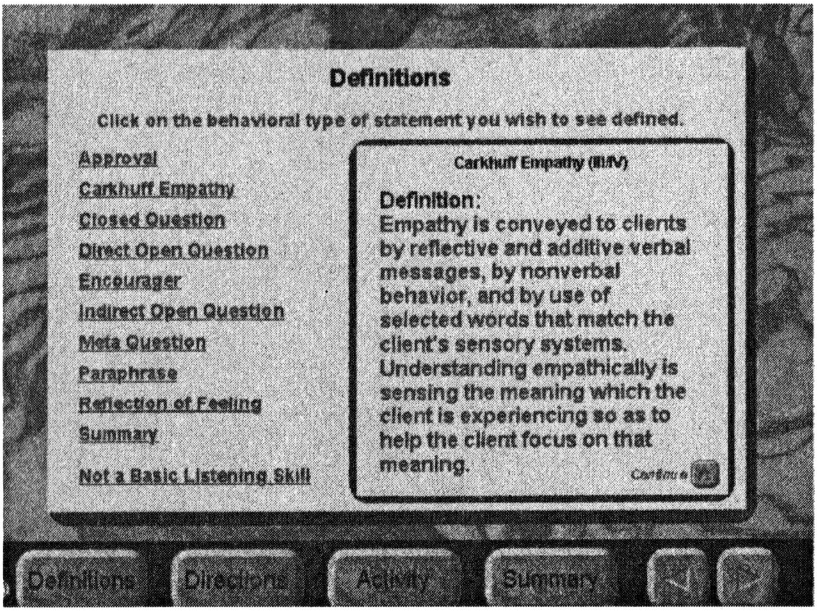

DOCUMENTATION

Instructor Manual: The instructor manual describes how to integrate the product into the curriculum, how to install the software, resources required in order to use the software, how to install CD-ROM, if they are using a videodisc player (connecting the videodisc player to the computer, which videodisc players are supported), how to generate reports for the instructor, and general overall maintenance of the package.

Student Worksheets: Each software activity has a worksheet the student uses while doing the activity which can either be turned in as an assignment or used as a basis for discussion in the classroom.

MINIMAL SKILLS NEEDED

There are four basic instructional software activities related to the videodisc. Each activity requires basic knowledge in order to participate successfully in the activity. The first is a basic listening sequence where the learner practices identifying counselor statements according to specific behaviors, such as encouragers, various types of questions, and responding and feeling skills. For coding the focus dimension, the learner needs to be able to identify the three dimensions that are included in the focus pattern: the subject, the verb and the time dimensions. For the identification of eliciting and reflecting meaning, the learner needs a thorough grasp of the overall concept of eliciting and reflecting meaning.

AUDIENCE

The field of practice is directed at any such program that is training persons in the basic interviewing and microcounseling skills areas. The Division of Counselor Education at the University of Iowa sponsors four sections each semester, including the summer session, of the course 7C:178 Microcounseling. Approximately 200 students are served each year. These students are graduate students in Counselor Education and related programs plus undergraduate students who are minoring in the area of Human Relations. In addition, The Center for Credit Programs at the University of Iowa offers the 7C:178 Microcounseling as a distance learning course available in print or online at *http://www.uiowa.edu/~ccp/c-a-g/cg7c178.htm.*

EVALUATION

During the one to one evaluation all the students were enthusiastic about using the computer videodisc activities to practice microcounseling skills they were learning and were unanimous in stating that the activities were interesting and useful. Students seemed to prefer doing the coding activities in small groups. They commented that they enjoyed discussing the coding with others and felt that they learned more through the discussions. Specific comments by the students on each activity are found in Appendix A (Engen, p. 296).

Revisions of the program were performed based on the users' feedback. (See Appendix A). After the revisions were made to the program it would again be evaluated by another user and feedback on the program received. The revising and evaluating of the program were conducted until the objectives of the lesson were able to be achieved and free of errors that would previously encumber the lesson (Alessi & Trollop, 1991). By using this method to evaluate a program, major problems could be identified and revised before testing in a small group situation.

In addition to the evaluation forms completed by the students, the student co-director of the project designed her doctoral dissertation around the interactive video project (Kenney, 1991; Engen, 1994). The study assessed the instructional effectiveness of an interactive videodisc simulation program. She has particularly addressed the program that was designed to aid students in a microcounseling skills training class in the acquisition of the interpersonal skills of eliciting meaning and reflection of meaning. The purposes of this study were: (1) to assess the instructional effectiveness of using instructional software and an interactive videodisc, and instructional software and no interactive videodisc for delivering a counseling simulation to teach counselor trainees the microcounseling skills of eliciting meaning and reflection of meaning; (2) to determine whether cognitive styles serve as a mediating variable to the acquisition of the microcounseling skills of eliciting meaning and reflection of meaning; and (3) to assess student perceptions of an interactive videodisc program and the microcomputer program of a counseling simulation used as a supplement to a typical microcounseling approach to instruction. Student trainees for the study were solicited from all those enrolled in three sections of the course 7C:178, Microcounseling. All participants were volunteers who had signed consent forms. All sections were taught by Professor Engen, Project Co-Director, and he remained blind as to those students who had volunteered to participate in the study.

Prior to the students going to the computer center, one of the four exercises was demonstrated in the classroom. The computer center has a reserved booth which contains the computer with its appropriate software installed, a videodisc player and a video monitor. All of the students were enthusiastic about using the computer videodisc activities to practice microcounseling skills they were learning and were unanimous in stating that the activities were interesting and useful. Students seemed to prefer doing the coding activities in small groups. They commented that they enjoyed discussing the coding with others and felt that they learned more through the discussions.

The second research question in the Kenney dissertation study was: What is the relationship of cognitive style to the use of the microcounseling skills of eliciting meaning and reflection of meaning? No relationship of cognitive style as measured by the Group Embedded Figures Test (GEFT) was found in this study. However, an interesting finding related to cognitive style was that of the 38 participants in the two experimental sections who were classified as field-dependent, all 11 were women. This is consistent with observations of sex differences related to the field-dependent dimension, i.e., that women tend to be more field-dependent than do men (Witkin et al., 1971).

APPLICATIONS FOR THE FUTURE

In the original creation of the Microcounseling Simulation, students would have used either the videodisc player or the CD-ROM. As technology has advanced, students are now able to practice directly on the Internet through a Web-based browser, such as Netscape or Internet Explorer. A database could be built into the site that would allow the instructor to track the progress of their students as they worked though the various exercises in the simulation. The results of the database would confirm to the instructor that the student has worked through all the exercises but would also let the instructor track the performance of the student. If an instructor sees that the student is not able to make the transition of the textbook to the simulation exercises, they can intervene and guide the student. As the technology progresses, it is not unlikely that an instructor would set up a meeting on-line where they observe a student, several states apart, taking the exercises and offering real time feedback and further microcounseling examples.

CONCLUSION

As history has shown, it is difficult to predict the future concerning changes in technology related to instruction. The development of the Microcounseling Simulation Computer Program reflects not only how technology has changed but how we must match this evolving technology as a tool for learning. From videodisc to the use of the Internet and distance learning, the media changed but the basic format remained constant. It is the task of educators to continue to improve instruction in training counselors and other helping professionals. In addition, it is necessary to keep informed of the technological advances, and to work toward integrating an essentially technological resource into an interpersonal process.

REFERENCES

Alessi, S.M. & Trollip, S.R. (1991). *Computer-based instruction: Methods and development* (2nd. ed). Englewood Cliffs, NJ: Prentice Hall.

Allen, D. (Ed). (1967). *Microteaching: A description.* Palo Alto, CA: Stanford teacher education program.

Engen, H. B., Finken, L.J., Luschei, N. S., & Kenney, D. (1994). Counseling Simulations: An interactive videodisc approach. *Electronic tools for social work practice and education.* New York: The Haworth Press, Inc.

Hannafin, M.J., & Peck, K.L. (1988). *The design, development, and evaluation: Instructional software.* New York: Macmillan Pub.

Ivey, A.E. (1971). *Microcounseling: Innovations in interviewing training.* Springfield, IL: Charles C. Thomas.

Kenney, D.M. (1991). *Meaning skills training for counselors using interactive videodisc and the influence of cognitive style.* Thesis (PhD)–University of Iowa.

Lantz, K. (1987). *The prototyping methodology.* Englewood Cliffs, NJ: Prentice Hall.

Sampson, J.P., Jr. (1986). The use of computer assisted instruction in support of psychotherapeutic processes. *Computers in Human Behavior*, 2, 1-19.

Spector, A., & Gifford, D. (1986). A computer science perspective of bridge design. *Communications of the ACM-29,* ACM, 268-283.

Witkin, H. A,, Olrman, P. K., Raskin, E., & Karp, S. A. (1971). Manual: Embedded Figures Test. Palo Alto, CA: Consulting Psychologist Press, Inc.

APPENDIX A

Evaluation of the Coding for Basic Listening Skills Activity:

"Immediate feedback would be good."
"Kept my attention and interest."
"With more practice I would get better."
"It made me realize that I need more practice."
"Some codes were never used."
"It was helpful to hear the responses."

Evaluation of the Coding for Focus Activity:

"Some of the responses were long and had lots of different codes."
"More specific feedback for each response."
"My listening skills were sharpened."
"I need more practice."
"I need a definition for the abbreviations."

Evaluation of the Identifying the Use of Eliciting and Reflecting Meaning Activity:

"I learned which responses I confuse."
"Good feedback."
"It was fun to discuss what you would say."
"The possible outcomes of different responses were unexpected sometimes."
"It was interesting to see how a client might respond to different counselor comments."

Better Listening: Paraphrasing and Perception Checking– A Study of the Effectiveness of a Multimedia Skills Training Program

Forrest C. Bud Hansen
Hy Resnick
Jerry Galea

SUMMARY. The authors describe a multimedia communications skills training CD-ROM for human service students and practitioners and evaluate its effectiveness with undergraduate social work students in Canada. *[Article copies available for a fee from The Haworth Document Delivery Service: 1-800-HAWORTH. E-mail address: <getinfo@haworthpressinc.com> Website: <http://www.HaworthPress.com> © 2002 by The Haworth Press, Inc. All rights reserved.]*

KEYWORDS. Communication skills, CD-ROM, multimedia, technological education

---

Forrest C. Bud Hansen, PhD, is Associate Professor of Social Work, University of Windsor School of Social Work, Windsor, Ontario.

Hy Resnick, PhD, is Professor of Social Work, University of Washington School of Social Work, Seattle, WA 98105.

Jerry Galea, MSW, is affiliated with the University of Washington School of Social Work, Seattle, WA 98105.

[Haworth co-indexing entry note]: "*Better Listening: Paraphrasing and Perception Checking*–A Study of the Effectiveness of a Multimedia Skills Training Program." Hansen, Forrest C. Bud, Hy Resnick, and Jerry Galea. Co-published simultaneously in *Journal of Technology in Human Services* (The Haworth Press, Inc.) Vol. 20, No. 3/4, 2002, pp. 317-331; and: *Human Services Technology: Innovations in Practice and Education* (ed: Hy Resnick, and Phoebe Sade Anderson) The Haworth Press, Inc., 2002, pp. 317-331. Single or multiple copies of this article are available for a fee from The Haworth Document Delivery Service [1-800-HAWORTH, 9:00 a.m. - 5:00 p.m. (EST). E-mail address: getinfo@haworthpressinc.com].

INTRODUCTION

This study seeks to determine the effectiveness with social work undergraduate students of a multimedia communication skills training program recently developed at the University of Washington School of Social Work.

Well known to the social work field is the use of certain skills to explore the client's problems, thoughts, and resources (Van Lieshout, 1993). Of the many skills social workers employ, two in particular ensure that the practitioner has heard and understood the content and the affective dimensions of the client's message. First, *paraphrasing* is employed "to provide feedback that the practitioner has grasped the *content* of a client's message . . . by [restating (with different words)] what the client has expressed" (Hepworth & Larsen, 1993, p. 46). Second, *perception checking* is the process by which the practitioner "provides feedback that [he or she] is aware of the *emotions* the client has experienced or is currently experiencing" (Hepworth & Larsen, 1993, p. 46). Use of these skills is also correlated with facilitating positive relationships with clients (Nugent, 1992).

Enter computer instruction. Once a hi-tech classroom novelty, instructional use grew from 1% in 1977 to 70% in 1997 of the total computer utilization in educational institutions (*T.H.E. Journal,* 1998). The reasons for the recent popularity of computers in higher education instruction are many and include cost-effectiveness, the increasing pervasiveness of computers in colleges and the workplace, and the notion of instruction-on-demand, whereby learning is fully controlled by the student. Learner control is a key factor in successfully teaching adults. Learners using multimedia instruction initiate, plan, and implement training in a time-frame that meets their schedules and lifestyles, offering increased autonomy for the learner (Caffarella, 1993 as cited in Stoney & Oliver, 1998). In addition, interactive multimedia has a direct impact on enhanced learning outcomes in adults by providing motivation and engagement in the lesson materials, since the student decides when and how much to study (Stoney & Oliver, 1998).

Teaching many social work practice skills, such as communication skills, can require the use of video. Although the technology needed to drive such multimedia applications has become commonplace in the past few years, there has been little use of computers for instruction in social work education. (See Hansen, 1981; O'Reilly, 1986; and Flynn, 1986 for early reviews. For a full review of technologies see Dorman, 1997, and Patterson & Jaffee, 1994. See also Schoeck & Belen, 1998, for an innovative use of technology to present information to workers in public agencies.) There are few CD-ROM titles reported in the literature or on the Web that specifically teach the skill of paraphrasing and perception checking (*New Technologies in the Human Services,* 1999; Resnick, 1999).

Resnick and colleagues developed a CD-ROM, *Better Listening: Paraphrasing and Perception Checking* (Resnick, 1998), to teach these basic listening skills. The prototype employs graphics to increase the attractiveness of the program and multiple video clips to model these skills. *Better Listening* took more than two years to design and produce, and was supported by a small grant from the University of Washington. Volunteers from a variety of computer companies, students, and university and school of social work technical staff, as well as the authors of this article, all contributed to the development of the CD. Final decisions were made by the senior author, who also served as the producer for the program.

Initially the university technical staff wrote the program in a software-authoring language, Authorware. A doctoral student in the school of music who was familiar with the authoring language completed the program. Graphics were designed and produced by a variety of graphic artists: in the university technical departments and professional graphic artists. An undergraduate student was hired for particular sections of the program, and also was responsible for the musical pieces in the introduction and transitions between segments of the program. All in all, over thirty persons participated in the design and production of the several versions of the program. They served as programmers, script writers, actors, directors, content specialists, lighting and video technicians, digitizers, graphic artists, sound technicians, music composers, narrators, and reviewers.

The prototype of *Better Listening* employs graphics to increase the attractiveness of the content and multiple video clips to model listening skills.

DESCRIPTION OF THE PROGRAM

Better Listening is a skills training program designed to instruct the social work and health professional in the skills of listening. The program design is interactive. For example, users participate by typing in a paraphrase after viewing an associated video clip, and in the perception checking section, by completing a quiz. The program runs approximately 35 minutes, although users may work at their own pace. The program specifically provides students and practitioners with:

- Working definitions of paraphrasing and perception-checking.
- The different methods of using these skills.
- Knowledge of the basic concepts underpinning the paraphrasing and perception-checking skills.
- Advantages, disadvantages, and incorrect uses of the two skills.
- Brief practical applications of skills in pharmacy, dental, social work, and medical contexts.

A variety of media including text, video clips, slides, audio, and graphics illustrate, highlight, and reinforce learning points. Video clips illustrate methods of paraphrasing and perception-checking, and clarify text explanations. Music dramatically introduces the program, and graphics humorously portray incorrect uses of these skills.

Better Listening consists of seven major technical or content components.

1. *Content, definition, and major concepts.* Students using *Better Listening* receive instruction which increases their skill in attending to the affective dimension of a communication as well as the cognitive message, making the program useful in preparing clinical practitioners.
2. *Comprehension checks* assess learning and understanding of the skills. Students' results are provided to the instructor via printouts or, in an advanced model, e-mail.
3. *E-mail* allows students to communicate with the instructor, receive feedback, ask questions, and provide the instructor with information about the overall effectiveness of the program.
4. *Interface* guides students through the program, informing them how to exit, continue, take comprehension checks, repeat screens, view other topics, use e-mail, and quit.
5. *Video vignettes, graphics, and cartoons* illustrate the paraphrasing and perception-checking skills more effectively than does text alone.
6. *Audio,* voice over, narration, and music dramatize learning points, and contribute to the students' engagement with the program.
7. A series of exercises to help users practice these skills.

RESEARCH METHOD

This was an intentionally small project aimed at only addressing whether this CD-ROM has the *potential* to teach paraphrasing and perception checking, and not whether the skills are actually employed or whether there is any impact on client well-being. The evaluation study employed a pretest/posttest design.

Typically, 67% of the students in the sample were 20 years of age or less, 85% were female, and 66% were majoring in pre-social work. Other majors reported were 11% in psychology, 7% in sociology, and 15% "other" majors. Full-time students account for 86% and 75% were in a daytime class. First year university students made up 65% of the class with another 20% being in their second year of studies. There are 4% who had a degree and were returning students.

Administration of the Pre- and Posttests

The sample was obtained from a first-year, undergraduate social welfare class in their first semester at the University of Windsor. Students were offered the opportunity to learn listening skills and to test *Better Listening*, and were offered a 5% increase in their class grades if they participated. They used a learning laboratory at the University of Windsor on an individual basis during the first two weeks of December 1998.

The pretest was taken immediately before they used the *Better Listening* program and the posttest was taken immediately after completion of the program. The pretest and the posttest were developed by Dr. Herman Resnick of the University of Washington and revised by Dr. Hansen at the University of Windsor (Appendix 1), who administered the program and was the instructor for the undergraduate classes from which the sample was obtained.

Development of Questionnaires

In order to evaluate changes in the students' knowledge and in their confidence concerning listening skills, the first two sections of the pretest and posttest were identical. This first section consisted of 12 multiple-choice questions relating directly to the listening skills presented. These questions evaluated students' mastery of the conceptual content of the program. The second section of the posttest included six open-ended questions that asked the students to rate (on a one to five-point scale) their confidence in their listening skills, and provided them the opportunity to comment on the usefulness of the program in increasing their confidence in their listening skills. The posttest included a third section which asked respondents to rate their perception of the overall helpfulness of the program (on a one to five point scale), to comment on items they liked the most and the least, and to recommend suggestions for the program.

Results

In the sample (N = 51), on the 12-item test of mastery of the listening skills, the mean score on the pretest was 4.24 (35.3%) with a standard deviation of 1.80. The mean score for the posttest on the corresponding section was 8.27 (68.9%) with a standard deviation of 2.62. The mean difference of 4.04 on the paired-sample *t*-test was statistically significant ($t(50) = 12.063$, $p < .001$), indicating that the difference was not likely to have occurred by chance.

On the 6-item self-rating of confidence in listening skills on the pretest, for the first sample, the mean rating overall was 3.34, with a standard deviation of 0.68. On the posttest, the mean was 3.83 with a standard deviation of 0.65. A mean increase of 0.48 is statistically significant on a paired-*t* test ($t(46) = 5.401$, $p < .001$), indicating that the increase in the self-rating is not likely to have occurred by chance.

In the third section the students rated the helpfulness of the *Better Listening* Program. Of the 49 respondents, 7 (14.3%) rated it as "some of the time helpful," 22 (44.9%) rated it as "a good part of the time helpful," and 20 (40.8%) gave it the highest rating of "most or all of the time helpful." No one rated it in the bottom two categories of "rarely or not at all helpful" and "a little of the time helpful." The mean rating was 4.27, with 5.0 being the highest possible rating, and with a standard deviation of 0.70, indicating that the students generally found the program helpful.

DISCUSSION

The evaluation of the *Better Listening* Program by use of the pretest/posttest design was intended to determine if there was an increase in students' mastery of the conceptual material. Because the respondents came from an introductory class, social welfare (N = 51), it was expected that they would achieve a low score on the pretest. Hence, mean scores of 4.24 (35.3%) and 4.57 (38.1%) correct responses were in keeping with the students' beginning level in the undergraduate social work degree program. Approximately 60% of the students were in their first year of University studies. Also, since they were introductory courses, no formal lecture material on listening skills was included in the course content prior to the administration of the trials. The posttest mean scores of 8.27 (68.9%) and of 8.87 (73.9%) correct responses, a mean increase of 4.04 (33.6%) and 4.30 (35.8%), indicates considerable improvement in their mastery of the conceptual material of the *Better Listening* Program, indicating that the program was at least partially effective for this novice group of students. A further question is raised as to how effective this program would be for upper level students. Presumably, the program would be even more appropriate for a beginning social work practice course, at either an undergraduate or a graduate level.

A similar, although less dramatic, result was indicated by an increase in the self-rating of the students' confidence in their listening skills. The 6-item self-rating 5-point scale produced a mean increase of 0.48 and 0.37 from the mean scores of 3.34 and 3.43 on the pretests to 3.83 and 3.80 on the posttests. While this increase in mean self-ratings shows a modest increase in confidence in their listening skills, it is possible that without a conceptual basis for assessing their listening skills, the students' pretest scores were somewhat inflated in comparison to their more-informed posttest ratings. The importance of this rating is that it is a measure that goes beyond the conceptual level to the students' self-perception of their skills level. A future step in the evaluation would be to provide testing of the students' actual skill achieved through live demonstration in a controlled simulation. Another step would be to compare this mode of social work skill training with more traditional modes of social work skill training.

The last part of the questionnaire asked for an overall evaluation of the helpfulness of the program. Demonstrated on a 1-5 point scale, with 5 as the most helpful, mean ratings were 4.27 and 4.21 respectively. These are very high ratings and attests to the potential of this multimedia approach to the teaching of these skills. It is consistent with the authors' experience with the use of video on CD-ROM to bring the reality of practice to the classroom. A summary of specific responses submitted as comments on the posttest is provided in Appendix 2.

NEXT STEPS

Further research is clearly indicated. What would be particularly interesting to document is whether use of CD-ROM multimedia is at all effective in stimulating social work personnel to use the skills in their practice. Since current social work thinking is increasingly centered on client outcomes, it will be important to study whether the use of the skills ultimately correlates with better client function. To address that issue, future researchers may consider employing *Better Listening* in a setting where client outcomes are easily tracked (perhaps in a private therapist's office where long-term clients are served).

Whatever the results from this study, given the beginning interest in technology in social work education, it is not unlikely that social workers would also begin to use multimedia in some form or fashion with clients. Thus, at the very least, this study is a gateway for the much larger inquiries into multimedia and social services yet to come.

REFERENCES

Caffarella, R. (1993). Self-directed learning. *New Directions for Adult and Continuing Education, 7*, 25-35.

Dorman, S. (1997). Technology briefs: CD-ROM use in health instruction. *Journal of School Health, 67*, 444-446.

Flynn, M. (1986). Computer assisted instruction and experiential learning. In G. R. Geiss & N. Viswanathany (Eds.), *The human edge: Information technology and helping people* (pp. 292-295). New York: The Haworth Press, Inc.

Hansen, F. (1981). *An evaluation of computer assisted instruction for teaching statistics to social work students*. Unpublished Doctoral Dissertation. University of Toronto.

Hepworth, D., & Larsen, J. (1993). *Direct social work practice: Theory and skills*. Pacific Grove, CA: Brooks/Cole.

New technology in the human services. http:www.soton.ac.uk/~chst/nths

Nugent, W. (1992). The affective impact of a clinical social worker's interviewing style: A series of single-case experiments. *Research on Social Work Practice, 2*, 6-27.

O'Reilly, C. T. (1986). Information technology and social work education. In G. R. Geiss & N. Viswanathany (Eds.), *The human edge: Information technology and helping people* (pp. 287-292). New York: The Haworth Press, Inc.

Patterson, D. A. & Jaffee, I. (1994). Hypermedia computer-mediated education in social work education. *Journal of Social Work Education, 30*(2), 267-277.

Resnick, H. (1996). IMM in the future social work classroom. *Tulane studies in social welfare: Modes of professional education 11: The electronic social work curriculum in the twenty-first century* (Vol. 20, No. 24). Tulane University.

Resnick, H. (1998). Information technologies: Teaching to use, using to teach in Paraphrase II: A listening skills training program for human services students. In F. Raymond, J. Ginsberg, & D. Gohagen (Eds.) *Computers in Human Services*, Vol. 15(2/3), New York: The Haworth Press, Inc.

Schoech, D. & Belen, R. (1998). The worker safety advisor: A performance support system. In F. Raymond, J. Ginsberg, & D. Gohagen (Eds.), *Computers in Human Services*, 15(2/3), pp. 143-158.

Stoney, S. & Oliver, R. (1998). Interactive multimedia for adult learners: Can learning be fun? *Journal of Interactive Learning Research*, *9*, 55-81.

University of Washington. (February 21, 1999). *University of Washington Bulletin* (USPS 078-880), General Series No. 1264. Seattle, WA: Author.

Van Lieshout, H. (1993). More than computers: The development of learning materials for information technology education in Dutch schools of social work. In B. Glastonbury & A. Van Gorcum (Eds.), *Proceedings of 3rd Husita Human Welfare Technology Conference* (pp. 238-239).

APPENDIX 1.
Better Listening Program Screens

Pre-test **Code#**

·_ _ _ _

Better Listening Questionnaire
(Please circle)

1. Effective paraphrasing confirms for a client that his or her message has been understood. True or False (circle one)
2. Paraphrasing should capture the essence of a client's comments. True or False
3. There is only one way to paraphrase. True or False
4. Effective paraphrasing involves an interpretation of the underlying motivations or emotions of a client. True or False
5. Using a metaphor as a paraphrase that is unclear can create ambiguity or increase the tension between a worker and a client. True or False
6. Sometimes it is ok to take notes while interviewing a client. True or False
7. When taking notes it is important to maintain eye contact. True or False
8. A lengthy restatement of a client's comments can be an effective paraphrase. True or False
9. The purpose of a paraphrase is to communicate to another your understanding of what the other person said. True or False
10. Paraphrasing can stimulate new ideas for the person who just spoke. True or False
11. Repeating exactly what a person just said is a good example of paraphrasing. True or False
12. Summarizing, i.e., capturing the essence of, what a person said by way of using a few words is a good example of paraphrasing. True or False
13. Metaphors are always good techniques to use when paraphrasing. True or False
14. Perception checking, i.e., telling or asking a person what they are feeling in response to a comment they made, is always appropriate. True or False
15. The advantage of perception checking is that it may help you understand a person's comments more fully. True or False

Post-test **Code#**

·_ _ _ _

Better Listening Questionnaire
(Please circle)

16. Paraphrasing should capture the essence of a client's comments. True or False
17. There is only one way to paraphrase. True or False
18. Effective paraphrasing involves an interpretation of the underlying motivations or emotions of a client. True or False

APPENDIX 1 (continued)

19. Using a metaphor as a paraphrase that is unclear can create ambiguity or increase the tension between a worker and a client. True or False
20. Sometimes it is ok to take notes while interviewing a client. True or False
21. When taking notes it is important to maintain eye contact. True or False
22. A lengthy restatement of a client's comments can be an effective paraphrase. True or False
23. The purpose of a paraphrase is to communicate to another your understanding of what the other person said. True or False
24. Paraphrasing can stimulate new ideas for the person who just spoke. True or False
25. Repeating exactly what a person just said is a good example of paraphrasing. True or False
26. Summarizing, i.e., capturing the essence of, what a person said by way of using a few words is a good example of paraphrasing. True or False
27. Metaphors are always good techniques to use when paraphrasing. True or False
28. Perception checking, i.e., telling or asking a person what they are feeling in response to a comment they made, is always appropriate. True or False
29. The advantage of perception checking is that it may help you understand a person's comments more fully. True or False

Evaluation

1. Was this Better Listening program helpful?

    5. Most of all of the time
    4. A good part of the time
    3. Some of the time
    2. A little of the time
    1. Rarely or not at all.

2. What aspects were the most helpful?

3. What aspects were the least helpful?

4. Any suggestions for improvement?

APPENDIX 2.
Comments (n = 51)

General Comments	Most Useful	Least Useful	To Improve the Program
	The conflict mediator segment.	All content was useful, but "guide" was distracting.	Slightly repetitive. On the whole, it was excellent.
A lot of what was said I learned in counseling training.			
	How to identify emotions.	Conflict resolution section.	This was a good study.
	Very important therapeutic methods of communication.		
	Examples in each section. Real life situations.	No notes to take away with use about what we learned.	Discuss program first. Tests at end of each segment. Give notes to take away.
It was an effective and informative video.	The acted out scenes with explanations that followed.		
I think it would be good to cover during a high school English class.	All aspects on paraphrasing and perception checking.	None	Nope, it was good.
	The tips to help improve skills. The video.		
	Summarizing each set of examples. Repetition. Clarity and conciseness.	N/A	Use different people to demonstrate each explanation in the videos.
	The conflict resolution.	Metaphors.	Make the viewers have more interaction.

APPENDIX 2 (continued)

General Comments	Most Useful	Least Useful	To Improve the Program
	The descriptions and examples shown as well as how to apply it.	They would all be helpful in helping one understand aspects of better listening.	Make the test longer to go more in depth.
	Video examples.	Having to type in answers.	
	Mediation. Wendell steps. Paraphrasing. Almost all parts were helpful.	None.	Give examples of mediators who mediate. Even if follow steps, didn't get message across.
Very good program, Helps a lot because of good and easy examples.	Videos.	None.	None.
	I had never learned about emotions perceptions before.	I already had taken listening programs but there was nothing wrong with this one.	Not really, it was very cute.
This is about interpersonal and group discussion skills. More groups skills in SW program.			
	It was easy to understand and therefore learn from.	Some parts were slow and too repetitive.	
Well put together. Organized, simple, to the point. Clear essence of what was being said.	Real life example help the viewer capture what was being spoken about.		None! Great job.
	The hands-on or interactive aspect made learning easy.	Some parts seem repetitive and annoying.	
Good job of receiving the info you need.	Having pre and post tests.		

General Comments	Most Useful	Least Useful	To Improve the Program
It was interesting.	Different aspects of listening.	Different aspects of communication because everyone is different.	More tests for the viewer.
	Videos helped learning to understand emotions portrayed, importance of paraphrasing.		Thought videos were helpful with "everyday" problems. The use of metaphors was beneficial.
	Videos of people paraphrasing, perception checking. Step-by-step info. Explanations at start.		
Effective use especially when dealing with people and listening skills.	The definition (concepts) were clear although they explained more when videos were played.	The self test at the end of watching a video was too easy.	Make the videos a little more challenging.
	Aspects that were most helpful included video clips as examples of what was being said.	Everything was helpful. Nothing was confusing or took you off track.	No suggestions for improvement.
Everything was fine! The video was quite interesting and easy to follow.	The aspects of paraphrasing. I now know better what paraphrasing is and when to use it.	Nothing, actually! The video was cool!	Nay!
Enjoyed the program. Liked sense of humor in it, easier to learn from instead of stiff texts.	Didn't use big confusing words to illustrate point. Video slip examples very effective.	N/A	N/A
	Giving these issues attention to help teach through CD was great.	Too long.	
Good.	All.	None.	No.
	All.	None.	No.

APPENDIX 2 (continued)

General Comments	Most Useful	Least Useful	To Improve the Program
	I understand more about what is actually expected and what the person wants to hear.	Not much.	
Program was helpful, interesting. Sometimes we feel we have mastered more than we have.	The different examples that were given. Also, that things were reviewed.	The examples at times were vague.	Pretest should have been done in a natural environment (classroom) than go to computer.
	Explaining the Wendell French method in 4 steps.		I have no suggestions. I found this to be an excellent program.
	Gave very clear answers about questions asked. The videos.	I can't say that anything wasn't helpful.	It was a good and interesting video.
	The stuff about perceiving what others say.	Paraphrasing because by 1st or 2nd year university, we should be very good at this.	No.
	All aspects were very helpful, especially for careers that deal with working with others.		Keep up the good work!
	Gave good ideas about how to increase your skills.	Too vague.	
	The summaries are helpful and the videos. Voice is clear and message gets across.		
	Both the narration and the videos.		

General Comments	Most Useful	Least Useful	To Improve the Program
	The aspects teamed with videos where students picked answers and judged.	The aspects that were simply listed. This didn't stimulate any kind of interest.	Use more videos and make the program more interactive. Other than that, it's great!
	The interview section where the other person's feelings were known.	Paraphrase practice summary was not helpful to me.	Try not to do all on the computer.
	The explaining of the meaning of perception/ paraphrasing, and little sitcoms.	None.	Good work overall.
	Going through each aspect clearly and providing role play very helpful.	None.	Provide these presentations to students as part of the course requirements.
The program was helpful especially for SW majors who will need the info in the future.	Most of the program was useful. The Wendell French method was most helpful for me.		
Some of the explanations were hard to follow and understand.	Videos.	N/A	N/A
	It was helpful when I had to participate in the program. It helped me remember more.		

Multimedia Interactive Training Development–*Journey: Discovering Social Services* CD-ROM

Alan D. Bookhagen
David P. Wegenast
Richard J. McCowan

SUMMARY. This article describes a multimedia 9-module training program which uses text, graphics, animation, narration, and video as well as a planned approach to the use of color, pace, tone, setting, and instructional activities to achieve its goal of orienting new workers to the complexity of a public social service agency. *[Article copies available for a fee from The Haworth Document Delivery Service: 1-800-HAWORTH. E-mail address: <getinfo@haworthpressinc.com> Website: <http://www.HaworthPress.com> © 2002 by The Haworth Press, Inc. All rights reserved.]*

KEYWORDS. Public welfare, orientation, multimedia, CD-ROM, evaluation

INTRODUCTION

This paper describes the development of *Journey: Discovering Social Services,* a self-instructional, interactive, multimedia CD-ROM developed for the New York State Office of Child and Family Services,

---

Alan D. Bookhagen, MS, is Director of Distance Learning, Center for Development of Human Services, Buffalo State College. David P. Wegenast, DSW, is Professor, Department of Social Work, Buffalo State College. Richard J. McCowan, PhD, is Professor Emeritus, Department of Education, Buffalo State College.

[Haworth co-indexing entry note]: "Multimedia Interactive Training Development–*Journey: Discovering Social Services* CD-ROM." Bookhagen, Alan D., David P. Wegenast, and Richard J. McCowan. Co-published simultaneously in *Journal of Technology in Human Services* (The Haworth Press, Inc.) Vol. 20, No. 3/4, 2002, pp. 333-343; and: *Human Services Technology: Innovations in Practice and Education* (ed: Hy Resnick, and Phoebe Sade Anderson) The Haworth Press, Inc., 2002, pp. 333-343. Single or multiple copies of this article are available for a fee from The Haworth Document Delivery Service [1-800-HAWORTH, 9:00 a.m. - 5:00 p.m. (EST). E-mail address: getinfo@haworthpressinc.com].

Office of Temporary and Disability Assistance, and Department of Health. *Journey* creates an awareness of the delivery of social services in a local community as opposed to a particular organization and reflects the delivery of social services in New York State with content relevant across its 58 unique counties. Other states will find the content relevant and useful though the organization and delivery of services may be different. *Journey*, an invaluable Staff Development Resource, assures depth, breadth and excitement to the orientation experience.

NEED FOR STATEWIDE SOCIAL SERVICES ORIENTATION PROGRAM

The Bureau of Training and Work Force Development, BTWD, is a state agency that supervises training for 58 county districts and New York City. In 1985, Center for Development of Human Services, CDHS, developed a *Social Service New Employee Orientation Resource Guide* for county departments. A needs assessment later revealed that it was not uniformly used in all counties (Wegenast, 1986). A few counties had no orientation program, while most offered half to full day programs mostly limited to personnel concerns. The nine generic social service topics included in the 1985 orientation manual were either not covered or covered in a non-uniform, inconsistent manner.

In 1995, BTWD announced an initiative to design technological applications for social service training (Miraglia, 1995). This initiative led to the development of the 9-module CD-ROM entitled *Journey: Discovering Social Services*.

TECHNOLOGY AND TRAINING: THEORETICAL FRAMEWORK

Computer-assisted training is best utilized as part of a larger, integrated set of learning activities. Interactive multimedia training has been effective (McNeil and Nelson, 1991). Well-designed educational programs can be delivered as computer assisted multimedia interactive training. Shapiro (1986) noted that computer-assisted multimedia interactive training has many benefits. Participants learn independently, interact during learning, re-work material to attain pre-set criteria, and receive high interest, multiple sensory input and individualized rewards (Reinoehl and Shapiro, 1986). They also are exposed to decision-making strategies that lead to "good judgment." Material can be synthesized and integrated more quickly (Phillips, 1983). In addition, learners can make protected mistakes (Alpert, 1986). Self instructional training was found effective in social services by Wegenast (1975), multimedia, interactive training in social services was found to be effective by Satterwhite and Schoech (1995).

Journey uses a combination of text, graphics, animation, narration, and video to bring real life to situations and to help in the transfer of learning. Its multi-sensory inputs as well as color scheme, tone, pace, setting, and instructional activities increase participant cues and attention and retention of information.

DESCRIPTION OF INTERACTIVE CD-ROM: JOURNEY: DISCOVERING SOCIAL SERVICES

Traditional training programs and staff orientations in social services organizations require an extensive commitment of staff developer time. These programs use print-based materials that typically focus on personnel issues and program overviews. Staff developers may not have program experience from which to describe the entire organizational picture. Self-instructional, multimedia computer-aided learning offers a consistent method of delivering media rich content to the learner that is effective and fun.

Journey is a self-paced, user-friendly, 9-module narrated orientation to social services that features videos, photographs, illustrations, and instructional activities that capture and maintain learner interest. Frequent embedded evaluations with corrective feedback reinforce key learning points while providing new employees with a broad understanding of social services.

The goal of the Customer module is to create an awareness of the wide array of customer needs using eleven video vignettes from a cross-section of social services customers. It also uses video interviews of "Sages," social service experts, to provide more in-depth information about the program being discussed. Customers include: young mother with two children, abandoned by the family wage-earner; an individual who has lost his job, can't find another, and has an eviction notice; a husband whose wife is in a nursing home and who can't afford the medical bills; a working mother who can't afford to get by without food stamps; a mother who suspects her son is being abused during visitations with his father; a teenage girl who lives in a foster home; a mother who needs help with her troubled, truant, acting-out son; a man who is concerned about his increasingly incompetent elderly neighbor; a mother who needs help from the department to collect child support payments; a father who is in a job-training program, trying to become self-sufficient; a man who suspects that his neighbor is committing welfare fraud.

The goal of the mission module is to create an awareness of the concept of mission, the department's mission and its relation to other community service providers, and the individuals part in carrying out the mission. It uses instructional games to accomplish this goal.

The goal of the *Staffing* module is to create an awareness of the variety of staff positions and programs within the department. This module uses an interview format to allow participants to expand their awareness of a cross-section of staff working at social services. Interview topics include job roles and responsibilities, rewards and frustration, and daily activities.

The goal of the *Facts* module is to create an awareness of the facts about poverty programs and work. *Facts* uses a television-game-show-style playing board to help learners discover facts about poverty and welfare and discover characteristics of families receiving public assistance, the connection between welfare and jobs, statistics about medical care, and the impact of welfare on taxes.

The goal of the *Values and Standards* module is to create an awareness of the core helping values of social services and their standards of professional practice. It uses interactive graphics and video clips to help users identify their own values, explore values conflicts, discover how their values align with values at social services, deepen their understanding of core social services values: respect, individuality, self-determination, confidentiality and their standards of customer service and practice.

The goal of the *Skills* module is to demonstrate best practices of common helping skills used in social services: Phone Skills, Interviewing, Case Management & Problem Solving, Managing Records, Supervision, Teamwork, and Information and Referral, used at social services.

The goal of the *Policy* module is to create an awareness of the concept of policy and its development process and the learners' part in the implementation of policy. Using an instructional game, it illustrates how resource allocation can affect policy decisions.

The goal of the *Jargon* module is to create an awareness of the jargon and acronyms frequently used at social services and the effect of its use on new employees. *Jargon* uses animation and video to allow users to explore jargon use in a work setting. It also provides a dictionary-style look-up to de-mystify acronyms and terms used in the social services arena.

The goal of the History module is to create an awareness of past responses to need. History uses animated illustrations and embedded evaluation to invite learners on a twelve-stop exploration of the colorful evolution of society's response to human need. Learners develop an appreciation and understanding of milestones in social services and child welfare history and information about the New Deal, Great Society, Title XX, Child Welfare, TANF, and Welfare Reform.

NAVIGATIONAL INTERFACE

Learners will find that *Journey* is not only fun but also easy to use. Fully narrated descriptions and directions guides learners throughout the program. Its accompanying workbook allows participants to record their thoughts, feelings, and training transfer plans as they progress through the program. Learners can, of course, redirect the program to replay important concepts or branch to points of special interest for enhanced understanding. The accompanying facilitator's guide provides easy reference for using *Journey* in single or multiple learner environments and relating training to the job.

CURRICULUM DESIGN AND DEVELOPMENT

Designer's Edge (Allen Communications, 1996, Instructional Systems Design, (ISD)) software was used in all phases of *Journey*'s development. This software uses a task and phase metaphor to manage and track the development of multimedia training interventions. This aspect made it possible for a diversely skilled team to use the same tool for different tasks. This model draws upon several similar but unique curriculum development models (Mager, 1988; Dick and Carey, 1996; Alessi and Trollip, 1991; Greer, 1992; Leshin and Reigeluth, 1992). It maintains that instruction is composed of a system of interrelated components, trainer, trainee, activities, delivery system, evaluation, and learning environment that provide relevant performance-based learning outcomes to the learner.

Phase 1: *Designer's Edge* was used in the needs analysis phase to produce forms for recording performance gaps. It was also used to generate and refine need statements, goals, and objectives obtained from focus groups and interviews. Interviewees included subject matter experts (SMEs) county staff developers, program experts, contract monitors, and technical experts. The developers used *Designer's Edge* wizards and expert advice to generate, refine, and associate curriculum design elements.

Phase 2: The Mission Phase involved identifying prerequisites for achievement of goals and prioritizing goals or determining the project's scope. *Journey*'s prerequisites were determined to be the ability to use a mouse and keyboard in a Windows environment. The *Designer's Edge* software helped the developers to prioritize goals. These goals would become the project scope though many more goals were identified in the needs analysis phase. *Journey* supports 9 of the 28 identified new-worker orientation competencies of social service staff (Erie Country, 1999). Each of these goals addresses a specific performance gap.

Other identified topics included professional development, sexual harassment, HIV information, union and contract functions, employee rights, fraud, protocol, computer skills, safety, danger, handling of difficult clients/violent behavior, handling of hazardous materials, communicable diseases, safety and building security. Project stakeholders determined these to be better addressed through traditional training (Erie Country Department of Social Services, 1999).

Phase 3: Audience profiling involves collecting information about the audience in order to design a product that fits the users' needs. Demographics collected for *Journey* included age, gender, education, and PC accessibility, capability, experience, and attitudes about computer based training. This data would be used in the design, development, implementation, and evaluation phases of the project.

Phase 4: This step involved writing behavioral objectives for goals generated earlier. Measurable objectives were written in the "A. B. C. D." format (McCowan and Wegenast, 1998). *A for Actor*: Who must meet the objective? *B for Behavior*: What behavior must be exhibited to meet the objective? *C for Condition*: Under what circumstances must the objective be met? *D for Degree*: What level of mastery indicates that the objective was met?

Behavioral objectives provide a logical foundation for building the course, indicating clearly what the course quantitative means for evaluating success (Mager, 1988). Performance-based objectives provide a job performance baseline to evaluate employee gain. Although success partially depends on learner ability, improvement in job performance is the best measure of successful training. Currently, *Journey*'s evaluation is based on pre/post testing, and embedded evaluation items. It may provide a measure of readiness to perform. Later studies might relate the *Journey* experience to job success indicators.

Phase 5: This involved content-gathering and research tasks. These tasks were prioritized according to identified audience needs and course goals and objectives. The content outline for *Journey* was based on summaries of information gathered through focus groups, interviews, agency records, and research. Team meetings utilized brainstorming to generate content outlines for modules. This information was synthesized into a project outline, and a project work plan in which development tasks and phase timelines were identified. The project work plan was developed and maintained using Microsoft Project. *Designer's Edge* was used to manage content assets and to ensure that content related to needs, goals, and objectives.

Phase 6: The developers used *Designer's Edge* to create a visual course map of the program. Using it, project staff could see how instructional components were associated. This course map made it possible to convey *Journey*'s complex structure to project stakeholders. The developers chose practice and drill strategies and games as the primary instructional strategies to link objectives to evaluation and feedback.

Phase 7: Treatment entailed defining theme, tone, pace, and setting. These are the motivational aspects of the course. It is where the "look and feel" of *Journey* came into being. Some of these decisions came from information collected during the needs analysis phase, while others came from project team experts. *Journey*'s theme is one of discovery. Its tone is one of friendly conversation where the learner can drive the direction of the instruction. *Journey* is set in a classic building. Structural elements allow users to access its modules in any order. During this phase, page layout and design standards were established, actors and media were selected, and media were critiqued for inclusion. Criterion for inclusion were relevance to content, conveyed desired mood, matched audience profile, and manageable file size.

Phase 8: The developers used *Designer's Edge* to prototype models of strategies to accomplish identified objectives. The developers selected pre-instructional, information presentation, student participation, instructional games, and embedded knowledge checks as instructional strategies. This phase culminated in the production of the design strategy document and *Journey* Prototype. The design strategy document was used to present data and design decisions collected during earlier phases to project stakeholders. The developers used it later to construct the *Journey* prototype. *Journey*'s prototype was a sample of the color scheme, interactions, navigation controls, sample content, and instructional strategies for the *Customers*, *Mission*, and *Staffing* modules. The design team selected a color theme that was soft, calming, and unobtrusive. Information is presented from left to right and top to bottom; body text, emphasis text, title text, and status text use the same font family with different sizes and strokes. Wherever possible, only one object requiring user input was presented on the page at any given time. *Journey*'s prototype served to demonstrate to key stakeholders the products look, feel, and operation. It also served as a basis for constructive feedback, to insure stakeholder interests, to build credibility for the newly developed project team with stakeholders. As such, stakeholders began to share a collective vision of the project.

Phase 9: Storyboarding began once the developers received signoff for the prototype from project stakeholders. With the help of the VISIO charting software, the developers created flow charts that provided a visual representation of the course direction, branching and links, data collection points, and data dictionary. *Designer's Edge* was then used to translate information from the design strategy documentation, course map, and flowcharts generated in earlier phases into a screen-by-screen story, storyboard. Storyboards indicated, to team members, relative sequence, positions, and timing of Journey's navigation, media, and feedback elements. When producing the initial prototype, each module was authored and tested as it was scripted.

Phase 10: Media Production in *Journey* had both Pre-production and Post-production tasks. The developers used *Designer's Edge* during both tasks. Media assets identified during the storyboarding phase and media shot lists for narrators and actors were managed using the *Designer's Edge* software. The *Facilitator Guide* and *Participant Workbook* performance support tools were developed concurrently by other team members in order to support the transfer of learning. During Post-production identified resources were logged into the *Designer's Edge* database by the graphics team as they were completed. This enabled the programmers to know when media elements had been completed and could be used. The developers spent a great deal of time determining optimum audio and video capture methods and compression ratios during Post-production.

Phase 11: Authoring is to a multimedia application as a conductor is to an orchestra. Each assembles and sequences components to create a whole greater than the sum of its parts. The authoring package chosen for *Journey* was *Multimedia Toolbook 5.0*. This development product was chosen for its robust interactivity capabilities. *Journey*'s metaphor is of exploration. This metaphor was carried throughout the application to provide an interesting learning environment. Project team members used the "Guidelines for Interface Design" developed by Microsoft to benchmark *Journey*'s interface design. These guidelines outlined details such as screen design, meaning of colors, placement of feedback, size and number of typefaces, and use of interactive objects.

Phase 12: Evaluation: Sixty-nine participants completed *Journey*'s pre/posttest. Frequency distributions for demographic and reaction items were completed. Matched participant pre- and posttest differences were measured to assess knowledge gain. Data analysis was based on a paired t-test that compared the pretest/posttest scores for sixty-nine trainees. The results showed a significant pre-post improvement for cognitive test items ($t = 2.47$; $df = 68$; $p > .01$).

Following the posttest, each participant indicated they understood the origins of social services. At pretest, only thirty-seven percent had a clear understanding of its origins. All participants indicated that they believed social services were vital to communities both at the pretest and the posttest levels. The pretest indicated that only thirty-one percent of the participants understood how the programs delivered by social services relate to the mission of the organization. Following the post-testing all participants indicated that they understood how thc programs delivered by social services were mission related. Fifty-seven percent of the participants in this study had no previous computer experience before. Ninety-one percent agreed that the program was interesting, and ninety percent said that they would recommend this program to others.

PROJECT TEAM

Sixteen staff worked part time on this project representing skills of coordination, curriculum development, producing, writing, graphic arts, editing, photography, videography, illustration, animation, and programming. Thirty-six performers and four commissioners of country departments were videotaped, twenty-two staff photographed, and sixteen voices recorded. A professional staff of four, a director, grip, and lighting and recording engineers, produced videotape segments. A professional recording studio, sound engineer, and narrator were utilized. Fourteen social service employees served on the advisory committee. The project was completed in three years.

CONCLUSIONS

These data suggest that interactive multimedia is an interesting and effective method for information delivery. Pre-posttest differences indicate a significant increase in learning. Participants expressed consistent satisfaction in using *Journey*. Users take about six hours to complete the program. It may have been useful to produce the project as three courses, thus reducing its magnitude and size. *Journey* is recommended as a supplement for traditional training and supervision, not as a replacement. Its effectiveness on performance is dependent on supervisory feedback and assistance in applying the content to the job.

FUTURE IMPLICATIONS

An outcome evaluation would document performance improvement and return on investment. A comparison of staff with social work undergraduate and graduate degrees to those without would assist in assessing the educational level and utility of the program in an educational and work setting. An item analysis will ensure item discrimination between high and low performers.

Other states or localities could adapt this program or modify it. Modification costs would be dependent on the nature of the changes. Changes to text are the least costly while changes to media are more costly. Content for six of the nine modules is generic. However, modules on mission, staffing, and jargon are directly related to the organization and delivery of social services in New York State.

Future plans include developing content for the other 19 identified new-worker orientation competencies, customizing *Journey* for other organizations, and delivering *Journey* via the Internet. *Journey*'s web page can be found at *http://www.bsc-cdhs.org/journey*. Evaluation copies are available for those who participate in on-going evaluations by contacting Dr. David Wegenast at *wegenadp@bscmail.buffalostate.edu*.

REFERENCES

Alessi, S.M., & Trollip, S.R. (1991). *Computer-based instruction: Methods and development*. Boston: Allyn and Bacon.

Alpert, D. (1986). A preliminary investigation of computer-enhanced counselor training. *Computers in Human Behavior*, *2*, 63-70.

Dick, W., & Carey, L. (1990). *The systematic design of instruction*. Glenview, IL: Scott, Foresman and Company.

Fritz, M. (1991). The world of virtual reality. *Training*, *28*(2), 45-50.

Glaser, R. (1984). Education and thinking: The role of knowledge. *American Psychologist*, *39*(2), 93-104.

Greer, M. (1992). ID project management: *Tools and techniques for instructional designers and developers*. Englewood Cliffs, NJ: Educational Technology Publications.

Leshin, C.J., & Reigeluth, C. (1992). *Instructional design: Strategies and tactics*. Englewood Cliffs, NJ: Educational Technology Publications.

Mager, R. F. (1988). *Making instruction work or skillboomers*. Belmont, CA: Lake Publishing Company.

McCowan, R. & Wegenast, D. (1998). *Defining competence*. SUNY Research Foundation, Center for Development of Human Services.

McNeil, B.J., & Nelson, K.R. (1991). Meta-analysis of interactive video instruction: A 10-year review of achievement efforts. *Journal of Computer-Based Instruction, 18*(1), 1-6.

Mott, M. (1992). "Interviewing for Social Services: An Interactive Video Disk." Western Washington University.

Phillips, J. (1996). ROI: The search for the best practices. *Training and Development Journal*, 28 (3), 64-75.

Reinoehl, R., & Shapiro, C.H. (1986). Interactive videodiscs: A linkage tool for social work education. *Journal of Social Work Education*, *22*(3), 61-67.

Satterwhite, R., & Schoech, D. (1995). "Multimedia Training for Child Protective Service Workers: Results of Initial Development and Testing." *Computers in Human Services*, 12 (1/2), 81-97.

Savicki, V., & Brown, R.A. (1981). *Working with troubled children.* New York: Human Sciences Press.

"Social Service Competencies," a monograph. Erie Country Department of Social Services, Buffalo, New York, 1995, 1999.

"Social Services Orientation Trainer's Manual" (1999). Erie Country Department of Social Services, Buffalo, New York.

Van Horn, M. (1986). *Understanding Expert Systems*. New York: Bantam.

Wegenast, D. (1975). *Assessment of Child Abuse: A Self Instructional Program.* Buffalo State College, Department of Social Work.

Wegenast, D. (1985). *Orientation for social services in New York State.* Buffalo State College, Department of Social Work.

The Development of a Multimedia Training Project: Rewards and Challenges of the Multidisciplinary Team

A. Elizabeth Cauble
Janice M. Dinkel

SUMMARY. This paper describes the development of Building Family Foundations, an interactive, multimedia training project for child welfare workers. In addition to this description, the collaborative process among professionals from various disciplines is examined. The authors recommend applying the social work helping process to the development of training projects that involve a large multidisciplinary team effort. The profession of social work is committed to ensuring that members regularly receive continuing education in order to enhance their knowledge and skills and keep current with trends in the various fields in which they practice. Social workers who practice in rural areas find it difficult to meet this commitment. Distance education, particularly multimedia instruction, offers an exceptional remedy to this situation (Thurston, Verschelden & Denning, 1996). This method of delivering training and

---

A. Elizabeth Cauble and Janice M. Dinkel are affiliated with Kansas State University.

This project was funded by a grant from the Kansas Department of Social and Rehabilitation Services. Portions of this manuscript were developed into an article and published in *Professional Development: The International Journal of Continuing Social Work Education*.

[Haworth co-indexing entry note]: "The Development of a Multimedia Training Project: Rewards and Challenges of the Multidisciplinary Team." Cauble, A. Elizabeth, and Janice M. Dinkel. Co-published simultaneously in *Journal of Technology in Human Services* (The Haworth Press, Inc.) Vol. 20, No. 3/4, 2002, pp. 345-367; and: *Human Services Technology: Innovations in Practice and Education* (ed: Hy Resnick, and Phoebe Sade Anderson) The Haworth Press, Inc., 2002, pp. 345-367. Single or multiple copies of this article are available for a fee from The Haworth Document Delivery Service [1-800-HAWORTH, 9:00 a.m. - 5:00 p.m. (EST). E-mail address: getinfo@haworthpressinc.com].

education, new to the social work profession, is both exciting and challenging in its development and implementation. The Kansas Department of Social and Rehabilitation Services in collaboration with Kansas State University developed a training curriculum to help address rural child welfare training needs. This project, which began in November 1992 and ended in June 1998, produced a significant training tool for the state of Kansas as well as contributed to the growing body of knowledge of multimedia development and multidisciplinary collaboration (Thurston et al., 1996; Cauble & Dinkel, 1999). *[Article copies available for a fee from The Haworth Document Delivery Service: 1-800-HAWORTH. E-mail address: <getinfo@haworthpressinc.com> Website: <http://www.HaworthPress.com>*

KEYWORDS. Participation, interactive videodisc, training, focus groups, public

The profession of social work is committed to ensuring that members regularly receive continuing education in order to enhance their knowledge and skills and keep current with trends in the various fields in which they practice. Social workers who practice in rural areas find it difficult to meet this commitment. Distance education, particularly multimedia instruction, offers an exceptional remedy to this situation (Thurston, Verschelden & Denning, 1996). This method of delivering training and education, new to the social work profession, is both exciting and challenging in its development and implementation. The Kansas Department of Social and Rehabilitation Services, in collaboration with Kansas State University, developed a training curriculum to help address rural child welfare training needs. This project, which began in November 1992 and ended in June 1998, produced a significant training tool for the state of Kansas as well as contributed to the growing body of knowledge of multimedia development and multidisciplinary collaboration (Thurston et al., 1996; Cauble & Dinkel, 1999).

The Beginning

The training project began with a statewide assessment of child welfare worker training needs. Focus groups were used in order to maximize the participation of the workers in the planning stage. Developers of the project required a high level of worker involvement in this phase of the project in order to establish that they (the workers) "owned" the project by helping with its design, implementation, and evaluation. Paralleling the social work helping process, this approach to development and implementation of the curriculum insured that the first step was "listening to the needs of the client and establishing rapport." The assumption that clients "have the capacity to consider and evaluate the accuracy of their needs and wants and can express these in the form of goals" (Fox, 1987) further supports the use of the focus group as a method of needs assessment and contrasts with those traditionally used in the child welfare field (Pecora et al., 1983b).

A paramount consideration when planning the needs assessment was not to burden the workers who have considerable demands on their time. Workers perceive surveys as time consuming and frivolous since they often do not see them as resulting in any changes in their work system. It was important, therefore, that this assessment involve the workers differently than the usual "pen and pencil" method, which often disappears in the system and fails to produce meaningful feedback for them. Workers were approached as adult learners who possessed knowledge of their own needs and ideas about how to meet those needs (Denning & Verschelden, 1993) and whose time was a precious resource.

The focus groups were held in six areas of the state; all child welfare supervisors and line workers were invited to participate. Care was taken to "advertise" the groups well in advance and emphasize the voluntary nature of participation. This method minimized resistance and further demonstrated the social work helping process by respecting the "rights" of the workers to choose not to participate. Approximately 75 supervisors and 495 social workers participated. Input from administration was sought from each of the twelve management areas. This group was not accessible for direct interview so they were asked to rate a list of 20 training topics that emerged as significant in the early focus groups, according to their perceptions of the importance of each to child welfare workers. At least one focus group for workers and one for supervisors was held in each of the state's 12 management areas–34 sessions (14 for supervisors and 17 for workers) in all.

The groups were divided into six discrete segments: brainstorming topics about which workers needed more training; organizing topics into units of training, or modules; establishing priorities within each module according to perceived needs for training; discussing training delivery methods; demonstrating multimedia, interactive computer-based training technology; and evaluating the focus group training session (Denning & Verschelden, 1993). Two project staff members, a social work faculty member and a project assistant, led each focus group. Rules for the conduct of each session were reviewed prior to beginning the actual work of the sessions. Participants were reminded that they were the experts and that the ideas of each person were valid and should be respected. Topics related to nontraining matters, such as too-large caseloads, and workplace dissatisfaction were disallowed in the focus groups. Participants were told that acceptable areas were those that related directly to their training needs: areas in which lack of knowledge, understanding, or skill disabled workers in the performance of their jobs. After brainstorming a list of topics about which they needed more training, the participants organized the list into training units by grouping like topics together. Each participant then prioritized the list and recorded demographic data related to their work role within the agency.

The fourth segment of the focus group was devoted to gathering information about previous types of training workers perceived as valuable and those that were not helpful. Participants were encouraged to talk about factors that seemed to contribute to training effectiveness. The fifth segment consisted of a demonstration of multimedia, interactive, computer-based training technology. During the demonstration, which took approximately 30 minutes, participants were encouraged to "try out" the technology. This segment introduced the idea that the latest in training technology was being considered to deliver the training curriculum. The facilitators noted the participants' reactions to the demonstration in order to assess their receptivity to using multimedia instruction.

The sixth and final segment of the focus group session was an evaluative component. Participants completed a feedback survey, which assessed the satisfaction of the participants with the experience. Participants rated the effectiveness of the facilitator, their sense of having their input respected, their preference for this format as compared to a written survey, their belief that their input would result in more training opportunities, and whether their participation was voluntary. Additional comments were encouraged.

RESULTS OF THE FOCUS GROUPS

The focus group method of conducting a needs assessment provided rich data for the project staff (Denning & Verschelden, 1993). The groups generated many ideas about the areas in which they wanted additional knowledge, understanding or skill. Table 1 summarizes the frequency with which topics were listed by the focus group participants. This list was later prioritized by workers and resulted in the training modules that comprise the Building Family Foundations curriculum (see Table 2).

TABLE 1. Workers' Training Needs According to Focus Groups

Training Needs	Number of Times Topic Appeared
Survival Skills for Workers	42
Time, crisis, and stress management	17
Survival skills	13
Personal and professional role	7
Worker safety	5
Abuse/Neglect	28
Sexual abuse	12
Sexual abuse investigation/intervention	8
Evidence/risk assessment	6
Emotional abuse	1
Overcoming effects of abuse	1
Legal/Court System	27
Families	19
Family dynamics/systems	7
Family preservation	4
Family types	2
Family services	2
Family interventions	2
Multi-problem families	1
Domestic violence	1
Adolescents	17
Oppositional/Resistant clients	17
Oppositional, resistant, violent clients	13
Mediation	3
Conflict resolution	1
Interaction/Interviewing Skills	16
Networking–Community Resources	16
Mental health	14
Writing Reports/Documentation	12
Cultural Differences	12
Child Development	11
Computer Training	11
Understanding SRS System	11
Special Populations/Special Education	9

Note. Number of times topic appeared is based on the number of times a topic appears on lists from 34 meetings.

TABLE 2. Building Family Foundations Modules and Content Areas

Child Development
Normal development–development at risk
Developmental disabilities and delays
Assessment
Professional Development
Ethical decision-making–work system survival skills
Stress Management
Time management–organizational skills
Preventing burnout and brownout–assessing stress
Family Issues
Families from other cultures–blended and reconstituted families
Families with members with disabilities–gay and lesbian families
Family-based Treatment Strategies
Family assessment–ecobehavioral approaches
Family strategies for child management–improving parent-child relationships
Teaching, motivating and supporting parents
Social Workers in Court
Role of justice system in child welfare–preparing for court
Testifying in court–writing court reports
Understanding the law–role of social worker in the legal system
Roles, responsibilities and goals of key players
Child Abuse and Neglect
Indicators of physical, sexual, and emotional abuse–situational and environmental factors
Indicators of neglect
Family strengths perspective
Effect of abuse on development
Separation and attachment issues
Practice Skills I
Basic interviewing skills–interviewing children
Writing case records and reports
Practice Skills II
Dealing with resistant/hostile clients–mediation and negotiation
Collaborative problem-solving
Adolescents
Adolescent development–treatment/management methods
Finding and maintaining placement–independent living
Adolescent sexuality issues
Juvenile offenders

Among the significant findings were the differences in the ways training was being delivered to rural and urban child welfare workers. Those traditional methods of instruction, such as workshops and courses, were largely inaccessible to the workers in the rural parts of the state. In order to travel the distances required to receive training, workers had to leave their caseloads for several days at a time. This burden and the lack of timeliness of the content were factors that seriously interfered with the social workers' access to and satisfaction with training.

Methods of training delivery were also discussed during the focus groups. The participants overwhelmingly indicated that they preferred interactive training versus a lecture or traditional classroom approach. They stressed the importance of variety and that they enjoy visual aids in training. Supplemental materials handed out during training were largely ignored after the training event, except those that could be copied and given to clients. The workers also expressed a clear desire that trainers should be practicing professionals who could relate case examples to the training topics. Knowledge of the SRS system was also considered a critical credential for the trainers to possess, even if they did not actually work for the agency.

Workers expressed their need for training that corresponded to their various levels of skill and knowledge. Training is usually entry level and not progressive to accommodate the experience level of the staff. The participants felt that ongoing training on specific issues rather than a "one shot" approach was more effective. They also emphasized that considerable "in-house" knowledge and expertise existed among the staff and regretted that they have few opportunities to share with others with the SRS system.

The responses to the demonstration of the multimedia method of training were overwhelmingly positive. This response, coupled with the specific training issues that surfaced relative to timeliness, geographic distance, variety and other presentation specifics, encouraged the project staff to pursue development of a multimedia curriculum.

THE MULTIDISCIPLINARY TEAM

The subsequent development and production of the multimedia training modules was a multidisciplinary, collaborative process. This process was simultaneously exciting and difficult. Collaboration among the many different disciplines created significant challenges as well as benefits, which will be described in this section. The key members of the team for each module were Subject Matter Expert (SME), Instructional Designer (ID), Computer Programmer (CP), and Graphic Designer (GD). There was also a video production team that included camera operators as well as producers, directors, and editors.

Competencies for each module were selected after review of the focus group results. These were then stated in terms of learning objectives. At this point in the process the SME began to research the topical areas and developed an outline for the module. The SME was either a social work faculty member or the special education faculty member on the project. Modules were assigned to each SME based on her areas of expertise. It was, however, necessary for the SME to identify additional resources within the professional community to help with the writing of specific sections of the modules. For example, while writing the content for the *Professional Development* module, the SME enlisted the help of a social worker in private practice who could write realistic scenarios to be used in the interactive section that demonstrated work system struggles and their resolution. These professionals were issued contracts through the university and paid a lump sum for their work. Since these professionals had never written material for any type of multimedia project, a great deal of coaching was required. It was, therefore, the SME's job to teach the writer to write for this particular type of medium. The difficulty with this was minimized when the SME was able to find a writer in the nearby community. Many who assisted, however, were several hours away, requiring that interactions occur over the telephone and through the mail.

Teaching about how to write for a multimedia script was difficult when the "teachers" (SMEs) had no experience doing so themselves. Often material would come back that was much too difficult to read and/or convey on the computer screen or through role-play. Special consideration had to be given to making the material simple and easily conveyed to the learner. On the other hand, community professionals are more in touch with day-to-day practice issues than are academics. Academic scholarship requires a writing style that does not lend itself to this medium.

In addition to writing the content, the SME was responsible for acquiring any copyright permissions that were necessary for her module. This proved to be a somewhat difficult task. Publishers who give permission for their materials to be reproduced for educational purposes were hesitant to grant permission for a computer program to be used by hundreds of social workers. Negotiations took place in order to reduce or eliminate the fees usually charged for copyright permissions. Some text had to be changed because of our inability to acquire copyright permission for material we thought important to include in the modules. This was often a time-consuming and frustrating endeavor, yet a very necessary one. It was difficult to cite the authors or use a copyright permission by-line within the text of the module, because doing so frequently deterred from the easy "readability" of the text on the computer screen. The compromise between appropriate citations and "readability" was to include an exhaustive list of references at the end of each module and to include the source of material as part of a sentence rather than parenthetically, which is common practice in scholarly writing. This was but another example of how our academic writing style and techniques became a hindrance as we prepared text for the multimedia format.

The Instructional Designer (ID) used his or her knowledge of multimedia instruction and adult learning to construct the most effective way to relate the content to the learner. These team members either had master's degrees in instructional design or were in the process of finishing their degrees while working on this project. These highly skilled and creative members of the team were informed by the SMEs about the challenges faced by child welfare workers in their daily jobs. This enabled the IDs to understand their audience. Their tremendous enthusiasm and creativity was sometimes tempered by the reality that child welfare workers might not be receptive to another training activity. Considerable time and effort went into this educative process, which essentially served as a socialization or acculturation process for the designers and other team members. The team was sometimes incredulous when they learned of the demands and restraints placed on the social workers as they attempted to carry out their day to day functions.

The first step after delivery of the content by the SME was for the ID to draw a "concept map," which is a navigation tool that graphically describes how the learner will move through the various segments or sections of the module (see Figure 1). The ID determined the best mode of delivery for each aspect of the content, such as a video segment, text on the computer screen, illustrations, computer graphics or animation, or a combination of those modes and creates the module script. A sample page from a script appears in Figure 2. Each page of script represents one computer screen.

After this step was accomplished the ID presented the concept map to the SME who often did not easily relate to the visual presentation. Instructional Designers had to exercise considerable patience when working with SMEs who were generally not visually creative and had difficulty understanding how the pieces would "all fit together."

The next major task of the ID was the development of the multimedia "script," a detailed description, of what will be happening with audio, video, and computer text throughout the module. At this point in the process the Computer Programmer and the Graphic Designer became integral parts of the team. Team meetings were held to review the script and to decide how the various team members would handle each segment. These meetings were of crucial importance because the script

FIGURE 1. Concept Map of Overall Flow Chart for *BFF Child Abuse and Neglect* module. Concept Map Was Produced Using VISIO Software by VISIO Corporation, 520 Pike Street, Suite 1800, Seattle, WA 98101-4001.

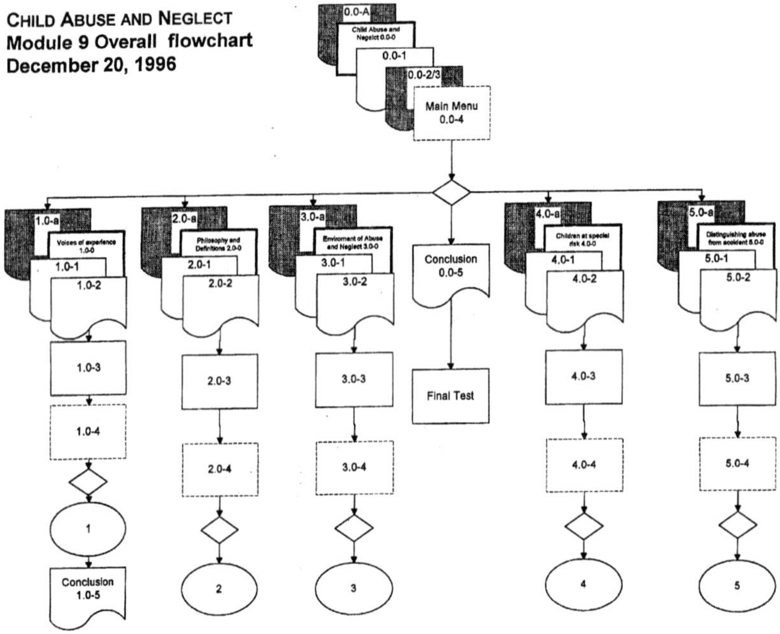

drives the production of the module. Sometimes fraught with frustration, these meetings were essential in that all team players had to agree on which discipline involved would handle discrete segments of the module.

Decisions about work allocation were sometimes based on availability of staff time and financial resources. For example, if the team agreed that the best treatment of a certain concept was to use graphics but the graphic designer was already overloaded with work, concessions had to be made. Additionally, the use of students finishing degrees in either graphic design, instructional design, or computer programming contributed to the frustrations when allocating work and designing the module. Students, with competing obligations of work and school, were sometimes unavailable at critical times during the module production.

The entire production team was dependent upon the SMEs for getting the content to them in a timely manner. SMEs, who had competing

FIGURE 2. Sample Module Script Page from *Child Abuse and Neglect* BFF module.

Module 9, Section 0: Child Abuse and Neglect

Section Title: Introduction			**Flowchart #:0.0-3**
Section Objective: Objectives screen/Module goals			
Treatment/Theme: Text			
Testing:			
Video Length:	**(A1) Audio Length:**		**(A2) Audio Length:**
# Photo/Audio CD's:	#Graphics: Pen in hand icons and menu button	Graphics Animation:	Graphics Vendor
LD Clip ID:	**LD Descriptor:**		LD Start/End Frame:
Remarks: Hot words: <Abuse>, <Neglect>			**Branch To:** 1.1-1 (section menu)

Computer text:

Module Goals

This is a module about Child <Abuse> and <Neglect>. The topics covered in this module include **Voice of Experience, Philospohy and Legal Definitions, The Environment of Abuse and Neglect, Children at Special Risk, and Distinguishing Abuse from the Accident.**

Each section of the module begins with an introduction and an overview of the learning objectives. You may choose the lessons in any order. However, we suggest that you go through them in the order they appear for the most comprehensive training. Reviews are given at the end of sections two through five. There is a final test you must take to complete the module.

Keep your workbook handy as you work your way through the training session. An icon will appear on the computer screen from time-to-time to give you the opportunity to break and go to a particular section for reference. The workbook includes, graphs, charts, and resources that may be helpful in your casework. Feel free to make copies of the information. You may exit the module at anytime. A bookmark is provided for your convenience.
The goals of this module are to:
✍ Make social work professionals aware of the breadth of child abuse and neglect.
✍ Help make social work professional decide whether to bring about intervention in child abuse and neglect cases.

Click here to go to the main menu. (button)

Visual (specify LD or CMP):
CMP

Description of Scene:

Audio (specify A1, A2, or None):
None

obligations of teaching, service and other research activities, sometimes struggled to meet writing deadlines set by the team. In order to impose realistic and firm deadlines, one of the project managers agreed to oversee the scheduling. She was able to effectively project time needed for completion of each phase and through constant encouragement hold the other SMEs accountable to their writing commitments. This adherence to schedule was critical because if one member of the team failed to meet a deadline, all others fell behind as a result.

The Graphic Designer (GD) was responsible for the visual presentation of the module. His work included selecting the color scheme for the entire curriculum and for each individual module. The GD also designed the project logo and specific themes for each module. A significant consideration of the GD was whether or not text could be easily read while maximizing the number of words on each computer screen. How much text on one screen was too much for the user? How big did the print need to be to accommodate young and old eyes? What specific shadings would enhance the readability of the text? These and many more considerations were the responsibility of the Graphic Designer as was the development of the supporting materials in the workbook. The following scenario illustrates the significance of the selections made by the GD:

> The team is meeting to provide input about what the logo for the entire curriculum should look like. Someone suggests that we use graphic depictions of "a family" since we have entitled the series "Building Family Foundations." Discussion ensues about what constitutes a "family." The GD is left with considerable input from his teammates and must invent a logo that offends no one yet captures the attention of the audience it's intended to attract.

The *Child Abuse and Neglect* module also presented similar design challenges. Creativity, common sense, and sensitivity to cultural stereotypes were important qualities possessed by the Graphic Designer.

The audio and video (A&V) production team, consisting of photographers, set builders, and designers, as well as audio and lighting technicians, was responsible for filming segments to be included in the modules and for editing segments from the script to the videotape. The team also made editorial comments about the script that made the dialog more realistic for filming purposes. After editing, the tape was pressed onto a first-draft videodisk called a "check disk." The A&V designer was responsible for the filming phase of the project. Persons held this position with master's degrees in photojournalism and mass communications. These professionals attended the module team meetings from the onset in order to conceptualize the module and make suggestions in the planning stages that would later impact video production. These suggestions were mediated by budget considerations because video production was one of the most expensive elements of the development of Building Family Foundations.

TESTING AND THE ROLE OF THE COMPUTER PROGRAMMER

The Computer Programmer's (CP) role was to program the text, graphics and animation. After the videotape was pressed onto a first-draft videodisk called a "check disk," the CP integrated the various components of the module to produce a completed check disk. The check disk was used to alpha test the modules. Alpha testing is a process of detecting errors and correcting them. During this testing phase of the project the Computer Programmer had a lead role. Other team members assisted the CP as he combed through every detail of the module and corrected errors. Some errors were as simple as spelling and grammar, while others required major revision to the text or the navigational program (the unseen programming that makes it possible for the user to easily go through the module). The CP's considerable technological skills were most obvious during this phase of the project. Less obvious, but as critical to the project's success, was his ability to "join" the social work culture in order to work effectively with the SMEs. Much patience was required of the CP as he translated computer language into a tongue that could be understood by the SMEs writing the content. One of the CP's concerns as he watched the development of the module and prepared for the programming was the final product's ease of navigation. While entertaining feedback from the team relative to the content and design, the CP was constantly appraising the module from the perspective of the user. Many creative suggestions and valid context considerations were discarded due to the CP's concerns about the ease with which the user could navigate through the module.

The second testing phase of the module was beta testing. Social work students and social workers from the community completed the module and gave feedback that helped identify problems with content or navigation. This input from the beta testing was then used to make modifications to the module. When this testing process was complete, the "master disk" was pressed and multiple copies were made.

IMPLEMENTATION

The final phase of the Building Family Foundations Training Project was implementation. This phase required that the project staff distribute machinery, install the programs, and provide training on the use of the technology. The entire curriculum package consisted of a videodisk, computer disk, and workbook. Additionally, the project was responsible for purchasing and delivering the equipment needed to run the curriculum. This consisted of a CPU, monitor, laser disk player, and speakers. Sixty SRS offices across the state received training units. The project had a staff person solely responsible for the delivery of the machinery, installation of the program, and training of SRS staff at each site. This staff person was critical to the project. Whether or not SRS staff used the modules depended on their perception of how easily they could "run the computer." The trainer was adept at reducing users' fears of the technology and instilling users' confidence in their ability to use the modules.

When considering the challenges of this phase of the project, it is important to consider the excitement of the project staff in being able to finally, after several years of hard work, deliver a "product" to the social workers. This excitement was tempered when delivery of equipment and training occurred. For example, even though our staff carefully prepared each office for receipt of their equipment, they would sometimes find that, after driving three hours to deliver, there would be no space allotted for the units. Training was set up well in advance of the deliveries, yet few workers would attend. One trip made for training after equipment delivery found the expensive computer equipment in a storage closet with water dripping on it from a leaky roof. These incidents were reminders to our staff that child welfare workers had much more on their minds than our exciting new training project.

In order to maximize the use of this training curriculum within the large SRS system, the project staff advertised its availability through the use of brochures and presentations at various conferences around the state. The presentations and visibility of project staff at statewide conferences informed workers of the availability and overall merit of the curriculum. Child welfare workers across the state began using the first training module in early 1994. Initial feedback was very positive and continued to be with the introduction of each new module. Use of the modules continues throughout the state as both mandatory training of new staff and continuing education for senior staff. Our excitement was restored when enthusiastic feedback from child welfare workers was received.

As part of implementation an evaluative plan was developed. It consisted of child welfare workers reporting their impressions of and comfort with the training and demographic data to determine patterns of responses to categories of learners. Further, social work students were given three instruments before and after viewing five of the modules. The instruments measure comfort level of workers using a computer, job satisfaction and level of self-confidence with the module content. It was found that interactive multimedia is an effective means of providing training in knowledge and skills necessary for social work practice. For a complete discussion of the evaluation process see *Using Interactive Multimedia to Build Child Welfare Competencies in Social Workers* (Thurston and Cauble, 1999).

COMPLEXITIES OF MULTIMEDIA INSTRUCTIONAL DESIGN

Delivering social work knowledge and skills in the classroom setting and teaching through technology are very different approaches. It was difficult and proved to be challenging for all involved. The development of interactive multimedia programs is complex, labor-intensive, and expensive. The costs in terms of exact dollar amounts, while possible to determine, would be misleading to the reader because technology has advanced considerably since this project was completed. These advancements in technology will allow others to develop projects such as this at considerably lower cost. Additionally, our project costs included purchase of the field units for 60 sites for the state agency; this greatly distorts the cost of the project. And, perhaps most important relative to cost, is that development and production costs were also high because this project had no map to follow. As stated earlier, much of the required technology was in its infancy. This, combined with no model to follow, resulted in high costs. Although no hard evidence exists, administrators report that, when examining costs over time, the overall expenses compare favorably with more traditional training programs.

Working within the university setting can reduce some of the costs. Rather than full-time professionals, educational technology graduate students from the College of Education were employed as instructional designers and programmers. An advantage of the university setting is the availability of resources including professors with expertise in a variety of fields, students who are available to do research and other necessary activities, and libraries. Conversely, the issues of dual role and relationships inherent in a university setting sometimes resulted in difficulty for our project. Difficulty arose when professors of instructional design courses were also responsible for the supervision of students while they were working as staff on the project. The students often felt demands were unreasonable and were concerned that if they complained it would negatively affect their class grade. Students and faculty have many responsibilities in addition to those of the project. At times, these competing obligations complicated and prolonged the production phase of the project. Reducing student involvement and using paid staff expedites completion.

COLLABORATION CHALLENGES

Collaboration between the departments of special education and the social work program was both rewarding and difficult. The integration of knowledge from the fields of education and social work is very useful for the development of training curricula that can meet the large and ongoing demand for social work training. However, such interdisciplinary work requires time for processing issues that arise due to different perspectives. Time was spent educating each other about how each discipline viewed a particular issue. For example, social workers have a commonly understood practice framework that constitutes a "culture of helping." The professionals from other disciplines had to be socialized into this culture in order for them to relate to the content and present it in a meaningful way to the social work learner. This included learning terminology and procedures. The time required to successfully accomplish a rewarding collaboration should not be underestimated.

UNDERSTANDING EACH OTHERS' LANGUAGE

A common working language must evolve when professionals from varied disciplines and backgrounds are brought together to create a successful project. Assuming that team members understand each other and share common goals is, to say the least, naive. The team must learn how to bridge communication barriers just as social workers must strive to form a language link with clients. All professions and technical trades have informal language or jargon. Considerable misunderstanding could have been prevented if time had been devoted to discuss the various professions' languages. Simply giving each other permission to not always understand the jargon could have reduced language confusion. We struggled to learn as we moved through the project development and were often confused. The videotaping process illustrates this language bewilderment. Video production staff uses the word "tape" when they are referring to the video recording process. The other disciplines referred to this as "filming." These differences, while seemingly benign, resulted in continual confusion among team members. Often, when staff spoke about something using their professional jargon, others would not understand what was wanted or needed. Instructional designers frequently asked subject matter experts (social workers and special education professors) "What do you want this to look like?" The assumption inherent in that question was that the writers knew what the possibilities were when, in fact, they had little knowledge of what was possible.

Staff supervision by the project administrators (social workers and a special education professor) was also challenging due to the absence of shared language. Administrators had difficulty with accountability and offering guidance to the technical production staff when they could not understand or speak their language. The credibility of administrators was a central issue during the first year of the project. Staff were incredulous when their "bosses" responded to their many questions with: "I don't know," or "I don't understand what you are talking about." The production team members struggled with administration's obvious lack of knowledge and experience in their areas of expertise. Simply stated, it is hard to supervise someone when you know very little, if anything, about what they do and can accomplish. It was both difficult to evaluate employees' job performances and to offer appropriate encouragement and meaningful feedback. Setting realistic time lines was also difficult, because administrators did not understand how long it might take to accomplish a task. This became less of a problem as staff learned that this project was the first of its kind and that there was no model to follow. It was critical that we educated one another about our respective disciplines. Eventually, a sense of "we're all in this boat together" emerged as we learned that we were breaking new ground. A more tolerant work environment was created when we developed empathy for each other's struggles.

PROFESSIONAL VALUE CONFLICTS

Ethical dilemmas are common in social work practice. The social work professionals on the team found that resolving ethical dilemmas that developed during the production of the modules was difficult. Resolution of ethical dilemmas was complicated due to the involvement of other disciplines, including those from non-helping fields, in the decision making process. Social workers have a Code of Ethics (1996) that both differentiates us from other professions and creates a code of conduct. As professional social workers we were clear about our need to protect the identity of anyone whose "story" was told in order to provide material for the modules. The local SRS offices produced case histories and carefully concealed and/or changed any identifying information about clients. Difficulty arose during production of the Family Issues module. The social workers on the team were concerned about how to use real life "client" stories without exploiting former clients. The production team wanted to tape testimonials from members of real-life gay/lesbian, single-parent, and the other family types being featured in the module. They insisted that, if the families gave informed consent, understood the project, and were made fully aware of the scope of the viewing audience, former clients and "real life" families should be used in the module. We, the professional social workers, felt it was our responsibility to protect the identities of these families, even if they agreed to participate. We felt strongly that the potential negative repercussions from "telling one's story" to thousands of unseen viewers greatly outweighed the benefits. We conceded that we were quite possibly being overly cautious but believed that our obligation was to keep our "clients" identities confidential. In doing so we disappointed the team whose understanding of our ethical standards was limited and whose creativity we stifled by our seemingly "rigid" stance.

THEORETICAL ORIENTATION CHALLENGES AMONG TEAM MEMBERS

The multidisciplinary collaboration greatly enhanced the scope and content of this training program. The special education input provided material that, as social work educators, we may not have included. Our special education colleague's behavioral theoretical orientation enabled us to include segments on parenting skills that were rich with examples from her work with parents and classroom teachers. As social workers, our perspective on change and how we view client problems differed from that of our behaviorist colleague. Her inclination was to assess problems primarily in terms of behavioral theory (Dettmer et al., 1996) while ours was inclusive of social, cultural, and other systems interfacing with the individual and family (Hartman & Laird, 1983). Integrating "our way" of looking at problems and resolutions with a perspective that, while not foreign or unappealing to us, was not the "lens" through which we view the world, was challenging. We developed respect for the value of both perspectives to train social workers after we processed the differences and talked about the similarities of our approaches. These sessions were intellectually stimulating and necessary for resolution of issues impeding the progress of the project.

MANAGING REACTIONS TO SENSITIVE MATERIAL

Differences in orientation and sensitivity among the production team members became quite obvious during production of the child abuse module. Slides showing various types of injuries to children were obtained from the American Pediatric Association. Their purpose was to help child welfare workers identify and differentiate those injuries that are caused by accidents from those that are suspicious of child abuse. Social workers are sensitized to these graphic depictions of injuries to children and are able to respond to them with some degree of objectivity. This was not true of our production team. They had difficulty with the graphic nature of these slides; some members said that they were having dreams about the pictures of the children who suffered these injuries. The instructional designers and programmers insisted that these pictures be quite small on the computer screen so as not to upset the learner (child welfare worker using the module). We argued that the slides needed to be as large as technology would allow in order to help the workers learn about the different types of injuries. We achieved compromise by using a screen that informed the learners that they would be viewing potentially disturbing material and that they could move to another screen at their own discretion. This experience reminded us that material child welfare workers are accustomed to seeing is often upsetting to the lay person who has not been sensitized to the subject matter. This discomfort and the delays that resulted could have been minimized if we had sensitized the entire staff to this difficult material.

ACCOMMODATING THE SPECIAL INTERESTS OF EACH DISCIPLINE

Each discipline involved in the production of BFF had its standards for performance. Accommodating the standards of each was challenging. For example, conflict arose when we, as social workers, evaluated the quality of the videotaping. Our professional video production team members wanted a "perfect" product, not unlike any that they would produce for a television program. We cared less about lighting and wardrobe than we cared about the dialogue being taped. One taping session stands out as particularly memorable. During this session fifteen (so it seemed!) minutes were spent on one of the talent's earrings. The video production staff was concerned about light reflection from the earring and worked to correct it. This, from the perspective of the video production team, was a reasonable concern. Others tired of the attention to detail. Since studio time is charged by the minute some of us felt as though this attention to detail was a waste of our time and resources. Both sides were frustrated as we considered how to proceed without compromising the standards of any discipline involved. It is difficult and can be inappropriate to ask people to lower their professional standards.

Competing professional agendas were noted during the production of the *Social Work Skills* modules. The video production team believed that a script should be used for all scenes. This approach worked well for most of the modules and involved using a teleprompter. The *Social Work Skills* modules feature interviewing scenes during which the social worker interacts with clients and demonstrates specific skills such as reflection, empathy, active listening, etc. Demonstration of these skills required a cast comprised of a professional social worker and actors (talents) who played family roles. In this way, the family could role-play while the social worker responded to them spontaneously. The video production staff doubted the ability of social workers to respond without a written script and believed that it would increase production time and costs. We eventually convinced the team that our instruction in the classroom prepared social workers to interact with the actors without a prepared script. Our credibility with the team was enhanced when this approach proved to be very successful.

DISCUSSION AND LESSONS LEARNED

Distance education holds great promise for rural social work training. The special needs of child welfare workers who practice in rural areas can be met through the use of new technologies. Our experience with Building Family Foundations convinces us that multimedia interactive training can be made readily available to the rural professional in a variety of fields. This methodology can overcome many of rural service delivery's common challenges identified by Merell, Pratt, Forbush, Jentzsh, Nelson, Odell, and Smith (1994), e.g., lack of specialists and lack of access to professional tools and materials. The technology and expertise is available to achieve advanced levels of training for all professionals no matter their location. Notwithstanding its potential, challenges do exist when transferring knowledge and skill training from the traditional classroom setting to a multimedia format of instruction. The development, implementation and subsequent evaluation of the Building Family Foundations training project highlights the challenges working with a multidisciplinary team to create multimedia interactive training.

Social workers have considerable training in the use of methods to help them establish helping relationships, assess strengths and needs, and develop plans to address these needs. These social work practice methods should be consciously applied during the planning and development of a project using a multidisciplinary team in order to maximize the effectiveness of the final product and minimize difficulties during the production process. Social workers are familiar with the need to carefully plan their interactions with clients. It is expected that workers may have considerable "differences" with clients, whether those differences are social, racial, ethnic, gender, or, in this case, professional. Social workers accept the responsibility of bridging differences and adjusting their language to effectively communicate with clients. Similarly, in planning a project using a multidisciplinary team, differences in language, values, and standards must be anticipated. A plan to mediate these differences would include initial sensitivity training, emphasizing education about each discipline's language and area of expertise to the project.

The use of the focus groups to assess training needs (Denning & Verschelden, 1993) initiated the Building Foundations training project and paralleled the first phase of the social work helping process. Workers were engaged through a process that encouraged their participation, emphasized their strengths, and asked them to voice their concerns and list their needs. This type of engagement and mutual planning must be continued as the multidisciplinary team is assembled for the production of the multimedia-training curriculum. Social workers typically contract with clients regarding the goals of the helping process and delineate the roles and responsibilities of each participant. Similarly, when working with a multidisciplinary team, clear roles must be established before the work is begun. Someone must be in charge even though the concept of "team" connotes an egalitarian effort. Many difficulties can result when administrative authority is shared. Misunderstandings and deadline lapses were common until we realized that we needed to become more "hierarchical" in our approach to team management. We suggest that one person on the team be designated as the overall head regardless of specific needs within each discipline.

Social workers providing direct services to clients understand the need to continually work on rapport and "building the relationship" in order to accomplish clients' goals. Working with a multidisciplinary team requires that this skill is used continually and that considerable time be allotted for the processing of issues related to value and theoretical differences among team members. Production deadlines and funding realities can be overwhelming and pressure the team to dispense with this critical phase of the process. Our experience convinces us that time spent processing differences is well spent and can prevent barriers to goal accomplishment.

The evaluation of BFF has resulted in enthusiasm for the future use of interactive multimedia instruction for social workers. Our periods of floundering and frustration have been instructive and have convinced us that when working with a multidisciplinary team, a conscious effort must be made to parallel the entire social work helping process. Application of common practice methods will maximize the efficiency of the multidisciplinary team and facilitate the production of an effective training program.

The lessons learned from BFF are many. In brief:

- Collaboration takes longer and produces a better result.
- Have a plan to educate the team about each discipline's values, professional standards, and language.
- Recognize each discipline's contribution to the finished product.
- Minimize student and volunteer involvement.

REFERENCES

Cauble, A. E., & Dinkel, J. (1999). Social workers and technology: Challenges of the multidisciplinary team. *Professional Development: The International Journal of Continuing Social Work Education*, *2*, 4-13.

Denning, J., & Verschelden, C. (1993). Using the focus group in assessing training needs: Empowering child welfare workers. *Child Welfare*, *72*, 569-579.

Dettmer, P., Dyck, N., & Thurston, L. (1996). *Consultation, collaboration, and teamwork for students with special needs.* (2nd ed.). Needham Heights, MA: Allyn & Bacon. 66-69.

Fox, R. (1987). Short term, goal-oriented family therapy. *Social Casework*, *68*, 494-499.

Hartman, A., & Laird, J. (1983). *Family-centered social work practice*. New York, NY: Free Press. 158-180.

Kush, S., & Campo, J. (1998). *Consultation and liaison in the pediatric setting*. Boston, MA: Allyn & Bacon.

Marans, S., Berkowitz, S., & Cohen, D. (1998). Police and mental health professionals: Collaborative responses to the impact of violence on children and families. *Child and Adolescent Psychiatric Clinics of North America*, *7* (3), 635-651.

Merrell, K.E., Pratt, S., Forbush, D., Jentzsch, C., Nelson, S., Odell, C., & Smith, M. (1994). Special education, school psychology, and community mental health practice in rural settings: Common problems and overlapping solutions for training. *Rural Special Education Quarterly*, *13*, 28-36.

National Association of Social Workers. (1996). *NASW code of ethics*. Washington, DC: Author. Available: *http://www.naswdc.org/CODE.HTM*.

Pecora, P. J. (1989). Improving the quality of child welfare services: Needs assessment for staff training. *Child Welfare*, *68*, 403-419.

Saloff-Coste, C., Hamburg, P., & Herzog, D. (1993). Nutrition and psychotherapy: Collaborative treatment of patients with eating disorders. *Bulletin of the Menninger Clinic*, *57*(4), 504-516.

Thurston, L.P., & Cauble, A.E. (1999). Using interactive multimedia to build child welfare competencies in social workers. *Journal of Research on Computing in Education*, *32*, 298-306.

Thurston, L.P., Verschelden, C., & Denning, J. (1996). Using interactive multi-media to address rural social work education needs. *Tulane Studies in Social Welfare*, *20*, 28-39.

Conclusion

Hy Resnick
Phoebe Sade Anderson

This edition introduced the human service reader to a beginning literature describing electronically driven programs–many high tech and some not so high tech–which are intended to enhance, or at least support, human service practice and education.

In the first section which focuses on practice, the software programs described have been designed to:

- improve physical access of clients for service (Finn, Rosenfield, Mielonen, Collie),
- increase psychological receptivity to service (Aymard, Cowen),
- provide increased engagement and understanding of medical and social problems and ways to prevent and/or resolve them to youthful clients (Wilder and Schoech, Gropper, Bosworth) and
- support and enhance the work of social workers, both clinical and administrative (Meier and Garcia & Lewis).

In the education section, articles, which describe electronically aided educational offerings (increasingly called online education and distance learning), highlight the following advantages:

- improving students access to information (a book contains pages, a CD-ROM contains up to 300,000 pages) (Engen, Resnick et al., Dinkel & Cauble and Wegenest), and

[Haworth co-indexing entry note]: "Conclusion." Resnick, Hy, and Phoebe Sade Anderson. Co-published simultaneously in *Journal of Technology in Human Services* (The Haworth Press, Inc.) Vol. 20, No. 3/4, 2002, pp. 369-371; and: *Human Services Technology: Innovations in Practice and Education* (ed: Hy Resnick, and Phoebe Sade Anderson) The Haworth Press, Inc., 2002, pp. 369-371. Single or multiple copies of this article are available for a fee from The Haworth Document Delivery Service [1-800-HAWORTH, 9:00 a.m. - 5:00 p.m. (EST). E-mail address: getinfo@haworthpressinc.com].

- the ability to overcome the traditional learning parameters of time and location (the Internet and the World Wide Web make synchronous as well as asynchronous learning possible, and students in remote areas can access formal education programs and trainings) (Seabury, Cummings & Bonk, MacFadden, and Hick).

Even though the level of sophistication of the electronically driven programs included in this collection represents a giant step forward compared to those programs presented in the first edition, it is still too early to predict just what impact electronic technology will have on what facet of the profession. With respect to social work education, there are now more than 50 schools of social work that regularly provide access to social work education through distance education modalities.[1] However, practice itself, i.e., face-to-face contact with clients, has yet to be significantly affected by electronic progress. It is not too early in the development of this technology, however, to suggest a number of areas which might be impacted and in what ways, assuming technology continues to be integrated into social work practice and instruction. It is possible a number of actors and institutions will be impacted as follows.

ACTORS

Practitioners, administrators, instructors, and students in our agencies and educational institutions will be increasingly inclined or pressured to modify their roles. For example, the role of Instructors may change from primarily information givers and resource providers to primarily facilitators and synthesizers of information. Students will find it more difficult to depend on the instructor for learning and will find conditions in schools of social work which will stimulate proactivity, accountability, and independence in learning. Administrators will become more knowledgeable regarding technology and will advocate appropriate changes in their budget requests. Technical Specialists will become more useful, visible and influential in facility construction and remodeling, curriculum building and student recruitment decisions. More specialists will be hired, creating a new cadre of social work oriented computer specialists probably at the doctoral or practitioner level.

Other areas that might be affected include:

- relations with the business community, especially computer firms,
- student body will contain more "techies" than in present today to "compete" with activists, clinicians and administrators,
- marginal students who learn poorly via traditional instructional methods may become more successful because of new electronically driven instructional methods, and
- educational institutions, buildings and interior spaces will be changed to make space for technology (larger offices to house computer equipment, electronically supprted classrooms, less office space as faculty can also do much work at home, etc).

Technology in social work education is here to stay and especially so in the last five or ten years. As Raymond and Ginsberg stated: "The decade of the nineties brought an explosion in the use of information and computer-based technologies. Higher education, in particular, is experiencing a significant impact from this rapid growth and diffusion." And yet, its influence is only now beginning to be felt and observed.

Although this volume has only minimally dealt with the ethical, legal, financial, personnel questions that technology has presented for us, these will continue to plague us in ways small and large. But whatever form these obstacles will take, electronic technology has insinuated itself into our world and we will (and can) deal with it.

NOTE

1. Raymond, F.B., Ginsberg, L, and Gohagen, D. eds. Teaching to Use and Using to Teach (1998). The Haworth Press, Inc.

Bibliography

In addition to the references included in most of the articles in this volume, we have compiled the following list. These references indicate the breadth of technological work within the social work field–an expansive list of articles and books from the last several years. We hope that you find them as useful as we have.

Aaronson, D. (1994). Computer use in cognitive psychology. *Behavior Research Methods, Instruments & Computers, 26*(2), 81-93.

Adams, L., & Grigsby, K. (1995). The Georgia state telemedicine program: Initiation, design and plans. *Telemedicine Journal, 1*(3), 227-235.

Ashery, R.S. (1999, September). *The utilization of technology in graduate schools of social work.* Paper presented at the 3rd Annual Technology Conference for Social Work Education and Practice, Charleston, SC.

Bailey, E. & Cotlar, M. (1994). Teaching via the Internet. *Communication Education, 43*(2), 184-193.

Barker, P., & King, T. (1993). Evaluating interactive multimedia courseware–A methodology. *Computers and Education, 21*(4), 307-319.

Barnett-Queen, T., & Zhu, E. (1999, September). *Distance education: Analysis of learning preferences in two sections of undergraduate HBSE-like human growth and development course: Face-to-face and web-based distance learning.* Paper presented at the 3rd Annual Technology Conference for Social Work Education and Practice, Charleston, SC.

Beasley, R. (1998-99). Interactive multimedia development: Pre-design analyses. *Journal of Educational Technology Systems, 27*(1), 23-42.

[Haworth co-indexing entry note]: "Bibliography." Co-published simultaneously in *Journal of Technology in Human Services* (The Haworth Press, Inc.) Vol. 20, No. 3/4, 2002, pp. 373-381; and: *Human Services Technology: Innovations in Practice and Education* (ed: Hy Resnick, and Phoebe Sade Anderson) The Haworth Press, Inc., 2002, pp. 373-381. Single or multiple copies of this article are available for a fee from The Haworth Document Delivery Service [1-800-HAWORTH, 9:00 a.m. - 5:00 p.m. (EST). E-mail address: getinfo@haworthpressinc.com].

Bertcher, H. (1994). *TELL-A-GROUP: How to set up and operate group work by telephone*. Unpublished.

Blakely, T. (1992). A Model for Distance Education Delivery. *Journal of Social Work Education, 28*(2), 214-221.

Blakely, T. (1994). Strategies for distance learning. *Journal of Continuing Social Work Education, 6*(1), 4-7.

Blakely, T., & Schoenherr, P. (1995). Telecommunication technologies in social work distance education. *Journal of Continuing Social Work Education, 6*(3), 8-12.

Blissett, G., & Atkins, M. (1993). Are they thinking? Are they learning? A study of the use of interactive video. *Computers and Education, 21*(1-2), 31-39.

Blood, G. (1995). A behavioral-cognitive therapy program for adults who stutter: Computers and counseling. *Journal of Communication Disorders, 28*, 165-180.

Boyd, P. (1991). Developing software for social workers. *New Technology in the Human Services*, 5(4), 19-25.

Brieff, R. (1994). Personal computers in psychiatric rehabilitation: A new approach to skills training. *Hospital and Community Psychiatry, 45*(3), 257-260.

Brouch, V. (1994). Navigating the arts in an electronic sea. *NASSP-Bulletin, 78*(561), 43-49.

Burda, P., Starkey, T., Dominguez, F., & Vera, V. (1994). Computer-assisted cognitive rehabilitation of chronic psychiatric inpatients. *Computers in Human Behavior, 10*(3), 359-368.

Caputo, R., & Cnaan, R. (1990). Information technology availability in schools of social work. *Journal of Social Work Education, 26*(20), 187-198.

Carlin, A., Hoffman, H., & Weghorst, S. (1997). Virtual Reality and tactile augmentation in the treatment of spider phobia: A case report. *Behavior Research Therapy, 35*(2), 153-158.

Clark, J., Lanphear, A., & Riddick, C. (1987). The effects of videogame playing on the response selection processing of elderly adults. *Journal of Gerontology, 42*(1), 82-85.

Conklin, J., & Osterndorf, W. (1995). Distance learning in continuing social work education: Promise of the year 2000. *Journal of Continuing Social Work Education, 6*(3), 13-17.

D'Andrea, M. (1995). Using computer technology to promote multicultural awareness among elementary school-age students. *Elementary School Guidance and Counseling, 30*(1), 45-55.

De Klein, R. (1997). The making of the CD-ROM Dementia. *New Technology in the Human Services, 10*(3), 15-18.

Dezendorf, P., & Green, R. (1999, September). *The impact of electronic social work (ESW) on rural practice.* Paper presented at the 3rd Annual Technology Conference for Social Work Education and Practice, Charleston, SC.

Dorman, S. (1997). CD-ROM use in health instruction. *Journal of School Health, 67*(10), 444-446.

Droste-Bielak, E. (1986). Two techniques for teaching interviewing. *Computers in Nursing, 4*(4), 152-157.

Engel, R. & McMurty, S. (1987). Computer content in education for human services administration. *Computers in Human Services, 2*(1/2), 51-62.

Falk, D., Shepard, M., Campbell, J., & Maypole, D. (1992). Current and potential applications of interactive videodiscs in social work education. *Journal of Teaching in Social Work, 6*(1), 117-136.

Fine, M., & McIntosh, D. (1986). The use of interactive video to demonstrate differential approaches to marital and family therapy. *Journal of Marital and Family Therapy, 12*(1), 85-88.

Finn, J. (1995). Computer-based self-help groups: A new resource to supplement support groups. *Social Work with Groups, 18*(1), 109-117.

Finn, J. (1995). Use of electronic mail to promote computer literacy in social work undergraduates. *Journal of Teaching in Social Work, 12*(1/2), 73-83.

Flynn, J. (1990). Using the Computer to Teach and Learn Social Policy: A Report from the Classroom and the Field. *Computers in Human Services, 7*(3-4), 199-209.

Franchi, J. (1994). *Virtual reality: An overview.* TechTrends, *39*(1), 23-26.

Furlong, M. (1989). An electronic community for older adults: The SeniorNet network. *Journal of Communication, 39*(3), 145-153.

Glantz, K. et al. (1997). Virtual reality and psychotherapy: Opportunities and challenges. *Presence, 6*(1), 87-105.

Glover, B. (1995). DINOS (drinking is not our solution): Using computer programs in middle school drug education. *Elementary School Guidance and Counseling, 30*(1), 55-62.

Gohagen, D. (1998, August). *A social work specific evaluation framework for using the internet in professional activities.* Paper presented at the Conference on Information Technologies for Social Work Education and Practice, Charleston, SC.

Groves, D. (1990). Computer assisted instruction with senior citizens. *Journal of Instructional Psychology*, *17*(3), 172-177.

Hallenbecker, C.E., Gallaher, R.B., & Warren, J.Q. (1977). The community mental health center management game: Teaching administrative skills by means of computer simulation. *Behavior Research Methods & Instrumentation*, *9*(2), 202-208.

Henderson, J. (1998). Comprehensive, technology-based clinical education: The "virtual practicum." *International Journal of Psychiatry in Medicine*, *28*(1), 41-79.

Hines, M. (1994). Using the telephone in family therapy. *Journal of Marital and Family Therapy*, *20*(2), 175-185.

Hoffman, D., & Duggan, W. (1989). *Guerilla Media: A citizen's guide to using electronic media for social change*. Princeton, NJ: Films for the Humanities.

Hornby, P., & Anderson, M. (1994). Computer use in psychology instruction: A survey of individual and institutional characteristics. *Behavior Research Methods, Instruments & Computers*, *26*(2), 250-254.

Jacobson, R. (1991, April). *Televirtuality: "Being there" in the 21st century*. Paper presented at the Silicon Valley Networking Conference, Santa Clara, CA.

Jones, A., & Petre, M. (1994). Computer-Based Practical Work at a Distance: A Case Study. *Computers and Education*, *22*(1-2), 27-37.

Juels, C., & Kramer, T. (1994). Psychiatric residency directors' use of computers in their training programs. *Academic Psychiatry*, *18*(2), 81-87.

Kautzmann, L. (1990). Introducing computers to the elderly. *Physical & Occupational Therapy in Geriatrics*, *9*(1), 27-36.

Kaye, L. (1988, March). *A social work administration model curriculum in computer technology and information management*. Paper presented at the symposium Information Technology and Social Work Education, Atlanta, GA.

Kenardy, J., & Adams, C. (1993). Computers in cognitive-behaviour therapy. *Australian Psychologist*, *28*(3), 189-94.

Kost, K., & Sturman, S. (1999, September). *Using technology to teach community practice*. Paper presented at the Third Annual Technology Conference for Social Work Education and Practice, Charleston, SC.

Kotwal, D., Burns, W., & Montgomery, D. (1996). Computer-assisted cognitive training for ADHD. *Behavior Modification, 20*(1), 85-96.

Lambert, M., Hedlund, J., & Vieweg, B. (1990). Computer Simulations in Mental Health Education: Two Illustrative Projects. *Computers in Human Services, 7*(3-4), 231-245.

Large, A., Beheshti, J., Breuleux, A., & Renaud, A. (1994). Multimedia and comprehension–A cognitive study. *Journal of the American Society for Information Science, 45*(7), 515-528.

Latting, J. (1994). Diffusion of computer-mediated communication in a graduate social work class: Lessons from "The class from Hell." *Computers in Human Services, 10*(3), 21-45.

Lindstrom, M. (1993). Computers in teaching in Danish social work schools: The past and present. *New Technology in the Human Services, 7*(1), 26-28.

Luse, F.D. (1980). Use of computer simulation in welfare management. *Administration in Social Work, 4*(3), 13-22.

MacFadden, R. (1989). Sexual abuse assessment training: Developing CAI in child welfare. *Computers in Human Services, 5*(3/4), 29-41.

Margalit, M. (1995). Social skills learning for students with learning disabilities and students with behavior disorders. *Educational Psychology, 15*(4), 445-456.

Maypole, D. (1991). Interactive videodiscs in social work education. *Social Work, 36*(3), 239-41.

McCue, A. (1980). Multi-media approach to group counseling with preadolescent girls. *Journal of School Health, 50*(3), 156-59.

Merickel, M. (1992, April). *A study of the relationship between virtual reality (perceived realism) and the ability of children to create, manipulate and utilize mental images for spatially related problem solving*. Paper presented at the Annual Convention of the National School Boards Association, Orlando, Florida.

Meyer, C., & Dunn-Roberts, R. (1992). Virtual reality: A strategy for training in cross-cultural communication. *Educational Media International, 29*(3), 175-80.

Myers, D. (1994). Communication technology and social movements: Contributions of computer networks to activism. *Social Science Computer Review, 12*(2), 250-260.

Newby, G. (1993). Virtual reality. *Annual Review of Information Science and Technology (ARTIST), 28*, 187-229.

Newman, M., Consoli, A., & Taylor, C. (1997). Computers in assessment and cognitive behavioral treatment of clinical disorders: Anxiety as a case in point. *Behavior Therapy, 28*, 211-235.

Noell, J., Biglan, A., Hood, D., & Britz, B. (1994). An interactive video-disc based smoking cessation program: Prototype development and pilot test. *Computers in Human Behavior, 10*(3), 347-358.

Norman, K. (1994). HyperCourseware for interactive instruction in the electronic classroom. *Behavior Research Methods, Instruments and Computers, 26*(2), 255-259.

Nurius, P. (1991). Classifying software to better support social work practice. *Social Work, 36*(6), 536-41.

Nurius, P., Hooyman, N., & Nicoll, A. (1991). Computers in agencies: A survey baseline and planning implications. *Journal of Social Service Research, 14*(3/4), 141-155.

O'Dell, J., & Dickson, J. (1984). Eliza as a "therapeutic" tool. *Journal of Clinical Psychology, 40*(4), 942-945.

Pacino, M., & Pacino, J. (1996). *Multimedia and cultural diversity.* T.H.E. Journal, vX, 70-71.

Pardeck, J. (1998). Rationalizing decision-making through computer technology: A critical appraisal. *Journal of Health & Social Policy, 9*(4), 19-29.

Pardeck, J., & Schulte, R. (1990). Computers in social intervention: Implications for professional social work practice and education. *Family Therapy, 17*(2), 109-121.

Patterson, D. et al. (1997). An experimental evaluation of HyperCDTX: Multimedia substance abuse treatment education software. *Computers in Human Services, 14*(1), 21-38.

Patterson, D. & Yaffe, J. (1994). Hypermedia computer-based education in social work education. *Journal of Social Work Education, 30*(2), 267-277.

Patterson, D., & Yaffe, J. (1993). Using computer-assisted instruction to teach Axis-II of the DSM-III-R to social work students. *Research on Social Work Practice, 3*(3), 343-357.

Petracchi, H., & Morgenbesser, M. (1995). The use of video and one-way broadcast technology to deliver continuing social work education: A comparative assessment of student learning. *Journal of Continuing Social Work Education, 6*(3), 18-22.

Poulin, J., & Walter, C. (1990). Interviewing skills and computer assisted instruction: BSW student perceptions. *Computers in Human Services, 7*(3-4), 179-197.

Quinn, C. (1991). Computers for cognitive research: A HyperCard adventure game. *Behavior Research Models, 23*(2), 237-246.

Rafferty, J. (1999). Changing to learn: Learning to change. In Raymond III, Ginsberg & Gohagen (Eds.). *Information Technologies: Teaching to Use: Using to Teach.* The Haworth Press, Inc.

Raffoul, P. (1993). DTREE, the electronic DSM-III-R. *Computers in Human Services, 10*(1), 61-64.

Raffoul, P. (1993). If you drink, an alcohol education program. *Computers in Human Services, 10*(1), 71-74.

Rebok, G., Rasmusson, D., & Brandt, J. (1996). Prospects for computerized memory training in normal elderly: Effects of practice on explicit and implicit memory tasks. *Applied Cognitive Psychology, 10*, 211-223.

Resnick, H. (1994). Future of electronic technology in human service practice and education. *Computers in Human Services, 11*(3/4), 379-384.

Reuben, D., Hirsch, S., Chernoff, J. et al. (1993). Project safety net: A health screening outreach and assessment program. *The Gerontologist, 33*(4), 557-560.

Reynolds, M. (1994). Decision-making using computer conferencing: A case study. *Behaviour & Information Technology, 13*(3), 239-252.

Root, L. (1996). Computer conferencing in a decentralized program: An occupational social work example. *Administration in Social Work, 20*(1), 31-45.

Rothbaum, B., Hodges, L., Jooper, R. et al. (1995). Effectiveness of computer-generated (virtual reality) graded exposure in the treatment of acrophobia. *American Journal of Psychiatry, 152*(4), 626-628.

Russell, C. (1972). Simulating the adolescent society: A validity study. *Simulation & Games, 3*(2), 165-188.

Scheibe, K., & Erwin, M. (1979). The computer as alter. *The Journal of Social Psychology, 108*, 103-109.

Schiller, S. (1993). Multimedia equipment for distance education. *Media and Methods, 30*(2), 36-37.

Schoenfeldt, L. (1994). Computer-assisted testing in organizational psychology. *European Journal of Psychological Assessment, 10*(1), 71-85.

Schopler, J.H., Abell, M.D., & Galinsky, M.J. (1998). Technology-based groups: A review and conceptual framework for practice. *Social Work, 43*(3), 254-267.

Seabury, B. (1993). Interactive video programs: Crisis counseling and organizational assessment. *Computers in Human Services, 9*(3-4), 301-310.

Seabury, B., & Maple, F., Jr. (1993). Using Computers to Teach Practice Skills. *Social Work, 38*(4), 430-39.

Seymour, G., Stahl, J., Levine, S., Ingram, J. et al. (1994). Modifying law enforcement training simulators for use in basic research. *Behavior Research Methods, Instruments and Computers, 26*(2), 266-268.

Shapiro, M. (1992). I'm not a real doctor, but I play one in virtual reality: Implications of virtual reality for judgements about reality. *Journal of Communication, 42*(4), 94-114.

Smyth, K. (1993). Using telecomputing to provide information and support to caregivers of persons with dementia. *The Gerontologist, 33*(1), 123-127.

Stafford, J., & Namorato, M.V. (1998). Multi-media computer technology in the classroom. *Computers in Human Services, 15*(2/3), 185-191.

Stagner, M., & Johnson, P. (1994). Understanding and representing human services knowledge: The process of developing expert systems. *Journal of Social Service Research, 19*(1/2), 115-137.

Steelman, J., Pierce, P., & Koppenahver, D. (1993). The role of computers in promoting literacy in children with severe speech and physical impairments (SSPI). *Topics in Language Disorders, 13*(2), 76-88.

Stefanescu, P. (1995). Using a computer network for social work training. *Computers in Human Services, 12*(1-2), 75-80.

Stodolsky, D. (1970). The computer as psychotherapist. *International Journal of Man-Machine Studies, 2*, 327-350.

Stoney, S., & Oliver, R. (1998). Interactive multimedia for adult learners: Can learning be fun? *Journal of Interactive Learning Research, 9*(1), 55-81.

Thyer, B., Polk, G., & Gaudin, J. (1997). Distance learning in social work education: A preliminary evaluation. *Journal of Social Work Evaluation, 33*(2), 363-367.

Tompkins, P., & Southward, L. (1998). Geographic information systems (GIS): Implications for promoting social and economic justice. *Computers in Human Services, 15*(2/3), 209-226.

Tovey, R., Savicki, V., & White, C. (1990). Electronic networking in human service agencies: A developmental analysis. *Child Welfare, 69*(2), 115-28.

Turner, A., Singleton, N., & Easterbrook, S. (1997). Developing sexual health software incorporating user feedback: A British experience. *Health Education & Behavior, 24*(1), 102-120.

Waltman, G. (1990). New options in continuing education: Professional development for rural social workers. *Human Services in the Rural Environment, 13*(3), 16-20.

Watson, M. (1995). On-line, CD-ROM and the Internet–new opportunities for social work education and practice. *New Technology in the Human Services, 8*(3), 25-27.

Weiss, L. (1994). Cognitive socialization by computer games in two cultures: Inductive discovery or mastery of an iconic code? *Journal of Applied Developmental Psychology, 15*(1), 59-85.

Weizenbaum, J. (1976). *Computer power and human reason*. San Francisco: W. H. Freeman.

Wetzler, S., & Marlowe, D. (1994). Clinical psychology by computer?: The state of the "art." *European Journal of Psychological Assessment, 10*(1), 55-61.

Wodarski, J., Bricout, J., & Smokowski, P. (1996). Making interactive videodisc computer simulation accessible and practice relevant. *Journal of Teaching in Social Work, 13*(1/2),15-26.

Zarr, M. (1994). Computer-aided psychotherapy: Machine helping therapist. *Psychiatric Annals, 24*(1), 42-46.

Index

